'This book argues that meeting the UN Sustainable Development Goals will require the united efforts of governments and the private sector. It injects a welcome note of realism into this hugely ambitious task.'

–Kichimoto Asaka, Professor of Law, University of Tokyo

'Digital innovation and financial technology, supported by the fourth Industrial Revolution technology such as Blockchain technology and others, have a critical role to play in meeting the United Nations Sustainable Development Goals. This exciting book explores how nations and businesses can join together to successfully achieve the goals.'

–Kanya Hirunwattanapong, International College of Digital Innovation, Chiang Mai University, Thailand

Sustainable Development Goals

Sustainable Development Goals

Harnessing Business to Achieve the SDGs through Finance, Technology, and Law Reform

Edited by Julia Walker, Alma Pekmezovic, and Gordon Walker

This edition first published 2019
© 2019 John Wiley & Sons Ltd

Registered office
John Wiley & Sons Ltd, The Atrium, Southern Gate, Chichester, West Sussex,
PO19 8SQ, United Kingdom

For details of our global editorial offices, for customer services and for information about how
to apply for permission to reuse the copyright material in this book please see our website at
www.wiley.com.

Wiley publishes in a variety of print and electronic formats and by print-on-demand. Some material
included with standard print versions of this book may not be included in e-books or in print-on-
demand. If this book refers to media such as a CD or DVD that is not included in the version you
purchased, you may download this material at http://booksupport.wiley.com. For more information
about Wiley products, visit www.wiley.com.

Library of Congress Cataloging-in-Publication Data is Available:

ISBN 978-1-119-54181-3 (hardback);
ISBN 978-1-119-54180-6 (ePDF);
ISBN 978-1-119-54184-4 (epub)

Cover Design: Wiley
Cover Image: From https://www.un.org/sustainabledevelopment/,
Copyright @ 2019 United Nations. Reprinted with the permission of the United Nations.

Set in 10/12pt WarnockPro by SPi Global, Chennai

Printed in Great Britain by TJ International Ltd, Padstow, Cornwall, UK

10 9 8 7 6 5 4 3 2 1

Contents

About the Editors

Julia Walker is a senior business executive with extensive experience in the private sector principally in finance, technology, and risk management. She currently runs market growth and strategy across Asia Pacific for Refinitiv, one of the world's largest providers of financial markets data, infrastructure and risk intelligence. Julia previously was a director at UBS Investment Bank in London and Singapore.

She is a member of the United Nations Secretary Generals Task Force on Digital Financing of the Sustainable Development Goals and a Professional Advisory Board member of the Asian Institute of International Financial Law. An advocate of gender equality, financial inclusion, and sustainable development, Julia believes the private sector can play a significant role in the SDG's. She has appeared in articles by Innovation Australia, Asian Private Banker and Risk.net; and is a frequent speaker at events including the World Economic Forum and Money2020. She is also a guest lecturer at Hong Kong University's Faculty of Law FinTech MOOC on Regulatory Technology.

Julia is an alumnus of the University of Canterbury, New Zealand and the University of Cambridge's Institute of Sustainable Leadership.

Dr Alma Pekmezovic is a consultant to the Asian Development Bank. Her key areas of expertise include capital markets law, corporate law and governance, and commercial law reform. She has published numerous law journal articles on these topics and is the coauthor of three books. During 2006–2015, Dr Pekmezovic taught corporate and commercial law at La Trobe University School of Law, Melbourne, Australia. She was a Lecturer in Law at Bucerius Law School in Hamburg (2015–2018) and a Visiting Research Fellow at the Max Planck Institute for Comparative and International Private Law in Hamburg, Germany.

Dr Pekmezovic is admitted as an attorney-at-law in New York, United States, and as a Barrister and Solicitor in Australia. She is a BA and LLB (Hons) graduate of the University of Melbourne School of Law, Melbourne, Australia, and holds an LLM degree from UCLA Law School, Los Angeles, United States, where she served as an editor of the UCLA *Pacific Basin Law Journal.*

Dr Gordon Walker, SJD (Duke) is an Emeritus Professor of La Trobe University, Melbourne, Australia; Adjunct Professor at Curtin University School of Law; Visiting Professor, University of Padua Law School, Italy; and an advisor to the Asian Development Bank (ADB) designated as International Business Law Expert and International Financial Sector Expert. His research contracts at the ADB principally involve law reform in the areas of securities regulation, company, secured transactions, and FinTech within the Private Sector Development Initiative (PSDI-III) in the South Pacific.

Professor Walker was formerly Professor of Law, Qatar Foundation, Doha, Qatar (2015–2016); Professor of Commercial Law (1999–2015) and Head of Law School (2004–2007) at La Trobe University School of Law; Paul Hastings Visiting Professor at Hong Kong University School of Law (2006); Wallace Fujiyama Visiting Professor at the University of Hawaii (2008 and 2010); Visiting Professor (MBA program) at Hong Kong University of Science and Technology (2009); Visiting Faculty, Duke University Law School Summer School Program in Hong Kong (2010); Visiting Professor at the University of Houston Law Centre (2009–2016); Adjunct Professor at Texas Tech University School of Law (2009–2016); and Consultant to the European Bank for Reconstruction and Development, London, UK (2011–2012). He has published widely on securities regulation and is best known internationally for the twin multivolume treatises on international securities regulation published by Westlaw in the United States – the eight-volume treatise *International Securities Regulation* and the five-volume treatise *International Securities Regulation Pacific Rim.*

Notes on Contributors

Dr Inna Amesheva holds a PhD in climate change law and policy from Hong Kong University Law School. She is an Associate at Arabesque S-Ray, where she focuses on mainstreaming sustainable finance through the power of technology, big data, and artificial intelligence. Inna has a background in innovation and entrepreneurship, gained throughout Europe and Asia. She also serves as a UN SDSN Youth Project Officer, focusing on Solutions Initiatives and developing Digital Ecosystems that foster SDG youth entrepreneurship. Inna is passionate about environmental sustainability and enhancing economic opportunity for all.

Dr Douglas W. Arner is the Kerry Holdings Professor in Law at the University of Hong Kong and one of the world's leading experts on financial regulation, particularly the intersection between law, finance, and technology. At HKU, he is Faculty Director of the Faculty of Law's LLM in Compliance and the Regulation, LLM in Corporate and Financial Law and the Law, Innovation, Technology, and Entrepreneurship (LITE) Programmes. He is a Senior Visiting Fellow of Melbourne Law School, University of Melbourne, an Executive Committee Member of the Asia Pacific Structured Finance Association, and an independent non-executive director of the Nasdaq-listed Aptorum Group. He led the development of the world's largest massive open online course (MOOC): Introduction to FinTech, launched on edX in May 2018, now with over 35,000 learners spanning every country in the world. From 2006 to 2011 he was the Director of HKU's Asian Institute of International Financial Law, which he cofounded in 1999, and from 2012 to 2018, he led a major research project on Hong Kong's future as a leading international financial centre. He was an inaugural member of the Hong Kong Financial Services Development Council, of which he was a member from 2013 to 2019. Douglas served as Head of the HKU Department of Law from 2011 to 2014 and as Co-Director of the Duke University-HKU Asia-America Institute in Transnational Law from 2005 to 2016. He has published 15 books and more than 150 articles, chapters, and reports on international financial law and regulation, including, *Reconceptualising Global*

Finance and Its Regulation (with Ross Buckley and Emilios Avgouleas; Cambridge, 2016) and *The RegTech Book* (with Janos Barberis and Ross Buckley; forthcoming, 2019). His recent papers are available on SSRN at https://papers.ssrn.com/sol3/cf_dev/AbsByAuth.cfm?per_id=524849, where he is among the top 150 authors in the world by total downloads. Douglas has served as a consultant with, among others, the World Bank, Asian Development Bank, APEC, Alliance for Financial Inclusion, and European Bank for Reconstruction and Development, and has lectured, co-organised conferences and seminars, and been involved with financial sector reform projects around the world. He has been a visiting professor or fellow at Duke, Harvard, the Hong Kong Institute for Monetary Research, IDC Herzliya, McGill, Melbourne, National University of Singapore, University of New South Wales, Shanghai University of Finance and Economics, and Zurich, among others.

Martin Blessing was appointed co-President of Global Wealth Management of UBS Group AG and UBS AG as of February 2018. Prior to this, he was President of Wealth Management, effective January 2018. He held the positions of President of Personal and Corporate Banking of UBS Group AG and President of UBS Switzerland, as well as President of the Executive Board of UBS Switzerland AG from September 2016 to December 2017. He became a member of the GEB in September 2016. Before joining UBS, he worked for 15 years for Commerzbank AG, from 2008 to April 2016 as Chief Executive Officer. Before, he held various senior management positions; from 2004 to 2008, he was Head of Corporate Banking and from 2006 onward was also responsible for IT & Operations. From 2001 to 2004, he was Head of Private Clients. Before joining Commerzbank, from 2000 to 2001 he was Chief Executive Officer of Advance Bank, a subsidiary of Dresdner Bank AG. From 1997 to 2000, he acted as Dresdner Bank's joint Head Private Clients. From 1989 to 1996, he worked for McKinsey & Company, the last two years as Partner. Martin Blessing holds an MBA from the University of Chicago and in 1987 graduated from the University of St. Gallen with a degree in business administration.

Ross Buckley is the KPMG Law – King & Wood Mallesons Professor of Disruptive Innovation and a Scientia Professor at UNSW Sydney. His research focus is FinTech, RegTech, and blockchain. His research on these topics has been downloaded more often from the Social Science Research Network than that of any other social scientist. His joint world-first research has (i) developed the generally accepted timeline for the evolution of FinTech; (ii) reconceptualised the true potential of RegTech; (iii) undertaken the first comprehensive analysis of the liabilities of blockchain; and (iv) analysed the rise and regulation of initial coin offerings, in a forthcoming article in the *Harvard Journal of International Law.*

He chairs the Digital Finance Advisory Panel of ASIC, and has consulted to government departments in ten countries, including Australia and the United States. He consults regularly to the Asian Development Bank, and has twice been a Fulbright Scholar, at Yale and Duke.

Emily Chew is Managing Director, Global Head of ESG, Manulife Investment Management. She leads Manulife Investment Management's team of dedicated ESG research and integration analysts to advance the firm's ESG agenda. She oversees the team of ESG analysts that work with portfolio management teams on progressing ESG integration processes and conducting ESG engagement with investee companies; works with Manulife Investment Management's sales and product teams on ESG strategy and marketing; and represents Manulife Investment Management on various industry groups and collaborative initiatives.

Before joining Manulife Investment Management, Emily was Head of ESG Research for Asia-Pacific at MSCI Inc., where she led a team of nine ESG analysts across the region, commencing her role in Beijing and later continuing in Hong Kong. Her team had oversight into research quality and issue identification for approximately 1,200 stocks, and under her leadership produced original research on the relevance of ESG to Asian and emerging markets, with a particular emphasis on China. Prior to that, she was a capital markets lawyer with Baker & McKenzie in Melbourne, Australia, with a focus on funds management, capital raisings, and REITs.

Emily holds an MBA from the University of Oxford, and Bachelor of Laws and Bachelor of Arts from the University of Melbourne. She is a member of the United Nations-sponsored Principles for Responsible Investment's Listed Equities Integration Subcommittee, and the Steering Committee for the Climate Action 100+ global collaborative investor engagement initiative. She previously served as chair of the Asian Investor Group on Climate Change's Member Working Group from 2016 to 2018.

Margaret Childe is the Director of Environmental, Social, and Governance (ESG) Research and Integration at Manulife Investment Management responsible for working with Manulife IM's Canada-based investment teams on ESG integration, identifying and managing ESG risks and opportunities for Canadian portfolios. Margaret also works on global ESG integration projects and methodologies for ESG product development, and represents Manulife IM's ESG capabilities among the local investment community.

Previously, Margaret was a senior manager of ESG advisory services at Sustainalytics, where she helped asset owners and investment managers in Canada and the United States to develop and implement sustainable and responsible investment strategies, including ESG integration and impact investing solutions. Earlier, Margaret managed RBC Capital Market's collateral management desk and was an associate on the Global Equity Linked Products desk. Margaret has also worked for Save the Children and the Intergovernmental Oceanographic Commission. Margaret is fluent in French.

Alex Clark is a climate finance analyst at the Climate Policy Initiative in San Francisco. He is also a Researcher at Harvard Kennedy School supporting Professor Henry Lee on electric vehicles, environmental economics, and other select topics. Alex is a former Henry Fellow at Harvard University and a graduate of Oxford University (MSc) and Warwick University (BA Hons. First Class), with an exchange at Sciences Po in Paris. He is also an advisor, and previously Project Leader for Operations, with UN SDSN Youth, and youth delegate to the COP21/COP22 climate conferences.

Helen Clark was Prime Minister of New Zealand for three successive terms from 1999 to 2008. She was the first woman to become Prime Minister following a General Election in New Zealand and the second woman to serve as Prime Minister.

Throughout her tenure as Prime Minister and as a Member of Parliament over 27 years, Helen Clark engaged widely in policy development and advocacy across the international affairs, economic, social, environmental, and cultural spheres. She advocated strongly for a comprehensive programme on sustainability for New Zealand and for tackling the challenges of climate change. She was an active leader of her country's foreign relations, engaging in a wide range of international issues.

In April 2009, Helen Clark became Administrator of the United Nations Development Programme. She was the first woman to lead the organisation, and served two terms there. At the same time, she was Chair of the United Nations Development Group, a committee consisting of all UN funds, programmes, agencies, and departments working on development issues. As Administrator, she led UNDP to be ranked the most transparent global development organisation. She completed her tenure in April 2017.

Helen Clark came to the role of Prime Minister after an extensive parliamentary and ministerial career. Prior to entering the New Zealand Parliament, Helen Clark taught in the Political Studies Department of the University of Auckland, from which she earlier graduated with her BA and MA (Hons) degrees.

Helen continues to speak widely and be a strong voice on sustainable development, climate action, gender equality and women's leadership, peace and justice, and action on noncommunicable diseases and on HIV. She serves on a number of advisory boards and commissions, including in the capacity of Chair of the Advisory Board of UNESCO's Global Education Monitoring Report. In June 2019, she assumed the Chairpersonship of the Extractive Industries Transparency Initiative. She is also the Patron of The Helen Clark

Foundation, which has been established as a think tank to support evidence-informed debate on issues which Helen has been passionate about all her life.

Brent Fisse has acted for clients on competition law in a wide range of industries, some in the public sector. Brent was a partner of Gilbert + Tobin in Sydney from 1995. Since retiring from Gilbert + Tobin in 2004, he has run his own practice (Brent Fisse Lawyers) and is also a Special Counsel at Resolve Litigation Lawyers.

Until 2019, he acted as consultant to the Asian Development Bank, mainly on competition law and policy reviews in Pacific Island economies, including Papua New Guinea and Fiji.

Brent was a professor of law at the University of Sydney from 1985 to 1995, and is now an Honorary Professor there and an Adjunct Professor, Australian School of Taxation and Business Law, UNSW Business School. He is the coauthor (with Caron Beaton-Wells) of *Australian Cartel Regulation* (2011) and author of various papers on competition law.

Brent is a member of the American Bar Association Antitrust Section and the Law Council of Australia's Competition and Consumer Committee.

Iason Gabriel is a Senior Research Scientist at DeepMind in the Ethics and Society team. Before joining DeepMind, he was a Supernumerary Teaching Fellow in Politics at St Johns College, Oxford, and a part-time researcher at the Mind, Behavior, and Development Unit of the World Bank.

Varun Gauri is Senior Economist in the Development Economics Vice Presidency of the World Bank, and Co-Head of the Mind, Behavior, and Development Unit (eMBeD), which integrates behavioural science into the design of antipoverty policies worldwide. He was Co-Director of the World Development Report 2015: *Mind, Society, and Behaviour*.

Dr Geoff Kendall is an entrepreneur whose experience spans sustainability consulting, high-tech start-ups, corporate communications, and academic research. Geoff holds a PhD in artificial intelligence, and has cofounded two software businesses. The second of these was acquired by a global technology company, where Geoff went on to serve as marketing director for three years.

Geoff switched careers in 2010, joining SustainAbility, a London-based think tank, and for four years he led the communications team and advised some of the world's biggest corporations on sustainable business models. In early 2014, Geoff left to set up the Future-Fit Foundation.

Guillaume Lafortune is Manager at the UN Sustainable Development Solutions Network (SDSN), where he leads the work on data and statistics for the SDGs, including the production of the SDG Index and Dashboards Report. Previously, he served as an economist at the Organisation for Economic Co-operation and Development (OECD), working on public governance reforms and statistics. Earlier, Guillaume worked as an economist at the Ministry of Economic Development in the Government of Quebec (Canada).

Julian Payne is an Associate at The Carbon Trust and Senior Project Advisor at UN SDSN Youth, focusing on green finance issues. Julian has also served as the Project Leader for SDSN Youth's work on Youth, Peace , and Security and as a member of its Research and Policy team. Previously, Julian worked as a Research Associate at the UCL Department of Science, Technology, Engineering , and Public Policy. He holds an MSc in Comparative Political Economy from the LSE and a BA in Philosophy and Linguistics from the University of Konstanz, with an exchange at the University of Durham.

Dr Mahmoud Mohieldin is a Senior Vice President at the World Bank Group, responsible for the 2030 Development Agenda, UN Relations and Partnerships. Before joining the World Bank Group, Dr Mohieldin held numerous senior positions in the Government of Egypt, including Minister of Investment from 2004 until 2010. He also served on several Boards of Directors, including the Central Bank of Egypt, as well as in the banking and the corporate sectors. Dr Mohieldin was a member of the Commission on Growth and Development, and was selected by the World Economic Forum as a Young Global Leader.

Dr Mohieldin is a Professor of Economics and Finance at Cairo University. He is also an Honorary Professor at Durham University, UAEU, and Nile University, and is member of the Advisory Board of the Durham Business School. Dr Mohieldin has held leading positions in national and regional research centres and think tanks. He has authored numerous publications and articles in the fields of international finance, growth, banking, financial development, and economic planning. He received his PhD in Economics from the University of Warwick; an MSc in Economic and Social Policy Analysis from the University of York; and a BSc in Economics, first in the order of merit, from Cairo University.

Suresh Nanwani is a CEDR Accredited Mediator; Honorary Associate Professor at Australian National University; Visiting Professorial Fellow at University of New South Wales; Honorary Research Fellow at Birkbeck University of London; and Visiting Fellow at Global Policy Institute in Durham University. He is a Member of Practitioners' Board at Global Policy; and Executive Council Member of the Society of International Economic Law. He has 30 years of development experience in international organisations, including the World Bank and was formerly Advisor at Asian Development Bank and Counsel at European Bank for Reconstruction and Development. He has published on international financial institutions, law and development, and governance and accountability.

Tom Naratil became co-President of Global Wealth Management of UBS Group AG and UBS AG in February 2018. In January 2018, he became CEO of UBS Americas Holding LLC. He was appointed President UBS Americas of UBS Group AG and UBS AG in January 2016. He previously served as President

Wealth Management Americas from 2016 to 2018. He became a member of the GEB in June 2011 and was Group CFO of UBS AG from 2011 to 2015. He held the same position for UBS Group AG from 2014 to 2015. In addition to the role of Group CFO, he was Group Chief Operating Officer from 2014 to 2015. He was President of the Executive Board of UBS Business Solutions AG from 2015 to March 2016. He served as CFO and Chief Risk Officer of Wealth Management Americas from 2009 until his appointment as Group CFO in 2011. Before 2009, he held various senior management positions within UBS, including heading the Auction Rate Securities Solutions Group during the financial crisis in 2008. He was named Global Head of Marketing, Segment & Client Development in 2007, Global Head of Market Strategy & Development in 2005, and Director of Banking and Transactional Solutions, Wealth Management USA, in 2002. During this time, he was a member of the Group Managing Board. He joined Paine Webber Incorporated in 1983 and after the merger with UBS became Director of the Investment Products Group. Mr Naratil holds an MBA in economics from New York University and a Bachelor of Arts in history from Yale University.

Martin Rich is a sustainability and impact investment specialist, with over 20 years' experience in both mainstream and social investment. Martin cofounded Future-Fit Foundation six years ago with a vision of helping to create a society which is environmentally restorative, socially just, and economically inclusive. The foundation's free-to-use tools enable businesses to take practical steps towards – and ultimately beyond – the SDGs, and empower investors to understand the total impact of their portfolios and thus direct capital accordingly.

Dr Guido Schmidt-Traub is Executive Director of the UN Sustainable Development Solutions Network (SDSN), which operates under the auspices of the UN Secretary-General to support the implementation of the Sustainable Development Goals and the Paris Climate Agreement. Guido leads the SDSN's policy work, including on long-term pathways for sustainable land-use and food systems, financing for development, and the SDG Index and Dashboards. He serves on the Governing Council of Future Earth and other advisory bodies.

Dr Jon Truby is Associate Professor of Law and Director of the Centre for Law & Development at the College of Law, Qatar University, Doha, where he manages several million dollars of research grants delivering solutions in fields related to law and technological innovation. A lawyer and legal academic, he specialises in law and policy related to digital and financial innovation, and the application of legal and fiscal tools in sustainable development policy. He joined Qatar University in 2010 from Newcastle University School of Law in the United Kingdom, where he taught and completed his doctorate in environmental taxation law. He is an avid publisher and is currently researching legal fields in blockchain, artificial intelligence, cybersecurity, and financial technology. He recently spoke at the United Nations on Blockchain's energy consumption problem.

Dr Benjamin Walker is a Senior Lecturer in the School of Accounting and Commercial Law at Victoria University of Wellington, New Zealand. He received his undergraduate degrees in Law and Finance from the University of Otago. He completed a Master of Laws in International Tax and a PhD (with honours) from the Vienna University of Economics and Business. He also has four years of experience in Australia, the United Kingdom, and Germany advising large companies on international tax issues. Benjamin currently teaches a number of undergraduate and postgraduate courses in Taxation and his research agenda explores various international tax issues.

Alastair Wilson is Managing Director and Head of Moody's Sovereign Risk Group. In this capacity, he leads Moody's global team of sovereign risk analysts, with responsibility for maintaining the quality of Moody's sovereign ratings and for the analytical leadership Moody's aims to provide to investors and issuers through its research. Until August 2014, Alastair was Chief Credit Officer in EMEA, responsible for the quality and consistency of Moody's credit standards and methodologies across all franchises within the region. He joined Moody's in September 2010 following 21 years at the Bank of England. At the bank, he worked in a variety of roles in banking supervision, FX and reserves management, banking operations, and financial stability. Alastair graduated from St John's College, Oxford University, in 1988, having studied Philosophy, Politics, and Economics. He is based in London.

Simon Zadek is currently Principal of Project Catalyst at the United Nations Development Program, where he has lead responsibility for the Secretary General's Task Force on Digital Financing of the Sustainable Development Goals. He was until recently Senior Advisor on Finance in the Executive Office of the UN Secretary-General, and prior to that ran an international inquiry on financial markets and sustainable development, where he co-led China's Green Finance Task Force with the People's Bank of China. He has held many academic posts, including Visiting Professor at the Singapore Management University and Copenhagen Business School, and Visiting Scholar at Harvard's John F. Kennedy School of Government and Tsinghua School of Economics and Management. He has been Senior Advisor to the World Economic Forum, and Senior Fellow at the Global Green Growth Institute. He founded and was until 2009 Chief Executive of the international think tank AccountAbility. Simon's book, *The Civil Corporation*, was awarded the Academy of Management's prestigious Best Book on Social Issues in Management, and his *Harvard Business Review* article, 'Paths to Corporate Responsibility' is widely used as a reference point in understanding emergent sustainability strategies. He has advised companies worldwide on sustainability issues.

Dirk Zetzsche is the ADA Chair in Financial Law (inclusive finance) at the University of Luxembourg and non-Executive Director at the Centre for Business and Corporate Law at Heinrich Heine University in Düsseldorf, Germany. His research focus is on alternative investment funds, corporate law, FinTech, RegTech, and blockchain. Professor Zetzsche is listed on SSRN within the Top 20 law scholars globally by downloads in the past 12 months. He is the author of more than 200 publications in English and German, among them some standard treatises on collective investment schemes, cross-border financial services, and corporate law. Professor Zetzsche has advised various regulators and supervisors around the world and functions, among others, as member of the European Securities and Markets Authority's (ESMA) Consultative Working Group on Financial Innovation ('FinTech Committee').

Foreword

Mahmoud Mohieldin

The 2030 Agenda for Sustainable Development and the 17 Sustainable Development Goals (SDGs) are ambitious and define global priorities and aspirations for 2030.

The SDGs seek 'to end extreme poverty in all its forms and to have in place the building blocks of sustained prosperity for all'. Their success relies heavily on action and collaboration by all actors, including governments at the national and subnational levels, in addition to civil society and the private sector.

Yet the path to achieving this 2030 Agenda is obstructed by daunting, overlapping challenges, including climate change, fragility and conflict, pandemics, and many others. The ambitious spirit of the SDGs requires an unprecedented mobilisation of financial resources, knowledge, and partnerships at the global, national, and subnational levels.

Mobilising the necessary financial resources is an essential component for achieving the SDGs, and there are many innovative developments that will contribute to the global efforts. In July 2015, Financing for Development entered a new era, when the global community agreed to the Addis Ababa Action Agenda. The global development community is committed to seeking new approaches to move the discussion from 'billions' in Official Development Assistance to 'trillions' in financial resources of all kinds: public and private, national and global. The world needs intelligent development finance that goes well beyond filling financing gaps and that can be used strategically to unlock, leverage, and catalyse private flows and domestic resources.

Notwithstanding the critical role finance plays in supporting countries to implement the 2030 Agenda for Sustainable Development, we need to complement these efforts with new approaches, new tools, to build momentum and accelerate progress.

We need to support countries in harnessing technology that is disrupting traditional economic markets. We can do this by embracing the power of technology in areas such as FinTech, to improve access to finance as well as to better harness the power of big data to support policy decisions linked to the SDGs. A recent World Bank Group World Development Report, entitled

'Digital Dividends', documents many examples where digital technologies have promoted inclusion, efficiency, and innovation. At the same time, technological advancements could leave millions behind. Our data shows that digital adoption by firms in developing countries has been slow. Automation is disrupting labour markets and will displace a significant number of jobs over the next few decades. And let's not forget that 3.6 billion people still have no internet access at all.

Leveraging technology for the public good requires global cooperation and partnerships to amplify its benefits, and to identify the risks and mitigate them. Ten years after the financial crisis, we have learned that preventing and dealing with risks early on is less costly in financial and human terms than tackling these issues too late.

Technology offers new opportunities but also introduces new risks, including increased inequality within and between countries. Urgent action is needed to maximise potential benefits and mitigate risks. We will need to help countries invest more – and more effectively – in their people to prepare for what is certain to be a more digitally demanding future. The need of the hour is for strong partnerships to build sustainable and technology-led economies, and to expand the capacity of people and institutions to thrive in this rapidly evolving environment.

This book is an excellent resource of information and cutting-edge research by leaders from the development institutions, academia, business, finance, and the startup and entrepreneurial community who have provided innovative ideas, solutions, and entrepreneurial insight into what it would take to achieve the SDGs. Now more than ever we need visionary global solutions, and this book is an important step in helping us achieve a future that is more prosperous and just for all.

Mahmoud Mohieldin
World Bank Group Senior Vice President for the 2030
Development Agenda, United Nations Relations,
and Partnerships

Foreword: Implementation of the SDGs

Rt. Hon. Helen Clark

The 2030 Agenda and the Sustainable Development Goals are bold and transformational in their quest for an inclusive and sustainable world. Achieving them requires accepting and acting on the principles on which they are based, making very large investments, and deploying innovations and technologies at prices affordable to the poorest countries. As well, a state of peace is vital for sustained development – sadly, citizens of countries mired in conflict, including refugees and the internally displaced, stand to be left behind while conflict continues.

To date, the level of commitment required for the SDGs to be achieved has not materialised. Much has changed geopolitically since the Goals were agreed upon in 2015. The political climate for advancing both the Goals and the related Paris Agreement on climate change is less conducive to prioritising these global agendas than it was then.

The main message of the 2018 *SDG Index and Dashboard* report of the Sustainable Development Solutions Network and the Bertelsmann Stiftung foundation was that *no country is on track* to achieve all SDGs by 2030. That is sobering.

So, what are the major barriers to progress? Conventional wisdom would point to ongoing significant levels of inequality, environmental degradation – including climate change – ongoing conflicts, and lack of finance as barriers. But so too are the often-insufficient political will and public support in countries rich and poor to take the steps required to advance sustainable development.

A core principle of the 2030 Agenda for Sustainable Development and the SDGs is to *leave no one behind*. Yet many are being left behind, to the extent that there is little hope at the current rate of progress – or lack of it – of eradicating either extreme poverty or hunger by 2030 as the SDGs aspired to do.

- On current trends, those living in *extreme poverty* on under US$1.90 a day will still number some 6% of the world population in 2030 – some 400–475 million people.

- World *hunger* has been rising for the past three years, affecting 821 million people in 2017, or one in nine of all people on earth.
- The world collectively is nowhere near meeting the ambition of the Paris Agreement to limit the global temperature rise to under two degrees Celsius, and preferably no more than 1.5 degrees.

The greatest concentration of challenges to sustainable development lies in the world's *fragile contexts*. According to the OECD definition, those living in such contexts number almost a quarter of the world's population – 1.8 billion people. That number is projected to rise to 2.3 billion people by 2030.

So – could this somewhat dismal outlook be turned around?

It is time for the United Nations and the international and regional financial institutions to spell out clearly the scale of the deficit in progress to date, and to step up advocacy for more commitment and action across the SDG agenda.

It would be unconscionable for the international community just to drift on, knowing that in 2030, just 11 years away, hundreds of millions of people will still be deeply impoverished, hungry, without access to basic services, and exposed to a world heading for a temperature rise of 3-plus degrees unless much greater efforts are made.

There would be considerable merit now in both *increasing international development cooperation and focusing it on those who are being left behind*. This is the thrust of the message of the '*Fragility, crisis and leaving no one behind*' report issued by the Overseas Development Institute of the United Kingdom and the International Rescue Committee last year. They advocate *inter alia* for prioritisation of policies, actions, and financing for those in fragile contexts, and also for filling data gaps – too often those who are caught up in crises, including refugees and the internally displaced, or those who are otherwise marginalised, are excluded from data collection, thus disguising the level of needs they have.

ODI and IRC have been blunt in saying that '*Failure to take action now means that the Sustainable Development Goals will not be met, undermining the credibility of the international community and leaving millions to die unnecessarily*'.

In the major effort required to move the SDGs forward, everyone has a role to play.

- *Development co-operation* from North and South will continue to be important, particularly for the poorest countries. Indeed, it will be essential in moving those last 400 to 475 million people out of extreme poverty as projected global growth alone will not do that. Support needs to be channeled directly into health, education, and social protection in an estimated 48 countries characterised as low income, developing, and fragile. The empowerment and full inclusion of women will also be vital for lifting human development across the board.

- On *climate change adaptation*, the most vulnerable countries need urgent support. The Green Climate Fund is grossly under-capitalised – yet it and the Global Environment Facility are trusted partners for developing countries and can do a power of good with adequate resourcing.
- On *mitigation*, two major areas of action need to be prioritised:

  1. The world must get over its addiction to *coal* and other fossil fuels. Global coal production and consumption increased in 2017 after two years of decline. New coal-fired energy plants continue to be built and financed by some development partners. That flies in the face of the Intergovernmental Panel on Climate Change warnings that there are just 12 years left in which to act to avoid climate catastrophe and that coal should be phased out entirely by 2050. That transition needs to start now.
  2. *Stopping tropical deforestation*, which currently contributes 15% of all global greenhouse gas emissions. That is equivalent to the emissions of all cars, trucks, and trains. The switch to biofuels in the United States is reported to have driven forest clearance for palm oil production in Indonesia. The year to July 2018 was the worst year in a decade for forest loss in the Amazon. Cooperation across governments, the private sector, communities, and consumers will be needed to halt deforestation and forest degradation.

- *The private sector has a very important role to play.* The gap in financing for the SDGs in key sectors in developing countries has been estimated to be as much as US$2.5 trillion per annum. That gap cannot be filled by international public finance – Official Development Assistance (ODA) from OECD countries in 2017 was only US$146.6 billion, and 18 out of 29 member countries of the OECD's Development Assistance Committee actually reduced their ODA that year.

Thus, a global private sector which is inclusive and sustainable, and is prepared to invest in countries with infrastructure and livelihood deficits, could have a very positive impact. If, for example, all companies committed to zero deforestation in their supply chains for commodities such as palm oil, soy, and beef, that would make a huge difference to climate change mitigation and to endangered species and habitat protection.

Civil society engagement matters enormously too, and was very important in the design of the SDGs. The 2030 Agenda broke new ground in SDG 16 in advocating for peaceful and inclusive societies that provide access to justice for all and have responsive, inclusive, participatory, and representative decision making at all levels. Citizens should be able to have input into the decisions that affect their lives, and their organisations should be able to advocate for them and hold governments to account. All governments committed to the SDGs. Civil society can help ensure that they go beyond words to implementation.

In conclusion:
While overall progress on the SDGs is far from adequate, there are some areas gaining traction. For example,

- Momentum is growing for *universal health coverage* as a basic right for all and a key target in SDG 3 on health. It must, however, incorporate strong action on the social and commercial determinants of health, or today's huge health challenges in the noncommunicable diseases will never be overcome.
- The drive for SDG 5 on *gender equality* has momentum. Our world badly needs more women at the decision-making table – in elected positions, public administration, and the multilateral organisations. I am supporting the *Global Health 50/50* initiative, which advocates for gender parity in the global health organisations. So often a photo of the leaders of those organisations will reveal that only one woman is included. It goes without saying that if women are left behind, the SDGs can't be achieved either.
- There is potential for an *energy transformation* that relegates fossil fuels to the proverbial dustbin of history. If countries commit to that quickly, we would be well on the way to reaching both SDG 7 on energy and the Paris Climate Agreement targets.

I continue, however, to be concerned by the state of fragility affecting a significant proportion of the world's peoples. This is cause for reflection by all responsible – for example, those who are parties to conflicts and those who arm them. Think of the horrific images of starving children in Yemen we have seen almost daily on our media screens – children being left behind to the point of death in one of the world's poorest countries.

We won't have achieved the SDGs if they are achieved only in zones of peace and prosperity – and a failure to extend inclusive and sustainable development to all will continue to have spill-over impacts on the peace, well-being, and security of all of us. For all these reasons, it's time to act on the SDGs as if our lives depended on them – because they do if we want an inclusive and sustainable future for all.

Rt. Hon. Helen Clark
Former New Zealand Prime Minister and
former United Nations Development
Programme Administrator

Preface

We begin by talking about the intended or desired audience. We wanted to write a book that was accessible to a wide range of engaged citizens worldwide – primarily business people – including professionals, policymakers, regulators, students, and teachers. We sought to reach a wide audience aiming – wherever possible – to present the views of our many contributors in plain, nontechnical, English.

In this Preface, we wish to say a little about our journey with this book project: where we started, how our thinking evolved, and the final design.

Gordon Walker and Alma Pekmezovic are lawyers; Julia Walker is a senior business executive with expertise in finance and regulatory technology. The origins of the book go back to 2015–2016 when Gordon was working with Qatar Foundation in Doha, Qatar and Alma was teaching at Bucerius Law School in Hamburg, Germany.

In 2015–2016, Gordon and Alma began researching fundraising regimes in Pacific Island nations (PINs). A key finding of that research was that there were only minimal legal concessions to enable fundraising by small and medium-sized enterprises (SMES). The effect of the absence of such laws is that SMEs are largely denied access to the capital market. In turn, this means that the role of SMEs in driving private sector employment is adversely affected. The problem is especially acute in the more fragile PINs. Later, when reviewing policy rationales for supporting SMEs, they encountered SDG 8, which explicitly calls for measures supporting SMEs and linked their analysis to that goal.

One way in which lawyers consider law reform is to ask what the law 'is' and then what the law 'ought' to be. Thus, the SDGs can be viewed as a set of 'ought' statements, a supporting set of policy rationales for law reform. This perception opens up exciting avenues for legal research by using the lens of the SDGs to examine the law as it is and also as it could be.

Nations report on their progress on achieving the SDGs and the reports make interesting reading. For example, contrast the conventional economic snapshots of a South Pacific island nation such as Fiji produced by The Economist Intelligence Unit with a progress report on the SDGs (or their predecessors).

The pictures produced are markedly different and force another way of looking at the country: for example, we confront measures of child poverty usually not captured in traditional analysis. The resulting change in perception cannot be underestimated. One aspect of that perceptual change is recognition that the public sector can only do so much to achieve the SDGs and that, in some instances, governments may hinder their realisation.

At this point, the main theme of the book emerged – the need to involve the private sector in achieving the SDGs. As a result, the input of a senior figure in the private sector was required. Julia Walker has an extensive background in the private sector, principally in banking and finance. She is well known for chairing Regulatory Summits across Asia and South Pacific and played a key role in developing and creating the general concept of the book. Her insights and contacts resulted in the rich roll call of private sector and NGO participation.

She looked at examples of how her peers in the private sector were incorporating the SDG's into their operations and practices and invited them to crystallize their position on how they can support the SDGs in a chapter contribution. Many welcomed the opportunity to formalise their thinking on the SDGs in a contribution to this book. An early initiative was to involve the UBS, for whom Julia had previously worked as a director. Similarly, Julia and Gordon had worked with Professor Douglas Arner at Hong Kong University (HKU) and his work on FinTech, RegTech, and the reconceptualisation of financial markets.

After discussions, we were able to secure a key chapter on FinTech and the SDGs by Dirk Zetschke, Ross Buckley, and Douglas Arner. The same can be said for all of the chapters from the private and NGO sectors, and that is how we came to the final design of the book.

We were delighted to bring the former Prime Minister of New Zealand, the Right Hon. Helen Clark, onboard to share her views on the need to accelerate implementation of the SDGs and provide a call to action. We are thankful to Mahmoud Mohieldin – the World Bank Group Senior Vice President for the 2030 Development Agenda, United Nations Relations, and Partnerships – for lending his support to our project and writing a foreword. Simon Zadek shared his perspective on how we can harness the power of digitisation to achieve the SDGs.

Simon Zadek shared his perspective on how we can harness the power of digitalisation to achieve the SDGs. Simon has lead responsibility for the United Nations Secretary General's Task Force on Digital Financing of the Sustainable Development Goals.

The many contributors to this book gave freely of their time and expertise to pursue the worthwhile goal of exploring how the private sector – broadly conceived – can facilitate the vision of the SDGs. We thank them again. We also thank Julius Gwyer of the World Bank Group for his constructive advice.

To assist readers, we have reproduced the full text of the UN Declaration in the Appendix to the book.

Introduction

The United Nations Sustainable Development Goals (SDGs) comprise a list of ambitious goals and targets; they are reproduced in full in the Appendix to this book. However, aspirations alone will be insufficient to realise the SDGs. We think it is the involvement of actors from the private sector together with new ways and means of implementing the SDGs that will provide the critical success factors. This is the central theme of this edited volume.

The book highlights the importance of the sustainable development agenda and addresses the key changes required in the global financial and economic system to bring about fundamental sustainability transformations. It surveys a range of issues and topics in order to demonstrate how business and the private sector can be harnessed effectively to achieve the SDGs. In particular, this book focuses on emerging concepts and solutions (including trends in banking, private investment, technology, innovation, law reform, and entrepreneurship), linking scientific research in the area of sustainability with insights and knowledge from industry (providing practical perspectives and case-based examples), in order to further global discussion on the SDGs and develop realisable solutions for their implementation. We seek to integrate perspectives from multiple fields and develop a cross-disciplinary approach to understanding the SDGs by generating knowledge about the goals and their diffusion and transformation into local contexts.

The changes the global community faces in response to the sustainability and development challenges of the twenty-first century are enormous, requiring a fundamental rethink of the SDGs agenda and its relevance for governments and business alike. While governments and regulators are key actors reaching the SDGs, the future role of the private sector, civil society, and philanthropic organisations cannot be understated. The private sector – owing to its vast financial resources and scale – is an especially powerful stakeholder in supporting the achievement of the SDGs. Moreover, current changes in international public financial flows further underscore the importance of motivating

Sustainable Development Goals: Harnessing Business to Achieve the SDGs through Finance, Technology, and Law Reform, First Edition. Edited by Julia Walker, Alma Pekmezovic, and Gordon Walker.
© 2019 John Wiley & Sons Ltd. Published 2019 by John Wiley & Sons Ltd.

support for the SDGs among the private sector and fostering greater synergies between the public and private sectors in the delivery of the SDGs.

The international development finance landscape is also undergoing a significant transformation. In 2015, the international community adopted a series of global agreements pivotal to the new development agenda. The agreements included three key milestones:

1) The adoption of the SDGs that replaced the Millennium Development Goals (MDGs);
2) A new framework for financing the development goals; and
3) Reaching a legally binding and universal agreement on climate.[1]

These agreements were concluded at a UN General Assembly meeting in New York, the third international conference on financing for development in Addis Ababa and the COP21 in Paris, respectively.[2] Together, they shape the core components of the post-2015 development agenda and usher in a new era in development.

Prior to the adoption of the SDGs and the Addis Ababa Action Agenda (AAAA), official development finance and other sources of financing for development – mainly domestic resources – were considered the main drivers of development finance.[3] Since 2000, however, it had become obvious that official development resources were insufficient to implement the new development agenda. The Addis Ababa agenda is considered groundbreaking as it focused not on how much official development assistance (ODA) is available to support sustainable development but on how it can be used to mobilise and catalyse financing from other sources. The AAAA called on the Multilateral Development Banks (MDBs) and governments to develop new approaches to financing development. Table I.1 gives an overview of the SDGs.

The SDGs will require substantial increases in development finance far exceeding the sums that were required for the predecessor MDGs. It is estimated countries will need to deploy up to $4.5 trillion per year between 2015 and 2030 to meet the SDGs and the AAAA. Other estimates place the investments required to meet the SDGs at US$5–7 trillion per annum, representing 7–10% of global GDP, and 25–40% of annual global investment.[4] Although there are sufficient resources

---

1 United Nations, *The Road to Dignity by 2030: Ending Poverty, Transforming All Lives and Protecting the Planet* (December 2014), 7.
2 United Nations, 'Transforming Our World: The 2030 Agenda for Sustainable Development', A/RES/70/1 (September 2015).
3 UN DESA (United Nations Department of Economic and Social Affairs). Addis Ababa Action Agenda of the Third International Conference on Financing for Development (2015).
4 Homi Kharas and John McArthur, *Links in the Chain of Sustainable Finance: Accelerating Private Investments for the SDGs, including Climate Action* (September 2016), 5. Available at: https://www.brookings.edu/wp-content/uploads/2016/09/global_20160919_sustainable_finance.pdf.

Table I.1 The UN Sustainable Development Goals

Goal 1	End poverty in all its forms everywhere
Goal 2	End hunger, achieve food security and improved nutrition, and promote sustainable agriculture
Goal 3	Ensure healthy lives and promote well-being for all, at all ages
Goal 4	Ensure inclusive and equitable quality education and promote lifelong learning opportunities for all
Goal 5	Achieve gender equality and empower all women and girls
Goal 6	Ensure availability and sustainable management of water and sanitation for all
Goal 7	Ensure access to affordable, reliable, sustainable, and modern energy for all
Goal 8	Promote sustained, inclusive and sustainable economic growth, full and productive employment, and decent work for all
Goal 9	Build resilient infrastructure, promote inclusive and sustainable industrialization, and foster innovation
Goal 10	Reduce inequality within and among countries
Goal 11	Make cities and human settlements inclusive, safe, resilient, and sustainable
Goal 12	Ensure sustainable consumption and production patterns
Goal 13	Take urgent action to combat climate change and its impacts
Goal 14	Conserve and sustainably use the oceans, seas, and marine resources for sustainable development
Goal 15	Protect, restore, and promote sustainable use of terrestrial ecosystems, sustainably manage forests, combat desertification, and halt and reverse land degradation and halt biodiversity loss
Goal 16	Promote peaceful and inclusive societies for sustainable development, provide access to justice for all and build effective, accountable, and inclusive institutions at all levels
Goal 17	Strengthen the means of implementation and revitalize the Global Partnership for Sustainable Development

Source: United Nations, 'Transforming Our World: The 2030 Agenda for Sustainable Development' (A/RES/70/1), September 2015.

available globally to finance development – with global savings amounting to $17 trillion – not all public and private resources are channelled in sufficient quantities towards investments that support sustainable development. [5]

The SDGs – which are intended to be universal in nature and target both developed and developing countries – consist of 17 goals and 169 individual

---

5 Development Committee (Joint Ministerial Committee of the Boards of Governors of the Bank and the Fund on the Transfer of Real Resources to Developing Countries), 'From Billions to Trillions: Transforming Development Finance', April 2015, 1–5.

targets and will require investments in development which go far beyond current available resources. Achieving the SDGs will require moving from billions to trillions in resource flows, and channelling resources and investments of all types – including public and private, national and international – into development. The 'billions' available in ODA must be used to unlock and mobilise 'trillions' of dollars from all sources of financing – including public, private, domestic, and international – to finance the implementation of the SDGs.[6] Table 1.2 illustrates the means of implementation envisaged for SDGs 1–16, in particular, highlighting the importance of development cooperation, international financial cooperation, and ODA:

Table 1.2 Means of Implementation (MOI) for SDGs 1–16

Goal 1a: End poverty in all its forms everywhere	Ensure significant mobilization of resources from a variety of sources, including through enhanced development cooperation, in order to provide adequate and predictable means for developing countries, in particular least developed countries, to implement programmes and policies to end poverty in all its dimensions
Goal 2a: Hunger and food	Increase investment, including through enhanced international cooperation, in rural infrastructure, agricultural research and extension services, technology development, and plant and livestock gene banks in order to enhance agricultural productive capacity in developing countries, in particular least developed countries
Goal 3c: Health and Well-Being	Substantially increase health financing and the recruitment, development, training, and retention of the health workforce in developing countries, especially in least developed countries and small island developing States
Goal 4c: Education	By 2030, substantially increase the supply of qualified teachers, including through international cooperation for teacher training in developing countries, especially least developed countries and small island developing States
Goal 5a: Gender Equality	Undertake reforms to give women equal rights to economic resources, as well as access to ownership and control over land and other forms of property, financial services, inheritance, and natural resources, in accordance with national laws
Goal 6a: Water and Sanitation	By 2030, expand international cooperation and capacity-building support to developing countries in water- and sanitation-related activities and programmes, including water harvesting, desalination, water efficiency, wastewater treatment, and recycling and reuse technologies
Goal 7a: Energy	By 2030, enhance international cooperation to facilitate access to clean energy research and technology, including renewable energy, energy efficiency, and advanced and cleaner fossil-fuel technology, and promote investment in energy infrastructure and clean energy technology

6 Ibid.

Goal 8a: Growth, Employment and Decent Work	Increase Aid for Trade support for developing countries, in particular least developed countries, including through the Enhanced Integrated Framework for Trade-Related Technical Assistance to Least Developed Countries
Goal 9a: Infrastructure Development	Facilitate sustainable and resilient infrastructure development in developing countries through enhanced financial, technological and technical support to African countries, least developed countries, landlocked developing countries, and small island developing States
Goal 9b: Technology	Support domestic technology development, research, and innovation in developing countries, including by ensuring a conducive policy environment for, inter alia, industrial diversification and value addition to commodities
Goal 10b: ODA	Encourage official development assistance and financial flows, including foreign direct investment, to States where the need is greatest, in particular least developed countries, African countries, small island developing States and landlocked developing countries, in accordance with their national plans and programmes
Goal 11b: Disaster Risk Management	By 2020, substantially increase the number of cities and human settlements adopting and implementing integrated policies and plans towards inclusion, resource efficiency, mitigation and adaptation to climate change, resilience to disasters, and develop and implement, in line with the Sendai Framework for Disaster Risk Reduction 2015–2030, holistic disaster risk management at all levels
Goal 12a: Sustainable Consumption and Production	Support developing countries to strengthen their scientific and technological capacity to move towards more sustainable patterns of consumption and production
Goal 13a: Climate Change	Implement the commitment undertaken by developed-country parties to the United Nations Framework Convention on Climate Change to a goal of mobilizing jointly $100 billion annually by 2020 from all sources to address the needs of developing countries in the context of meaningful mitigation actions and transparency on implementation and fully operationalize the Green Climate Fund through its capitalization as soon as possible
Goal 14: Sustainable Use of Oceans	Enhance the conservation and sustainable use of oceans and their resources by implementing international law as reflected in the United Nations Convention on the Law of the Sea, which provides the legal framework for the conservation and sustainable use of oceans and their resources, as recalled in paragraph 158 of 'The Future We Want'
Goal 15a: Biodiversity and Ecosystems	Mobilize and significantly increase financial resources from all sources to conserve and sustainably use biodiversity and ecosystems
Goal 16a: Governance	Strengthen relevant national institutions, including through international cooperation, for building capacity at all levels, in particular in developing countries, to prevent violence and combat terrorism and crime

Source: United Nations, 'Transforming Our World: The 2030 Agenda for Sustainable Development' (A/RES/70/1), September 2015.

Since the new Global Development Goals are interrelated and cover complex concepts that overlap (ending extreme poverty and hunger, climate change, sustainable cities and community, gender inequality, and wider inequality), they cannot be funded separately as stand-alone goals and require a holistic approach to funding. Indeed, the successful implementation of the SDGs will depend on both the quality and quantity of finance, along with regulatory change at the local, national, and international level. Table 1.3 highlights the key components of SDG Goal 17.

While concessional resources will continue to play a role in many countries – including low-income countries (LICs), low-middle income countries (LMICs), many landlocked countries, small island developing states (SIDS), and countries affected by conflict – it is important to bear in mind limitations to the present financing framework governing development. For example, achieving zero extreme poverty – defined as living on less than $1.25 a day – in Asia and the Pacific alone would require $51 billion, while raising the poverty standard to $2 per day would boost the sum required to $323 billion.[7]

Access to finance is a key determinant in the field of development and growth. Moreover, both public and private sources of finance are needed to facilitate economic growth. Owing to the vast resources necessary to meet the

Table 1.3 Strengthening the Means of Implementation (SDG Goal 17)

Goal 17.1	Strengthen domestic resource mobilization, including through international support to developing countries, to improve domestic capacity for tax and other revenue collection
Goal 17.2	Developed countries to implement fully their official development assistance commitments, including the commitment by many developed countries to achieve the target of 0.7% of gross national income for official development assistance (ODA/GNI) to developing countries and 0.15 to 0.20% of ODA/GNI to least developed countries; ODA providers are encouraged to consider setting a target to provide at least 0.20% of ODA/GNI to least developed countries
Goal 17.3	Mobilize additional financial resources for developing countries from multiple sources
Goal 17.4	Assist developing countries in attaining long-term debt sustainability through coordinated policies aimed at fostering debt financing, debt relief, and debt restructuring, as appropriate, and address the external debt of highly indebted poor countries to reduce debt distress
Goal 17.5	Adopt and implement investment promotion regimes for least developed countries

Source: United Nations, 'Transforming Our World: The 2030 Agenda for Sustainable Development' (A/RES/70/1), September 2015.

---

7 ADB, UNESCAP and UNDP, *Making It Happen: Technology, Finance and Statistics for Sustainable Development in Asia and the Pacific* (28 May 2015), vi. Available at https://www.unescap.org/publications/making-it-happen-technology-finance-and-statistics-sustainable-development-asia-and.

SDGs and the AAAA, there is a clear need to move beyond ODA, domestic, and public finance to novel forms of financing which provide incentives for the private sector to participate in development.

The SDG financing framework as endorsed by the multilateral development banks (MDBs) – including the World Bank Group (WBG), the Asian Development Bank (ADB), the African Development Bank (AfDB), the European Investment Bank (EIB) – and other regional development banks together with international bodies such as the European Commission envisages stronger linkages between public and private finance, domestic and international resources. In moving forward with the post-2015 development agenda, countries will be required to use a combination of public, private, domestic, and international sources of financing to fund the SDGs.

A key question goes to the ways private capital can be connected to public finance and directed to development. Private capital has the potential to generate profit for its investors while at the same time delivering a significant development impact in developing countries. However, current levels of private sector investment related to SDGs are relatively low with only a fraction of assets of banks, pension funds, insurers, foundations, and transnational corporations being directed towards sectors critical to the SDGs.[8] The question here is how to translate and channel private funds into SDG-compatible investments in sectors such as telecommunications, water, and sanitation (SDG 6), which have significant financing shortfalls in developing and fragile and conflict states (FCSs).[9] For example, the World Bank has estimated that global infrastructure alone would require at least $2.5 trillion dollars each year until 2030 to achieve the SDGs.[10] Yet, emerging markets are only spending $1 trillion a year currently on infrastructure.[11]

The 2002 Monterrey Consensus on Financing for Development recognised the importance of promoting private international capital flows into developing countries, and complementing developing efforts funded through domestic resources and ODA. Globally, there is a consensus that ODA from member countries of the OECD's Development Assistance Committee (DAC), on its own, is insufficient to finance the post 2015-development agenda and ensure the successful achievement of the SDGs.[12] ODA amounts to roughly about $135 billion annually, and is incapable of funding

---

8 UNEP, *Blended Finance: A Primer for Development Finance and Philanthropic Funders* (2015), 6.
9 UNCTAD, World Investment Report 2014. *Investing in the SDGs: An Action Plan* (2014), 23. Available at: https://unctad.org/en/PublicationsLibrary/wir2014_en.pdf.
10 Ibid., 140.
11 Ibid., 140. See also World Bank, *Financing for Development Post 2015* (October 2013), 16.
12 OECD, 'Global Outlook on Aid: Results of the 2014 DAC Survey on Donors' Forward Spending Plans and Prospects for Improving Aid Predictability' (2014), 9. Available at: http://www.oecd.org/dac/aid-architecture/GlobalOutlookAid-web.pdf. See also OECD, *Geographical Distribution of Financial Flows to Developing Countries* (22 February 2019) available at: https://www.oecd-ilibrary.org/development/geographical-distribution-of-financial-flows-to-developing-countries_20743149.

the new development agenda.[13] It is estimated that 28% of ODA is allocated to least developed countries, and roughly 72% to middle-income countries.[14] Consequently, it is important to develop new and innovative funding mechanisms to increase the pool of financial resources available to support development in the world. Moreover, it is crucial to leverage ODA with private finance, as the bulk of development finance will need to ultimately come from the private sector. In Asia and the Pacific, for example, private sources could provide around $10 trillion for developing countries.[15]

In addition, developing countries will be required to increase their own spending on SDG-related investments. A key pillar of the new development agenda is enhancing domestic resource mobilisation (DRM) in developing countries.[16] Domestic resources constitute the largest pool of resources available to developing countries and mobilised $7.7 trillion in 2012, primarily through taxes, duties, and natural-resource concessions.[17] In fact, mobilising domestic resources is at the heart of the financing for development debate, as domestic resources dwarf developing countries' all other resources including ODA, foreign direct investment (FDI), and capital market capitalization from international flows which roughly amount to $600 billion and $300 billion respectively,[18] underscoring the importance of further expanding DRM as source of finance.[19] Even if all non-DRM related sources of funding were trebled, they would still be too small compared to the domestic resources available.[20] Unless DRM resources are utilised most efficiently and effectively at the country level, the desired SDG-related outcomes will not be achieved.[21]

At another level, another aim of this book is to bring together various strands of development finance and develop a holistic understanding of the post-2015 development finance landscape. For example, blended finance (defined as the strategic use of development finance and philanthropic funds to mobilise private capital flows to developing markets) is widely regarded as an effective catalyst for promoting sustainable development in nascent markets in developing countries.

---

13 Development Committee, above note 5, 7. A United Nations target is that developed countries should devote 0.7% of their gross national income to ODA.

14 See generally OECD, *Net ODA* (2019), available at: https://data.oecd.org/oda/distribution-of-net-oda.htm (last accessed 10 March 2019). See also World Bank, *Financing for Development Post 2015* (October 2013), 15–23.

15 ADB, *Making Money Work: Financing a Sustainable Future in Asia and the Pacific* (2015). Available at: https://www.adb.org/publications/making-money-work-financing-sustainable-future-asia-and-pacific.

16 World Bank, Domestic Resource Mobilization (4 October 2018). Available at: http://www.worldbank.org/en/topic/governance/brief/domestic-resource-mobilization.

17 Development Committee, above note 5, 7.

18 Ibid., 7.

19 World Bank, *Financing for Development Post 2015* (October 2013), 16.

20 Development Committee, above note 5, 7.

21 Ibid.

The book also draws attention to the necessity and importance of building appropriate legal and regulatory frameworks for supporting private sector development. While blended finance is an effective tool for catalysing private equity flows into developing markets, it should be utilised as part of a broader reform programme to support an enabling policy and institutional environment which will de-risk private investment in such markets. An enabling environment is essential for moving more private resources towards sustainable development. Private investments are determined by risk-reward considerations, which, in turn, are driven by public policies globally, as well as policies in host and source countries. Channelling greater private inflows in development will hence require the right policy mix.

It is important to explore the policy interventions available to governments of developing countries. Generally, governments have several options available to them to 'crowd in' greater private finance and investing including: (i) establishing a policy environment that reduces barriers to private investments (referred to as creating an 'investment-grade policy infrastructure'); (ii) adopting policies which facilitate access to finance by private investors; and (iii) coinvesting directly with the private sector.[22] MDBs engaged in policy-based lending and the IMF can support countries to develop the necessary institutions, capital markets, and capacity to support private investment into development by providing financial support, technical assistance, and policy advice.[23] This book is structured into four main parts as outlined further below.

Part One: Overview and Context

Part One of the book outlines the purpose and scope of this book. It provides a roadmap to the SDGs and sets the scene for subsequent discussion of the goals. It consists of the following chapters:

- **Chapter 1: Alma Pekmezovic, 'The UN and Goal Setting'. – From the MDGs to the SDGs'.** This chapter looks more closely at the notion of 'sustainable development' and the components of the post-2015 development agenda. It provides a road map to the Sustainable Development Goals (SDGs) that were adopted by Member States during the United Nations General Assembly in September 2015.

---

22 UNTT Working Group on Sustainable Development Financing, Chapter 4, 'Public Support to Private Investment for Sustainable Development: Challenges and Opportunities, with Emphasis on the Environmental Pillar,' 4. Available at: https://sustainabledevelopment.un.org/content/documents/2111Chapter%204-public%20support%20to%20private%20investment.pdf (last accessed 7 March 2019). This chapter is part of a report produced by the UN Working Group on Financing for Sustainable Development under the UN System Task Team (UNTT).
23 Development Committee, above note 5, 2–3.

- **Chapter 2: Suresh Nanwani, 'SDGs and the Role of International Financial Institutions'.** This chapter discusses the impact of the SDGs and how international financial institutions (IFIs) have shown their collective and individual responses on implementing the ambitious post-2015 development agenda, and in assisting their member countries in implementing the SDGs. The analysis is based on various IFI references including annual reports, strategies, project documents, press releases, and other sources; international and bilateral documents and reports; and civil society organisation inputs and reports to demonstrate the role played by IFIs in implementing the SDGs. The chapter concludes with recommendations on how implementation progress can be improved or augmented to meet the SDG goals and targets.
- **Chapter 3: Iason Gabriel and Varun Gauri, 'Towards a New Global Narrative for the Sustainable Development Goals'.** This chapter looks at the question of how best to motivate support for the SDGs. It asks how the goals can be made compelling for a variety of stakeholders including national governments, the staff of international organisations, and ordinary citizens. To this end, the chapter looks in more detail at the goals themselves, asking how they should be understood and the mechanisms by which they are meant to take effect.
- **Chapter 4: Simon Zadek, 'Overcoming Scarcity – the Paradox of Abundance: Harnessing Digitalization in Financing Sustainable Development'.** This chapter addresses the links between digital finance and the 2030 Agenda. It reviews today's finance system, systemic failures and the need to focus on system design. It takes into consideration the role of technologies such as big data, artificial intelligence, online and mobile platforms, blockchain, and the Internet of Things and its impact on the digitization of finance. It provides examples of applications of digital finance to sustainable development outcomes and provides suggestions on what can be done to further mobilise digital finance to support the SDGs.

Part Two: Where Will the Money Come From? Financing the SDGs

As stated, future development finance will require bringing in more actors and new innovative financing techniques to support development. Part Two of the book considers the role the private sector can play in the post-2015 sustainable development agenda. It discusses the implications of the SDGs for the private sector. Part Two consists of the following chapters:

- **Chapter 5: Alma Pekmezovic, 'The New Framework for Financing the 2030 Agenda for Sustainable Development and the SDGs'.** This chapter considers the new development framework for the period 2016–2030 and the role envisaged for the SDGs. The focus of the discussion is on the challenges and complexities associated with financing the new development agenda. Different types of finance must be used holistically and complementarily to support sustainable development and economic growth. The main types of finance available are: domestic public, domestic private, international public finance, and international private finance. Sustainable development finance must be designed to maximise synergies across all these financing sources. A major focus of the chapter is on private development finance, and on how public and private sources of finance can be mobilised to end extreme poverty and advance the sustainable development agenda. The chapter addresses four key questions: (1) What does the post-2015 financing framework look like? (2) What are the specific roles and challenges of the various types of finance in the development context? (3) Who are the new private players in development finance? And (4) What does it take to mobilise them? In addressing these questions, the chapter considers the shift currently taking place in the landscape of finance, namely a shift from an aid-centric approach on development to a more holistic and broader framework of financing for development that links both public and private resources together. To move from the 'billions' in ODA to the 'trillions' needed for the implementation of the SDGs, the global community and developing countries will need to utilise investments of all kinds, including private public, national, and global, and take advantage of the specific characteristics and strengths of all sources.

- **Chapter 6: Martin Blessing and Tom Naratil, 'The Contribution of the International Private Sector in a More Sustainable Future'.** UBS has observed that private investors increasingly appreciate the power of sustainable investment to satisfy their financial and societal goals simultaneously. According to the authors, there are two main drivers of this trend. First, private investors are increasingly aware that doing good for society can deliver superior risk-adjusted financial returns, compared to strategies that do not account for environmental and social factors. A substantial body of scientific study supports this relationship. One paper reviewed more than 2,000 academic studies from the past 40 years that examined factors related to sustainable investing. It concluded that integrating sustainability factors either improves financial performance or has no negative impact upon it. This finding holds true across all asset classes. Corporations are also embedding social and environmental impact into their operations. Case studies are provided from KKR, Align 17, the World Bank, Hermes Investment Management, and MPM Capital. Supporting sustainable development enables firms not only to manage social and environmental risks to their profitability. It can also boost profits by unlocking new commercial opportunities in underserved parts of the world or helping firms to manage costs more effectively.

- **Chapter 7: Alma Pekmezovic, 'Reorienting the Global Financial System Towards Sustainability'.** If financial market participants are to switch to long-term investment horizons and other sustainable forms of investments, financial regulation and governance frameworks must provide the necessary incentives and the right policy mix to facilitate such a change. This chapter discusses various examples of hard and soft financial regulation (including the sustainability reporting standards, the G20/OECD Principles of Corporate Governance, and other relevant principles, and frameworks), and discusses how these can be further amended and revised to reflect sustainability considerations. In doing so, the chapter aims to develop a sound policy and legal infrastructure – a global framework – that can underpin sustainable investing and enable this form of investment to grow in the future. The overarching theme of this chapter focuses on maximising the social utility of private capital and creating the necessary policies that can help move the financial system toward sustainability.
- **Chapter 8: Emily Chew and Margaret Childe, 'How Asset Managers Can Better Align Public Markets Investing with the SDGs'.** This chapter explores the reasons why the SDGs could prove to be a powerful framework to propel the next phase of responsible and sustainable investment. The authors illustrate an approach developed by Manulife Asset Management that applies the SDGs to public market investing, shares the results of applying this approach to a US large-cap universe of companies, and foreshadow likely SDG-related developments and initiatives for public markets investing in coming years.
- **Chapter 9: Alistair Wilson, 'The Significance of Sustainable Development Goals for Government Credit Quality'.** This chapter explores how the SDGs and the ESG factors to which they are linked underscore sovereign credit quality by fostering sustained growth, reducing income inequality, supporting social stability, promoting stronger governance, and mitigating environmental risk. They also illustrate the observed quantitative relationship between ESG considerations and rating factors and the key role of governance.

Part Three: Technology, Innovation, and Entrepreneurship

Part Three of the book focuses on the importance of channelling technological innovations to finance sustainable development. To advance sustainable development financing, policymakers need to focus on the benefits that financial technology can provide. FinTech covers everything from mobile payment platforms to high-frequency trading (HFT), from crowdfunding and virtual currencies to blockchain.

Here, we explore the ways in which FinTech can be leveraged to serve sustainable development. FinTech allows investors to make a greater set of choices with respect to how to allocate their funds and has the potential to allow consideration of ethical, social, and governance criteria (ESG) and other sustainability factors. It also increases the potential for mobilising funds directly from investors in developing countries. This chapter sets out the links between FinTech and sustainable development and outlines the constructive role that FinTech can play in realigning the financial system with the Sustainable Development Goals.

Part Three consists of the following key chapters:

- **Chapter 10: Dirk A. Zetsche, Ross P. Buckley, and Douglas W. Arner, 'FinTech for Financial Inclusion: Driving Sustainable Growth'.** The full potential of FinTech for financial inclusion will only be realised with a staged and progressive approach in which each stage builds upon the former. Drawing from experiences in a range of developing countries, this chapter suggests that the best way to think about such a process is in four stages. The first stage requires the building of digital identity and e-KYC systems. Once these are established for individuals and businesses, they provide a solid foundation for the next stage of open electronic payments systems. The third stage is government account opening strategies supported by government electronic social payments. And the fourth and final stage is that of a broad digital financial infrastructure, which supports securities trading, clearing and settlement, and other more sophisticated financial functions. This is a long-term journey for any nation but is also one with much to offer to enhance financial inclusion and promote economic growth more generally.

- **Chapter 11: Jon Truby, 'Financing and Self-Financing of SDGs through Financial Technology, Legal, and Fiscal Tools'.** The focus of this chapter is upon two imperatives for the developing world: first, the need to develop innovative SDG financing solutions that can be designed to simultaneously produce benefits going towards the achievement of related SDGs; and second, the need to develop clean energy and low emissions solutions to achieve sustainability in the developing world. The chapter provides a selection of innovative legal and policy solutions designed to offer policymakers realistic choices for achieving and financing SDGs. The focus throughout is on the developing world, and the chapter is divided into three sections based upon the type of policy tool or solution and the purpose behind it, with each section subdivided into differing thematic solutions. The first two parts of the chapter focus on how developing countries can finance SDGs in a self-sufficient manner, without (or with limited) dependence on foreign contributions. The first section of the chapter studies the choices available to reform taxation and the administration of taxation to self-finance and achieve SDGs.

The second section continues on the subject of realising means of self-financing, by considering how both the digitisation of money and the formation of digital identities can benefit the developing world and go towards the achievement of SDGs. The third section of the chapter focuses upon financial technology solutions to achieving and financing SDG 7 and related SDGs.

- **Chapter 12: Guillaume Lafortune and Guido Schmidt-Traub, 'SDG Challenges in G20 Countries'.** This chapter looks at the biggest SDG challenges facing G20 countries and suggests key ways to tackle the required transformations including integrated pathways (as a tool for problem solving), directed innovation and technological change.

- **Chapter 13: Geoff Kendall and Martin Rich, 'The Future-Fit Business Benchmark: Flourishing Business in a Truly Sustainable Future'.** This chapter explores the Future-Fit Business Benchmark, a free business tool designed to guide real progress toward a flourishing future and to make the SDGs a reality. Built upon more than 30 years of scientific research, the Benchmark consists of 23 social and environmental goals which together identify the extra-financial breakeven point every business must reach to ensure it protects people and the planet. The benchmark also shows how all businesses can make credible positive contributions to the SDGs, while simultaneously working to ensure that they are not inadvertently undermining progress elsewhere. Furthermore, businesses are able to convey their journey toward future-fitness through consistent, comparable, forward-looking data, enabling investors to identify which ones are on the right trajectory and increasingly direct their capital accordingly.

- **Chapter 14: Inna Amesheva, Alex Clark, and Julian Payne, 'Financing for Youth Entrepreneurship in Sustainable Development'.** The 2030 Sustainable Development Agenda emphasises the role of young people as 'critical agents of change'. Young people are the workers and entrepreneurs who hold the responsibility of building a brighter future for their countries and the planet. Providing them with education, employment, and entrepreneurial opportunities, particularly in the poorest countries and communities, will prove critical to leveraging the demographic dividend and the unique potential of an ever-increasing youth demographic to deliver on the SDGs.

- **Chapter 15: Julia Walker, 'Transparency in the Supply Chain'.** The forces of globalisation and outsourcing have increased the complexity of managing supply chains. Left unchecked, forced labour and modern-day slavery can operate unnoticed inside supply chains. This chapter looks at the opportunity digitisation provides and – in two case studies – considers the opportunities around (a) supplier onboarding tools and (b) blockchain for transparency and provenance.

Part Four: Facilitating the SDGs by Legal Infrastructure Reform

Part Four considers how law reform measures might promote the SDGs. This part of the book explores the potential of institutional and legal change for sustainability transformation. Generally speaking, the legal measures discussed in this part are directed at SDGs 8 and 9. The key contributions included discuss fundraising law, competition, and consumer law, as well as tax law, providing a discussion on how law reform can be leveraged as a tool for enacting transformative change.

- **Chapter 16: Gordon Walker, 'Facilitating Sustainable Development Goal 8 by Legal Reform Measures'.** This chapter considers how law reform mechanisms can facilitate SDG 8 and targets 8.3 and 8.10 especially as regards law reform to enable FinTech. After an introduction outlining the scope of the chapter, a set of contextual issues (legal families, law reform in common law countries, the roles of policymakers and regulators and constraints in implementation such as corruption) and a key constraint (the MSME funding problem) are identified. The chapter then turns to briefly consider the whole of government initiative ('digital nation') advanced by Estonia (best of breed e-government). Two case studies are then offered. Both relate to the facilitation of fundraising via FinTech. The first considers the position in Hong Kong. The second looks at how a small, island developing state can enable FinTech alternative financing platforms within its existing legislation.
- **Chapter 17: Benjamin Walker, 'Facilitating SDGs by Tax System Reform'.** This chapter outlines the role that tax plays in facilitating the SDGs. Tax is a fundamental pillar of a nation that has political, economic, financial, and societal ramifications that are often unrealised, but felt by its citizens. If countries are serious about achieving their SDGs, a comprehensive evidence-based approach to tax is needed to foster and complement other areas of development. The central question of this chapter is: what are the key tax factors that are relevant for sustainable development? This chapter aids all stakeholders developing and implementing tax policy in developing countries. Furthermore, the chapter provides a critical analysis of tax and sustainability.
- **Chapter 18: Brent Fisse, 'Facilitating SDGs by Competition and Consumer Law and Policy Reform: Aspirations and Challenges in Papua New Guinea'.** This chapter outlines the main features of the competition and consumer reforms proposed in Papua New Guinea (PNG) ('Proposed PNG Reforms') and relates these initiatives to SDG 8 and SDG 9. Further sections address five of the challenges that arise in developing competition and consumer law and policy fit for purpose in PNG and capable of facilitating

SDG 8 and SDG 9: (1) tailoring law and policy to the particular needs and circumstances of PNG; (2) removing statutory and regulatory barriers to entry; (3) designing competition rules that are practical and avoid excessive technicality; (4) harnessing consumer protection laws to protect and promote small business in ways that competition rules cannot; and (5) using enforcement mechanisms that have some chance of working in PNG.

Part I

Overview and Context

1

The UN and Goal Setting

From the MDGs to the SDGs

Alma Pekmezovic

Introduction

This chapter looks closely at the notion of sustainable development and the components of the post-2015 development agenda. It provides a road map to the Sustainable Development Goals (SDGs) adopted by Member States during the United Nations General Assembly (UNGA) in September 2015. The SDGs envision a world that is 'comprehensively sustainable: socially fair; environmentally secure; economically prosperous; inclusive; and more predictable',[1] and call for a concerted effort to build a future based on 'sustainability'. The SDGs encompass social, economic, and environmental objectives, and target both developed and developing countries. They replace the former Millennium Development Goals (MDGs) and establish a new financing framework for development.

The analysis in this chapter centres on the notion of sustainability that underpins the SDGs and is central to the 2030 development agenda. More specifically, this chapter is concerned with two key themes: first, what is development; and, second, why does sustainable development matter? The chapter considers the importance of development, identifies relevant theories of development, and considers the determinants of development. As we shall see, development can be defined in both human and economic terms, with different implications for the development agenda. Over the past decade, a range of theories have been developed to explain the determinants of development. This has sparked an extensive debate about the relationship between law, political institutions, and economic development.

Third, the chapter considers the value of development objectives such as the SDGs. It considers the purposes and premises of the SDGs and discusses their underpinnings. In doing so, this chapter lays the groundwork for subsequent discussion in this book. The main purpose is to outline the 17 SDGs and their implications for scaling up development finance.

---

1 Business and Sustainable Development Commission, *Better Business. Better World* (January 2017), http://report.businesscommission.org/report, 5.

Sustainable Development Goals: Harnessing Business to Achieve the SDGs through Finance, Technology, and Law Reform, First Edition. Edited by Julia Walker, Alma Pekmezovic, and Gordon Walker.

What Is Development?

There is no generally agreed-upon criteria for classifying countries as developed or developing countries.[2] This is because there are different measures of development. We can measure development across a range of variables, including economic, social, and political and trade factors. Accordingly, different international institutions employ different criteria for measuring development and classifying countries. Most OECD members are considered high-income countries, and, membership of the OECD is taken as a criterion for developed status. Moreover, the term *developing country* is not a legal term *per se*, but it does appear in some international treaties and agreements, most obviously in the provisions of some WTO agreements and the UN Framework Convention on Climate Change in developing countries. For instance, Article XVIII(1) of the General Agreement on Tariffs and Trade (GATT) defines developing countries as those 'economies which can only support low standards of living and are in the early stage of development.'

The World Trade Organization's Self-Selection Principle allows WTO member countries to unilaterally announce whether they are developed or developing countries (referred to as 'unilateral declarations'). Self-selection can take place on an ad hoc basis. However, such an announcement is open to challenge by other WTO members. In addition to references in the GATT to 'developing countries', some international environmental treaties also refer to developing countries. However, they adopt different classification criteria. For example, the Kyoto Protocol divides countries into four main groups: (i) members of the OECD; (ii) countries with economies in transition; and (iii and iv) countries outside these two categories, which are mainly developing countries and the least developed countries (LDCs).

Other terms may be used in the development literature. Reference may be made to First World Countries, as opposed to Second, Third, and Fourth World Countries. In addition, a differentiation is made between the Global North and the Global South. The term *Global South* is taken to refer to developing countries in the Southern Hemisphere. Here, the Global South would include Latin America, South and Southern Asia, the Middle East, Africa, and the Pacific Region, whereas the Global North includes North America, Western Europe, and Japan. Core States are generally defined as the Group of Seven plus One, or G7 + 1 (Russia); Group of Eight or G-8; and Group of Twenty or G-20. Furthermore, the IMF distinguishes between 'advanced markets' and 'emerging markets', with emerging markets being a new category of countries that arises from the category of developing countries – they are partners and competitors of some developed countries.

---

2 Michael J. Trebilcock and Mariana Mota Prado, *What Makes Poor Countries Poor? Institutional Determinants of Development* (Edward Elgar Publishing, 2012), 2.

The term *development* does not have a fixed definition that is accepted universally. There are different visions of development. Generally speaking, the notion of 'development' is understood to refer to progressive social, political, and economic change in developing countries. Often, development is associated with economic growth – the latter concept being understood as an increase in the capacity of an economy to produce goods and services, compared from one period of time to another. The term is generally taken to refer to the ability of firms to produce goods and services at an efficient and optimal level.

According to the Commission on Growth and Development – which includes a broad group of eminent economists and policymakers – countries with high, sustained growth exhibit five common characteristics:

1. *Strategic integration with the world economy:* High-growth countries benefit from the world economy in several ways: they import ideas, technology, and knowhow from the rest of the world, while at the same time exploiting global demand for their goods.
2. *Mobility of resources, particularly labour*: In high-growth economies, capital, and especially, labour moves rapidly from sector to sector, industry to industry. This mobility of resources was found to be a feature of all the 13 high-growth countries considered in the Growth and Development Report.
3. *High savings*: Sustained economic growth is typically backed up by high domestic savings.
4. *High investment rates.*
5. A *capable government committed to growth.*[3]

We can juxtapose economic conceptions of development such as economic growth with more holistic conceptions of development, such as human well-being or freedom. In *Development as Freedom,* Nobel Prize–winning economist Professor Amartya Sen views development as the process of expanding real freedoms and removing major sources of 'unfreedom' – demonstrating a strong correlation between poverty and lack of freedom.[4] The achievement of such freedoms is seen as the primary end of development. Although this book accepts the view that the attainment of such freedoms is an important dimension of development and instrumental to social progress, its primary focus will be on sustainable economic growth. Sustainable economic growth is not seen as the ultimate end of development, but rather one dimension of it.

---

3 Commission on Growth and Development, *The Growth Report: Strategies for Sustained Growth and Inclusive Development* (Washington, DC: World Bank, 2008).
4 See Amartya Sen, *Development as Freedom* (New York: Knopf, 1999).

Is There a Right to Development?

The UNGA Declaration on the Right to Development of 4 December 1986 defines the concept as 'an inalienable human right by virtue of which every human person and all peoples are entitled to participate in, contribute to, and enjoy economic, social, cultural and political development, in which all human rights and fundamental freedoms can be fully realized' (at Art. 1). The right to development includes, but goes beyond, the neoclassical model of economic growth measured by increases in gross domestic product (GDP) or per capita income.

The right to development was proclaimed in the Declaration on the Right to Development adopted in 1986. The right is also recognised in some other international instruments that are nonbinding resolutions. It has therefore been argued that the right to development does not create binding obligations in international law.

Measuring Economic Development

As stated, different international institutions employ different criteria to measure development. A frequently used indicator is a change in total economic output expressed as GDP. Based on GDP and economic output, we can further subcategorise countries into high-income, middle-income, low-income, and low-middle income countries.

For the 2019 fiscal year, low-income economies are defined as those with a GNI per capita, calculated using the World Bank Atlas method, of $995 or less in 2017; lower middle-income economies are those with a GNI per capita between $996 and $3,895; upper middle-income economies are those with a GNI per capita between $3,896 and $12,055; high-income economies are those with a GNI per capita of $12,056 or more.[5] The World Bank conventionally refers to low-income and middle-income countries as developing countries, and to high-income countries as developed countries.

According to some estimates more than 80% of the world population lives in developing countries.[6] These countries produce only 20% of the world's products and services. Low-income countries have markedly different economies from higher-income countries. More than half of the countries are in Sub-Saharan Africa.

---

5 World Bank, World Bank Country and Lending Groups, https://datahelpdesk.worldbank.org/knowledgebase/articles/906519-world-bank-country-and-lending-groups (last accessed 28 February 2019).

6 World Bank, 'Nearly Half the World Lives on Less than $5.50 a Day' (Press Release, 17 October 2018), https://www.worldbank.org/en/news/press-release/2018/10/17/nearly-half-the-world-lives-on-less-than-550-a-day.

Among developing countries, the subcategory of least-developed countries (LDCs) is recognised in international practice. The UN Economic and Social Council (ECOSOC) designates a list of LDCs, which is updated every three years. The three criteria employed for the identification of LDCs are low income, weak human resources (based on indicators of nutrition, health, education, and adult literacy), and economic vulnerability (based on the instability of agricultural production, instability of export, the economic importance of nontraditional activities, handicap of economic smallness, and the percentage of the population displaced by natural disasters). Countries with populations exceeding 75 million are not included in the list.

Measuring Non-Economic Aspects of Development

The Human Development Index (HDI) has been used since 1993 by the UN Development Programme (UNDP). The HDI measures a country's achievements in three principal dimensions: health and longevity, measured by life expectancy; education, measured by the percentage of adult literacy and the combined enrolment ratio for primary, secondary, and tertiary schools; and standard of living, measured by GDP per capita.[7]

Second, there is a multidimensional poverty index which was developed by Oxford University in conjunction with UNDP (the United Nations Development Programme). This index seeks to quantify the nature and extent of poverty in each country. The purpose of this index is not only to reveal how many people are poor but also to ascertain the nature and intensity of the prevailing poverty. Thus, the Multidimensional Poverty Index (MPI) captures measures such as child mortality, years of schooling, access to water, sanitation, electricity, health, and living standards.[8] The MPI is often used to reveal acute poverty in countries.

Another multidimensional approach is exemplified by the MDGs, which have now been replaced by the SDGs. The MDGs used various indicators to monitor development progress, setting a number of targets including: (i) to eradicate poverty and hunger; (ii) achieve universal primary education; (iii) promote gender equality and empower women; (iv) reduce child mortality; (v) improve maternal health; (vi) combat HIV/AIDS, malaria, and other diseases; (vii) ensure environmental sustainability; and (viii) develop a global partnership for development. The MDGs also focused on the importance of developing an open trading and financial system, addressing the special needs

---

7 UN Development Programme, The Human Development Index (HDI), http://hdr.undp.org/en/content/human-development-index-hdi.

8 Sabine Alkire and Maria Emma Santos, 'Acute Multidimensional Poverty: A New Index for Developing Countries'. OPHI Working Paper No. 38 (2010): 7.

of small-island developing States, dealing with debt problems of developing countries and making the benefits of new technologies such as information and communication technologies available in developing countries. Unlike the SDGs, however, the MDGs targeted developing countries only.

The MDGs and their framework for accountability have led to substantial improvements in certain areas. The developing countries increased their focus on reaching the 8 MDGs, and created specific funds to achieve certain goals (such as advancing education/health, combating malaria, etc.). Most notably, the mortality rate of children under five was cut by more than half since 1990.[9] Moreover, as a result of the MDGs, the number of people living in extreme poverty has declined by more than half from 1.9 billion in 1990 to 836 million in 2015.[10] Compared with 1990, however, there are now more poor people in Sub-Saharan Africa and fewer in East Asia and the Pacific.

The Sustainable Development Goals (SDGs)

The SDGs were developed through a bottom-up and consultative process, and are intended to be holistic and universal in nature, in the sense that they encompass social, economic, and environmental goals. The SDGs were first formally discussed at the United Nations Conference on Sustainable Development held in Rio de Janeiro in June 2012 (Rio+20). During the conference, the UN Member States agreed to establish an intergovernmental process to develop a set of 'action-oriented, concise and easy to communicate' goals to help drive the implementation of the sustainable development agenda. The Rio+20 outcome document, *The Future We Want*, also called for the goals to be coherent with the UN development agenda beyond 2015.[11] A 30-member Open Working Group (OWG) of the General Assembly was tasked with preparing a proposal on the SDGs, as well as a concrete list of targets and measurable indicators to ensure that progress against the SDGs can be tracked. On 25 September 2015, the United Nations General Assembly accepted the OWG's proposals and used them as a basis for developing the 2030 Agenda.

---

9 United Nations, *The Millennium Development Goals Report* (2015), http://www.un.org/ millenniumgoals/2015_MDG_Report/pdf/MDG%202015%20PR%20Key%20Facts%20Global.pdf.
10 Ibid.
11 United Nations, *The Future We Want*. Outcome document of the United Nations Conference on Sustainable Development, Rio de Janeiro, Brazil, 20–22 June 2012, https:// sustainabledevelopment.un.org/content/documents/733FutureWeWant.pdf.

The new SDGs came into effect in September 2015.[12] They replace the MDGs and, unlike the MDGs, apply to all countries including developed and developing countries, regardless of their level of development. The goals and targets set out an exceptionally ambitious and transformational vision, envisaging a world free of poverty, hunger, and disease, and also free of fear of violence – a world with universal literacy and equitable and universal access to quality education, health care, and social protection, promising more peaceful and inclusive societies. The Preamble to the SDGs states as follows:

> . . . We envisage a world of **universal respect for human rights and human dignity, the rule of law, justice, equality and non-discrimination**; of **respect for race, ethnicity and cultural diversity**; and of equal opportunity permitting the full realization of **human potential** and contributing to **shared prosperity**. A world which invests in its **children** and in which every child grows up free from violence and exploitation. A world in which every **woman and girl** enjoys full gender equality and all legal, social and economic barriers to their empowerment have been removed. . . .
>
> We envisage a world in which every country enjoys **sustained, inclusive and sustainable economic growth and decent work** for all. A world in which consumption and production patterns and use of all **natural resources – from air to land, from rivers, lakes and aquifers to oceans and seas – are sustainable**. One in which **democracy, good governance and the rule of law, as well as an enabling environment at the national and international levels**, are essential for sustainable development, including sustained and inclusive **economic growth, social development, environmental protection and the eradication of poverty and hunger**. . . .
>
> In its scope, however, the framework we are announcing today goes **far beyond the Millennium Development Goals**. Alongside continuing development priorities such as **poverty eradication, health, education and food security and nutrition**, it sets out a wide range of economic, social and environmental objectives. . . It also, crucially, defines means of implementation.[13]

---

12 The SDGs can be downloaded from https://sustainabledevelopment.un.org/post2015. See also United Nations, 'Transforming Our World: The 2030 Agenda for Sustainable Development' A/RES/70/1 (September 2015), https://sustainabledevelopment.un.org/content/documents/21252030%20Agenda%20for%20Sustainable%20Development%20web.pdf.
13 Ibid., 3–6.

The SDGs are more complex than the MDGs and significantly expand the scope of the former goals. The focus is not simply on development but sustainable development or 'development that meets the needs of the present without compromising the ability of future generations to meet their own needs.'[14] Another definition used in the 2002 Convention for Cooperation in the Protection and Sustainable Development of the Marine and Coastal Environment of the Northeast Pacific defines sustainable development as:

> . . . the process of progressive change in the quality of life of human beings, which places them as the centre and primary subjects of development, by means of economic growth with social equity and transformation of production methods and consumption patterns, sustained by the ecological balance and life support systems of the region. This process implies respect for regional, national and local ethnic and cultural diversity, and full public participation, peaceful coexistence in harmony with nature, without prejudice to and ensuring the quality of life of future generations.[15]

The concept integrates economic and social developmental as well as environmental protection. In addition to being a guiding principle in the SDGs, the notion of 'sustainable development' is part of the 'object and purpose' of a growing number of international treaties, and thus relevant to the interpretation of these instruments.[16] The term appears often in economic, social, and environmental treaties, which make explicit reference to developed and developing countries.[17]

According to some commentators, the new SDG agenda is likely to displace current country groupings, such as developed or developing countries, with new country classifications according to variables such as: per-capita income levels (low, middle, or high-income countries), specific conditions (e.g. post-conflict,

---

14 World Commission on Environment and Development, *Our Common Future* (Oxford: Oxford University Press, 1987), https://www.sustainabledevelopment2015.org/AdvocacyToolkit/index.php/earth-summit-history/historical-documents/92-our-common-future.

15 The 2002 *Convention for Cooperation in the Protection and Sustainable Development of the Marine and Coastal Environment of the Northeast Pacific* (18 February 2002).

16 See D. French, *International Law and Policy of Sustainable Development* (Manchester: Manchester University Press, 2005), 168.

17 See M.C. Cordonier Segger and A. Khalfan, *Sustainable Development Law: Principles, Practices & Prospects* (Oxford: Oxford University Press, 2004), 31. Examples of treaties which use the notion of 'sustainable development' include the 1992 UN Convention on Biological Diversity, the 2000 Cartagena Protocol, the 1992 UN Framework Convention on Climate Change, the 1997 Kyoto Protocol, as well as the 2000 Cotonou Partnership Agreement between the European Union and the African Caribbean and Pacific Countries.

small-island, or landlocked), or specific problems (e.g. highly polluting, ecological footprint).[18]

The new SDGs are broadly formulated and consist of 17 goals (16 substantive goals and one goal that calls for the 'means of implementation' to achieve the 16 goals) and 169 targets. Thus, SDG 1 calls for the end of extreme poverty and builds on the poverty-reduction efforts of the MDGs, while SDG 2 focuses on hunger eradication. Development under the new SDG agenda will commence once extreme poverty is eradicated. Other substantive gaols include universal health coverage (SDG 3), universal quality education (SDG 4), ending gender discrimination (SDG 5), universal access to water (SDG 6), access to modern energy (SDG 7), sustainable economic growth (SDG 8), sustainable infrastructure (SDG 9), environmental sustainability (SDGs 11–15, e.g. reducing exposure to climate-related extreme events; combating climate change through low-carbon energy systems as addressed by SDG 13), and reduced inequalities (SDG 10).

These broad goals link with specific targets, and address a wide range of issues that are interlinked. For instance, Goal 1 (eliminating poverty) is related to inequality in Goal 10, which again is related to gender equality in Goal 5, which, in turn is related to decent work – Goal 8 – and quality education – Goal 4. The goals and targets should be viewed as an integrated, indivisible whole and not separately, and it is important to recognise the linkages between and within the goals.

A key difference between the SDGs and the MDGs is that the SDGs tackle a dual challenge: they seek to (1) overcome poverty (which is captured in SDG 1), and (2) promote sustainable development that encompasses economic, social, and environmental dimensions.

Sustainable Development Goal 8 specifically addresses the importance of sustainable economic growth, and refers to the importance of promoting development-oriented policies that support entrepreneurship and encourage the formalisation and growth of micro-, small, and medium-sized enterprises (MMSEs).[19] The achievement of SDG 8 will require effective domestic resource mobilisation (DRM) and extensive private sector investment.

---

18 Adolf Kloke-Lesch, 'The G20 and the Sustainable Development Goals (SDGs): Reflections on Future Roles and Tasks'. Third Annual G20 Think Tank Summit 'Global Governance and Open Economy' (August 2015), available via Sustainable Development Solutions Network Germany, https://www.die-gdi.de/fileadmin/user_upload/pdfs/dauerthemen_spezial/20150730_Kloke-Lesch_The_G20_and_the_Sustainable_Development_Goals.pdf, 2.

19 See SDGs generally, http://www.un.org/ga/search/view_doc.asp?symbol=A/RES/70/1&Lang=E (last accessed 28 February 2019) at para. [8.3].

Situating the SDGs in the International Legal Framework

The SDGs are a statement of aspirations intended to guide global development efforts. The Goals are not part of a binding legal treaty, but part of a revitalised global partnership intended to work in the spirit of global solidarity. They represent voluntary guidelines like the predecessor MDGs and are intended to inspire policy and legislative action over the next 15 years in areas of critical importance. Since the goals are not enshrined in a treaty, countries are not legally obliged to implement them. The implementation of the SDGs, therefore, will largely depend on civil society and citizens exerting pressure on their respective governments to implement the goals. Furthermore, global engagement in support of the implementation of the goals and targets will be essential for the achievement of the SDGs, as recognised in the UN Resolution:

> We recognize that *each country has primary responsibility* for its own economic and social development. The new Agenda deals with the means required for implementation of the Goals and targets. We recognize that these will include the *mobilization of financial resources as well as capacity-building* and the *transfer of environmentally sound technologies* to developing countries on favourable terms, including on concessional and preferential terms, as mutually agreed. *Public finance*, both domestic and international, will play a vital role in providing essential services and public goods and in catalysing other sources of finance. We acknowledge the role of the diverse *private sector*, ranging from micro-enterprises to cooperatives to multinationals, and that of civil society organizations and philanthropic organizations in the implementation of the new Agenda.[20] [emphasis added]

The SDGs, although integrated and indivisible, global in nature, and universally applicable, take into account different national realities, capacities, and levels of development. Each government will need to set its own national targets guided by the global level of ambition but taking into account national circumstances. Furthermore, each government will decide how these aspirational and global targets should be incorporated into national planning processes, policies, and strategies. Although SDGs are not legally binding, governments are expected to establish national frameworks to achieve the goals.

---

20 United Nations, 'Transforming Our World: The 2030 Agenda for Sustainable Development' A/RES/70/1 (September 2015), 10.

Enabling legal frameworks will therefore be crucial for the implementation and achievement of the SDGs. The Goals, in particular, are intended to help the policy-setting process, which typically consists of political parties setting out a policy agenda (i.e. determining country-specific objectives, goals, and milestones via a national development plan, thus providing policy leadership) and legislating to achieve these policies. This, in turn, is expected to ensure meaningful national ownership of the SDGs.

Not all SDGs, however, will be of equal importance in every country or regions of a country. In deciding upon the relevant Goals and targets, each country is likely to face specific challenges to achieve sustainable development. These challenges will differ depending on the countries' own priorities and needs. Furthermore, some SDGs will require legal innovations – for example, passing specific laws to achieve the SDGs. It might also be crucial to review all proposed legislation through a sustainable development lens and mainstream the SDGs in this manner (e.g. referencing the SDGs and explaining how a piece of legislation contributes to the achievement of the SDGs). This will assist in the dissemination of the SDGs.

Another important tool for disseminating the SDGs will be free trade agreements. For example, Chapter 16 of the Japan–EU Free Trade Agreement includes all of the key elements of the European approach on sustainable development and provides for certain agreements – including the UN Framework Convention on Climate Change and the Paris Accord, as well as commitments to the conservation and sustainable management of natural resources, addressing biodiversity (including combating illegal wildlife trade), forestry (including fighting against illegal logging), and fisheries (including combating illegal, unreported, and unregulated [IUU] fishing); and the promotion of Corporate Social Responsibility and other trade and investment practices supporting sustainable development.[21]

Theories of Development: Towards a New Theory of Sustainable Development

While it is beyond the scope of this chapter to consider various theories of development in depth, the key theories will be shortly considered in this part. These theories can be grouped into four categories: (1) economic theories of development; (2) cultural theories of development; (3) geographic theories of development; and (4) institutional theories of development. Except for the latter theory, generally speaking, the theories tend to marginalise the importance

---

21 EU-Japan Economic Partnership Agreement 18.4.2018 COM (August 2018), 192 final. See Article 16.1, http://trade.ec.europa.eu/doclib/docs/2018/august/tradoc_157228.pdf#page=440.

of a country's institutions to development. Furthermore, the theories do not consider the relevance of sustainable development.

Economic Theories of Development

Economic theories of development can be categorised into a number of sub-theories. For example, some theories adopt a *linear stages approach* to development. According to these theories, countries need to mobilise domestic savings and foreign investment to enhance GDP growth.[22] *Structural change theories*, on the other hand, proceed from the assumption that economic growth requires the transformation of domestic economic structures from a 'heavy emphasis on traditional subsistence agriculture to a more modern, more urbanized, and more industrially diverse manufacturing and service economy'.[23] Hence, the implication of this group of theories is that the state needs to implement policies that promote industrialisation, mechanisation of the agricultural sector, the creation of a strong education system, urban planning, and infrastructure investments.[24] The significance of the institutional framework for development, however, is largely left out in such models.

The same criticism can be made of *dependency theories* that emerged in developing countries. These theories look to external and historical influences as a central determinant of economic development, but do not address the importance of the institutional framework.[25] The theories advocate important substitution industrialisation policies with high levels of tariff protection to restrict the flow of imports and foster the development of local industries.[26]

Cultural Theories of Development

Cultural theories of development assert that societies perceive the notion of development differently. For example, radical relativists argue that Western standards or benchmarks should not be used to measure development, as such benchmarks may be incompatible with the underlying culture of some societies.[27]

---

22 Michael Todaro and Stephen Smith, *Economic Development* (Boston, San Francisco, New York: Addison Wesley, 2012, 11th ed.), 110–111.
23 Ibid., 115.
24 Trebilcock and Mota Prado, *What Makes Poor Countries Poor?*, 9.
25 Dennis Conway and Nikolas Heynen, 'Classical Dependency Theories: From ECLA to Andre Gunder Frank', in V. Desai and R. Potter (eds), *The Companion to Development Studies* (London: Oxford University Press, 2002), 97.
26 John Coatsworth, 'Structures, Endowments and Institutions in the Economic History of Latin America', *Latin America Research Review*, 40, no. 3 (2005): 126.
27 A. Escobar, 'Introduction: Development and the Anthropology of Modernity' in *Encountering Development: The Making and Unmaking of the Third World* (Princeton, NJ: Princeton University Press, 1995), 3–20.

Another variant of this view is that substantive cultural change is crucial for the promotion of Western conceptions of development in some developing countries as such countries may have a progress-resistant cultural outlook that prevents development.[28] A third strand argues that development policies need to be formulated in light of divergent cultural contexts.[29] The implication is that it is impossible to develop overarching, universal policies; policies need to be tailored to particular contexts and must be country-specific.

Culture and 'informal institutions', therefore, are viewed as an important factor in developing strategies. Thus, the new institutional economics expressly recognises the role of culture in development. As Douglass North points out:

> Institutions are the rules of the game of a society, or more formally, are the humanly devised constraints that structure human interactions. They are composed for formal rules (statute law, common law, and regulation), informal constraints (conventions, norms of behavior and self-imposed codes of conduct) and the enforcement characteristics of both.[30]

However, one criticism which can be made in this context is that the theories do not go beyond a mere recognition of culture as an important factor in the development discourse. Culture is, hence, often treated as a black box in the institutional analysis.[31] For example, it is unclear to what extent culture influences the operation of formal institutions, and *vice versa*. To what extent does culture influence the rule of law and democratic accountability, for example? Moreover, can formal institutions change culture?

Geographic Theories of Development

According to a third group of theories, the geographic location and condition of a country geography matters and has an impact on development. For instance, tropical countries are more likely to be underdeveloped for several reasons: their tropical climate might impact on productive economic activity, especially in sectors such as agriculture due to lower fertility of tropical soils, the high prevalence of crop pests and parasites, and the high evaporation of water.[32] Similarly, land-locked countries face barriers to engaging in

---

28 L. Harrison and S. Huntington, *Culture Matters* (New York, NY: Basic Books, 2000) 158–76.

29 Amartya Sen, 'How Does Culture Matter?' in Vijayendra Rao and Michael Walton (eds), *Culture and Public Action* (Stanford University Press: 2004), 39.

30 Douglass North, 'The New Institutional Economics and Third World Development', in J. Harris et al. (eds), *Economics and Third World Development* (London: Routledge, 1995).

31 D. Cemoglu and S. Johnson, 'Unbundling Institutions', *Journal of Political Economy* 113 (2005): 5.

32 Trebilcock and Mota Prado, *What Makes Poor Countries Poor?*, 19.

international trade and are often 'hostages to their [coastal] neighbors' depending on them for access to the coast and trading routes.[33] While geography is not seen as the sole cause of lack of development, it is considered a barrier to development. Geographic theories of development suggest that barriers to development arise because of: (i) transportation costs (especially high in the case of landlocked countries); (ii) the presence of diseases (especially prevalent in tropical countries); and (iii) poor soil fertility.[34] Thus, Jeffrey Sachs takes the view that material factors – such as resource endowments, disease burdens, climate, and geographical location – are determinants of economic growth.[35]

The criticism which has been raised in this context, however, is that natural resource endowments are only important for providing favourable conditions for the emergence of certain types of institutions. The 'institutions themselves remain the proximate causes of growth, and in many cases can be shown to be exogenous to the material conditions under which a given society develops.'[36]

Institutional Theories of Development

A fourth school of thought – new institutional economics – is based on the view that institutions have a direct impact on growth and development. Thus, per the institutional perspective, countries should not consider themselves captive to factors such as history, culture, climate, and geography and natural resource endowments.[37] Rather, it is the institutions and their quality that matters. They are the proximate causes of growth. As North notes:

> The institutional framework dictates the kinds of skills and knowledge perceived to have the maximum pay off. . . . If the institutional matrix rewards piracy (or more generally redistributive activities) more than productive activity, then learning will take the form of learning to be better pirates.[38]

---

33 Paul Collier, *The Bottom Billion* (Oxford: Oxford University Press, 2007), 55.

34 Jeffrey Sachs, 'Institutions Matter, But Not for Everything: The Role of Geography and Resource Endowments in Development Shouldn't Be Underestimated', *Finance and Development* 40, no. 2 (2003).

35 Ibid.

36 Francis Fukuyama, 'Development and the Limits of Institutional Design' in Global Development Network, http://depot.gdnet.org/gdnshare/pdf2/gdn_library/annual_conferences/seventh_annual_conference/Fukuyama_plenary1.pdf(last accessed 28 February 2019).

37 Trebilcock and Mota Prado, *What Makes Poor Countries Poor?*, 26.

38 Douglass North, 'The New Institutional Economics and Third World Development' in J. Harris et al. (eds), *Economics and Third World Development* (London: Routledge, 1995), 17.

Similarly, Holden et al. state:

> There is growing evidence that the most plausible explanation for the disappointing failure of most developing countries to grow and prosper is the inadequate institutions that underpin private sector development.[39]

Institutional quality can be measured along six dimensions: (1) voice and accountability (the extent to which citizens are able to participate in political processes); (2) political stability (the likelihood that the government in power will be destabilised); (3) government effectiveness (as measured by the quality of public service provision, the quality of bureaucracy, independence of civil service sector from political pressures); (4) regulatory quality (this includes the incidence of market-unfriendly policies such as price controls, inadequate bank supervision, and perceptions of the burden imposed by excessive regulation in areas such as foreign trade and business development); (5) the rule of law (including the effectiveness and predictability of the judiciary, the enforceability of contracts); and (6) the control of corruption (measures the frequency of additional payments to get things done, the effects of corruption on the business environment).[40]

These measures, for example, are used in the World Bank Governance Project. The project uses these measures in addition to a composite 'governance' index that measures the overall quality of governance in a given country. According to the World Bank Governance group, improvements in overall governance and institutional quality correspond to increases in per capita income. Thus, Kaufmann notes:

> Indeed, the effects of improved governance on income in the long run are found to be very large, with an estimated 400 percent improvement in per capita income associated with an improvement in governance by one standard deviation, and similar improvements in reducing child mortality and illiteracy. To illustrate, an improvement in the rule of law by one standard deviation from the current levels in Ukraine to those 'middling' levels prevailing in South Africa would lead to a fourfold increase in per capita income in the long run ... Similar results emerge from other governance dimensions: a mere one standard deviation improvement in voice and accountability from the low level of Indonesia to the middling level of Mexico, or from the level of Mexico to that of Costa Rica, would be associated with an estimated fourfold increase in per capita incomes, as well as similar improvements in reducing child mortality by 75 percent and major gains in literacy.[41]

---

39 Paul Holden et al., *Swimming against the Tide* (ADB Report, 2004), 99.
40 World Bank, 'Governance Matters' (World Bank Policy Research), Working Paper No. 2196 (1999).
41 Daniel Kaufmann, 'Governance Redux: the Empirical Challenge'. Available at: https://papers.ssrn.com/sol3/papers.cfm?abstract_id=541322.279, if acceptable? (last accessed 20 February 2019).

Moreover, Kaufmann and Kraay find there is a direct causal effect from better governance to improved development. The implication of these findings is that it is of fundamental importance for countries to engage in sustained interventions to improve governance and the quality of their institutions. The empirical evidence supports the conclusion that strong institutions bring about improvements in development indicators.[42]

A New Theory of Sustainable Development

Central to the notion of sustainable development is the idea that development should promote the human development of people without compromising the integral human development of people tomorrow. A theory of sustainable development would therefore necessarily insist, for example, that nonrenewable resources be used modestly and eventually be entirely replaced by renewable resources, since the exploitation of certain resources would have long-term implications for the survivability of humanity, especially in light of ecological conditions of climate change.

Measuring Progress Towards the SDGs

A study by the Bertelsmann Foundation examines how high-income countries are currently performing against the SDGs.[43] The study presents the first 'stress test' of rich countries for the SDGs and presents a new SDG Index to assess country performance on the goals. The SDG Index illustrates the overall performance of each OECD country based on the 17 goals and 34 indicators examined in the study. It offers detailed profiles of the strengths and weaknesses of each country and highlights best practices for achieving the SDGs.[44]

Looking at the performance of the countries against the 17 SDGs, the study concludes that OECD countries currently vary greatly in their capacity to meet the SDGs. In fact, no country performs outstandingly on all goals, and not all countries are ready for the SDGs. Each country faces its own challenges in implementing the SDGs and countries will need to implement domestic reforms in order to meet the SDGs. As a group, the OECD countries face some

---

42 Daniel Kaufmann and Aart Kraay, 'Governance and Growth: Causality Which Way? Evidence for the World in Brief' (Washington: WBI, 2003). Available at http://citeseerx.ist.psu.edu/viewdoc/summary?doi=10.1.1.201.2315.
43 Christian Kroll, 'Sustainable Development Goals: Are the Rich Countries Ready?' (2015), https://www.bertelsmann-stiftung.de/de/publikationen/publikation/did/sustainable-development-goals-are-the-rich-countries-ready/.
44 The overall SDG Index was calculated as an unweighted arithmetic mean of the 34 individual indicators. For each indicator, a score of 10 is the best and a score of 1 the worst result possible.

common challenges, such as fostering inclusive economic growth (meeting SDGs 8 and 10) and promoting sustainable consumption and production patterns (SDG 12). Another challenge for OECD countries is drawing energy from renewable sources, as half of all OECD nations currently obtain less than 11% of their energy from renewable sources.[45] The top five performers on the SDG Index include Sweden, Norway, Denmark, Finland, and Switzerland.[46] These countries are considered fit for implementing the SDGs and in a good position to further drive improvements in terms of sustainable development. Sweden, for example, has cut its already low greenhouse gas emissions relative to GDP by more than 35% since 2006.[47]

Conclusions

The SDGs are ambitious in both scope and vision. They represent a universal set of inspirational goals for all countries. The success of the SDGs, however, will depend on the implementation of the goals across both developed and developing countries. Since the SDGs are not part of a binding treaty, countries are not legally obliged to implement the goals. Therefore, it is essential for countries to have the right governance and policy structures in place that will facilitate the implementation of the sustainable development agenda and contribute to the achievement of the SDGs.

---

45 Ibid., 5.
46 Ibid.
47 Ibid.

2

SDGs and the Role of International Financial Institutions

Suresh Nanwani

Introduction

The Sustainable Development Goals (SDGs) constitute the post-2015 development agenda, replacing the Millennium Development Goals (MDGs), the previous framework for international development. The post-2015 development agenda is different from past global development agreements as it applies universally to all countries and recognises that no country has yet achieved sustainable development together with the added SDGs pledge in the preamble of the 2030 Agenda that 'no one will be left behind'. This chapter discusses the impact of the SDGs and how international financial institutions (IFIs) have shown their collective and individual responses in implementing the ambitious post-2015 development agenda and in assisting their member countries in implementing the SDGs.

The IFIs covered include the World Bank, Asian Development Bank (ADB), and European Bank for Reconstruction and Development (EBRD) and other institutions such as International Finance Corporation (IFC). The views and contributions by other development actors in relation to the work of the IFIs are also considered. These include bilateral donors (Sweden); international organisations and agencies (UNESCAP, UNDP, and UNCTAD); and civil society organisations (CSOs) such as Oxfam because they provide insights on how these development actors view IFI implementation. The analysis is based on various IFI references including annual reports, strategies, project documents, press releases, and other sources; international and bilateral documents and reports and CSO inputs and reports to demonstrate the role played by IFIs in implementing the SDGs. The first section focuses on the response and implementation on the SDGs by IFIs. The second section relates how IFIs internalise their project processing in relation to the SDGs and take other actions to implement the SDGs, and responses from other development actors. The final section concludes with recommendations on how implementation progress

Sustainable Development Goals: Harnessing Business to Achieve the SDGs through Finance, Technology, and Law Reform, First Edition. Edited by Julia Walker, Alma Pekmezovic, and Gordon Walker.
© 2019 John Wiley & Sons Ltd. Published 2019 by John Wiley & Sons Ltd.

can be improved or augmented to meet the goals and targets set in the Agenda 2030's 'supremely ambitious and transformational vision.'[1]

Response and Implementation of the SDGs by IFIs

On the same day as the adoption of the SDGs, seven IFIs – African Development Bank (AfDB), Asian Development Bank (ADB), Inter-American Development Bank (IADB), European Bank for Reconstruction and Development (EBRD), European Investment Bank (EIB), International Monetary Fund (IMF), and the World Bank Group (WBG) – published a joint press release stating they (i) supported the new development agenda, (ii) are 'fully committed to stepping up their support to ensure its success', and (iii) 'vowed to examine how they could increase their own financing and also to work to ensure a greater mobilization of domestic resources and expanded funding from the private sector.'[2]

The SDGs balance three dimensions of development: economic, social, and environmental. The post-2015 sustainable development agenda recognises that extreme poverty is the greatest global challenge and is an indispensable requirement for sustainable development. Goal 1 is eradicating poverty for all people everywhere, currently measured as people living on less than US$1.25 a day (SDG 1.1). The 2030 development agenda also builds on the multilateral development banks, (MDBs) agreement in Addis Ababa in 2015 to a collective US$400 billion in development spending from 2016 to 2018 as well as measures to promote domestic resource mobilisation. Also, in December 2015, the global climate change agreement at COP21 (Conference of Parties) was reached in Paris, France, where there is restriction of warming to well below 3 degrees Celsius and agreement to pursue efforts to limit the temperature increase to 1.5 degrees Celsius.

Within a year, the number of IFIs widened by giving support on delivery of the SDGs, from seven in September 2015 to 11 in October 2016. The joint statement, 'Delivering on the 2030 Agenda' by the heads of the seven IFIs and the heads of additional four IFIs – Asian Infrastructure Investment Bank (AIIB), Islamic Development Bank (IsDB), International Finance Corporation (IFC), and New Development Bank BRICS (NDB) – also demonstrated enhanced IFI commitment with coordinated efforts taken by the 11 IFIs in working collectively on their delivery of the SDGs. Additionally, the MDBs agreed to (i) launch the first Global Infrastructure Forum in April 2016 with the second forum in April 2017, focusing on inclusive, sustainable infrastructure; and (ii) through

---

1 United Nations, 'Transforming Our World: The 2030 Agenda for Sustainable Development', A/RES/70/1 (September 2015), para. 7 (our vision).
2 World Bank press release (25 September 2015), http://www.worldbank.org/en/news/ press-release/2015/09/25/international-financial-institutions-global-development-agenda.

a joint Task Force, advance on harmonising methodologies and common metrics to quantify private finance catalysed by their institutions.

On climate change, the MDBs were developing a joint climate action partnership aimed at a more collaborative and coherent approach to working with countries to implement their Nationally Determined Contributions (NDCs) and develop their adaptive capacities. The joint statement noted that (i) the institutions would redouble their efforts to scale up financing for development as well as the capacity to achieve the SDGs by leveraging, mobilising, and catalysing resources at all levels; and (ii) the SDGs will require building a financing framework that channels more resources from more sources, particularly the private sector as the 2030 Agenda is a trillion-dollar one. The joint statement ended with the affirmative note that the 11 IFIs 'will individually and collectively bring in emerging and existing global, regional, sub-regional and national partner institutions and, together, contribute to the success of the 2030 Agenda, helping countries to leverage the financing and knowledge of the MDBs and the IMF to address their most pressing development challenges and, as such, contribute to achieving the transformative outcomes that the SDGs entail.'[3]

In 2017, WBG Senior Vice President Mahmoud Mohieldin provided directions taken by the institution on its need to change the way it works and fundamentally change the approach to development finance, with the adoption of the SDGs and the Paris Agreement under the UN Framework Convention on Climate Change (UNFCCC). The WBG would be 'crowding-in the private sector' whenever possible, combining this with its technical and local knowledge to make that capital work for those who need it most. Under this 'cascade' approach, when assessing new investments, WBG seeks to first mobilise private sector finance and where risks remain high, there would be use of guarantees and risk-sharing instruments. WBG would also work with governments on regulatory and policy reforms to improve project bankability and feasibility, and only where market solutions are not possible would official and public resources be used. This 'cascade approach' is a 'profound departure from the conventional lending practice' at the WBG but was seen as essential to reach the trillions necessary to finance the SDGs.[4]

Table 2.1 illustrates the involvement of six IFIs in implementing the SDGs with each institution's alignment to the SDGs, key activities, and examples of specific interventions.

The WBG has taken a leading role in the implementation of the SDGs for various reasons including: the financial resources available for public sector lending (IBRD and IDA) and private sector operations (IFC and MIGA) on a

---

3 Ibid., para. 8.
4 World Bank speech (22 May 2017), http://www.worldbank.org/en/news/speech/2017/06/06/speech-as-prepared-by-world-bank-group-senior-vp-mahmoud-mohieldin-at-the-un-ecosoc-forum-on-financing-for-development-may-22-2017-new-york.

Table 2.1 IFIs and Their Involvement in Implementing the SDGs.

Bank	The Institution's Alignment with the SDGs; and Key Activities	Examples of Specific Interventions
African Development Bank	1) The bank's mission is to promote sustainable growth and reduce poverty in Africa. 2) In 2016, the bank focused on five development priorities – the 'High 5s': light up and power Africa, feed Africa, industrialise Africa, integrate Africa, and improve the quality of life for the people of Africa within the framework of its 10-Year Strategy (2013–2022) aimed at promoting inclusive and green growth. The objectives of the High 5s are consistent with the SDGs, creating a platform for transforming the lives of the people of Africa through rapid, sustainable, and inclusive growth.	In 2016, it approved a New Deal on Energy for Africa 2016–2025 and its target of providing universal access for Africa by 2025. Complementing the New Deal is the Africa Renewable Energy Initiative (AREI) launched in 2015 at COP 21 and this initiative seeks to boost Africa's renewable energy generation capacity by 10GW by 2020 with the bank mandated by the African Union to host the AREI's independent delivery unit and to act as a trustee.[5]
Asian Development Bank	1) The bank's aim is to free Asia and Pacific from poverty. 2) New corporate strategy 'Strategy 2030' will guide the bank's engagement with borrowing countries until 2030 and is expected to define how the bank's operations will align with the SDGs and the 2015 Paris global climate agreement. 3) Effective January 2017, the merger of lending operations of Asian Development Fund (ADF) (special resources) and Ordinary Capital Resources resulted in more development assistance available to countries in need. 4) In 2016, ADF replenishment increased, which provided more grant support to ADB's poorest borrowing countries by 70% with the levels provided in 2013–2016 to support the SDGs and combat climate change.	In 2016, it approved a second policy-based program to Indonesia worth US$500 million to reduce income inequality by better aligning the public expenditure framework with the government's SDGs in education, health, infrastructure, and social protection.[6]

5 African Development Bank Annual Report 2016, 9.
6 Asian Development Bank Annual Report 2016, 32.

Inter-American Development Bank	1) The bank's Institutional Strategy accompanying the ninth general increase in the bank's resources (IDB-9) has two pillars: (1) reducing poverty and inequality and (2) supporting growth that is both sustained and sustainable in economic, social, and environmental terms. 2) In 2016, the bank expanded its role as coordinator for Latin America and the Caribbean of the global UN initiative Sustainable Energy for All (SE4All), which seeks universal access to sustainable energy service. 3) Effective January 2017, the bank integrated resources of the Fund for Special Operations to resources of the bank's ordinary capital boosting the bank's lending capacity and strengthening the bank's concessional assistance to its poorest and most vulnerable member countries.	In 2016, it approved the Peace and Sustainability Development Facility for Colombia where IADB is responsible for technical and fiduciary administration and financing will come from international donors (including IADB), with the potential to mobilise US$600 million.[7] This facility follows from the bank's support of the launch of Sustainable Colombia and the initiative will focus on rural development, environmental sustainability, and climate change in areas characterised by armed conflict.[8]
European Bank for Reconstruction and Development	1) The bank's Strategic and Capital Framework of May 2015 focuses on three themes one of which is helping member countries fight global challenges such as climate change by making their economies more sustainable. 2) With its Green Economy Transition (GET) approach implemented in 2016, the bank aims to raise the level of environmental investment to 40% of its total financing by 2020.	In 2016, it strengthened its support for infrastructure projects responding to the need for innovative ventures that mobilise private sector resources through the development of a Green Cities Framework which helps municipalities address their environmental priorities. The regionwide framework's initial focus is on Armenia, Georgia, and Moldova, and the first project under this framework is a loan to the administration of the Moldovan capital Chisinau for energy improvements to public buildings.[9]

(Continued)

7 Inter-American Development Bank (IADB) Annual Report 2016, 17.
8 IADB news release (1 December 2015), https://www.iadb.org/en/news/news-releases/2015-12-01/idb-supports-launch-of-sustainable-colombia-initiative%2C11342.html.
9 European Bank for Reconstruction and Development Annual Report 2016, 24–25.

Table 2.1 (Continued)

Bank	The Institution's Alignment with the SDGs; and Key Activities	Examples of Specific Interventions
World Bank Group (WBG)	1) WBG's mission of twin goals is to (1) end extreme poverty by 2030 (by decreasing the percentage of people living on less than US$1.90 a day); and (2) boost shared prosperity by fostering income growth for the poorest 40% in every country. 2) There are three priority areas in pursuing WBG's goals: (1) accelerating sustainable and inclusive growth, (2) investing in people to build human capital, and (3) fostering resilience to global shocks and threats. 3) Appointment of WBG Senior Vice President for the 2030 Development Agenda, United Nations Relations, and Partnerships. 4) In 2017, 'Atlas of SDGs' launched as a tool to track progress on achieving the SDGs. 5) In fiscal year (FY) 2016 (1 July 2016–30 June 2017), there was a record US$75 million for IDA replenishment after leveraging IDA's equity by blending donor contributions with internal resources and funds raised through debt markets – this innovative financing helps with reaching out to the poorest countries. 6) In 2017, the World Bank launched the first-ever bonds directly linked to the SDGs, which directly link returns to the stock market performance of companies in the Solactive Sustainable Development Goals World Index.	It introduced in 2016 an innovative financing and solution in its partnering with the World Health Organization (WHO), the private sector, and development partners to develop the Pandemic Emergency Financing Facility (PEF). The PEF can release up to US$500 million to pandemic responders in the poorest countries. Also, through the PEF, the World Bank will issue the first pandemic bonds and create a new market for pandemic risk insurance.[10]

---

10 World Bank Annual Report 2016, 18.

Asian Infrastructure Investment Bank	1) The bank's mission is to improve social and economic outcomes in Asia and beyond. There are three thematic priorities in the bank's investments: (1) promoting sustainable infrastructure and supporting countries to meet their commitments under the SDGs, (2) cross-border connectivity, and (3) private capital mobilization. 2) On infrastructure, the bank addresses all dimensions of sustainable development – economic, social, and environmental.	In 2016, it approved a project targeted at improving the living conditions of 9.7 million people who live in slums in 154 cities in central and eastern parts of Indonesia.[11]
International Finance Corporation (dealt separately from WBG as IFC is focused on private sector operations)	1) IFC's new strategic framework 'IFC 3.0' is a response to the challenge of converting billions to trillions of development finance to meet the financing needs under the SDGs. 2) In 2016, IFC developed a new framework – Anticipated Impact Measurement and Monitoring (AIMM) to measure and articulate the development impact of each project and to focus scorecards and incentives on the delivery of each impact. 3) IFC serves as secretariat for the Sustainable Banking Network, a global knowledge-sharing group of banking regulators and banking associations, to help develop guidance and capacity for banks to incorporate environmental and social risk management into credit decision making. 4) It launched the world's biggest green-bond fund dedicated to emerging markets in FY2017 – $2 billion Green Cornerstone Bond Fund aimed at unlocking private funding for climate related projects.	In FY16, it made climate-related investments totaling US$3.3 billion, including funds mobilised from other investors. The mobilised funds included nearly US$390 million in climate-related commitments investment through its advisory work on public–private-partnership projects.[12]

11 Asian Infrastructure Investment Bank Annual Report, 2016, 17.
12 International Finance Corporation Annual Report 2016, 41.

global (and not just regional) basis; being a UN specialised agency; its rich development experience over the past 70 years of operations and its appointment of Senior Vice President Mahmoud Mohieldin (formerly Corporate Secretary and President's Special Envoy, WBG) to WBG Senior Vice President for the 2030 Development Agenda, United Nations Relations, and Partnerships. The other IFIs also play pivotal roles and those with a regional focus have the value-added experience gained from their regions, together with other development actors, in moving forward on implementing the SDGs. IFC and EBRD are well placed to play key roles in providing advice on private sector initiatives in implementing the SDGs with their catalytic role in involving the private sector in foreign direct investment.

Project Processing and Actions Taken by IFIs to Implement the SDGs, and Responses from Other Development Actors

The project cycle for IFIs, such as the World Bank and ADB, ensures that they follow specific processes in a project financed by them commencing from ADB's Country Partnership Strategy (CPS) or the World Bank's Country Partnership Framework (CPF) to due diligence to approval of the project by the board of directors followed by implementation and completion, and ending with evaluation. ADB and the World Bank have used the SDGs as a crucial reference in their CPS/CPF documents and also in the project documents (Report and Recommendation of the President [RRP] for ADB and Project Appraisal Document [PAD] for the World Bank) where these project documents are sent to the board of directors for approval.

The following analysis is based on documents and projects processed at these institutions after the adoption of the SDGs in 2015. In the World Bank, the latest CPF for the Lao People's Democratic Republic dated 2 March 2017 referenced the WBG's twin goals; the country's commitment to the SDGs; and the country's 15-year vision, 10-year strategy, and 5-year 8th National Socio-Economic Development Plan (NSEDP) all of which reinforce the country's commitment to a larger paradigm shift, naming green growth and sustainability that will guide the government in reaching its goal towards becoming an upper-middle-income country by 2030. The document shows that the SDGs have been mainstreamed into the 8th NSEDP, and the other strategic planning documents for the country such as its Vision 2030. There are annexes attached containing links between the 8th NSEDP, the SDGs, and the CPF; and complementarity of activities between the WBG, ADB, and UN in Lao PDR, which demonstrates interagency planning and coordination.[13] ADB's Country

---

13 World Bank Group, Country Partnership Framework for Lao People's Democratic Republic FY2017–2021 (2 March 2017), 1, 2, 4–5, and Annexes 6 and 7.

Partnership Strategy for Lao PDR 2017–2020 is broadly similar in approach with some nuances in that it has references to the 8th NSEDP, and has provisions on how ADB operations will help the government achieve the SDGs, for example, stating that proposed ADB operations on sustainable natural resource management and climate resilience will help the government achieve SDG 12 (responsible consumption and production), SDG 13 (climate action), and SDG 15 (life on land).[14]

When RRPs/PADs are prepared by ADB/World Bank, there are cross references to the equivalent country partnership documents prepared by ADB or World Bank. For example, in the World Bank's Central Highlands Connectivity Improvement Project, the IDA's project document (PAD) and the WBG's Vietnam CPF are cross-referenced to show that the bank's operation is consistent with the CPF FY18–FY22, and that these interventions are broadly consistent with the World Bank's support of the country in implementing its SDGs, with paragraph 9 of the PAD expressly referring to the country's UN commitments and citing that the proposed project supports the Intended Nationally Determined Contribution plan of Vietnam to the UNFCCC.[15] In the case of ADB's Secondary Green Cities Development Project in Vietnam, the ADB's project document goes further than the World Bank's project document by specifically citing which SDGs are being targeted under the project – in this case, SDG 6 (clean water and sanitation) and SDG 11 (sustainable cities and communities).[16] The practice at ADB in citing the targeting of SDGs is not just in loan projects but also covers Technical Assistance (TA) which is usually grant and not covered by loan. For example, in TA Reports there are references to how the TA project is aligned with the country's CPS (which would link to the SDGs) and have clear SDG targeting in the TA project, such as SDG 5 (gender equality) and SDG 8 (decent work and economic growth) in the TA on Preparing the Sindh Secondary Education Improvement Project in Pakistan.[17]

IFIs have also interacted with development partners within or outside their region to work on implementing the SDGs. This activity is driven by various

---

14 Asian Development Bank. Country Partnership Strategy for Lao PDR, 2017–2020 (August 2017), 1, 8.

15 World Bank, Project Appraisal Document on Central Highlands Connectivity Improvement Project (1 June 2017), paras. 6–9; and WBG, Country Partnership Framework for the Socialist Republic of Vietnam FY18–FY22 (4 May 2017), 1.

16 Asian Development Bank, 'Report and Recommendation of the President to the Board of Directors for the Socialist Republic of Viet Nam: Secondary Green Cities Development Project' (October 2017), Project at a Glance page; and Asian Development Bank, Country Partnership Strategy for Viet Nam 2016–2020 (September 2016), 7.

17 Asian Development Bank, Technical Assistance Report. Pakistan: Preparing the Sindh Secondary Education Improvement Project (October 2017). Transactional Technical Assistance at a Glance page, 1.

conferences, publications, and so on. For example, ADB partnered with UN ESCAP and UNDP, together with 'contributions made by more than 100 experts' in the preparation of the Asia-Pacific Sustainable Development Goals Outlook report.[18] This publication shows how the partnership among the three institutions can build 'its experiences to achieve the 2030 Agenda' and at the same time 'foster new ideas by providing an informed overview of where [the three institutions] stand as a region in relation to the SDGs and by highlighting those issues that will require a concerted effort to fulfil the dream of a region without poverty.'[19] The following recommendations were made: (1) governments will confront many common and fundamental challenges as they work to advance sustainable development; and (2) implementing the SDGs in a transformative agenda requires new government capacities with localised indicators, data collection, and monitoring systems reflecting the interactions between the goals.[20] The report's preliminary stocktaking effort in the Asia-Pacific region demonstrates action taken by ADB and development partners in studying the challenges facing governments, regional agencies, and other development actors, while highlighting that the 'indicators are incomplete, and data are limited'[21] so there is a need for more data information to have a better understanding in implementing and monitoring the implementation of the SDGs.

AfDB has also been working on discussing the challenges and opportunities of implementing the SDGs, and an example is its hosting a workshop on SDG 16 (peace, justice, and strong institutions) in fragile situations in Africa within AfDB's High 5 priority areas highlighted earlier. This workshop involved UN, African Union, and AfDB to identify concrete actions to strengthen their partnerships to implement SDG 16 in Africa at national and regional levels, with emphasis on West Africa. The seminar involving AfDB, UN, African Union, and other African stakeholders – practitioners, civil society actors, and policymakers – was to discuss how to strengthen their partnership to implement SDG 16 in Africa, based on their comparative advantages and mandates, with AfDB's 'leadership around the High 5s agenda and its long-standing engagement as a trusted and neutral broker in fragile situations, position[ing] the institution as a critical partner to achieve the SDGs in Africa.'[22]

---

18 Asia-Pacific Sustainable Development Goals Outlook (Thailand: UNESCAP-ADB-UNDP publication, 2017), 5.
19 Ibid., 11.
20 Ibid., 13, 16, 17.
21 Ibid., last page.
22 African Development Bank news (15 March 2016), https://www.afdb.org/en/news-and-events/the-afdb-the-un-and-african-stakeholders-to-discuss-the-implementation-of-the-sdg-16-and-the-high-5s-in-fragile-situations-in-africa-15468/.

The WBG published its 'Implementing the 2030 Agenda 2017 Update' which highlighted two salient aspects: (1) the 'need to work in partnership with multi-lateral organizations, governments, the private sector, civil society, foundations, and other stakeholders at the global, local, and sub-national levels'; and (2) WBG's conclusion that 'there are two other factors critical to success: the availability of quality data (including monitoring and evaluation); and evidence-based implementation which grows from a shared commitment with country partners, and which leverages multistakeholder partnerships to deliver results.'[23] This report showcases the 2017 Atlas of SDGs charting progress that societies are making towards the SDGs with goal-level and country-level perspectives on the SDGs, and articulates the actions taken by the WBG in each of the 17 SDGs, underscoring the complexity of challenges in this global agenda.

The report also highlights critical action needed to have data for development, monitoring, and reviewing the SDGs, and how the WBG works at the country level (which is important as it is the countries that are the owners as they plan their SDGs). It indicates that the WBG has about 300 active projects to support data improvements, and is providing about US$200 million a year in financing for upgrades to key data collection. In 2015, the WBG committed to helping countries complete at least one household survey every three years with a focus on IDA countries, with an estimated 111 surveys to be completed between 2017 and 2019.[24] The document serves as a good basis for other IFIs to use as a template in their annual reporting on implementation of the SDGs and perhaps there could also be a consolidated single update document prepared under the auspices of WBG given its lead role or by another entity as an objective evaluator engaged by the IFIs.

On responses from other development actors, these range from bilaterals, international agencies, and civil society. Sweden, through its Ministry for Foreign Affairs, published a report in 2017 on its actions towards achieving the 2030 Agenda and the SDGs, and this report is useful in that it highlights how the Swedish government is taking actions at various levels – country and international – to demonstrate the country's 'policy coherence for development' in accordance with the 2030 Agenda and the SDGs.[25] It shows, through extensive operational examples, the country's own commitments to the SDGs at a national level, and its contributions to various SDGs through various operational agents in Sweden (such as civil society partners) and outside Sweden (such as UN agencies, IFIs like the World Bank and the MDBs, private sector partners, civil society partners, and national government implementing entities).

---

23 World Bank Group, 'Implementing the 2030 Agenda 2017 Update' (Washington, DC, 2017), 2.
24 Ibid., 12.
25 Government Offices of Sweden, Ministry of Foreign Affairs, 'Report to the Financing for Development Forum' (FfD Forum) in New York, May 22–25, 2017, 9.

In November 2017, at an intergovernmental group of experts on Financing for Development at UNCTAD in Geneva, a background paper was prepared on whether MDBs are bridging the infrastructure gap. This paper noted the initiatives of MDBs to raise their lending capacity and presented the AIIB model as 'as an alternative to leverage resources for infrastructure development' which 'gives the bank greater capacity to finance different sorts of projects in infrastructure and other productive economic sectors, which are at the core of its mission.'[26] The significance of this paper is that the debate on IFI financing is still open for discussion on how best IFIs can innovate and scale up finance for the SDGs to meet the significant infrastructure gap financing.

CSOs as development actors have also seized the opportunity to comment on IFIs, for example, AIIB's sustainable energy for Asia strategy which was open for public consultation. In June 2017, Oxfam commented on AIIB's draft energy sector strategy prior to AIIB launching at its upcoming annual meeting its energy strategy, and gave its recommendation that AIIB does not fund new coal plants or lifetime extensions of existing plants either through direct or indirect lending.[27] Oxfam cited AIIB's core values of 'clean, lean, and green' and advanced arguments under the Paris Climate Agreement and the adoption of the SDGs as coal would fatally undermine the temperature goal of the Paris Agreement. This CSO input had impact because at the AIIB's annual meeting in June 2017, the bank president 'stressed the Bank's role in facilitating the implementation of the Paris Agreement on climate change and implementing the 2030 Agenda for Sustainable Development' and 'noted the absence of coal projects in the AIIB's pipeline and that it will not consider proposals "if we are concerned about their environmental and reputational impact".'[28] The contribution from CSOs is important as it shows that comments from development actors can have an impact on IFIs in applying its strategies to finance projects and implement the SDGs.

Conclusion and Recommendations for IFIs to Meet SDG Goals and Targets

The doors have been opened wide with the broad remit of the SDGs and the all-embracing mantra in the preamble of the 2030 Agenda that 'no one will be left behind'. There is always room for debate and improvement, and contributions

---

26 Ricardo Gottschalk, UNCTAD, and Daniel Poon, 'Scaling up Finance for the Sustainable Development Goals: Experimenting with Models of Multilateral Development Banking,' by UNCTAD, 23 (8–10 November 2017), http://unctad.org/meetings/en/SessionalDocuments/tdb_efd1_bp_GP2_en.pdf.

27 Oxfam Briefing Note (June 2017), 13, https://d1tn3vj7xz9fdh.cloudfront.net/s3fs-public/file_attachments/bn-the-aiibs-energy-opportunity-150617-en.pdf.

28 International Institute for Sustainable Development (IISD) news (20 June 2017), http://sdg.iisd.org/news/aiib-to-step-up-support-for-renewable-energy-sustainable-infrastructure-development/.

from external sources (such as universities and other knowledge institutions, academe, national authorities, private sector, and civil society) are very useful in that these external sources may view things differently from IFIs and can provide constructive feedback.

First, developing initiatives within the country are important as national ownership is key to achieving sustainable development. The example of initiatives such as Pakistan's Sustainable Development Policy Institute (SDPI), whose mission is to catalyse the transition towards sustainable development, in organising the institute's Twentieth Sustainable Development Conference in December 2017, showcases the path of the country in mapping out its SDGs through discussion of various topics covered in the SDGs ranging from harnessing private sector roles for sustainable development to pathways to realise health-related SDGs, and improving data foresight for economic policy decisions. This conference had the benefit not only of government officials, and local researchers and academics, but also representatives of IFIs such as the World Bank, bilaterals such as UK's Department for International Development (DFID), and UN agencies including ESCAP.[29]

Second, the need for having suitable data for development, monitoring, and reviewing the SDGs, which in turn impacts on the evaluation activities of IFIs in their lending operations. For example, in the WBG's Independent Evaluation Group (IEG) the IEG's role is to assess the development effectiveness of the institution (WBG), and not for each or all of its shareholders. But with the adoption of the SDGs, the IEG and other evaluation offices of IFIs would have to rethink, and IEG's 2015 evaluation report in learning from the predecessor MDGs for the next 15 years, highlights that the WBG 'requires balancing its global mandate with its country engagement.'[30] Caroline Heider, director general of IEG, identifies the challenging tasks ahead: 'the reality, as many development experts and evaluators have pointed out is that the international community will need to take a holistic look at the SDGs to ensure [we] achieve them in ways that create positive synergies rather than negative tradeoffs.' She highlighted three important lessons in evaluating WBG's work that would be relevant for the SDGs: (i) the importance of building country ownership; (ii) creating an environment where countries can learn from each other and tap into the best advice and solutions available globally; and (iii) the need to develop the right instruments as well as realistic national medium and long-term targets and programs.[31] IFIs are continuing to discuss evaluation of the

---

29 Sustainable Development Policy Institute, Pakistan, Conference programme, (15 January 2018), http://www.sdpi.org/contents/files/Detailed%20Agenda_SDC%202017-15Jan2018.pdf.
30 World Bank Group. Independent Evaluation Group. 'Transforming Our World – Aiming for Sustainable Development: Using Independent Evaluation to Transform Aspirations to Achievements' (Washington, DC: The World Bank, 2015), 21.
31 World Bank Group. Independent Evaluation Group (19 September 2017), http://ieg.world bankgroup.org/blog/staying-track-sustainable-development-goals-what-evaluation-can-teach-us.

SDGs, and in December 2017, IADB cohosted, together with other agencies such as national authorities and IFAD, a joint conference on evaluation for the SDGs with an emphasis on Latin America and the Caribbean where independent evaluation offices from other IFIs such as AfDB and ADB were also invited to exchange evaluation experiences.

Third, the implementation of the SDGs also raises critical issues such as that of corruption. Corruption is a systemic barrier to sustainable development that impacts the neediest of households as identified by the joint 2017 UN ESCAP-ADB-UNDP report. This report states that an estimated 40% of investments in electricity, water, and sanitation are lost due to corruption.[32] Additionally, 'global losses to corruption, money laundering, and tax evasion is estimated at US\$800 billion to US\$2 trillion every year – an amount that could instead be used by developing countries to achieve their [SDG] commitments.'[33] There is an even more imperative need to stem corruption in line with the zero tolerance approach taken by IFIs in their fight against corruption, and to cooperate more with member countries as these losses cost them more in trying to meet their obligations under the SDGs.

Fourth, joint IFI statements on their commitment to implementing the SDGs and giving help to their members on fulfilling the SDG targets and goals demonstrate the critical role played by these IFIs. In the 17 October 2016 joint statement, there were four additional IFIs that joined the seven IFIs in the 2015 joint statement. To capture that 'no one is left behind', it is suggested that other IFIs such as the Caribbean Development Bank (CDB) and others having similar development mandates join this collective initiative. CDB is also entering into partnership agreements with UN agencies on implementing the SDGs.[34] There is more synergy having these IFIs on board as they can share information with the other 'major' IFIs and all will benefit from shared experiences.

Fifth, getting more involvement of stakeholders such as International Development Finance Club (IDFC), governments, academe, civil society, and policy experts and other relevant stakeholders through various fora is heading in the right direction in moving forward on the challenges in implementing the SDGs. In November 2015, a joint statement by 6 MDBs at COP 21 was issued where these MDBs sought to share lessons based on their years of experience to 'measure the impact of [their] work in partnership with others,

---

32 Asia-Pacific Sustainable Development Goals Outlook (Thailand: UNESCAP-ADB-UNDP publication, 2017), 14.

33 Asian Development Bank news release (8 December 2017), https://www.adb.org/news/adb-president-calls-stronger-efforts-fight-corruption.

34 Caribbean Development Bank news release (14 July 2017), http://www.caribank.org/news/cdb-un-agencies-partnering-achieve-sdgs-caribbean.

35 Joint Statement by the Multilateral Development Banks at Paris, COP 21 (28 November 2017), http://www.eib.org/attachments/press/joint-mdb-statement-climate_nov-28_final.pdf.

including the International Development Finance Club [IDFC].'[35] The IDFC is a group of development banks of national and subregional origin comprising 23 members, which in turn represent 69 countries, and acts as financier, advisor, partner, and implementer to mobilise finance and expertise for development projects in emerging and developing countries. In December 2017, a joint IDFC-MDB statement was issued at the One Planet Summit in Paris, where IDFC and the MDBs 'commit to deepen their collaboration with each other and with other interested parties' in order to pursue the development of processes including the 'development of a common framework for tracking progress towards achieving resilience, to be shared by COP 24.'[36]

Another instance is MDB assistance in having a joint workshop, in coordination with development partners such as ESCAP and UN Environment, to share knowledge and strengthen aspects of SDGs for member countries. An illustration is the knowledge-sharing workshop organised by ADB, ESCAP, and UN Environment in February 2018 in Bangkok. Government officials from ADB member countries, as well as international experts, and representatives from academia and civil society involved in environmental sustainability and planning, were invited to share preliminary findings under an ADB TA project to equip policymakers with knowledge and tools to integrate select environment-related goals (SDGs 12, 14, and 15) and targets into their development plans, policies, and programmes. The workshop will provide benefits such as exchanging experience and discussing issues and challenges encountered in implementing the environment dimensions of the SDGs and identify tools and methods that can be used for integrating the environment dimensions of the SDGs into national and local contexts.[37] More engagement by IFIs in their assisting member countries on SDG implementation will be necessary as there will be thematic reviews of the SDGs at the high-level political forum under the auspices of ECOSOC on sustainable development.

Sixth, the SDGs are a milestone and provide an opportunity for the IFIs to recalibrate their existing strategies to align with the new international development agenda while also maximizing benefits, avoiding duplication of activities, and saving costs by harmonising their activities in line with the Paris Declaration on Aid Effectiveness (2005) and the Accra Agenda for Action (2008).

Finally, use of innovative approaches by IFIs in implementing the SDGs and spreading the word through more public outreach in conjunction with interested stakeholders are both very helpful. These include organising

---

36 European Bank for Reconstruction and Development Bank news (2017), http://www.ebrd.com/news/2017/together-major-development-finance-institutions-align-financial-flows-with-the-paris-agreement.html.

37 Asian Development Bank. Knowledge Sharing Workshop, 21–22 February 2018, https://www.adb.org/sites/default/files/related/103096/regional-workshop-environment-sdg-program.pdf.

youth competitions on financing for development[38] to promote youth involvement in the future of development and posting through the institution's website, communications to civil society through the CSO units established by IFIs, and social media on matters such as youth and the SDGs.[39] Such initiatives serve as an invaluable source for knowledge dissemination to get on board a broad representation of civil society – youth and females – so they are also made aware of their role in their country's path to sustainable development under the SDGs.

---

38 'Financing Sustainable Development: Ideas for Action 2017' edited by Mahmoud Mohieldin and Djordjija Petkoski (World Bank Group), https://openknowledge.worldbank.org/bitstream/handle/10986/28445/120228-WP-IdeasforActionWeb-PUBLIC.pdf?sequence=1&isAllowed=y.
39 Asian Development Bank article (18 August 2017), https://www.adb.org/news/features/youth-and-sdgs-12-things-know.

3

Towards a New Global Narrative for the Sustainable Development Goals

Iason Gabriel and Varun Gauri[*]

* We would like to thank David Hudson, Jennifer Hudson, Niheer Dasandi, Homi Kharas, Elizabeth Stuart, Jennifer Rubenstein, Thomas Black, and Yiannis Gabriel, for their help and contributions when preparing this chapter. The views and findings expressed in this chapter do not necessarily represent those of the World Bank or its Executive Directors.

Introduction

In 2015 the Sustainable Development Goals (SDGs) came into effect, replacing the Millennium Development Goals (MDGs) as the main international framework for coordinating global development activities. While some commentators praised the inclusive process that gave rise to the goals, others immediately expressed concern about their extraordinary scope and number.

Comprised of 17 goals, 169 targets, and 231 indicators in total, the SDGs call upon the international community to eradicate poverty, end hunger, achieve universal access to health and education, tackle inequality, and solve the problem of environmental degradation and global warming – all within the space of 15 years. *The Economist* compared the goals unfavourably with the Ten Commandments brought down by Moses from Mount Sinai.[1] Meanwhile Charles Kenny, from the Centre for Global Development, was prompted to ask whether the authors had 'lost the plot'.[2] As he went on to note, 'whereas the power of the original MDGs to motivate was in their simplicity and clarity, the process that has created the proposals for the new set of goals has guaranteed

---

1 *The Economist*, 'The 169 Commandments' (25 March 2015), http://www.economist.com/news/leaders/21647286-proposed-sustainable-development-goals-would-be-worse-useless-169-commandments.
2 Charles Kenny, 'MDGs to SDGs: Have We Lost the Plot?', Center for Global Development (27 May 2015). https://www.cgdev.org/publication/mdgs-sdgs-have-we-lost-plot.

Sustainable Development Goals: Harnessing Business to Achieve the SDGs through Finance, Technology, and Law Reform, First Edition. Edited by Julia Walker, Alma Pekmezovic, and Gordon Walker.

the opposite outcomes. The overwrought and obese drafts. . . almost ensure that the post-2015 goals will have comparatively limited value and impact.'[3]

This concern that the SDGs are destined to remain motivationally inert is well founded. To begin with, in an organisational context, reliance upon inflated targets often creates significant risk. Among other things, Ordonez et al. note that the proliferation of goals can inhibit organisational learning, reduce employees' intrinsic motivation, and lead to confusion and poor decision making as they struggle to balance different aims, sacrificing certain objectives altogether so others can be achieved.[4] From a motivational standpoint the number of goals and targets is also challenging. Reflecting on the MDGs, the UN Secretary General concluded that 'mobilized public advocacy has been essential in moving governments to take direct actions and adopt policy frameworks that may translate into effective means of implementation of the international goals and targets'.[5] Yet, in order for mobilisation to be successful the message must be heard, it must be understood, and it must be appealing.[6]

In this regard, the cognitive demandingness and rhetorical weakness of the SDGs represent significant constraints.[7] Psychologists who study the phenomenon of 'cognitive load' have found that there is only so much information the human brain can process at one time before the capacity of our working memory is exceeded. In a famous article, G.A. Miller argued that the upper threshold was about seven pieces of information.[8] A more recent study found that when the 'chunks' of information are larger, people might only be able to juggle two or three pieces of information at a time.[9] Bearing this in mind, efforts to understand and internalise the SDGs appear to demand a great deal from

---

3 Ibid.

4 Lisa Ordonez, Maurice Schweitzer, Adam Galinsky, and Max H. Bazerman, 'Goals Gone Wild: The Systematic Side Effects of Over-Prescribing Goal Setting', Working Paper 09-083, Harvard Business School (January 2009), https://www.hbs.edu/faculty/Publication%20Files/09-083.pdf.

5 MDG Gap Task Force, *MDG Gap Task Force Report 2015: Taking Stock of the Global Partnership for Development* (New York: United Nations, 2015), 3. http://www.un.org/en/development/desa/policy/mdg_gap/mdg_gap2015/2015GAP_FULLREPORT_EN.pdf.

6 Neta Crawford, *Argument and Change in World Politics: Ethics, Decolonization, and Humanitarian Intervention* (Cambridge: Cambridge University Press, 2002), 32–33.

7 Varun Gauri, 'MDGs That Nudge: The Millennium Development Goals, Popular Mobilization, and the Post-2015 Development Framework', Policy Research Working Paper 6282, The World Bank Group (November 2012), http://documents.worldbank.org/curated/en/383261468162862118/pdf/wps6282.pdf.

8 George Miller, 'The Magic Number Seven, Plus or Minus Two: Some Limits on Our Capacity to Process Information', *Psychological Review* 63, no. 2 (March 1956), 81–97.

9 Fred Pass, Alexander Renkl, and John Sweller, 'Cognitive Load Theory and Instructional Design: Recent Developments', *Educational Psychologist* 38, no. 1 (June 2003): 1–4.

people at a time when attention is stretched thin.[10] Furthermore, preliminary studies suggest efforts to mobilise public opinion around the goals have come up short, with 94% of US nationals and 96% of people in the United Kingdom reporting 'little knowledge' or 'no knowledge' of the goals.[11]

This chapter looks at the question of how best to motivate support for the SDGs. It asks how the goals can be made compelling for a variety of stakeholders including national governments, the staff of international organisations, and citizens around the world. To this end, we look in more detail at the goals themselves, asking how they should be understood and at the mechanism by which they are meant to take effect.

The chapter is structured as follows. The first section asks whether the SDGs can function as SMART goals and looks at the implications of this approach for delivery. Finding this approach ill-suited to the task at hand, the second section considers whether a 'stretch goal' approach is better suited to the goals' aims and aspirations. The third section shifts attention to the public-facing aspirational nature of the goals, looking at the way they intersect with global public opinion. The fourth section evaluates existing efforts to distill the meaning of the SDGs into simple slogans. The final section argues that the goals must be embedded in a new global narrative about their overarching goal and purpose if they are to achieve influence in the long run.

How SMART Are the SDGs?

SMART goals are specific, measurable, achievable, relevant and time-bound. These qualities help motivate compliance in a number of ways. The fact that they are specific and measurable means it is possible to create oversight regimes that track and rank the performance of different actors over time. This process, known as 'governance by indicators', frequently leads to improved results because those who fall behind know their progress is being monitored and that they must do better in order to avoid negative appraisal or sanction. The motivating potential of SMART goals is even stronger when they are alloyed to a scheme of positive fiscal incentives. Agents are then motivated not only by the desire to avoid public disapproval, but also by the knowledge that success will be rewarded in material terms.

---

10 World Bank, *World Development Report 2015: Mind, Society, and Behavior* (Washington, DC: World Bank, 2015), 165. http://documents.worldbank.org/curated/en/645741468339541646/pdf/ 928630WDR0978100Box385358B00PUBLIC0.pdf.
11 Martijn Lampert and Panos Papadongonas, *Mapping People's Awareness and Opinions about Poverty Eradication the Global Goals in China, France, Germany, India, UK and USA* (presentation obtained from the authors).

To address what was perceived to be widespread underperformance in the aid sector, the MDGs built upon these insights 'in a very direct fashion'.[12] The framers, who were largely Development Assistance Committee countries operating under the auspices of the OECD, set out to develop a concise list of global priorities that could be monitored and achieved with the support of a fresh round of development financing. They therefore avoided hard-to-measure outcomes such as participation and inclusion. They also avoided setting goals that were thought to be too demanding, something that can be seen in the dilution of the antipoverty target.[13] In the aftermath of the MDGs, several studies found that this approach was partially successful. In return for access to new funds, most low-income countries included the MDGs in their Poverty Reduction Strategy Papers and focused on achieving these objectives.[14] To deliver on their promise, donor nations also supported the MDGs by an increase in their overseas development assistance.[15]

Like the MDGs, the SDGs demonstrate a concern with measurement and data. The Inter-Agency Expert Group on SDG indicators (IAEG-SDG) has identified over 230 indicators that, if operationalised, would help governments track their progress towards the 169 targets. Yet in other ways the SDGs have thrown off the shackles imposed by results-based public management altogether. To begin with, almost all of the SDGs are general and encompass multiple targets. They are also, without fail, hugely ambitious. Whereas the MDGs focused on reducing the proportion of people living in poverty and increasing access to services, the SDGs focus on 'zero targets' such as ending poverty and eradicating hunger altogether. Commenting on the feasibility of these objectives, a recent report by the Overseas Development Institute (which looked at 14 representative targets) found that nine of them require 'revolution', where this means 'progress needs to be speeded up by multiple current rates to meet the goals', and a further five require the outright reversal of current global trends.[16]

---

12 David Hulme, 'The Making of the Millennium Development Goals: Human Development Meets Results-Based Management in an Imperfect World', Brooks World Poverty Institute Working Paper Series, BWPI, The University of Manchester (2007), 17.

13 Whereas the initial formulation required the international community to halve the number of people living in extreme poverty, the final version required only that they halve the proportion of people living in extreme poverty with progress being backdated to 1990 as the baseline year. Thomas Pogge, *Politics As Usual: What Lies Behind the Pro-Poor Rhetoric* (Oxford: Wiley, 2010), 58–59.

14 Kenny, 'MDGs to SDGs', *supra* note 2.

15 Ibid.

16 Furthermore, the targets that are most likely to be met (i.e. poverty and growth) are only likely to be met by drawing upon processes that frustrate the attainment of other goals (i.e. inequality and climate change). Susan Nicolai, Chris Hoy, Tom Berliner, and Thomas Aedy, *Projecting Progress: Reaching the SDGs by 2030* (London: ODI, 2015), 10.

During the consultation period, parties to the SDGs also rejected efforts to introduce a rigorous scheme of monitoring and evaluation. The goals do not form part of a treaty containing legal provisions for enforcement.[17] Nor will the High Level Political Forum, which is charged with monitoring country performance, produce public rankings of achievement. Indeed, a common complaint leveled at the MDGs was that they treated poor countries unfairly because they did not take into account variation in national contexts.[18] This meant that while they demanded little of high-income countries, they proved to be unachievable for most of sub-Saharan Africa. The backlash created by this effect meant that by the time the SDGs were negotiated, low- and middle-income countries were prepared to accept only weak forms of monitoring and oversight.[19]

Finally, there is no clear incentive scheme for the SDGs that supports compliance. In contrast with the MDGs, it is unlikely that aid can perform this function again. The new goals are going to cost considerably more than their predecessors, with low-end estimates suggesting required expenditure of $1.4 trillion per year.[20] There is also much less aid money to go around. As the Secretary-General has noted, 'global efforts are being undertaken in an increasingly difficult environment', characterised by volatile capital flows, a drop in commodity prices, escalated geopolitical tensions, and a refugee crisis that has seen 'the largest crisis of forced displacement since the Second World War'.[21] Against this backdrop, official development assistance to the least developed countries declined in 2014, something that looks set to continue in the future.[22]

---

17 Initial proposals made human rights more central, with the idea being that claim-making by citizens could drive SDG implementation. One idea was to build upon existing frameworks for human rights monitoring such as the Human Rights Council's process of Universal Periodic Review, which combines universality and peer-review with regular reporting and modalities of participation that include civil society. However, the major concern was that this would ultimately degenerate into forms of 'mud-slinging' and 'naming and shaming'. Kate Donald and Sally-Anne Way, 'Accountability for the Sustainable Development Goals: A Lost Opportunity?', *Ethics and International Affairs* (Summer 2016), 201–13.

18 William Easterly, 'How the Millennium Development Goals Are Unfair to Africa', Working Paper 14, Brookings Global Economy and Development (November 2007), https://www.brookings.edu/wp-content/uploads/2016/06/11_poverty_easterly.pdf.

19 The monitoring led by the High Level Political Forum is weak in the sense that reporting is voluntary; it is also heavily resource constrained – meeting for only eight days per year. Donald and Way, 'Accountability for the Sustainable Development Goals', 201–202.

20 Guido Schmidt-Traub, 'Investment Needs to Achieve the Sustainable Development Goals: Understanding the Billions and Trillions', Working Paper, Sustainable Development Solutions Network (September 2015).

21 UN Economic and Social Council, 'Monitoring Commitments and Actions in the Addis Ababa Action Agenda of the Third International Conference on Financing for Development' (Note by the Secretary General, United Nations Economic and Social Council, 18–20 April 2016), 4.

22 MDG Gap Task Force, *Taking Stock of the Global Partnership for Development* (New York: United Nations, 2015), 12.

The SDGs will therefore require the mobilisation of diverse funding streams, including domestic resource mobilisation and private capital flows.[23]

Bearing these constraints in mind, we may wonder whether the SDGs can be made SMART-er. On an organisational level, this would mean breaking the SDGs down into a set of more achievable interim goals, accompanied by clear lines of responsibility and metrics for evaluating performance. Measures would also need to be put in place to strengthen publicity effects and incentivise high levels of performance. Commenting on these dynamics, the Secretary-General has noted that 'monitoring per se, no matter how well undertaken, does not by itself deliver the cooperation promised by the global partnership for development. There needs to be a willingness of policymakers to act on the findings of the monitoring – a willingness that has ebbed and flowed over the past 15 years.'[24] To this end, civil society could focus on developing public scorecards that track overall performance, and nonfiscal incentives (such as technological transfer) could be leveraged to incentivise performance.[25]

Nonetheless, several concerns remain. First, the development of a large apparatus for monitoring and oversight risks over-burdening the data-collection facilities of developing countries. It is far from clear whether national audit offices are up to the task of supervising SDG implementation in the way required by SMART goals, given the severe capacity constraints they operate under, or if there are other bodies who can take on this task.[26] Second, and relatedly, the scale of this undertaking risks creating *information paralysis*. When organisations are subject to stress in the form of demanding targets combined with great uncertainty, they sometimes enter a state of *hypervigilence,* characterised by exhaustive efforts to know everything before even simple decisions can be taken. Third, a focus on establishing reliable metrics and

---

23 Susan Nicolai, Chris Hoy, Tom Berliner, and Thomas Aedy, 'Projecting Progress: Reaching the SDGs by 2030', (London: Overseas Development Institute, 2015); H. Kharas, A. Prizzon, and A. Rogerson, 'Financing the Post-2015 Sustainable Development Goals' (Overseas Development Institute, London, 2015).

24 MDG Gap Task Force, *Taking Stock*, 7.

25 The fact that the SDGs are universal, and automatically indexed to national benchmarks, means the fairness objection has less purchase than it did in the past. The creation of public scorecards is also one of the few ways to motivate performance by high-income countries. In the words of Donald and Way, 'direct monitoring and pressure from civil society and social movements could be developed to generate accountability and to empower, engage and inform national actors' (Donald and Way, 'Accountability', 208). A major concern raised by parties to the Addis round of development financing was that the uneven distribution of technology represents a major barrier to sustainable development.

26 Gijs de Vries, 'How National Audit Offices Can Support Implementation of the SDGs', *Public Financial Management Blog*, International Monetary Fund (28 June 2016), http://blog-pfm.imf. org/pfmblog/2016/06/national-audit-offices-should-support-implementation- of-the-sdgs.html?utm_source=feedburner&utm_medium=email&utm_campaign=Feed%3A+pfm blog+%28PFM+blog%29.

monitoring performance against them can lead to status quo bias given that the most reliable indicators we have tend to track elements of the traditional development agenda, rather than outcomes such as equality or sustainability which the SDGs introduce for the very first time. Fourth, even with a focus on key indicators or a subset of targets, the SDGs remain too ambitious to fit easily into a SMART goal framework. Any effort to reduce their scope, or create a functional division of labour, risks returning to the heavily siloed approach to development practice that hampered efforts to promote a sustainability agenda before. Lastly, it is not clear that the SMART goal approach is appropriate for a development regime that is now more egalitarian both in fact and in principle. There is a clear sense that international development and cooperation in the twenty-first century can no longer be about donor nations leveraging the aid regime to maximum effect. If these goals are to be achieved they require action by many countries that are neither significant donors nor recipients of aid. Indeed, Homi Kharas has calculated that the majority of signatories to the SDGs – some 130 countries – fit in this camp.[27]

Goals That Stretch

Stretch goals are targets that appear to be impossible to achieve, but which organisations pursue nevertheless – with the hope of stimulating radical improvements in performance. Commenting on their deployment in a business environment, Sitkin et al. argue that they have two important properties. First, stretch goals specify outcomes that are extremely difficult to achieve.[28] They are, in short, organisational goals 'with an objective probability that may be unknown but is seemingly impossible given current capabilities (i.e., current practices, skills, and knowledge)'.[29] Second, stretch goals are also characterised by extreme novelty. Because there is no known way to achieve these goals, the only way to pursue them is to break free from existing routines and assumptions.

In many regards, the SDGs fit the template for stretch goals. Of course, not everything they do is completely new. Nor are they the remit of a single

---

27 He calculates that of the 190 countries that attended the Addis, 30 were chronic 'donors' and up to another 30 are likely to remain aid dependent until 2030. However, this leaves 130 countries – or in his words a 'crushing majority' – who fit into neither category (Homi Kharas, Annalisa Prizzon and Andrew Rogerson), *Financing the Post-2015 Sustainable Development Goals: A Rough Roadmap* (London: ODI, 2014), 7.

28 Sim Sitkin, Kelly See, Chet Miller, Michael Lawless, and Andrew Carton, 'The Paradox of Stretch Goals: Organizations in Pursuit of the Seemingly Impossible', *Academy of Management Review* 36, no. 3 (July 2011): 544–566, https://ssrn.com/abstract=1698304.

29 Ibid., 547.

organisation aiming to improve performance. As part of an agenda that was agreed to by 193 countries, their function is to coordinate as well as to stretch. Nonetheless, their scale and ambition is beyond question. For example, goals such as the requirement signatories 'achieve full and productive employment and decent work for all women and men, including for young people and persons with disability, and equal pay for work of equal value' require the discovery of new technologies and the reversal of global trends.[30] By raising the bar at a time of fiscal constraint, there can be little doubt the SDGs encourage us to think about new and more radical solutions.

Unlike SMART goals, stretch goals do not need to be realistic in order to be successful: instead of focusing on monitoring and incentives, the main ways through which they produce change are *cognitive* and *emotional*. Under the right conditions, the decision to commit stretch goals can serve as a 'shock to the system', capturing the attention of employees, and shifting them towards new ways of thinking. When used to good effect, stretch goals also inspire employees, encouraging them to be more open to risk and to avoid the sunk costs fallacy – which often reproduces negative aspects of the status quo. These are biases that affect development professionals and nonprofessionals alike.[31]

However, the decision to set seemingly impossible targets is also part of a high-risk strategy that must be deployed with care. Stretch goals specify objectives that are both objectively difficult, which means the chances of success are slim, and are also known to be difficult – something that means that they may easily backfire by generating anxiety, cynicism, or despair among those tasked with their pursuit. Research into stretch goals therefore yields important lessons for the SDGs. Importantly, to stand a chance of success, stretch goals must focus on the right kind of problem, be assigned to organisations that are up to the task, and be accompanied by a narrative that reduces the chance of provoking negative emotional reactions among employees.

Taking these points in turn, the first lesson suggests that organisations cannot stretch in all directions: these objectives must be calibrated to the right kind of task. The SDGs are difficult to realise for a number of reasons: there are *knowledge gaps* regarding how certain goals can be achieved, *measurement gaps* for certain outcomes, and *mobilisation gaps* in areas where implementation will be costly or hard to coordinate. Stretch goals are best suited to the first kind of difficulty. They can help address knowledge gaps by encouraging experimentation and discovery. However, they are unlikely to make headway

---

30 For low-income countries the goal of full formal employment has long been a pipe dream. There is also concern that high-income economies will shed jobs in the next 15 years because of increasing automation. See James Ferguson, *Give a Man a Fish: Reflections on the New Politics of Distribution* (Durham, NC: Duke University Press, 2015).
31 Sheheryar Banuri, Stefan Dercon, and Varun Gauri, 'Biased Policy Professionals', Policy Research Working Paper 8113, World Bank (June 2017).

when the problem involves measurement or lack of coordination and political will. This is because in order to focus attention in the right way, stretch goals must specify outcomes that are well defined. The difficulty of achieving stretch goals also means that they can exacerbate coordination problems, leading actors to buck-pass or burden-shift due to the likelihood of failure. In sum, stretch goals should only be deployed *selectively* – when more traditional approaches are not up to the task. One area in which they may be appropriate concerns the climate goals. To meet these targets it is not enough, Nicholas Stern has argued, to think only 'about incremental initiatives that can be attached to existing development plans. The management of climate change requires deep structural and systemic change, implemented over many decades'.[32]

The second lesson that can be gleaned from the literature about stretch goals is that they are appropriate only for certain agents. According to Sitken et al., the two most important variables are an organisation's recent performance and the availability of 'slack' resources that can be dedicated to the task. Recent performance is the main factor affecting whether stretch goals 'shift organisational attention in a way that is focused productively or counterproductively'. At the same time, spare resources create the space required for staff to experiment and explore new options. Unfortunately, these conditions are often not met in practice. It follows from this that stretch goals should be delegated only to specific agencies or working groups who have had recent success in some area. Given the breadth of the SDGs, these actors must have a clear mandate and additional resources must also be found to support their work. Fortunately, because the correct use of stretch goals is highly selective, their work can be supported by special funds even at times of general scarcity. Indeed, a promising outcome of the Addis Agreement was the creation of a number of new financing mechanisms to support priority areas.[33]

Lastly, if stretch goals are to have a positive cognitive, emotional, and behavioral impact, steps must be taken to counteract the perception within organisations that the SDGs are *unachievable* or *unworthy* of support. What matters in this regard is not only that there have been recent successes, but also that these successes are recognised and celebrated. The nineteen years since the millennium have seen the fastest reduction in poverty in human history and significant inroads made in the fight against child mortality and hunger. To motivate support for the SDGs, employees must be able to recall recent victories and fit

---

32 Samuel Fankenhauser and Nicholas Stern, 'Climate Change, Development, Poverty, and Economics', Working paper, CCCEP and Grantham Research Institute on Climate Change and the Environment (October 2016).

33 In terms of recent history, the '3 by 5' initiative launched under the auspices and backed by funds from PEPFAR and the Global Fund is an important precedent, managing to double the amount of poor people receiving access to anti-retroviral therapy in the space of just two years.

them into a narrative about how change occurs. This is a central task for leadership in organisations.

Steps much also be taken to guard against the risk that the SDGs are 'unloved' – which is to say achievable but not worthwhile. In this regard, effort should be made to make the goals morally compelling for people working in the sector. We will shortly turn to consider the public-facing dimension of the SDGs, but it is important to develop the right moral message internally as well. Like the public at large, employees of international organisations are likely to draw inspiration from a powerful narrative, one that combines urgency with the substantive value of the goals that are being pursued. Ideally, the SDGs would come to be internalised as part of an employee's professional ethos, so that 'doing the job well' comes to mean taking them seriously – particularly when the goals demand novelty in response to shortcomings that have affected the sector in the past.[34]

Nonetheless, the stretch goals approach is also fraught with difficulty. The great paradox of stretch goal pursuit is that the organisations that are most likely to use them are often those who are the least likely to succeed.[35] All too often they embark on these projects as a 'Hail-Mary pass', when the situation is already desperate and the pursuit of impossible outcomes represents the only way to stave off disaster.

Goals That Inspire

What we term 'aspiration goals' are statements of shared belief about the aims and values that a community intends to pursue. Aspiration goals are normative in two senses. First, they tell us something important about how we *ought* to behave and the state of affairs we should try to bring about. Second, they help establish norms and *shared expectations* about behaviour of others in the community, and about what constitutes acceptable conduct. To perform these tasks successfully, aspiration goals do not need to be realistic. Unlike stretch goals, which must be realisable, at least in theory, aspiration goals can have a fairly utopian character and still be effective – in at least two ways.

To begin with, aspiration goals may influence the conduct of states and their representatives directly by contributing to the emergence of new global norms and expectations. In this regard, a major achievement of the MDGs was to change the way that donors and international institutions talked about

---

34 Commenting on the importance of moral framing, Jim Kim notes that the '3 by 5' initiative got going in force once people recognised that inequality in access to health care 'presented unacceptable economic, political, moral, and epidemiological consequences'. Jim Kim Yong, and Arthur Ammann, 'Is the "3 by 5" initiative the best approach to tackling the HIV pandemic?' *PLoS Medicine* 1.2 (2004): e37.

35 Sim Sitkin, Chet Miller, and Kelly See 'The Stretch Goal Paradox', *Harvard Business Review* (February 2017), https://hbr.org/2017/01/the-stretch-goal-paradox.

development, moving them away from the preoccupation with economic indicators towards an approach that focused on human development.[36] In this way the MDGs helped place the welfare of people living in poverty at the centre of the picture.

Beyond this, the process of articulating goals and committing to them in public has political consequences when it leads to public mobilisation and the development of new supporting coalitions. Important historical examples of this phenomenon include the goals set forth by abolitionists and those endorsed by the civil rights movement.[37] Moreover, despite the use of aid-heavy messaging, the MDGs were relatively successfully in this regard – notably in the United Kingdom where mass mobilisation at the time of the Gleneagles summit prompted the government to meet the 0.7% GDP development-finance target for the first time. In this context, public mobilisation was a powerful driver of social change.

In both respects, the SDGs show some degree of promise. Given the inclusive nature of the process that produced them, and their widespread endorsement, these goals should be understood as part of an emergent consensus about the kind of development policies that are acceptable. Taken seriously, they point to a world in which national plans, infrastructure development, and aid that is blind to environmental concerns, or that further entrench inequality, are no longer held to be morally acceptable.[38] The significant effort expended on informing people about the SDGs suggests that they are also meant to stimulate public engagement and debate. At the time of their launch, 500 million children were taught about the goals through 'the world's largest lesson' and text messages were sent to almost a billion people.

Yet in order to have an impact on public attitudes to development, the message contained by the SDGs must be heard, must be understood, and must be persuasive.[39] In each respect the SDGs encounter serious obstacles. To begin with, public knowledge and awareness around the SDGs continues to be

---

36 Hulme, 'The Making of the MDG' and Sakiko Fukuda-Parr and Alicia Ely Yamin, *Millennium Development Goals, Capabilities and Human Rights: The Power of Numbers to Shape Agendas* (London: Routledge, 2015).

37 Neta Crawford, *Argument and Change in World Politics*, and Joshua Cohen, 'The Arc of the Moral Universe', *Philosophy & Public Affairs* 26, no. 2 (1997): 91–134. http://www.jstor.org/stable/2961947.

38 In this regard future investment is key. Whereas total overseas development aid is around $140 billion per year, Nick Stern suggests that governments will have to make decisions about $100 trillion of infrastructure investment over the next 15 years. Whether this money is invested in ways that support efforts to prevent climate change and support the environment is decidedly important for the fate of our planet.

39 According to Neta Crawford whether an argument succeeds or not is a product of both extrinsic and intrinsic factors. The extrinsic factors affecting success are (1) whether its advocates have been heard, (2) whether it has been made by savvy political actors who mobilise support, (3) historical accident (e.g. the skill of the leadership), and (4) whether it coheres with the pre-existing context (*Argument and Change*, 79), *supra* note 37, note 79.

worryingly low. As mentioned previously, recent surveys suggest that one year after their launch 94% of people living in the United States and 96% of people living in the United Kingdom had little or no knowledge of the goals.[40] Beyond this, the sheer number of goals presents a challenge when it comes to crafting a successful communications strategy. The fact that there are 17 of them makes them cognitively demanding and functions as a barrier to intelligibility. Without any hierarchy or internal structure to guide general interpretation, their collective meaning is elusive. Finally, efforts to make the goals motivationally compelling may have actually backfired. Preliminary research from the *Narrative Project* suggests that their heavy reliance upon total targets – such as 'ending poverty', 'ending hunger', and 'achieving gender equality' – has created an air of unreality about the goals that could prove difficult to dispel.[41]

Sloganising the SDGs

What can be done to address this situation? Efforts to distill the SDGs into a compelling message must have three properties. First, they must create a message or narrative that is simple and helps to reduce their *cognitive demandingness*: a successful message must make the goals easier to understand and unite around on a collective basis. Second, a successful message must demonstrate *fidelity*: it must capture what is important about the SDGs and reflect their underlying purpose. Third, the message must *resonate* with existing beliefs and attitudes. This is because efforts to cajole and persuade the public to support new initiatives or ideas do not start with a blank slate. Instead, advocates must develop arguments that 'fit' with existing webs of belief, while also providing a fresh account of who we are or where we aspire to be.[42]

There have been various efforts to distill the message of the SDGs into a simpler form. How well do they fare against the standards set out? One of the most cogent and powerful efforts to bestow a simple meaning on the SDGs focuses on the pledge that 'no one will be left behind'. Signatories state that 'we wish to see the goals and targets met for all nations and peoples and for all segments of society. And we will endeavor to reach the further behind first'. This message is emotionally and psychologically powerful. To begin with, the idea of being left behind is itself psychologically vivid. It has emotional resonance and encourages its audience to undergo a perspective shift – to identify with those at the bottom – when encountered for the first time. The idea that

---

40 Martijn Lampert and Panos Papadongonas, *Mapping People's Awareness and Opinions about Poverty Eradication the Global Goals in China, France, Germany, India, UK and USA* (presentation obtained from the authors).
41 The Narrative Project website, accessed August 30, 2018, https://www.narrativeproject.org/.
42 Neta Crawford, *Argument and Change in World Politics*, 113–14.

we should leave no one behind (LNOB) also appeals to the widely held moral intuition that the worst-off members of society have the strongest claim to assistance, and encourages a sense of solidarity with them.

From a practical standpoint, LNOB was also crafted with a specific purpose in mind. It spoke to a worry among the signatories that MDGs had worsened inequality by creating a system of perverse incentives that encouraged governments to focus on easy-to-reach populations and ignored vulnerable groups.[43] The information contained by LNOB therefore helps to fill an important gap in the SDGs insofar as it proposes an approach to implementation.[44] However, LNOB also has certain weaknesses. Most obviously, it is a very partial reading of the SDG agenda. Whereas the SDGs are process-light and content-heavy, LNOB espouses a largely procedural aim. More seriously still, it is a message designed with the development sector in mind: it tells us *how* we should go about addressing poverty, but is silent about climate change and other environmental concerns.

A second attempt to distill meaning from the SDGs holds that they are all about 'empowering women and girls'. When different messages were tested in the United States, Britain, France, and Germany, the single most compelling one was found to be that 'women and girls everywhere deserve an equal chance to thrive. We must address the imbalance that is holding them back and let them take control of their lives'.[45] Like LNOB, this message is simple and compelling. It stresses the values of equality and autonomy that people care about, and it has significant global appeal – finding strong support in India and in LICs. Furthermore, the message has fidelity. It is pretty much a direct statement of SDG 5, and it focuses attention on an important crosscutting issue. For the first time, the SDGs acknowledge the entrenched and interlocking factors that perpetuate women's disadvantage, proposing comprehensive reforms including measures to tackle institutional discrimination and stigma.[46]

Nevertheless, a focus on women and girls still excludes a great deal. The SDGs are centrally concerned with other marginalised groups such as youth, the disabled, the LGBT community, and people who are geographically isolated or socially marginalised. Importantly, the idea that the environment and human development are inexorably connected is still missing. Finally, there is concern that the focus on women and girls encourages the dangerous

---

43 Edward Anderson, 'Equality as a Global Goal', *Ethics & International Affairs* 30, no. 2 (2016): 189–200. doi:10.1017/S0892679416000071, 189.

44 Nicolai et al., 'Projecting Progress'.

45 The Narrative Project, 'A Battle between Belief and Reason: Building Public Awareness and Support for Global Development in the US, UK, France, and Germany' (PowerPoint presentation, July 2014).

46 Sandra Fredman, Jaakko Kuosmanen, and Meghan Campbell, 'Transformative Equality: Making the Sustainable Development Goals Work for Women', *Ethics & International Affairs* 30, no. 2 (2016): 177–187. doi:10.1017/S089267941600006X.

propensity of the development community to think in terms of a 'silver bullet' or panacea for global problems. These approaches have failed in the past – and seem likely to fail again if they are pursued.[47]

Finally, there have been several attempts to develop more composite and inclusive messages. For example, the declaration presents a summary of its content in terms of 'five Ps': people, planet, prosperity, peace, and partnership. This summary is both accurate and comprehensive. However, it does not resonate or simplify the SDGs in the right way. Crucially, the 5Ps read like a list of platitudes. Each concept is vague and their collective meaning is elusive. More recently *Project Everyone*, the organisation given responsibility to promote the SDGs, has argued their purpose is to 'end poverty, fix climate change, and tackle inequalities'. This message is a marked improvement on the '5Ps'. It successfully identifies what is new in the SDGs – while also simplifying the agenda and breaking it down into a manageable form. Furthermore, while it lacks the emotional resonance of LNOB, the tripartite message has rhetorical power, introducing a measure of action-orientation and dynamism that the 5Ps lack. Of course, this message is still not perfect. People living in affluent countries tend to be sceptical of pledges to end poverty despite the great progress that has been made. More important, the message is *not yet a narrative*. It needs to be developed further, and successfully embedded, if it is to have genuine motivational power.

Towards a New Global Narrative?

One of the main ways in which aspiration goals lead to new forms of collective action and agency is through *narrative* and *narrative embedding*. On one hand, aspiration goals work best when they form part of a compelling story about the challenges we face, what we aim to achieve, and the steps that need to be taken. On the other hand, they must be embedded in meta-narratives which contain contextual information that orientates an audience and shapes their underlying ascriptions of purpose and value. Taken together, narratives help simplify complex events and responses, containing knowledge that is both easily shared and, for the listener, condensed.[48] They are also important from the standpoint

---

47 For example, microfinance was previously thought of as the 'silver bullet' that could end poverty, which led to greater investment in these types of intervention. However, that notion was later attenuated. See Robert Cull and Jonathan Morduch, 'Microfinance and Economic Development' (Policy Research Working Paper 8252, World Bank Group, November 2017), http://documents.worldbank.org/curated/en/107171511360386561/pdf/WPS8252.pdf, and the announcement by the Microfinance Impact and Innovation Conference, 'A First Look at New Research On Microfinance Impact and Innovation', News, CGAP (19 October 2010), http://www.cgap.org/news/first-look-new-research-microfinance-impact-and-innovation.
48 Jean-Francois Lyotard, *The Post-Modern Condition: A Report on Knowledge* (Manchester: Manchester University Press, 1979, 1986), 21.

of motivation, because as Stephen Denning notes, 'the best way to get human beings to venture into unknown terrain is to make that terrain familiar and desirable by taking them there first in their imaginations.'[49]

In this regard, the authors of the MDGs were particularly fortunate. For all their shortcomings, the goals were able to draw upon the idea of a 'millennial moment' – with advocates claiming it represented a one-shot opportunity to rid the world of poverty and disease. Allied with strong leadership, and a set of fortunate global circumstances, they argued that wealthy nations could use their resources to 'make poverty history' and that they would do so with suffi-cient public support. According to this message, all that was needed was for those living in rich countries to show they *cared enough* – and campaign for this specific programme to be implemented. Clearly, much about this narrative is problematic. It supposes a hierarchical relationship between donors and recipients, appealing to the beneficence of people living in affluent countries in a way that resonates with long-held beliefs about the special role and purpose of the West in the context of global civilisation. It also failed to take account of the inevitable disappointment and heightened cynicism that would result when these goals were not met. But from a motivational standpoint, the narra-tive was compelling, leading to widespread social mobilisation and support for this specific development agenda.

By way of comparison, the SDGs lack an equivalent narrative. Furthermore, they have been launched at a time when narrative resources are thin on the ground. On the one hand, turn-of-the-century optimism has given way to something far more ambiguous and complex. In place of the liberal narrative that posited humanity as a collective agent steadily progressing towards greater freedom, we now witness renewed scepticism about cosmopolitanism in high-income countries and pessimism about aid. According to Hudson et al., the 'unrelentingly shocking and dehumanizing framing of global poverty' has undermined 'people's sense of *efficacy* in addressing global poverty, and conse-quently their engagement.'[50] On the other hand, we have seen the rise of new counternarratives. In the international arena, Hobbesian narratives that fore-ground national security and the control of borders have regained the upper hand. These worldviews see the international arena as an inherently hostile place, in which the strong dominate the weak, and countries can only rely upon their own ingenuity to flourish.[51] Furthermore, in the United States, there has been a sustained assault on the notion of scientific knowledge, as demonstrated

---

49 Steve Denning, 'Telling Tales', *Harvard Business Review,* 7 May 2004.
50 Surveys support this conclusion. When asked about their views, only 9% of British people and 19% of Americans believe that individual action can make a significant difference in this area (The Narrative Project, and David Hudson, Jennifer van Heerde-Hudson, Niheer Darsandi, and Susan Gaines), 'Emotional Pathways to Engagement with Global Poverty: An Experimental Analysis' (Working Paper, University College London, 24 April 2016).
51 Alexander Wendt, *Social Theory of International Politics* (New York: Cambridge University Press, 1999), 259.

by the phenomenon of climate change denial, which had previously formed an important part of Enlightenment narratives about human progress. And globally, we might suspect that there has been a fragmentation of grand narratives themselves, followed by the rise of local voices that lack a single unifying theme.[52]

What hope is there, then, for a new global narrative built around the SDGs? Despite these obstacles, there are three reasons to be optimistic. First, the prevalence of anticosmopolitan beliefs and attitudes is overstated. Indeed, surveys suggest that the SDGs embody certain *universally recognised human values*. For example, a survey by Ipsos-MORI found that 95% of people globally believe 'it is important to preserve the planet for future generations.'[53] Efforts to end hunger, promote clean water and sanitation, meet health targets, and provide universal access to education meet with similarly high levels of global acclaim. This tells in favour of the SDGs' unifying potential and against the thesis of narrative fragmentation.[54]

Second, research from experimental psychology demonstrates that there are emotionally engaging *messages that command widespread support* and are properly adjusted to the world in which we live. In place of the traditional appeals, which focus on the role of sympathy, pity, and guilt to motivate action against a backdrop of hierarchical relations, Hudson et al. have tested a variety of new messages and found that *hope* is as influential as anger and more powerful than guilt when it comes to motivating people to action.[55] It is also a more beneficial emotion to tap into because it is empowering, improving people's sense of personal efficacy and avoiding repulsion – which has been a byproduct of more traditional approaches.[56] Building upon these insights, researchers at the *Narrative Project* found that the most effective stories – when it comes to changing behaviour – jettison the hierarchical relationships of the past and stress the value of autonomy and partnership in the global context. When it comes to engaging the public around the SDGs, we should focus on the

---

52 Lyotard, *Post-Modern Condition*, 41.

53 Ipsos-MORI, '17 Country Study of Foreign Aid and the Sustainable Development Goals', 24 September 2015. Available at: https://www.ipsos.com/en-us/17-country-study-foreign-aid-and-sustainable-development-goals.

54 At a deeper level it fits with the view of theorists such as Stephen Pinker who argue that exogenous factors are shifting the allocation of moral intuitions away from community, authority, and purity, and towards fairness, autonomy, and rationality (639–40). Ultimately, Pinker suggests that we should 're-evaluate our views about modernity and about where we are.' Steven Pinker, *The Better Angels of Our Nature: The Decline of Violence in History and Its Causes* (New York: Penguin, 2011), 692.

55 Hudson et al., 'Emotional Pathways'.

56 Andrew Darnton and Martin Kirk, *Finding Frames: New Ways to Engage the UK Public in Global Poverty* (London: Bond, 2011), 23.

unequal distribution of global opportunity and the need to unlock potential, as well as on the values that unite us.

Third, while public attitudes to global problems vary significantly by geographical location, people tend to be *particularly hopeful* in low- and middle-income countries. For example, whereas only 10% of people living in the United Kingdom and 17% of Americans believe that it is possible to end extreme poverty by 2030, 40% of people living in India believe this is the case – something that corresponds closely to their lived experience.[57] Thus, while the tendency to focus on public opinion in the Global North might lead us to conclude prematurely that the liberal idea that people can 'rise up in dignity and freedom through knowledge' no longer resonates, these ideas remain a powerful source of inspiration for many around the world today.[58] The SDGs should therefore make use of these ideas and place them on a more egalitarian footing so that they command widespread support. Around the world, people tend to be enthusiastic about the idea of an effective global partnership working together to address and end extreme poverty and protect the planet for the next generation.[59] This is the message that needs to be heard.

Conclusion

The SDGs are meant to perform multiple functions, motivating the staff of development organisations, shaping national priorities and plans, and stimulating the public to engage with global issues. In each context, their complexity and the question of how to translate them for different audiences loom large. To varying degrees, the mechanisms supporting compliance with stretch goals, SMART goals, and aspiration goals can be used to help address these problems. For example, the SMART goal methodology can be used to track progress toward priority objectives, stretch goals can be used to stimulate innovation, and aspirational goals can be used to galvanise political action. In each case, choices need to be made. For example, stretch goals and SMART goals use different mechanisms to motivate compliance and are suited to different aims. There is a need to delegate responsibility for achieving the SDGs accordingly.

At the same time, there are certain qualities or characteristics that have the potential to enhance the motivational power of the SDGs across multiple

---

57 The Narrative Project, and Hudson et al., 'Emotional Pathways'.

58 Lyotard, *The Post-Modern Condition*, 34.

59 This final message is found in Susanna Gable, Hans Lofgren, and Israel Osorio Rodarte, *Trajectories for the Sustainable Development Goals: Framework and Country Applications* (Washington, DC: World Bank, 2015), ix. See also Narrative Project, 'A Battle between Belief and Reason', 34–37.

domains. The first is *concreteness*. While this is usually thought to be a virtue of SMART goals, the ability to specify clearly what the desired outcome would look like also helps organisations focus attention in the right way on the task at hand, and provides the public with assurance that goals are not hopelessly utopian. The second is *prioritisation*. Prioritisation not only helps us determine which goals to focus on, it can also help bestow order – and hence meaning – upon complex schemes, enhancing their communicative power. The third, and perhaps the most important property, is the development of a strong *moral message* embedded in a narrative that commands widespread support. This is essential for public support and mobilisation but can also be used to inspire project managers and policymakers. While further research is needed in this area, we have suggested that an egalitarian, progressive, and hopeful narrative may work best in this context.

4

Overcoming Scarcity: The Paradox of Abundance

Harnessing Digitalisation in Financing Sustainable Development

Simon Zadek

This chapter argues that the reshaping of financial and capital markets resulting from digitalisation offers an opportunity to accelerate the alignment of the financial system with sustainable development goals. Advancing financial inclusion through digitalisation illustrates this opportunity, but is the thin edge of a far greater wedge into the current dynamics between finance and the long-term needs of an inclusive, sustainable economy. Digitalisation, however, brings with it downsides and the likelihood of unintended consequences. Furthermore, it may temporarily disrupt whilst not transforming more problematic aspects of today's financial and capital markets. In this formative stage, therefore, there is a unique opportunity, and need, to shape how the digitalisation of finance in practice impacts sustainable development.

Scarcity: The Paradox of Abundance

There is widespread agreement that there is inadequate financing flowing to support the achievement of the Sustainable Development Goals (SDGs) and the goals underlying the Paris Agreement on climate.[1] The cost of this collective failure cannot be understated, from the impacts of inequality on prospects of localities and nations to the existential challenges facing humanity in the event of continued increases in surface temperatures and the collapse of life-giving ecosystems.

Inadequate financing is not, however, the result of insufficient finance. Global savings today, at US$7 trillion annually, are more than enough to finance the transition to sustainable development. Indeed, the decade since the financial

---

1 United Nations Environment Programme, *The Financial System We Need: Aligning the Financial System with Sustainable Development*, 2015, http://unepinquiry.org/publication/inquiry-global-report-the-financial-system-we-need/.

Sustainable Development Goals: Harnessing Business to Achieve the SDGs through Finance, Technology, and Law Reform, First Edition. Edited by Julia Walker, Alma Pekmezovic, and Gordon Walker.

crisis has been one characterised by hyper-liquidity, historically unprecedentedly low interest rates in many countries, and a steady deterioration in the prospects of savers and pension holders in the face of low, risk-adjusted returns.

In short, there is plenty of financial capital desperately seeking almost any financial returns.

The paradox of this low-cost abundance is that capital has remained scarce and costly where it is most needed and could be most productive. Even in wealthy countries, such as Germany and the United States, there has been a serious underinvestment in everything from twenty-first-century infrastructure to education and health promotion. Likewise, in most developing countries, critical, productivity-enhancing infrastructure investment has not taken place in anything like the volume required, even before taking into account qualitative design issues concerning, for example, equity, low-carbon, and climate-resilient outcomes.[2]

Financing shortfalls are, therefore, constructed, or at least an outcome, of how financial and capital markets allocate capital. That is, despite the extraordinary sophistication of our global financial system, we have constructed conditions of financial capital scarcity in exactly those areas critical to delivering long-term financial returns underpinned by a healthy global economy, society, and planet.[3]

Such shortfalls, if sustained, will make it impossible to effectively implement the 2030 Agenda, including the Paris commitments on climate. This in turn creates substantial risks for communities, nations, and ultimately humankind, both directly, through, for example, the ravages of climate change, and indirectly, through the endemic effects of growing inequality.

Financing: A Systemic Challenge

Many factors underpin this apparently paradoxical shortfall and its effects. Often noted are weaknesses in finance-using countries. Suggested, especially in developing countries, is an insufficient or too risky investment pipeline, and insufficient or poorly used public finance in seeking to meet development financing needs. Also highlighted are inadequate and inappropriate incentives, including weak enforcement of environmental regulations, corruption, and the negative effects on fiscal space of illicit financial flows.

---

2 OECD, UNEP, and World Bank, *Financing Climate Futures: Rethinking Infrastructure*, 2018, http://unepinquiry.org/publication/financing-climate-futures-rethinking-infrastructure/.
3 S. Zadek, *An Economics of Utopia: the Democratisation of Scarcity* (Avebury Books, 1994); N. Xenos, 'Liberalism and the Postulate of Scarcity', *Political Theory* 15, no. 2 (May 1987): 225–243.

Until recently, less focus has been placed on the systemic features of today's global financial and capital markets. It is the financial system that, alongside other functions, has the role of intermediating global savings to ensure adequate financing for the long-term health of the real economy. Even through a narrow, fiduciary lens, failure in effecting this role means that the owners of capital ultimately suffer the consequences, most directly because one cannot sustain financial returns indefinitely from a weakening global economy. Some such consequences are of a long-term nature, such as the manner in which climate risk might disrupt some of the world's largest, deepest, and most liquid capital markets. Others, however, take place in the shorter term, exemplified by the impacts of an over-focus on mortgage lending and debt (rather than equity) in the aftermath of the most recent financial crisis, and arguably the next one, respectively.

There is little doubt that action is needed, with progress needed to:

- *Overcome financial system weaknesses,* domestically and internationally, that constrain financing for the 2030 Agenda, such as short-termism, and narrow approaches to financial risk assessment.
- Take into account broader development *impacts in internationally relevant, economic, and particularly financial policy-making.* Quantitative easing, for example, may well have played a critical role in ensuring financial liquidity but might also impact inequality, just as Basel III's banking regime might well negatively impact investment in clean energy.

There is an inevitability of such complex impact dynamics, positive or negative, of developments across the financial (and monetary) system. The implication is that the challenge of financing for the SDGs needs to be understood not simply as a matter of flows, let alone 'more' flows. Rather, the challenge needs to be understood as one of system design, or, more properly, the evolution of its design features over time.

Such a frame of reference is far from purely interesting or conceptual. The need to focus on system design can be illustrated across many aspects of the financial system. Measuring and providing effective information on risk, for example, is the lifeblood – indeed, some would say the existential core – of financial and capital markets. Yet it is now widely accepted, building on the work of the Financial Stability Board's Task Force on Climate-Related Risk Disclosure,[4] that fundamental risks, such as the impacts of climate change on asset valuation, are in the main mis-valued and often simply ignored. Such

---

4 Task Force on Climate Related Financial Disclosures, *Final Report: Recommendations of the Task Force on Climate-Related Financial Disclosures*, 2018, https://www.fsb-tcfd.org/.

distortions are, crucially, not randomly distributed. They are influenced, for example, by short-term investor horizons and associated incentives, and a lack of standardised metrics and methodologies.

In conclusion, then, effectively addressing the challenge of financing the SDGs requires that focus be placed on the design of the financial system, which needs to be aligned to the needs of sustainable development.

Action on System Design

Increasing action is being taken to address these broader, systemic failures in the financial system. UNEP's Inquiry into Design Options for a Sustainable Financial System ('the Inquiry') has mapped and advanced these developments since 2014.[5] There is a growth in the development of national-level roadmaps for green and sustainable finance in countries, by many counts exemplified in China[6] and subsequently across such diverse cases as Indonesia, Italy, Morocco, and Singapore.[7] Specialised sustainable finance regulations and guidelines have also been developed. Bangladesh, China, Vietnam, and Pakistan have developed guidance for banks to include environmental and social factors into risk management.

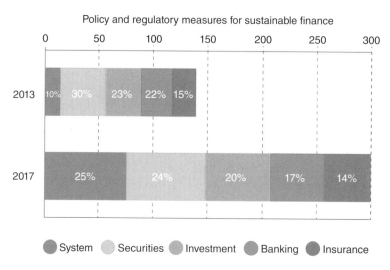

The doubling in policy and regulatory measures for sustainable finance, 2013–2017.
Source: Illustration based on original downloadable at: www.unepinquiry.org.

---

5 UNEP, *Making Waves: Aligning the Financial System with Sustainable Development*, 2017, http://unepinquiry.org/making-waves/.
6 People's Bank of China/UNEP, *China Green Finance Task Force Report*, 2015, https://unepinquiry.org/publication/establishing-chinas-green-financial-system/.
7 Many of these roadmaps have been produced in collaboration with the UNEP Inquiry into Design Options for a Sustainable Financial System, which can be downloaded from www.unepinquiry.org.

UNEP, with the World Bank Group, has reviewed these developments, and noted their account of ways to:[8]

- *Enhance market practice*, including efforts that mainstream sustainability factors into financial decision making and correct for market failures (such as unpriced environmental externalities).
- *Support market growth*, including policy frameworks and standards that promote the issuance of sustainability-aligned financial products (e.g. SDG bonds).[9]
- *Promote transparency and efficiency*, by improving flows of sustainability information through the financial system through voluntary guidance, labelling schemes, or mandatory requirements.
- *Strengthen risk management*, by integrating sustainability factors (such as physical and transition-related climate risks) into both the considerations of financing institutions and supervisory bodies.
- *Clarify legal frameworks*, including the fiduciary responsibilities of financial institutions, with respect to long-term risks and opportunities (such as climate change).
- *Enhance conduct and behaviour*, with codes of conduct and guidelines for environmental issues and compacts with financial institutions.

The G20 has taken increasing note of developments in sustainable finance. Initially, during China's G20 Presidency, the Green Finance Study Group was established in the G20 Finance Track. During Germany's G20 Presidency, this work was deepened, with a focus on enhancing risk management and the role of publicly available environmental data. Finally, during Argentina's G20 Presidency, the scope was broadened from green to sustainable finance,[10] with deeper dives, including a review of progress on sustainable finance across the G20[11] and a focus on the role of digital in advancing financing for the 2030 Agenda.[12]

Market action is now emerging in response to growing awareness, pressure, and policy and regulatory moves focused on the need to align the financial system with sustainable development. There is a growth in actions by individual investors, lenders, and insurers, including a volume increase in the scale of

---

8 UNEP and World Bank Group, *Roadmap for a Sustainable Financial System*, 2018, http://unepinquiry.org/publication/roadmap-for-a-sustainable-financial-system/.

9 A. Mohammed and S. Zadek, 'From Green Bonds to Sustainable Development: The Case of Nigeria', in R. M. Desai, H. Kato, H. Kharas (eds), *From Summits to Solutions: Innovations in Implementing the Sustainable Development Goals*, (Washington, DC: Brookings Institution), https://www.brookings.edu/wp-content/uploads/2018/03/FSTS_chapter3.pdf.

10 G20, *Sustainable Finance Synthesis Report*, 2018, http://unepinquiry.org/wp-content/uploads/2018/11/G20_Sustainable_Finance_Synthesis_Report_2018.pdf.

11 UNEP, *Progress on Sustainable Finance*, 2018, http://unepinquiry.org/wp-content/uploads/2019/03/Sustainable_Finance_Progress_Report_2018.pdf.

12 Sustainable Digital Finance Alliance, *Digital Technologies for Mobilizing Sustainable Finance*, 2018, http://unepinquiry.org/wp-content/uploads/2018/10/Digital_Technologies_for_Mobilizing_Sustainable_Finance.pdf.

so-called impact investors. Similarly, there is a growth in new products such as green and now SDG bonds, as well as numerous sustainability-related ratings, tracker funds, and indexes, including the newly established, Aviva-led World Benchmarking Alliance.[13] Likewise, there is a growth in collective action, such as the investor coalition or Climate Action 100+.[14]

Digital Financing of the SDGs

Finance is not static, and neither is the financial system. Measures to align financial flows with the 2030 Agenda and the Paris Agreement needs to take account of major changes in the nature of finance and the shape and functioning of the financial system. One of the most important is the growing impact of the digitalisation on finance, taking account of developments across a broad range of technologies including big data, artificial intelligence (AI), online and mobile platforms, blockchain, and the Internet of Things (IoT). Today, digitalisation is increasingly demonstrating its ability to overcome key barriers to advancing finance for inclusive, sustainable development. PwC estimates that AI alone could lift global GDP by US$15–20 trillion by 2030.[15] McKinsey estimates that digital finance could boost the GDP of emerging economies by US$3.7 trillion by 2025, translating into GDP growth in India, Brazil, Mexico, and China of almost 12%, 5.5%, 5%, and 4.2%, respectively.[16]

Digitalisation is a tsunami coursing its way through society, transforming everything in its path. It most directly changes finance through its ability to make the availability, processing, and analysis of larger amounts of complex data cheaper, faster, and more accurate. There is, however, a more complex, and, indeed, entangled set of pathways along which digitalisation can impact the nexus of finance and decisions that impact sustainable development.

- *Externalities*: Perhaps most directly and importantly, the improved breadth and quality and cheapness of data opens the door to understanding the nature of the impacts of financing decisions that are currently externalities, which in turn allows for those impacts to be valorised, whether through policy interventions, risk pricing, and/or the preferences of the owners of capital.

---

13 https://www.worldbenchmarkingalliance.org/.
14 http://www.climateaction100.org/.
15 PwC, *Sizing the Prize*, 2017, https://www.pwc.com/gx/en/issues/analytics/assets/pwc-ai-analysis-sizing-the-prize-report.pdf.
16 McKinsey Global Institute, *Digital Finance for All: Powering Inclusive Growth in Emerging Economies*, September 2016.

- *Innovation*: Drives new business models, products, and services, as well as markets that drive financing towards SDG outcomes. Kenya's iconic M-PESA has delivered a quantum uplift in financial inclusion[17] and has triggered M-KOPA, a business delivering distributed solar energy to poorer households without a credit record,[18] and M-AKIBA, the world's first government bond subscribed to exclusively by citizens through mobile payments platforms.[19]
- *Behaviour*: Digitalisation can shift values, incentives, and behavioural outcomes in ways that better align finance with SDGs. Ant Financial Services, working with UNEP and the Sustainable Digital Finance Alliance, has engaged more than 300 million Chinese users of Alipay in carbon saving activities by offering individualised, real-time carbon-use data based on algorithms of financial transaction data.[20]
- *Power*: Digitalisation can change the power of citizens in the financing value chain, including those traditionally disadvantaged in finance and economy.[21] Pension policyholders, for example, might make values-based choices opened to them through the more extensive use of robo-investors, whilst savers more generally can direct their savings into specific assets and businesses through peer-to-peer lending and crowdsourcing.
- *Governance*: Opens spaces for new mandates, policies, regulations, standards, and norms that better align finance with SDGs. FinTech, for example, opens the possibility of more sophisticated policy engagement in credit creation at a time where Positive Money[22] and others argue for a reduced role for commercial organisations in this public-goods critical role.[23]

These drivers, in combination, offer multiple potential benefits in advancing sustainable finance, by, for example:

1) Reducing the costs of obtaining timely material information relevant to sustainability impacts and investments' financial risks.
2) Increasing transparency and effective accountability.
3) Supporting public institutions in more effectively tracking the regulatory aspects of sustainable development.

---

17 https://en.wikipedia.org/wiki/M-Pesa.
18 http://www.m-kopa.com/.
19 http://www.m-akiba.go.ke/.
20 Sustainable Digital Finance Alliance, *Digital Technologies for Mobilizing Sustainable Finance*, 2017, https://www.sustainabledigitalfinance.org/initiatives-publications.
21 UNEP, *Digital Finance and Citizen Action* (consultation draft), 2018, http://unepinquiry.org/publication/digital-finance-and-citizen-action/.
22 https://positivemoney.org/.
23 M. Wolf, 'Strip Private Banks of their Power to Make Money', *Financial Times*, 24 April 2014, https://www.ft.com/content/7f000b18-ca44-11e3-bb92-00144feabdc0.

Box 4.1 Sustainable FinTech: early practices across the G20[24]

- **Argentina:** *Crowdear*[25] is a rewards-based crowdfunding platform. Its main objective is to unlock new sources of finance and encourage entrepreneurs to focus on projects applying technology to education, health, and environment outcomes.
- **Australia:** *Macquarie* has acquired Green Investment Bank and offers flat-fee digital investment advice services. *Acorns*, a micro-investing robo-advisors app, developed a socially responsible 'Emerald Portfolio' that allows users to invest more sustainably.[26] The *Green Crowd* offers traditional crowdfunding services at a fee, but specifically focuses on arts, community, and technology within the green niche.[27] *RateSetter*[28] is a P2P green lending platform for businesses and individuals.
- **Brazil:** *Kickante* is a leading collective platform that focuses on financing projects with a social impact. It has hosted more than 8,000 campaigns with artists, charities, and entrepreneurs, including an ecological sanctuary association in São Paulo. *Catarse* is another crowdfunding platform focused on raising collective finance for ventures that have social and environmental impacts, including low-carbon development, solid waste, and infrastructure.[29]
- **Germany:** *EcoCrowd*[30] is a crowdfunding platform specialised in green projects and sustainable initiatives. The goal is to use the platform to provide both financing and support to further develop the project.
- **Italy:** *Ecomill*[31] is an equity crowdfunding platform where households and firms can finance projects and new ventures in energy efficiency, sustainable mobility, renewables, smart grids, local economic development, and environmental services. Additionally, the platform supports projects using its professional network to provide analysis for the development of the venture and during the launch of their funding campaign.
- **Japan:** *NPO Bank* has been an advocate of crowdfunding activities and as such has been used to fund social investment and impact investment. For example, investing in a local business engaged in the revival of forests in the

---

24 Adapted from Sustainable Digital Finance Alliance, *Digital Technologies for Mobilizing Sustainable Finance*, 2017, https://www.sustainabledigitalfinance.org/initiatives-publications.
25 https://www.crowdium.com.ar/?gclid=CPaksozz-9ICFQcFkQod31kNlg.
26 World Economic Forum, *Beyond Fintech: A Pragmatic Assessment of Disruptive Potential in Financial Services*, 2017, http://www3.weforum.org/docs/Beyond_Fintech_-_A_Pragmatic_Assessment_of_Disruptive_Potential_in_Financial_Services.pdf.
27 Green Entrepreneurship, *6 Green Crowdfunding Platforms*, 2017, www.greenentrepreneurship.com/green-crowdfunding-platforms/.
28 https://www.ratesetter.com/.
29 IDG, *Crowdfunding Grows in Latin America with a Creative Twist*, 2017, http://www.idgconnect.com/abstract/16092/crowdfunding-grows-latin-america-creative-twist.
30 https://www.ecocrowd.de/en/.
31 https://www.ecomill.it/en.html.

village of Nishiawakura, Okayama Prefecture, the domestic crowdfunding market has expanded to ¥20 billion.[32]

- **Republic of Korea:** Start-up *YOLK*[33] used crowdfunding to raise over US$1 million for a solar charger it developed.
- **Saudi Arabia:** The research arm of the *Islamic Development Bank* plans to use blockchain technology to develop sharia-compliant products, aiming to promote financial inclusion across its member countries. Its goal is to leverage blockchain technology to meet demand from Muslim investors, with firms from Indonesia to Canada. Such features, besides assisting in eliminating counterparty risks, would allow instantaneous clearing and settlement of transactions and assets exchanges.[34]
- **South Africa:** *Thundafund* is an online channel through which entrepreneurs can access capital and establish an initial market for their products and services. Thundafund combines financing with business mentorship to support businesses' success. *StartMe* has been designed for entrepreneurs, schools, and communities to utilise a crowdfunding platform to raise funding for projects. Via PayFast, anyone in South Africa can raise funding for a project. These crowdfunding business models vary in terms of repayment. Some models utilise rewards (products or services) as compensation, whereas others use interest or equity structures to compensate investors.[35]
- **UK:** *Abundance*[36] is an investment platform that allows anyone to invest in green energy projects. It also offers an online marketplace where investments can be traded in funded projects at any stage of the investment term.
- **United States:** *GreenFunder*[37] is a global crowdfunding site for green and socially responsible projects. Investors are rewarded with perks. GreenFunder charges a 5% fee for fully funded projects and 9% for partially funded projects. On top of this, a 3–5% processing and administration fee applies.
- **EU (Netherlands):** *Oneplanetcrowd*[38] is a crowdfunding platform focusing on sustainable projects. The crowd finances the loan, which can then be converted to shares for institutional investors. It is currently Europe's leading sustainable crowdfunding platform, with more than 25,000 investors; it has raised over EUR20 million since its launch in 2012 and has provided seed money and growth capital for more than 175 projects.

---

32 Japanese Sustainable Investment Forum, *White Paper on Sustainable Investment in Japan*, 2015, http://japansif.com/2015whitepaper.pdf.

33 https://www.kickstarter.com/projects/1398120161/solar-paper-the-worlds-thinnest-and-lightest-solar?ref=nav_search.

34 Reuters, 'Saudi Arabia's IDB Plans Blockchain-based Financial Inclusion Product', 2017, https://www.reuters.com/article/us-islamic-finance-fintech/saudi-arabias-idb-plans-blockchain-based-financial-inclusion-product-idUSKBN1CP08W?il=0.

35 *Innovative Finance in Africa*, Bertha Centre for Innovation and Social Entrepreneurship. University of Cape Town.

36 https://www.abundanceinvestment.com/about.

37 https://www.crunchbase.com/organization/greenfunder.

38 https://www.oneplanetcrowd.com/en.

4) Raising citizen awareness about the environmental and social implications of consumption and investment patterns, which incentivises more sustainable behavioural choices.

5) Unlocking new sources of finance, both 'bottom-up' and by 'matching' investors with sustainable investment opportunities.

6) Encouraging digital applications that mobilise and deploy capital for sustainable technologies and business models with great potential for improving the environment.

Diverse examples of applications of digital finance to sustainable development outcomes are provided in Table 4.1.

Dilemmas: Digitalisation and Dark Financing

Digitalisation of finance can help in progressing financing of the SDGs. Before turning to the question of 'how much', however, it is important to explore the converse, or dark side, of the upside illustrations offered in the previous section. Michael Lewis, in one of his best-selling exposes of the financial industry, *Flash Boys*, focuses on the emergence of high-frequency trading and its consequences.[39] Whilst not intended as a technical analysis, the book sets out a compelling story of how traders using very high-speed computation power linked to new digital transmission pathways effectively front-run slower-moving, long-term investors, thereby pushing up prices and charging them a premium to buy financial assets intended to deliver returns to pay for pensions and insurance claims.

Mr Lewis's key message, since then reiterated by many others, is that digitalisation can distort financial markets in ways that profit those with no interest whatsoever in their underlying purpose, namely to effectively intermediate savings with financing needs that deliver private returns and support the long-term health of the global economy.

More broadly, today's financial and capital markets have evolved to particularly benefit large corporations, which have exceptional access to capital and debt, and financial markets actors, which derive the greatest benefit from creating returns from secondary and tertiary financial products rather than returns on the primary source of value creation in the real economy.[40] Such features go a long way in explaining the lack of affordable capital available for

---

39 M. Lewis, *Flash Boys* (WW Norton & Co, 2014); A. Ross, 'Flash Boys by Michael Lewis – A Review', *The Guardian*, 16 May 2014, https://www.theguardian.com/books/2014/may/16/flash-boys-michael-lewis-review.

40 Thanks to Sofie Blakstad for her insights on the nexus between broader, systemic features of financial and capital markets and FinTech.

real value creation at the same time as an abundance of finance. Whilst Mr Lewis is right in pointing out that digitalisation can worsen this situation, it can also help to flatten these markets by revealing through traceability and auditability the largely unproductive source of profitability of such market behaviour. At the same time, digitalisation should allow for engagement of players in capital markets who in the past could not participate in capital markets, from consumers and small investors on the buy side to many possible sell side entrants, such as collectives of primary producer microbusinesses in developing economies or actors involved in biodiversity preservation.

The case of illicit financial flows once again illustrates this contingent, multifaceted impact of digitalisation. Illicit financial flows undermine development by enabling corruption, reducing fiscal resources, impacting currencies, and distorting resource allocations. Estimates of the extent of such flows, and their causes, vary considerably,[41] with estimates by Global Financial Integrity of the outflow from developing countries as high as more than US$1 trillion annually.[42] Most illicit financial flows, whatever their volume, are enabled by pathways through the financial system. Refinitiv estimates that 'a staggering 80% of illicit financial flows from developing countries are made through trade-based money laundering.'[43]

Digitalisation of financial flows allows for improved tracking, reporting (and, so, accountability), and in principle greater cooperation between state authorities, encouraged for example through such platforms as the OECD's Global Forum on Transparency and Exchange of Information for Tax Purposes.[44] Yet digitalisation can also make it easier to avoid taxes, and indeed more broadly perpetrate profitable illegalities, as the OECD highlights, for example, in its report on tax challenges associated with digitalisation.[45]

Ant Financial Services has become one of the world's largest lenders to small and medium-sized businesses (SMEs) in China. It has adopted its so-called '3-2-1' approach, in which it takes three minutes to apply, one minute for a decision to be made, and all loans requiring zero collateral. Enabling this, clearly, is the vast pool of data that Ant can access on SMEs through its parent company, Alibaba, and its capacity to use artificial intelligence to profile to the smallest detail the factors determining creditworthiness.

---

41 M. Forstater, *Pinning Down Illicit Financial Flows: Why Definitions Matter?*, 26 March 2018, Center for Global Development, https://www.cgdev.org/blog/pinning-down-illicit-financial-flows-why-definitions-matter.

42 https://www.gfintegrity.org/issue/illicit-financial-flows/.

43 https://www.refinitiv.com/en/resources/expert-talk/trade-based-money-laundering-hidden-in-plain-sight.

44 http://www.oecd.org/tax/transparency/.

45 OECD, *Tax Challenges Arising from Digitalisation – Interim Report*, 2018, http://www.oecd.org/tax/tax-challenges-arising-from-digitalisation-interim-report-9789264293083-en.htm.

Big data and AI-driven credit scores can have some notable pitfalls. Algorithms of creditworthiness can, of course, block particular groups from accessing credit, either unintentionally because of learned, pathway effects, or intentionally if lending decisions are not exclusively based on delinquency probabilities. Particular ethnic groups might unintentionally or otherwise be downgraded as groups, for example. Moreover, such credit systems have opened the door to 'social credit' systems, generally developed by governments with an interest in spotting unwanted social deviations and seeking to incentivise their mitigation.[46]

Digitalisation, like any other innovation, is not inherently neutral. In some instances, this may offer some development advantage, for example in enabling certain types of financial inclusion by virtue of reduced costs of data, knowledge, and, so, risk pricing. In some cases, the broader impacts are complex and uncertain. High-frequency trading, for example, may seem problematic to Mr Lewis, but is vaunted by others as increasing market liquidity and so improving market efficiency and thereby reducing the cost of capital. Similarly, automated credit scoring through profiling, which may threaten some freedoms but also provides access to finance to many millions of small businesses that make up a huge proportion of the demand for workers and so the providers of livelihoods.

Preconceptions, in short, of the merits of digitalisation are in the main misconceived, as its impacts are contingent on how it is used and for what purpose. This highlights the need to shape innovation and practice through collaboration and policy interventions within a clear normative framework for the evolution of digitalisation of finance based on accepted norms, goals such as the SDGs and universal rights.

Sizing the Prize

Digitalisation may change everything, but not at the same time, the same way, or in the same sequencing. Key questions remain as to what the main opportunities are that need to be harnessed and the risks that need to be mitigated, and how much difference and in what ways digitalisation will make to financing the SDGs.

Today, we do not know the scale of opportunities or risks offered by digitalisation of finance, or the critical factors determining whether they would be realised and/or mitigated. It is true that digitalisation has long been on the G20

---

agenda, and is increasingly present as a core pillar across its many work streams and topics. Digital already intersects in the G20 with various aspects of the 2030 Agenda. Most obviously, digital is at the core of its treatment of financial innovation for inclusion. The G20 during Argentina's Presidency in 2018 considered for the first time the cross-cutting relevance of digitalisation in advancing sustainable finance, both through its Sustainable Finance Study Group[47] and through T20's Task Force on the 2030 Agenda.[48] By introducing this topic into the Sustainable Finance Study Group, Argentina took an important step in extending the field of inquiry beyond the important but limited lens of 'financial inclusion'.

We are not yet in a position to even reasonably speculate on the importance of the linkages to, say, climate or gender or anti-poverty goals. As a result, we also do not really know what measures might be taken to avail ourselves of opportunities and mitigate risks.

Conceptually, the findings of the work undertaken by Argentina's knowledge partner, the Sustainable Digital Finance Alliance,[49] a public-private partnership founded by UNEP and Ant Financial Services, was usefully framed as follows:

- *At the bottom of the pyramid*, digital finance's power to make large amounts of data available at high speed and low cost increases opportunities for investments in sustainable assets, notably for institutional investors by improving pricing of environmental risks and opportunities at a lower cost; reducing search costs; and improving, measuring, tracking, and validating the application of sustainability criteria.

- *Moving up the pyramid*, digital finance unlocks greater inclusion and innovation in access to sustainable finance options, including the facilitation of citizens' active involvement in sustainable finance and mobilisation of new sources of finance for sustainable development, at the institutional and retail levels.

- *At the top of the pyramid*, the interaction between innovations in digital finance and innovations in the real economy facilitate new investment configurations and business models, reducing sustainable business model risks, and creating opportunities to scale sustainable investments, particularly by PE/VCs. At the same time, interactions between sustainable development and the efficient use of capital at the top of the pyramid may be more complex and create unintended trade-offs.

47 G20, *Sustainable Finance Synthesis Report,* G20 Sustainable Finance Study Group, 2018, http://unepinquiry.org/wp-content/uploads/2018/11/G20_Sustainable_Finance_Synthesis_Report_2018.pdf.
48 S. Zadek and H. Karas, *Policy Brief on Sustainable Finance: Aligning Financial System Architecture and Innovation with Sustainable Development*, T20 Task Force on Agenda 2030 for Sustainable Development, New York, 2018, https://www.g20-insights.org/policy_briefs/aligning-financial-system-architecture-and-innovation-with-sustainable-development/.
49 https://www.sustainabledigitalfinance.org/.

Table 4.1 Extent to which digital technologies are being used to achieve sustainable outcomes.

	Systems and data	Sustainable choices	New sources of finance	Innovation for the SDGs
Machine learning/ AI	High adoption	Early adoption	Prevalent	Early adoption
Big data	Prevalent	Early adoption	Prevalent	Early adoption
Mobile/financial applications	Prevalent	Prevalent	High adoption	High adoption
Blockchain	Nascent	Nascent	Nascent	Nascent
IoT	Nascent	-	Nascent	Nascent

Source: Based on data from Sustainable Digital Finance Alliance, 2018.

The study undertaken for the G20 by the Sustainable Digital Finance Alliance offered a qualitative view as to the extent to which the digitalisation of finance is being harnessed today in pursuit of the 2030 Agenda, as summarised in Table 4.1. In short, it is early days and there is much to come going forward.

A key step in the right direction has been the decision by the UN Secretary General to champion a Task Force on Digital Financing for the SDGs.[50] This task force comprises about 20 members drawn from the private and public sectors, with a focus on representatives from major financial institutions and policymakers.[51] Led by the United Nations Development Programme (UNDP) with the United Nations Capital Development Fund (UNCDF), it will release an initial report by September 2019 and complete its overall work by mid-2020, focusing on answering three questions:

1) Analysis of the potential of digital financing.
2) Barriers to realising that potential and how best to overcome them.
3) Relevant roles of different actors, including the UN itself.

What Next?

It is early days in our understanding of and practice at the nexus of digital, finance, and sustainable development. This is simultaneously insufficient and

---

50 The Secretary General's Task Force was announced on 25 September 2018 at a high-level finance event at the time of the UN General Assembly, and formally launched on 29 November, https://www.un.org/sg/en/content/sg/personnel-appointments/2018-11-29/task-force-digital-financing-sustainable-development.
51 https://digitalfinancingtaskforce.org/.

an opportunity to shape the evolution of tomorrow's financial system to be better aligned with the financing needs of an inclusive, environmentally sustainable, and prosperous society.

There is much to be done, and many actors that need to be involved, a landscape for action that is being shaped by the UN Secretary General's Task Force on Digital Financing for the SDGs, and worked on downstream by many others. Some of the key elements that could be advanced would include:

- *Purpose, values, and principles:* Although finance is not an end in itself, the purpose of finance needs to shape the evolution of not only guiding policies and regulations but also market innovation itself, including the effects of digitalisation.
- *Standards, instruments, and metrics:* Digitisation will lead to a new generation of metrics, risk, and other instruments and ultimately standards, which need to be shaped by purpose and principles.
- *Innovation:* There is an opportunity to support innovation at the nexus of policy and regulatory development (sandboxes), business innovation (FinTech hubs), and sustainable development, at the local and national levels, connected through knowledge and financing networks.
- *Governance:* The governance of financial and capital markets is evolving in response to digitalisation, which offers a once-in-a-generation opportunity to embed sustainable development at the heart of these developments.
- *Thematic applications:* Exploring the application of digital finance to specific thematic domains and challenges, such as enhancing livelihood opportunities for migrants and refugees and the valorisation of biodiversity conservation, is supported.

Concluding Comments

Financing sustainable development is a keystone of how we invest our accumulated financial wealth in transitioning to an approach to development that matches our aspirations for generations to come. The urgency to act is well-matched by the financial resources that exist, but not by the mechanisms we have evolved to connect the dots.

Much must be done to connect the necessary dots, from carbon markets, to wealth redistribution, to technological progress and deployment, to improved health and education, rights, and governance and accountability. The financial system, as the lifeblood of the global economy, has a unique role to play, and is currently not fit for purpose. Improving the alignment of its current features will help, but only if these improvements are relevant in the future. Such relevance depends on understanding how the financial system will be recast, particularly – although not exclusively – as a result of digitalisation. Prediction, however, is a deeply flawed way of imagining the future, ever more so with the growing complexity of our world. Far better is that we create the future by harnessing such disruptions as digitalisation in ways that align the financial system with sustainable development.

Acknowledgements

This chapter benefits from the author's on-going role in the work of the UN Secretary General's Task Force on Digital Financing of the Sustainable Development Goals. It draws extensively on the work of the UNEP's Inquiry into Design Options for a Sustainable Financial System, and the Sustainable Digital Finance Alliance. It draws from 'La digitalización de las finanzas: oportunidades para los ODS', a lecture prepared by the author for the Inter-American Development Bank.

Acknowledged and appreciated are the comments on drafts of this chapter by a number of people, including Sofie Blakstad, Tillman Bruett, Marianne Haahr, Cornis can der Lugt, and Julia Walker. All errors and omissions remain the responsibility of the author.

Part II

Where Will the Money Come From? Financing the SDGs

5

The New Framework for Financing the 2030 Agenda for Sustainable Development and the SDGs
Alma Pekmezovic

Introduction

Development finance includes a wide range of diverse actors, including multilateral development banks and other international financial institutions, multinational corporations, philanthropic organisations, and sovereign wealth funds, as well as financial intermediaries, such as institutional investors and public and private pension funds. The aim of this chapter is to provide an overview of the key sources of development finance available and capture the dynamics of development finance.

A major focus of the chapter is on private development finance, and on how public and private sources of finance can be mobilised to end extreme poverty and advance the sustainable development agenda 2030. The chapter addresses four key questions: (1) What does the post-2015 financing framework look like? (2) What are the specific roles and challenges of the various types of finance in the development context? (3) Who are the new private players in development finance? and (4) What does it take to mobilise them?

In addressing these questions, the chapter considers the paradigm shift currently taking place in the landscape of finance, namely a shift from an aid-centric approach on development to a more holistic and broader framework of financing for development that links both public and private resources together. To move from the 'billions' in Official Development Assistance (ODA) to the 'trillions' needed for the implementation of the SDGs, the global community and developing countries will need to utilise investments of all kinds – including private, public, national, and global – and take advantage of the specific characteristics and strengths of all sources.[1]

---

1 United Nations Development Programme, 'UNDP Sees Public-Private Partnerships for Investments in Infrastructure as Vital for Achieving Sustainable Development', press release (9 February 2015), http://www.undp.org/content/undp/en/home/presscenter/ articles/2015/02/09/undp-sees-public-private-partnerships-for-investments-in-infrastructure-as-vital-for-achieving-sustainable-development.html.

Sustainable Development Goals: Harnessing Business to Achieve the SDGs through Finance, Technology, and Law Reform, First Edition. Edited by Julia Walker, Alma Pekmezovic, and Gordon Walker.

In this context, it will be necessary to consider the emergence of new financing tools and instruments to support development in developing countries. As we shall see, Multilateral Development Banks (MDBs) have developed new financing tools to spur sustainable economic growth in developing countries. These tools have been developed for different financing purposes ranging, from public-private partnerships (PPPs) to newer forms of finance, including blended finance, as well as new bond instruments such as green bonds (GBs), social impact bonds (SIBs), and development impact bonds (DIBs). These new financial instruments are aimed at increasing the supply of private capital to developing countries and offer significant potential to close the financing gap that currently exists in the developing world. In particular, blended finance is likely to become a key component in development finance and one of the main pillars of the international financing framework developed to support the post-2015 sustainable development agenda.[2] ODA, on the other hand, is likely to remain critical for low-income and fragile countries.

Sources of Development Finance

Domestic Public and Private Sources

Development finance includes a wide range of flows from private and public resources. Private resources – domestic and international – include foreign direct investment (FDI), equity and debt finance, private transfers (remittances), and private philanthropy. A distinction is drawn between private commercial funding – which can encompass finance supplied by sovereign wealth funds as well as public and private pension funds – and non-commercial funding. A key feature of commercial private finance is that it is profit-oriented and seeks a market-rate return, whereas non-commercial funding from governments or private donors is provided below market-rate returns. Hence, a crucial obstacle in the development context is ensuring that private finance achieves both commercial interests and public policy goals. Any public-sector measures must either encourage incentives for private investments or alternatively reduce perceived risks.

Domestic Resource Mobilisation (DRM)

Domestic public resources are the primary source of development finance available in developing countries. Despite international public resources in the form of ODA plying a crucial role, countries have the primary responsibility for

---

2 OECD, *Blended Finance Vol. 1: A Primer for Development Finance and Philanthropic Funders* (September 2015), 5.

advancing and self-financing their own development. Countries must add to the flows of DRM – in the form of taxes, fees, or other available resources – and ensure that domestic policies in place (legal, tax, institutional, economic, regulatory, or otherwise) enhance the effectiveness of DRM, making the best use of this form of funding via national, subnational, and municipal entities. More specifically, it is critical for governments to improve the efficiency of government spending and mobilise their domestic resources.[3] Improving DRM creates fiscal space for additional development funding, while at the same time reducing aid dependency and helping to raise the creditworthiness in many countries.[4]

Nevertheless, DRM in many developing countries (in particular, low-income countries) is problematic. Although DRM in low-income countries has increased significantly in recent years with developing countries growing significantly faster (at a rate of 6.1%) than developed countries (rate of 1.2%) from 2002–2012, and some developing countries graduating from upper-middle income to high-income countries, domestic public resources remain scarce.[5] In 2012, DRM in emerging and developing economies amounted to US$7.7 trillion, $6 trillion more than in 2002.[6] The gap between GDP per capita in Latin America and Sub-Saharan Africa and that of developed countries is greater today than 30 years ago.[7] This is often due to poorly designed spending, high subsidies, poor taxation, poor cash management, inadequate financial reporting, and capital flight. Energy subsidies in developing countries, for example, amounted worldwide to $480 billion in pre-tax and $1.9 trillion in post-tax subsidies.[8] Accordingly, implementing efficient subsidy reform could generate significant cost savings for many countries.

Moreover, many developing countries must do more to collect tax, as they are lagging behind the developed world in their ratio of tax revenues to GDP. For example, developing Asian countries have an 18% tax-to-GDP ratio, compared to 29% worldwide.[9] At the same time, illicit financial outflows are high in developing Asia, with many countries losing an average of 3.8% of their

---

3 Rathin Roy, Antoine Heuty, and Emmanuel Letouzé, 'Fiscal Space for What? Analytical Issues from a Human Development Perspective', UNDP (30 June 2007), 1, http://www.undp.org/content/dam/aplaws/publication/en/publications/poverty-reduction/poverty-website/fiscal-space-for-what/FiscalSpaceforWhat.pdf.

4 For example, well-targeted government spending programmes in Thailand facilitated remarkable fiscal expansion, allowing the country to access an upper middle-income status. See Roy, Heuty, and Letouzé, 'Fiscal Space for What?', 8, http://www.undp.org/content/dam/aplaws/publication/en/publications/poverty-reduction/poverty-website/fiscal-space-for-what/FiscalSpaceforWhat.pdf.

5 Intergovernmental Committee of Experts on Sustainable Development Financing, *Report of the Intergovernmental Committee of Experts on Sustainable Development Financing* (2014), 1.

6 World Bank, *Financing for Development Post-2015* (October 2013), 9.

7 Ibid.

8 Intergovernmental Committee of Experts on Sustainable Development Financing, see note 5, 12.

9 Asian Development Bank, *Making It Happen: Technology, Finance, Statistics for Sustainable Development in Asia and the Pacific. Asia-Pacific Regional MDGs 2014–15 Report* (29 May 2015), viii.

GDP in illicit outflows.[10] The IMF estimates the cost of bribery at roughly 2% of global GDP, and illicit flows from developing countries at over US$1 trillion.[11] Raising more tax and reducing illicit outflows would allow substantial funds to be channelled towards development.[12] An important pillar of the post-2015 development agenda therefore entails enhancing the capacity of developing countries to improve their tax systems, raise domestic revenues from business, and bolster non-tax resources to expand their resource base.[13] ODA plays an important role as well, since developing countries can utilise ODA to improve their fiscal and tax administration capacities, strengthen international tax cooperation, and implement other measures, such as beneficial ownership registration and adopting the Financial Action Task Force Standards (FATFS) or standards such as those in the Extractive Industries Transparency Initiative (EITI), aimed at improving transparency and reducing illicit flows.

In addition, there is significant scope in many countries to improve the efficiency of state-owned enterprises (SOEs) and public administration. Similarly, domestic private finance in developing countries is subject to various constraints. Many developing countries primarily rely on the banking sector as a supplier of finance – domestic corporate bond markets and equity capital markets tend to be small and underdeveloped.[14] Alternative vehicles for financing micro, small, and medium-sized Enterprises (MSMEs) and start-ups such as venture capital funds and angel investors are thus largely absent from developing countries.[15]

At the same time, debt finance supplied via the banking sector is primarily short term rather than long term.[16] In Africa, for instance, short-term credit accounts for up to 90% of bank financing.[17] The absence of long-term financing severely constrains the ability of some countries to support long-term investments in sustainable development and has led many countries to establish national development banks and other public institutions to support long-term

---

10 Ibid.

11 International Monetary Fund (IMF), *Corruption: Costs and Mitigating Strategies. IMF Staff Discussion Note* (11 May 2016), 5.

12 Ibid, 12.

13 A goal is to create a 'virtuous circle' whereby good governance, including reducing illicit outflows and corruption, promotes further development. See Irène Hors, 'Fighting Corruption in the Developing Countries', *OECD Observer* (2000), http://oecdobserver.org/news/archivestory.php/aid/291/Fighting_corruption_in_the_developing_countries.html.

14 For example, multiple countries in Africa have either an inactive or no stock exchange at all, and only one country on that continent has a stock exchange valued at over $100 billion. PWC, *2016 Africa Capital Markets Watch*, (2017), 2, https://www.pwc.co.za/en/assets/pdf/africa-capital-markets-watch-2016.pdf.

15 Ibid., 26.

16 Ibid.

17 Ibid, 13.

investment. The latter can play a significant role in strengthening capital mar-kets, financing MSMEs and leveraging investments in infrastructure and other sustainable projects (e.g. by issuing green bonds).[18] In 2010, the combined assets of the International Development Finance Club – a group of 20 national, bilateral, and regional development banks – amounted to over $2.1 trillion.[19]

International Public and Private Finance

The mix of resources flowing to many developing countries has changed dra-matically over the past decade, and varies substantially between LICs, middle-income countries, and SIDs.[20] The latter, such as the South Pacific Island nations, for example, are subject to unique development constraints due to their special geography, size, and climate change–related pressures.

Overall international resource flows to developing countries have grown from around US$1 trillion in 1990 to US$2.1 trillion in 2011.[21] This is largely due to an increase in: (i) international private finance, in the form of FDI, bonds, and syndicated bank-lending; (ii) migrant remittances; (iii) private phi-lanthropy from foundations and corporations; and (iv) new forms of official financing, such as financing from the BRIC countries (Brazil, Russia, India, China, and South Africa).[22] ODA, which was once the largest resource flow to almost 100 developing countries in the 1990s, has become the largest resource for only 43 developing countries in 2011 due to an expansion in FDI, lending, and increased remittance flows into the countries.[23]

Lending is an important source of finance for developing countries, which received net loan disbursements totalling US$340 billion in 2011.[24] More eco-nomically advanced countries such as Brazil and Mexico, for example, received the largest disbursements of long-term loans. China, on the other hand, accounted for 72% of net-short term loans disbursed to developing countries in 2011.[25]

---

18 Ibid, 23. Anthony Williams, *EBRD Approves Participation of Up to US$100 Million to Support Development of Green Bond Markets*, European Bank for Reconstruction and Development (12 December 2017), http://www.ebrd.com/news/2017/ebrd-approves-participation-of-up-to-us-100-million-to-support-development-of-green-bond-markets.html.
19 Ibid.
20 Case studies show countries have more funding options, policy space, and increasing options for development finance from an ever-larger pool of players with more instruments at work. OECD, *The New Development Finance Landscape: Developing Countries' Perspective* (25 June 2014), 45.
21 European Parliament Directorate-General for External Policies, *Financing for Development Post 2015: Improving the Contribution of Private Finance* (2014), 12.
22 World Bank, see note 6, 5.
23 Ibid. Remittances tend to be used for consumption rather than investment and are not discussed in this chapter.
24 Ibid., 13.
25 Ibid.

Most loan disbursements (three-quarters) were channelled towards the private sector in developing countries. Public sector institutions received or guaranteed a total of US$113.4 billion (roughly 22%).[26]

Lastly, remittances provide another significant source of finance. They are, however, mainly short-term oriented, restricted to private-to-private transfers, and generally not used to support government policies or development goals. Remittances are largely inappropriate to support long-term investments in sustainable development.

The Role of International Official Development Assistance (ODA)

ODA remains an important financing source and, in fact, the largest resource flow for countries with the highest levels of poverty (the least developed countries), and countries with the lowest levels of domestic resources such as fragile states. It is estimated that about 40% of ODA benefits the least developed countries.[27] In 2011, ODA made up 9.1% of the gross national income (GNI) of low-income countries (LICs).[28] These countries use ODA to support the delivery of essential services, such as health and education.[29] For example, Mozambique and Uganda rely heavily on aid funds to finance over 40% of their health budget.[30] Some lower-middle income countries (LMICs) also rely on donor funds to support government spending. Aid makes up 47.5% of government spending in Nicaragua, 42.5% in Laos, 21.5% in Ghana, and 16.8% in Georgia.[31] In 2010, Asian middle-income countries where nearly 63% of people live on less than $2 per day, received 19.3% of total net traditional ODA.[32] Africa, on the other hand, received 38.7% in 2012.[33]

The advantage of ODA funds generally is that they are less volatile than external private funds.[34] Moreover, ODA can be used to promote sustainability, human rights, and gender equality.[35] It is a critical source of finance for

---

26 Ibid.

27 *Report of the Intergovernmental Committee of Experts on Sustainable Development Financing,* see note 5, 14.

28 Ibid., 18.

29 Ibid.

30 Ibid.

31 Ibid.

32 Asian Development Bank, *Making Money Work: Financing Sustainable Future in Asia and the Pacific* (2015), 23, https://www.adb.org/sites/default/files/publication/158432/making-money-work-main-report.pdf.

33 Ibid.

34 Ibid.

35 Clair Apodaca, *Foreign Aid as Foreign Policy Tool,* Oxford Research Encyclopedia of Politics (April 2017), http://politics.oxfordre.com/view/10.1093/acrefore/9780190228637.001.0001/acrefore-9780190228637-e-332?print=pdf.

funding infrastructure gaps and building capacities, especially in LDCs and fragile states.[36] As the Monterrey Declaration points out:

> ODA plays an essential role as a complement to other sources of financing for development, especially in those countries with the least capacity to attract private direct investment . . . For many countries in Africa, least developed countries, small island developing states and landlocked developing countries, ODA is still the largest source of external financing and is critical to the achievement of the development goals and targets of the Millennium Declaration and other internationally agreed development targets.[37]

Nevertheless, ODA funds are small in comparison to funds held in private hands. In Asia and the Pacific, total ODA amounted to $26 billion[38] and government revenues at $3 trillion a year, compared to $205 billion in remittances, $568 billion in foreign direct investment flows, $6 trillion in private savings, and $3.5 trillion in assets held in pension and sovereign wealth funds.[39] The key challenge in the Asia-Pacific region is to mobilise these available resources for development purposes.

Historically, ODA has never reached the internationally agreed target by donors of 0.7% of gross national income.[40] Although ODA levels reached $135 billion in 2013, ODA has been continually on the decline. Furthermore, funding via OECD-DAC donors has become a less important source of development finance at the global level. ODA in future therefore is likely to be used to crowd-in other funding sources, primarily for LICs. Consequently, it is crucial for countries to look beyond ODA as a financing source and expand other funding channels including DRM, foreign private, and public finance.

Private Philanthropy

Private philanthropy is another source of vital importance in development finance.[41] Foundations such as the Gates Foundation, for example, which has

---

36 OECD, Development Aid Rises Again in 2016 but Flows to Poorest Countries Dip (4 November 2017), http://www.oecd.org/newsroom/development-aid-rises-again-in-2016-but-flows-to-poorest-countries-dip.htm.

37 Monterrey Consensus on Financing for Development, *Monterrey Consensus of the International Conference on Financing for Development* (2002), 14.

38 Remittances to Mexico from the US in 2016 alone approximated this regional value of ODA. See Anthony Harrup, 'Remittances to Mexico Hit Record $27 Billion in 2016,' *The Wall Street Journal* (1 February 2017).

39 Asian Development Bank, *Making Money Work*, xiii.

40 Asian Development Bank, *Asia-Pacific Regional MDGs 2014–15 Report*, viii.

41 Private foundations also bring valuable expertise; they play a critical part in pursuing goals towards combating poverty. The World Bank, 'Foundations Bring Philanthropy, Know-How, Vision' (May 28, 2013), http://www.worldbank.org/en/news/feature/2013/05/28/foundations-bring-philanthropy-know-how-vision.

made major contributions to health and agriculture in developing countries, have emerged as increasingly important players in the development arena.[42] Private philanthropy has therefore the potential to significantly fast-track development, as North-South contributions from foundations based in OECD countries have grown over a decade from US$3 billion in 2003 to US$29.7 billion in 2013.[43]

The OECD has launched a Global Network of Foundations Working for Development to facilitate knowledge sharing and global policy dialogue between foundations, with the aim of creating greater synergies between foundations. The network focuses on key development challenges such as inclusive growth, basic service delivery, and governance and institutions. Members include foundations from OECD and non-OECD countries.[44]

Sovereign Wealth Funds, Pension Funds, Insurance Companies, and Investment Funds

A survey by Thomson Reuters shows that the world's top 38 sovereign wealth funds globally invest nearly $900 billion in listed public equities and allocate more than a third of the total to emerging markets at $383 billion.[45] Impact-investing funds – a special subcategory of investment funds – have amassed more than $77 billion in assets under management.

Thus, there are significant resources available from institutional investors.[46] A lack of financial resources, in fact, is not an impediment for institutional investment. Nevertheless, institutional investors' resources are not directed towards development projects or infrastructure. Investment by institutional investors often remains limited in both the developed and developing world.[47] Furthermore, although national and domestic private funds are growing in developing countries, banking finance continues to dominate the markets.

---

42 Cécile Sangaré and Tomáš Hos, *Global Private Philanthropy for Development Preliminary Results of the OECD Data Survey*, *OECD*, OECD, https://www.oecd.org/dac/financing-sustainable-development/development-finance-data/Preliminary-results-philanthropy-survey.pdf.

43 OECD, Private Philanthropy for Development (May 2018), https://oecd-development-matters.org/2018/05/09/the-new-world-of-development-foundations/.

44 Examples of philanthropic foundations include the Emirates Foundation for Youth Development (Abu Dhabi, UAE), Fundación Empresarial EuroChile (Santiago, Chile), Instituto Ayrton Senna (São Paulo, Brazil), Mo Ibrahim Foundation (London, UK), Novartis Foundation for Sustainable Development (Basel, Switzerland), Robert Bosch Foundation (Stuttgart, Germany), Rockefeller Foundation (NYC, USA), Shell Foundation (London, UK), The Alexandria Trust (London, UK), The African Capacity Building Foundation (Harare, Zimbabwe).

45 Natsuko Waki, 'Analysis: Sovereign Funds' Fortunes Turn as Emerging Assets Sour', Reuters (21 August 2013).

46 Institutional investors hold an estimated $75 to $85 trillion in assets. UNTT Working Group on Sustainable Development Financing, *UN System Task Team on the Post–2015 UN Development Agenda Working Group on 'Financing for Sustainable Development'* (2013), 5.

47 Ibid.

When investing in developing countries, international institutional investors are generally looking for high returns, and diversification. Similarly, sovereign-wealth funds, pursue risk-reward objectives, although they typically have longer investment time horizons and are more flexible than other types of investors. Some SWFs have entered innovative coalitions with other SWFs, multinational corporations, and governments, and, in addition, to financial dividends, are motivated by political-security and industrial-policy considerations for their home countries.

Barriers to Greater Private Investment

Despite significant increases in private flows of capital to developing countries over the past decade, only a small percentage of these flows are used to finance sustainable development. There are several reasons for this.[48] First, there is a high degree of competition for capital in the global markets, with funds primarily directed to more developed countries.[49] Private sector investors often lack the necessary knowledge and understanding to identify investment opportunities in foreign countries.[50] Second – and this is widely considered to be the main obstacle for greater private investment – private investors may perceive the potential returns associated with certain development projects as too low relative to risks.[51] Many sustainable development projects are therefore often regarded as insufficiently profitable to attract private funding.[52]

Private investors, however, often have short-term investment horizons, but may wish to align their investment practices with sustainable and more inclusive development objectives. The World Economic Forum (WEF) is promoting a systematic transition from a short-term investment outlook to one based on long-term considerations with considerable social and environmental impact.[53] The main aim of the WEF initiative is to increase the flow of private investments into impact investing. SDG target 12.6 also encourages UN Member States to 'encourage companies, especially large and transnational companies, to adopt sustainable practices and to integrate sustainability information into their reporting cycle.'[54] Under the Addis Ababa agreement on financing for sustainable development, Member States also agreed to pursue policies and

---

48 Ibid.
49 OECD, *Development Aid Rises Again in 2016 but Flows to Poorest Countries Dip* (4 November 2017), http://www.oecd.org/newsroom/development-aid-rises-again-in-2016-but-flows-to-poorest-countries-dip.htm.
50 Ibid., 10. Owing to limited market data (such as historical financial returns in certain industries), investors may find it difficult to assess risk and make informed investment decisions.
51 Ibid.
52 Asian Development Bank, *Making Money Work*, xviii.
53 The WEF, *Shaping the Future of Impact Investing*, a https://www.weforum.org/projects/mainstreaming-sustainable-and-impact-investing.
54 SDG Target 12.6.

'regulations that promote incentives along the investment chain that are aligned with long-term performance and sustainability indicators, and that reduce excess volatility.'[55]

Third, foreign private investors face substantial transaction costs to familiarise themselves with new markets, and country-specific constraints. The transaction costs associated with capital intensive and risky projects may be especially high, because of lengthy transactions times, corporate governance risks, and funding shortfalls.

Fourth, private investors often face various other disincentives due to ineffective or unfavourable institutional and governance frameworks in place to facilitate investment.[56] In the absence of adequate legal and regulatory protections, private investors are unlikely to assume the risks associated with investing in many low-income or middle-income countries. For example, they may be reluctant to enter contracts that cannot be enforced and lack transparency. Political and economic instability also play a role in this context.

Another key constraining factor is illiquid local capital markets. Capital markets in emerging economies are often insufficiently developed, lacking the requisite infrastructure, expertise, and pools of capital to seamlessly connect supply to demand. This, in turn, results in greater liquidity risk for investors unable to refinance or exit investments. Owing to under-developed and illiquid equity and bond markets in emerging economies combined with a lack of strong, and transparent institutional frameworks, investors may opt to channel funds to less challenging environments. Accordingly, there is a real need to help investors overcome a wide range of barriers to private sector investment in developing countries.

The Role of Private and Blended Finance in Development

Blended finance – though not new in bilateral and multilateral development finance – is gaining increased prominence in this field and has come to be regarded as a key solution to the SDG financing gap. According to a survey of 74 blended-finance vehicles, blended finance is an effective tool for expanding the pool of capital that is available for development finance – every dollar of public money invested typically attracts a further $1–20 in private investment.[57] The purpose of this section is to explain the concept of blended

---

55 UN Addis Ababa Action Agreement (2015) at para. [38].
56 UNTT Working Group on Sustainable Development Financing, see note 46, 28.
57 *The Economist*, 'Trending: Blending' (23 April 2016), http://www.economist.com/news/finance-and-economics/21697263-fad-mixing-public-charitable-and-private-money-trending-blending.

finance, and shed light on the role that blended finance plays in promoting sustainable development.

The World Economic Forum and OECD define blended finance as 'the strategic use of development finance and philanthropic funds to mobilize private capital flows to emerging and frontier markets.'[58]

A key advantage of using blended finance in international development efforts is that blended finance enables a range of different stakeholders including public, philanthropic, and private actors to work together toward set development goals. Private investors can identify investment opportunities in the developing world and thus enhance their portfolio diversification, whereas 'development funders' can mobilise additional sources of finance stemming from the private sector.[59] In this way, blended finance helps to overcome the barriers that private investors face in developing countries (especially by improving the risk-return potential of development projects for private investors), while at the same time allowing development funders – i.e. philanthropic donors, development finance institutions and foundations – to enhance the impact of their investment and accelerate progress towards the achievement of the SDG.[60] The main objective of blended finance, therefore, is to generate additional funds and finance by crowding in commercial finance, that would be otherwise unavailable for SDG-related investments (so-called 'nondevelopment finance'). The public resources function as an enabler of private resources.

Blended finance is, therefore, best understood as an ecosystem of finance, that increases the overall availability of financing available for development purposes.[61] There are several key features worth pointing out about blended finance. First, in the blended finance model, private capital is not used as a substitute for public capital but rather in a strategically complementary manner. Second, blended finance is not intended to replace ODA. Third, the concept can be used across a range of different sectors (most frequently, climate resilience and clean energy, financial services, food and agriculture, health care, and infrastructure), and can be combined into a range of different

---

58 OECD, see note 2, 4.

59 Blended finance helps mitigate barriers that otherwise would prevent commercial investors from entering a region towards promotion of SDGs. Paul Horrocks, Wiebke Bartz-Zuccala, and Irene Basile, *Blended Finance – Mobilizing Resources for Sustainable Development and Climate Action in Developing Countries*, OECD (October 2017), 6, http://www.oecd.org/cgfi/forum/Blended-finance-Policy-Perspectives.pdf.

60 Paul Horrocks, *Blended Finance Bridging the Sustainable Development Finance Gap*, OECD, 1, https://www.oecd.org/dac/financing-sustainable-development/development-finance-topics/Blended-Finance-Bridging-SDG-Gap.pdf.

61 Blended finance could have strong impact if applied to ODA. Chris Clubb, *Blended Finance: Critical Steps to Ensure Success of the Sustainable Development Goals*, OECD (20 December 2016), https://oecd-development-matters.org/2016/12/20/blended-finance-critical-steps-to-ensure-success-of-the-sustainable-development-goals/.

instruments. Basic financial instruments can include debt, equity, grants (financial award with no expected repayment or compensation over a fixed period) and guarantees. Fourth, a blended financial transaction is still intended to generate a financial return, while contributing toward meeting the SDGs in an emerging or frontier market. Fifth, the incentives of investors in such a transaction will not necessarily be aligned, with some investors being attracted by diversification, returns, or strategic opportunities in a market. In this context, it is also important to point out that the concept of blended finance should not be conflated with 'public-private partnerships' (PPPs). PPPs constitute a subset of blended finance and are generally used to contract out responsibilities carried out by public sector bodies to the private sector.

The Development Impact and Risks of Blended Finance

Given the relative novelty of blended finance, it is difficult to predict the impact that blended finance will have in the long term. Though blended finance will undoubtedly play a significant role in diversifying the development finance landscape and mobilising new capital sources to achieve the SDGs, it is uncertain whether blended finance will help developing countries meet the SDGs by 2030.[62]

There are various risks associated with blended structures.[63] For example, poorly designed PPPs may result in misallocation of risks between public and private partners, with public partners carrying a disproportionate burden of the risks, and the private partners retaining all profits. It is thus important to ensure that blended finance is an attractive and financially viable proposition for both the public and private partners. Furthermore, careful consideration needs to be given to the transparency of blended finance transactions. Private partners in blended transactions should be selected as part of a fair and open process.

Moreover, private capital mobilised through blending is most likely to be channelled toward infrastructure and the productive sectors. As a corollary,

---

62 While more blended finance flows to lower middle-income countries than foreign direct investment, that amount is still significantly less than ODA. Harpinder Collacott, *What Does the Evidence on Blended Finance Tell Us about Its Potential to Fill the SDG Funding Gap?* OECD (24 November 2016), https://oecd-development-matters.org/2016/11/24/what-does-the-evidence-on-blended-finance-tell-us-about-its-potential-to-fill-the-sdg-funding-gap/.
63 The European Network on Debt and Development, *Private-Finance Blending for Development, Risks and Opportunities*, Oxfam (February 2017), https://www.oxfam.org/sites/www.oxfam.org/files/bp-private-finance-blending-for-development-130217-en.pdf.

traditional ODA will continue to be needed in countries and sectors that do not benefit from extensive blended finance inflows.

Currently, it is estimated that private capital mobilised via blending is likely to reach US$42 billion by 2020, and US$252 billion by 2030.[64] DAC Members have launched 140 blended finance funds and facilities from 2000 to 2014, with total assets under management of these facilities estimated to be approximately US$30 billion.[65] All funds and facilities in place utilised concessional support from DAC Members as well as philanthropic organisations.[66] Two thirds of the total assets were directed toward the infrastructure and the financial sector.[67] Two global platforms were recently launched to match investors with projects.

One example of such a fund is the EU-Africa Infrastructure Trust Fund that was created in 2007 and combines grants from some EU Member States (including Austria, Germany, the Netherlands, and the UK) and the European Commission with long-term loan finance from select public and private finance providers. The main objective of the Fund is to promote investment in regional infrastructure in Sub-Saharan Africa, including access to transport and communications services, water, and energy. The fund committed US$113 million for 17 projects in the energy and transport sectors in 2012.[68]

There is a need to apply blended finance in low-income countries and key development sectors such as education, health, and agriculture, as well as water and sanitation (SDG 6). At present, private investments mobilised through blended finance are generally higher in middle-income countries than developing countries.

An Overview of Blended Finance Mechanisms

There are various forms of blended finance. In this section, some common forms of blended finance are discussed. For example, blended finance may take the form of an ODA loan alongside an institutional investor loan, allowing the use of concessional public funds to attract nonconcessional private capital. Alternatively, blended finance may entail the use of 'public sector partial guarantees'. The latter are provided to investors to leverage public funds. There has

---

64 OECD, 'What Does the Evidence on Blended Finance Tell Us about Its Potential to Fill the SDG Funding Gap?' (24 November 2016), http://www.oecd.org/officialdocuments/publicdisplayd ocumentpdf/?cote=DCD/DAC(2017)9&docLanguage=En.

65 Ibid.

66 Ibid.

67 Ibid.

68 European Investment Bank, EU-Africa Infrastructure Trust Fund, http://www.eu-africa-infrastructure-tf.net/.

been an increase in the amounts mobilised from the private sector because of the use of such guarantees. From 2009 to 2014, the total volume of bilateral guarantees rose from 25% to 40%.[69] In the past decade, the World Bank has approved 28 guarantees worth a total of $1.4 billion.[70] The guarantees, in turn, have stimulated more than five dollars of private capital for every dollar spent by the World Bank.

A third form of blending occurs when concessional private funds – for example, grants from private foundations – are used together with grants from nonconcessional financing from private investors. Fourth, blended finance may also involve the blending of nonconcessional public funds with nonconcessional private capital as a part of one transaction.

Two examples of blended finance discussed below are: social impact bonds (SIBs) and development impact bonds (DIBs).[71] In a nutshell, DIBs allow private investors to provide upfront finance for development programmes, with international development banks or country governments making repayments if the evidence shows that the development programmes achieve pre-agreed societal outcomes.

Innovative Financing Tools: Social Impact Bonds (SIBs) and Development Impact Bonds (DIBs)

SIBs and DIBs involve the use of a series of interrelated contracts to secure funding in an innovative manner. Both are bond-driven funding mechanisms that can be used, for example, to secure funding for an education project. SIB and DIB investors are thus often referred to as 'social impact investors' who consider not only economic returns, but are also interested in supporting social causes and benefits. These investors may range from individual philanthropists, philanthropic organisations, pension funds, mutual funds, insurance companies, financial institutions to high-net worth individuals. The other key stakeholders in a SIB or DIB funding transaction include intermediaries, governments, assessors and evaluators, constituents, a local community or society at large, advisors, and various service providers.

Initially, the social impact investors will fund the SIB or DIB up-front, and the government is responsible for repaying the principal and the interest to the

---

69 Chris Clubb, *Blended Finance: Critical Steps to Ensure Success of the Sustainable Development Goals*, OECD (20 December 2016), https://oecd-development-matters.org/2016/12/20/blended-finance-critical-steps-to-ensure-success-of-the-sustainable-development-goals/.

70 World Bank, *Innovative Finance for Development Solutions*, 7, https://www.worldbank.org/en/about/annual-report/innovative-finance.

71 UNDP, Social and Development Impact Bonds, http://www.undp.org/content/sdfinance/en/home/solutions/social-development-impact-bonds.html.

social impact investors, if the project funded via the SIB or DIB is deemed successful. In this type of transaction, an intermediary – often a special-purpose type entity established either by the public or private sector – will typically connect the government with the social impact investors, as well as other relevant stakeholders, such as the service providers who are responsible for carrying out the project. For example, the service provider may provide the relevant education facility or programme. In a SIB/DIB finance structure, the parties will set performance criteria, so-called success metrics, which can be qualitative and quantitative in nature, to determine if the project being funded has been successful.

The task of an external, independent evaluator then is to determine if the stated objectives of the SIB/DIB have been met, while the key target group for which the financing is being sought via the SIBs/DIBs are often referred to as the constituents. The constituents are a subset of the local community, and the primary beneficiaries of the project being financed.[72] Finally, advisors play a key role in this type of capital structure, since they are responsible for providing guidance and advice on how to set up and implement the SIB/DIB structure and what kind of performance criteria to include.

Funding with SIBs/DIBs is associated with notable risks, and a minimum funding threshold amount should generally be reached, before the SIB/DIB structure can be considered a viable alternative for the stakeholders involved. Another prerequisite for success is that the parties involved are familiar with structured bond issues that are involved in a typical SIB/DIB, and that they fully understand the benefits and risks with a SIB/DIB structure. One of the main risks for the private sector SIB/DIB investors is that they initially provide the entire funding for the project. This funding will be repaid later (together with interest) only if the project is successful. Payment, in other words, is contingent on the quantitative and qualitative success metrics being achieved. Hence, the economic benefit of a return on the investor is not guaranteed. Second, a SIB/DIB transaction gives rise to significant set-up and administrative costs for the services of the intermediaries, advisors, and other parties.[73] Third, there are transactional risks involved, making it difficult to assess the likelihood of success of a funding project, as few SIB/DIB transactions have been completed to date.

The legal agreements used to support a SIB/DIB structure include: an outcomes contract which specifies the success metric (a key contractual concern for the parties) and outlines the relationship between the funders (both public

---

72 UNDP, 'Social and Development Impact Bonds', http://www.undp.org/content/sdfinance/en/home/solutions/social-development-impact-bonds.html.
73 Emily Gustafsson-Wright, Sophie Gardiner, and Vidya Putcha, *The Potential and Limitations of Impact Bonds: Lessons from the First Five Years of Experience Worldwide*, Brookings (July 2015), 35, https://www.brookings.edu/wp-content/uploads/2016/07/Impact-Bondsweb.pdf.

and private) and the intermediaries; an investment agreement concluded between the intermediary and the investors which specifies the terms and conditions under which investors are paid; a memorandum of understanding (MOU) which sets out the aspirations of the parties and may not necessarily be legally binding; an advisory agreement between the advisor, intermediary, and related parties that details the advisory services to be supplied; a service provider agreement that specifies the obligations of the service providers; and lastly, a measurement agreement between the investors and the external evaluation who is contracted to determine if the performance criteria have been achieved. The legal agreements may cross-reference terms and conditions.

In addition, the parties may enter a swap agreement, including a credit default swap (CDS) arrangement between each other. As part of such an agreement, the parties may set out 'trigger events' that will initiate a swap. Using a CDS, an SIB/DIB issuer (an intermediary) can transfer its credit risk (i.e. failure to pay owed obligations) to a CDS provider (which can be either a public or private entity). This is for the benefit of the SIB/DIB issuer as well as the investors who provide funds for the SIB/DIB structures. The CDS provider would assume the credit risk in exchange for a CDS premium, generally paid periodically (either quarterly, half-yearly, or yearly). In the result, the CDS contract can be compared to an insurance policy, and CDS premiums are comparable to insurance premiums. The principal benefit of using a CDS is that it lowers credit risk, and hence increases the incentives for enhanced private-public sector co-investment.

Although swap agreements are currently used in SIB/DIB structures, there is potential for greater use. Moreover, it has been argued that credit ratings should be used in connection with SIB/DIBs. Thus, one way of improving the transparency and risks associated with future SIB/DIB issuances is by allocating credit ratings. The credit rating would be based on the certainty of future promised cash flows from the SIB/DIB issuer to the investors of SIB/DIBs and could be provided by a broad array of potential credit rating agencies.

Another question worth exploring in this context is whether it is misleading for SIB/DIBs to be called 'bonds' as SIB/DIBs do not have the same features as a traditional bond. Unlike a 'bond', they are not a fixed-income product, entailing principal protection and specified returns. SIBs provide variable returns, and do not offer principal protection. SIBs are not securities and are structured as multiparty contracts. Moreover, because SIB/DIBs rely on privately negotiated, and customised contractual arrangements, it is difficult to make comparisons across SIB/DIBs. Stephen Foley, writing on the topic in the *Financial Times*, has thus noted that 'if the nascent investment vehicle is to become a big asset class, it needs a new name among other things.'[74]

---

74 https://www.ft.com/content/5eee5f46-293e-11e5-8613-e7aedbb7bdb7.

Finally, a regulatory constraint that is severely hampering the impact potential of SIB/DIBs is that SIB/DIBs are offered only as private placements limited to accredited and institutional investors. This is because they are considered 'restricted securities' and thus cannot be easily transferred between investors.

Best Practices for Engaging the Private Sector

One of the risks of blended finance is that it may be used to unduly subsidise the private sector. Accordingly, it is important to develop proper transparency and risk frameworks to address the risks associated with this form of finance. The provision of blended finance should not be used to distort competition in markets and provide unjustifiable subsidies to the private sector. Hence, one of the recommendations that has been made in connection with blended finance is that subsidies to the private sector should be made only in situations where the social returns on an investment exceed private returns, and where financial returns are insufficient to attract private investment. Further, private participation ought to enhance a project.

Moreover, it is important to understand the circumstances in which it is most appropriate to resort to blending concessional public with private finance. The use of blended finance should ideally be assessed on a case-by-case basis and occur at the country level rather than donor level, as countries need to prioritise how and where to allocate scarce public financial resources.

A key issue concerns the monitoring and transparency of blended finance instruments. It is important to not only identify the amount of public and private finance leveraged, but also the contribution made to sustainable development. Accordingly, blended finance must be guided by overarching principles of transparency and accountability, which apply to all actors in blended finance, and avoid undue risk to the public sector (in the form of contingent liabilities, for example).

Conclusions

In the post-2015 world, it is necessary for the developed and developing countries, MDBs, IFIs, the private sector, enterprises, and markets to work in a complementary way to achieve the SDGs and reorient available finance channels towards development. Developing countries will need to increase funding from various sources including DRM, FDI, bond issuances, and institutional investors. This will require improving national policy frameworks to create appropriate incentives for private sector investment. The private sector will play a pivotal role in financing the implementation of the SDGs and substituting for scarce public resources, as well as declining ODA.

6

The Contribution of the International Private Sector to a More Sustainable Future[1]

Martin Blessing and Tom Naratil

Sustainability is a simple idea. It aims to maximise shared prosperity today, without compromising the prosperity of future generations. Building a more sustainable future requires resolving the world's most pressing social and environmental problems.

The private sector's contribution to sustainable development is arguably not a 'nice to have' but rather a 'must have'. Limited resources demand that public and private sectors specialise to build a better world.

Private investors have long engaged in funding a more sustainable future. Previously their efforts to solve major societal problems through philanthropy satisfied their societal goals. But they did not try to satisfy their investment portfolio goals at the same time.

Charitable giving will remain an important tool for businesses and individuals in their efforts to support certain causes, especially those whose solution lies outside of financial-market mechanisms. But we argue that today this segregation between giving and investing for good need not continue.

The private sector can find sustainable investments that generate benefits for people and planet both, as well as competitive financial returns. Private investors are far from reaching their full potential to fund sustainability. Doing so will require time and talent that propel sustainable investments from the margin to the mainstream.

---

1 The views and opinions expressed in this chapter include those from external, non-UBS sources. Hence such views and opinions do not necessarily reflect those of UBS or any of its affiliates or agents, nor does UBS necessarily endorse the products and/or services mentioned or offered by any non-UBS entities. UBS AG and its affiliates accept no liability whatsoever for any statements or opinions contained in this chapter, or for the consequences which may result from any person relying on any such opinions or statements.

Sustainable Development Goals: Harnessing Business to Achieve the SDGs through Finance, Technology, and Law Reform, First Edition. Edited by Julia Walker, Alma Pekmezovic, and Gordon Walker.
© 2019 John Wiley & Sons Ltd. Published 2019 by John Wiley & Sons Ltd.

Ready and Able to Invest

UBS has observed that private investors increasingly appreciate the power of sustainable investment to satisfy their financial and societal goals simultaneously.

We believe there are two main drivers of this trend. First, private investors are increasingly aware that doing good for society can deliver superior risk-adjusted financial returns, compared to strategies that don't account for environmental and social factors.

A substantial body of scientific study supports this relationship. One paper reviewed more than 2,000 academic studies from the last 40 years that examine factors related to sustainable investing.[2] It concludes that integrating sustainability factors either improves financial performance or has no negative impact upon it. This finding holds true across all asset classes.

Corporations are also embedding social and environmental impact into their operations. Supporting sustainable development enables firms not only to manage social and environmental risks to their profitability, but also to boost profits by unlocking new commercial opportunities in underserved parts of the world or helping firms to manage costs more effectively.

UBS has explored this topic in a recent white paper.[3] We found that day-to-day consideration of sustainability can boost shareholder returns, better align business activities with investor demands, and help firms meet society's expectations that industry contribute to a more sustainable world.

Driving and Protecting Value through Sustainability

Ken Mehlman and General (Retd.) David H. Petraeus Members, KKR

The private sector has an indisputable role to play in building a more sustainable future for all. At KKR, we not only believe in doing well (financially) *while* doing good, but maintain that we can do good *and* still do well – by investing in companies whose core commercial offering addresses a global societal challenge. Since 2008, when we began integrating the management of environmental, social, and governance ('ESG') issues into our investment processes for our private markets business, we have seen a significant increase in global challenges facing our companies and the communities in which they operate.

(Continued)

---

2 G. Friede, T. Busch, and Alexander Bassen, 'ESG and Financial Performance: Aggregated Evidence from More Than 2000 Empirical Studies', *Journal of Sustainable Finance & Investment* 5, no. 4, (2015): 210–233, https://doi.org/10.1080/20430795.2015.1118917.
3 UBS Chief Investment Office Wealth Management, 'Business with Impact', UBS White Paper (September 2017), https://www.ubs.com/global/en/wealth-management/chief-investment-office/key-topics/2017/business-with-impact.html.

Increasingly, we have found ourselves investing in businesses that are working to address pressing societal issues as part of their core business model. We have invested more than US$4.6 billion behind sustainable solutions-oriented themes since 2008. These specific areas include industrial and infrastructure solutions, environmental management, next-generation energy, responsible production and consumption, and innovative learning resources and workforce development. Each of these areas represents opportunities to address evolving societal needs and support the advancement of the United Nations' Sustainable Development Goals.

A good example of one such investment is our acquisition of Resource Environmental Solutions (RES), one of the largest providers of ecological restoration and water resource solutions in the United States. As infrastructure and economic development intensifies, arable land and biodiversity are being lost. There is an increased role for business to play in protecting, improving, and restoring the environment. Innovative in their approach, RES provides cost-effective sustainability strategies that improve environmental outcomes, facilitate economic development, and mitigate regulatory risks. Since 2007, RES has restored, enhanced, rehabilitated, preserved, and conserved more than 290 miles of streams and more than 58,000 acres of wetlands in environmentally sensitive habitats.

Since our 2016 investment in RES, we have partnered with the company's leadership team to improve stakeholder engagement strategies, enhance branding, and educate key regulators on the importance of ecosystem restoration to both the environment and businesses.

RES is just one of many examples where we are helping our companies grow their business, manage their risks, and create value for their shareholders and stakeholders. Over the past decade, KKR has been a leader in driving and protecting value throughout our private markets portfolio through thoughtful ESG management, as well as extensive measuring and reporting of ESG performance and metrics for our investors. This experience of responsible investment combined with a changing landscape of global challenges has led to our decision to create a dedicated Global Impact investment vehicle. Our impact strategy will focus on identifying and investing behind global opportunities with positive social or environmental impacts, thus continuing to prove that investors today can be part of the solution to the shared challenges we face.

Commercial and Investment Benefits

Anecdotally, many of the client entrepreneurs with whom UBS speaks see the commercial benefits of operating sustainably. Aligning their business management strategy with their personal wealth strategy, this group is also committing more money to sustainable and impact investments.

A second reason for rising interest in sustainable investment is that the private sector is increasingly well placed to seize investment opportunities that other institutional or governmental investors cannot.

Governments, non-governmental organisations, and large institutional investors are often subject to strict regulatory restraints. High risk weightings on long-term investments may stop banks from investing in infrastructure. Insurance firms, especially life insurers, may struggle to fund long-term sustainability projects due to regulation governing the maximum tenor and minimum credit rating of debt instruments under Solvency II legislation. This is in spite of the natural match between long-term sustainability assets and the long-term liabilities that life insurers have to fund.[4]

By contrast UBS observes that the international private sector has greater flexibility.[5] We find that private investors, especially ultra-high-net-worth ones, often have scope to consider sustainable investment instruments that fall outside of traditional asset classes. They may be able to commit capital to risky or less liquid sustainable investments. Furthermore, they often build businesses or financial portfolios for the sake of future generations, matching the required timeframe needed to solve deep social and environmental problems.

What Is Needed to Mobilise Private Sector Money?

The international private sector is not yet meeting its full potential. Readiness and the ability to support sustainable development are high. However, supply-side inefficiencies prevent more meaningful flows of money into purposeful investments.

UBS has identified three categories of market failures that hold back greater private sector capital mobilisation.

First, sustainable development finance markets require rationalisation. Simply put, formal conventions or rules need to replace inconsistent terms and misunderstood motivations for acting sustainably.

Many investors are confused about how to quantify social and environmental impact. A rational sustainable development finance market should measure social and environmental outcomes with the same consistency that corporate financial metrics do financial ones. Common evaluation methods also need to be adopted.

Second, sustainable development finance markets need industrialisation. They still lack efficient matching between buyers and sellers. Appropriate

4 'Mobilizing Private Wealth for Public Good', UBS White Paper for the World Economic Forum Annual Meeting 2017 (January 2017), 12.
5 UBS Global Wealth Management, 'The Great Opportunity: Great Wealth Investment Report' (July 2017).

networks could overcome this problem, connecting willing investors with impactful projects.

We argue that sellers and buyers should also have ready access to other resources that support an efficient marketplace. Legal and accountancy advisors, due diligence expertise, and non-governmental organisations are all needed. Many networks exist for the largest investors; few do for private wealth investors. None has critical scale.

Successful industrialisation depends upon standardisation of financial markets. A lack of it continues to hinder private sector capital mobilisation in sustainable development financial markets. Let's take the example of infrastructure investments. They need greater efficiency and transparency to reach the equivalent scale as conventional asset markets. The Institute for International Finance's Council for Asset and Investment Management noted that the sector is subject to widely varying deal terms. Debt instrument structures lack consistency. Liquidity conditions vary in secondary debt markets, due to their different paths of development.[6]

Standardised infrastructure should also underpin this industrialisation. The sustainable development finance market misses such 'plumbing'. Benchmarks and a fully developed derivatives market are vital tools for serving large pools of sustainable development assets. Both improve market efficiency and promote market-making efforts; a fully fledged derivatives market also supports stickier investment in sustainable instruments by enabling market participants to hedge risks more effectively throughout the market cycle.

Third, sustainable development financial markets should be democratised and open to all. The mainstream adoption of sustainable and impact investing depends upon greater choices of financial instruments to tackle specific social and environmental causes that align with private investors' values or reflect their personal passions.[7] While a wide range of financial instruments exist to tackle some issues (such as climate action), there are few or no ways to invest in others (e.g. education, and clean water).

Easier substitution of sustainable asset classes for 'conventional' ones is a necessary step to more mainstream adoption of sustainable and impact investments. But it is not sufficient. Sustainable investing can only become the norm if the financial services industry adopts these new asset classes as a core part of doing business. To do so requires a more comprehensive sustainable and

---

6 Institute for International Finance, 'Top 10 Impediments to Long-Term Infrastructure Financing and Investment', Institute for International Finance's Council for Asset and Investment Management (June 2014), https://www.iif.com/press/ iif-identifies-top-10-impediments-long-term-infrastructure-financing-and-investment-0.

7 UBS, 'Partnerships for the Goals: Achieving the United Nations' Sustainable Development Goals', 32 (January 2018), https://www.ubs.com/global/en/wealth-management/chief-investment-office/key-topics/2018/five-lessons-on-sustainability-un-sdg-wef.html.

impact investment market. There are significant supply gaps in various sustainable asset classes, including US corporate, high yield, and emerging market debt, syndicated loans, sustainable real estate, and hedge funds.[8]

No one corporation or organisation can work alone. Drawing more private sector capital into sustainable development will depend on partnerships.

Partnerships for a More Sustainable Future

UBS has sought partners with the capabilities to draw more private sector capital into sustainable investments. To achieve this objective, public and private sectors need to work together to build a rational, scalable, and open-access sustainable investment marketplace. UBS is proud and privileged to draw upon its own public- and private-sector clients, its global resources, and its position as the world's leading wealth manager to promote sustainable investing's transition from margin to mainstream. We encourage other institutions and investors to work with us in mobilising private wealth for the public good.

Partnerships to Rationalise Sustainable Investment Markets

Greater private sector participation in sustainable investment rests on making a strong financial investment case. UBS has found that the most successful of its sustainable and impact investment launches stand up as compelling financial investments in their own right. The expected social and environmental benefits sway some investors to commit capital while serving as a bonus for others. Nevertheless, a 'dual bottom line' approach can widen the appeal of sustainable and impact investing to a broader investor base.

One reason investors still believe sustainability jeopardises performance is ignorance of the evidence. Part of the problem lies in the variety of sustainable and impact instrument types, whose expected financial and social impact returns can differ considerably. Another part of the problem lies in semantics.

UBS is working to redefine philanthropy and sustainable investing in a clearer, more intuitive way. We define sustainable investments as financial instruments that seek to generate risk-adjusted returns comparable to 'conventional' investments. There is no reason today's investors in sustainable and impact investment need to make return concessions for nonfinancial reasons (such as achieving social and environmental outcomes). We regard projects that deliver submarket rates of financial return as 'giving' or philanthropic ventures.

---

8 Ibid., 28.

Suggested definitions for sustainable giving and investment opportunities.

Philanthropy

	Charitable Giving	Strategic Philanthropy	Social Finance
Description	Making donations to nonprofits to enable them to achieve their vision. Hands off, no/low strategy, low resource intensity	Strategic donations into a variety of solutions to help achieve their philanthropic vision. Hands on, robust strategy, high resource intensity	Investing with the explicit intention to generate a measurable environmental and social (E&S) impact, alongside a (typically below-market) financial return
Desired primary outcome	Perceived positive environmental and social (E&S) impact	Demonstrable positive environmental and social (E&S) impact	Environmental and social (E&S) impact plus some financial return
Financial return			
Environmental and social (E&S) outcomes			

Sustainable Investing

	Exclusion	Integration	Impact Investing
Description	Excluding companies or industries from portfolios where they are not aligned with an investor's values	Integrating environmental, social, and corporate governance (ESG) factors into traditional investment processes to improve portfolio risk/return	Investing with the intention to generate measurable environmental and social (E&S) impact alongside a financial return
Desired primary outcome	Market returns non-underperformance	Competitive risk-adjusted financial returns, outperformance	Environmental and social (E&S) impact plus competitive risk-adjusted returns
Financial return			
Environmental and social (E&S) outcomes			

Source: UBS.

A second important distinction is between sustainable and impact investing, the latter being a subset of the former. UBS defines impact investing[9] as an investment that tries to generate positive financial *and* societal returns, with the additional criteria that these returns are *intentional* (on the part of both

---

9 UBS, 'Doing Well by Doing Good: Impact Investing', UBS Wealth Management Chief Investment Office (May 2016), https://www.ubs.com/global/en/wealth-management/chief-investment-office/our-research/sustainable-investing/2017/sustainable-impact-investing.html

issuer and investor); *measurable* (based on preagreed metrics); and *verifiable* (as a direct consequence of the investment).

UBS has partnered with the Impact Management Project to describe, measure, and communicate impact consistently. Working alongside more than 700 institutions, we have developed a consistent impact assessment methodology. Using these conventions, investors can embed impact into their standard investment processes. UBS suggests that a subsequent essential step is for other market participants to accept these definitions and adopt them as market conventions.

Adopting a 'dual bottom line' approach and delivering on it yields results. We would argue that this equal emphasis on positive financial and societal returns drove our successful partnership with impact investment specialists TPG Growth on distributing the Rise Fund to our non-US clients. UBS raised US$325 million of private wealth contribution to the fund, making it the largest private impact investment fund to date.

The process of industrialising sustainable investment markets begins with building networks. UBS has supported the development of Align17. This independent, open-architecture, impactful direct investment platform was initiated by the World Economic Forum's Young Global Leaders.[10] Its potential advantages include transparency on investment supply and demand, more effective connection across the sustainable development sector, and optimally designed incentive structures for private client investors.[11]

Better Connections to Spur Impact Investing

Georgie Benardete Co-founder and CEO of Allign 17

Impact investment is at a tipping point. In today's rapidly changing world, the process of deploying financial capital as a force for good as well as return is moving to centre stage. However, the path to impact investing has been challenging because of both a lack of coordination and a resistance to adopting the necessary technologies to achieve scale.

Bringing consistency and scale to the impact investment space is at the core of what Align17 does. As a World Economic Forum Young Global Leader I was privileged to meet people and institutions that originated attractive investment

(Continued)

---

10 UBS will not have any involvement in the selection of private investments made available on the Align17 platform. Nor will UBS perform due diligence or suitability reviews with regard to such investments. References to Align17 herein therefore should not be considered as an endorsement, solicitation, or referral to any investment made available on Align17.

11 UBS, January 2017, op. cit., especially chapter 5.

opportunities with clear positive social and environmental aims. To make a real contribution to sustainability these deal creators needed capital. The private wealth sector lagged others in making its mark, despite its real thirst to do well with its money.

Among those doing advanced thinking on this topic, UBS explored the barriers to greater private sector participation in funding the UN Sustainable Development Goals in its 2017 white paper for the World Economic Forum. Its research provided a blueprint on how we can crowd in more individuals and family offices to bring scale and build a more sustainable future.

Taking a lead from this insight, Align17's success will rest on connections, partnerships, and collaboration. At its core, we are connecting private investors to deals that tackle the sustainability issues they most care about. We are working with professional partners like Linklaters and PwC to build a structure that matches private wealth's ambitions and needs. We are also collaborating with Hamilton Lane on a transparent due diligence structure. Our collective efforts are then powered by the next generation of tech tools to increase efficiency, relevance, and scale. All these developments support Align17 in linking investors with projects that satisfy their need for competitive financial returns on investment and their passion for sustainable causes that are close to their hearts.

The ultimate reason why we are doing this is that it is recognised that solutions to the world's biggest problems need time and considerable financial resources to tackle – between US\$5 trillion and \$7 trillion per year, by one estimate. Solving these problems will require devoting strategically and systematically allocated capital, advanced skills, and energy to where they're needed most. We have a shared responsibility to improve the life of this planet. That is why we are asking other institutions and individuals to partner with Align17.

Efficient markets also need standardised infrastructure. UBS has worked with Solactive to launch new benchmarks for World Bank and other highly rated development bank debt issuers. These indexes should enable the private sector to allocate more funds to development bank debt than they would by following traditional fixed income benchmarks. A typical highly rated fixed income index comprises just 2.1% of multilateral development bank debt.[12] Furthermore, benchmarks can help deepen liquidity and issuance in development bank debt markets.

---

12 UBS, January 2018, op. cit., 18. UBS Global Wealth Management Chief Investment Office analysis, based on Barclays Aggregate data.

Partnerships to Democratise Sustainable Investment Markets

UBS has worked with a number of partners in the sustainability field to create fully sustainable, investing-focused cross-asset portfolios for private clients. These portfolios illustrate how financial institutions can provide access to sustainable development finance markets for the international private sector. World Bank securities, a subset of the multilateral development bank (MDB) debt market, form an integral part of our 100% sustainable cross-asset portfolios. UBS worked directly with the World Bank on two investment vehicles purpose-built to the specific liquidity and duration requirements of private client investors.

UBS suggests that MDB debt can play a role in all multiasset or fixed-income portfolios, in light of how comparable its risk-adjusted financial returns are to those of conventional high-quality government debt. Positive client responses to such vehicles imply that greater supply and a deeper MDB market would likely meet strong private sector demand.

Engaging Private Wealth with World Bank Debt

Heike Reichelt

Head of Investment Relations, World Bank

An end to extreme poverty. Boosting shared prosperity. These are the twin goals of the World Bank, which has a long history of issuing debt, in the form of World Bank bonds, to fund activities in support of them. Monies raised from debt sales fund investments in projects that aim to achieve these goals, such as by investing in health care, education, and sustainable infrastructure in the world's emerging and developing countries. Our investors look to the World Bank to provide a liquid and high-quality investment whose financial returns compare to those of top-rated government bonds and whose proceeds contribute to positive outcomes for society. Increasingly these investors are also looking to invest in World Bank bonds as a way to contribute to the Sustainable Development Goals that are aligned with the World Bank's mission.

The World Bank has support from its owners, our 189 member governments, other development agencies, and the private sector. UBS approached us with a unique opportunity to engage private wealth investors more actively. This collaboration enables the World Bank and UBS to raise awareness about multilateral development bank bonds and to develop new investment solutions together, both of which give investors easier access to World Bank bonds.

(Continued)

> We have decades of experience in funding and designing sustainable development projects and measuring and reporting on their social and environmental outcomes. Private sector investors can benefit from this increased transparency on how their money is being used and the impact it helps achieve. We have worked closely with UBS to better understand the requests of private investors and their desire to make a positive contribution and combat social and environmental challenges in addition to achieving their investment goals. We have gained deeper insight into private clients' investment timeframes and appetite for risk, whether related to interest rates, credit quality, or liquidity.
>
> Together the World Bank and UBS have created two dedicated investment vehicles for private investors to access World Bank debt. Opening up our debt markets to a broader audience has the power to extend our reach and amplify impact in developing countries by building awareness about sustainable investment opportunities. Together we've found a unique way for more investors to make a difference.

Increasing the availability of impactful public equity instruments is also important. Few sustainable public equity strategies have demonstrated the intentionality, measurability, and verifiability of societal returns that define an impact investment. Private sector investors with public market mandates have instead been limited to focusing on exclusion strategies or ones that integrate environmental, social, and corporate governance (ESG) criteria.

UBS has worked with Hermes Investment Management to define and develop a public equity strategy that enables more investors to deliver positive impact. The strategy employs shareholder engagement techniques. Hermes engages with corporate managers in small- and medium-sized companies in emerging markets. The firm's objective is to press for improvements in ESG factors.

Engagement can deliver positive results for people, planet, and profits. Academic analysis concludes that successful engagement on ESG factors delivers total excess returns of 7.1% in the year after shareholders and corporate management agree on changes.[13]

---

13 Elroy Dimson, Ouzhan Karaka, and Xi Li, 'Active Ownership', *The Review of Financial Studies* 28, no. 12 (1 December 2015): 3225–68.

Harnessing Shareholder Engagement to Meet the SDGs

Andrew Parry

Head of Sustainable Investment at Hermes Investment Management

We have worked with UBS to create an innovative Sustainable Development Goals (SDG) corporate shareholder engagement fund. It aims to give investors easy access to a truly impactful public-equity strategy in global markets. SDG engagement strategies provide investors with valuable additional insights into financial risks and opportunities as well as answers to questions central to sustainability. How a firm manages scarce resources, how it rewards its workforce, and how it drives supply-chain efficiency are all key elements of business practice, as well as critical social and environmental issues. Gathering information across the whole value chain, we also find great potential to engage with corporate boards and executives, identify areas where ESG factors can be improved, and support companies in driving positive change for people, planet, and profits.

Tangible and measurable examples of positive engagement include more inclusive hiring practices for ex-offenders and homeless people at the world's second-largest concessions operator; efforts to widen financial access for underbanked individuals in Peru; and collaboration between Hermes and Peru's largest bank to implement robust ESG due diligence on the bank's lending book, in a bid to align financial flows with projects that promote positive social and environmental outcomes for the Peruvian economy.

The success of an engagement strategy rests on productive partnerships between investors, Hermes Investment Management, and the firms in whom we invest client capital. Working closely with our portfolio companies, we are supporting a more standardised framework for assessing firms' SDG opportunities and systematically identifying improvement points. Creating this new engagement solution with sustainability experts at UBS, we wanted to apply 'industrialised' engagement techniques to small- and mid-cap global stocks. And through collaboration with UBS and its Global Wealth Management franchise, Hermes Investment Management has the potential to open up this impactful public-equity strategy to a wider group of investors, helping more private sector capital to make a positive impact.

Social enterprises also have an important role to play in mobilising more private wealth. These business owners often identify local sustainability problems. Their businesses combine business acumen and personal purpose to affect change. The best way of promoting social entrepreneurship to private investors is likely by bringing them together with financial services firms, matching powerful ideas with powerful investment capabilities.

UBS followed such an approach when setting up the UBS Oncology Impact Fund in 2015. Rising cancer rates around the world and the desire of clients to find cures drove UBS to consider ways to direct money to early stage oncology treatments. UBS designed an impact investment initiative that seeks to support this underfunded part of the market. Working with manager MPM Capital, UBS raised US$471 million from non-US investors to fund the vehicle that represents the largest health care impact investment ever.

The first full year of operation (2017) delivered compelling risk-adjusted financial returns and resulted in US$2.5 million being donated to health care improvement initiatives, including the UBS Optimus Foundation's impact philanthropy programs for children's health care.

Fighting Cancer with Impact . . . And Financial Returns

Bard Geesaman

Former Managing Director, UBS Oncology Impact Fund, MPM Capital

Few sustainability topics are as powerful as human health and wellness, particularly the search for cancer therapies that result in cures. Beyond the clear positive impact on human health and social well-being, investment in oncology-focused companies can offer some of the most attractive financial returns within the pharmaceutical industry. That's because cancer-focused biotech companies are developing therapies that have a dramatic impact on our ability to fight and even defeat a patient's cancer. The scientific basis for this new generation of oncology drugs originates from basic research conducted in top academic institutions around the world. The bottleneck for getting these innovations to patients is funding, both for driving cancer research and for commercialisation of these findings by drug-developing startup companies. Early-stage oncology treatments still lack vital private sector capital, therefore offering potential financial rewards for investors with a certain risk and liquidity tolerance.

Scientific developments have revolutionised cancer treatment since I trained as a physician. Back then, response rates for courses of chemotherapy treating late-stage melanoma were below 10%. These responses typically lasted for six months, followed by disease progression and death. Today, thanks to research breakthroughs in academia and companies financed with investor capital, 20–30% of late stage melanoma patients can enjoy cures, harnessing extraordinary developments such as using a patient's own immune system to treat the cancer.

In 2015, UBS and its clients noted the need for more private sector capital to support innovative cancer research and treatment. In a unique partnership between MPM Capital, UBS, and far-sighted private investors, we launched the UBS Oncology Impact Fund. Closing in 2016, it raised a record US$471 million from non-US investors, the largest health care impact investment ever.

(Continued)

Long-term success depends on mobilising even greater sums of investment. The world's cancer burden is set to grow heavier without the intervention of technology. The World Health Organization estimates that, globally, cancer causes around 17% of deaths today, a figure set to climb towards 29% over the next 20 years.

We expect that impactful oncology investments will continue to deliver both financial and social returns to investors. We believe that, through aggressive investment in innovative oncology companies, 50% of currently fatal cancers may be cured in 20 years' time. I am personally grateful to UBS as an institution and to specific individuals at UBS who share our determination in helping to reach this lofty goal.

We expect that impactful oncology investments will continue to deliver both financial and social returns to investors. These are powerful catalysts for greater private capital mobilisation into oncology, especially for those investors who want to make money and build a better world.

No one can afford to focus solely on short-term profits in today's world. Sustainable development is an integral part of long-term success for individuals, institutions, and society as a whole.

UBS expects the international private sector to play a critical role in building a more sustainable world. We are partnering with others to support greater private capital mobilisation for the public good. And we encourage others to join our partnerships to maximise our shared prosperity today and for generations to come.

7

Re-Orienting the Global Financial System Towards Sustainability

Alma Pekmezovic

Introduction

This chapter discusses how the global financial system, as a whole, could be re-aligned with sustainability purposes. The chapter is divided into the following parts: first, it explores the types of actors engaged in sustainable finance and draws attention to the key attributes of impact investing and its related phenomena: responsible investing, sustainable and/or community, ethical, or ESG investing. Second, it considers the enabling environment needed to allow sustainable investment to take place, and third, it draws attention to the key stakeholders involved in advancing these types of investments such as investors, governments, regulators, international standard-setting bodies (SSBs), stock exchanges, and issues. More specifically, this chapter comments on the legal and regulatory framework governing sustainable finance in the European Union. The chapter deals with (a) the sustainability disclosure requirements applying in the EU, and (b) investors' duties and sustainability.

As we shall see, institutional investors and asset managers are uniquely placed to channel a greater share of investable capital towards sustainability purposes. They have in recent times emerged as a significant potential source of sustainable development finance, primarily because of their growing assets under management and their ability to provide long-term finance.

This chapter therefore considers efforts to direct private sector financial investments via institutional investors, such as pension funds, sovereign wealth funds, pension funds, mutual funds and other similar vehicles to social or public purposes. The main question posed in this chapter is: what potential do new investment tools and strategies such as impact investing or sustainable investing hold for sustainable development, and what can policymakers do to transform such forms of investments into a large-scale practice for financing

Sustainable Development Goals: Harnessing Business to Achieve the SDGs through Finance, Technology, and Law Reform, First Edition. Edited by Julia Walker, Alma Pekmezovic, and Gordon Walker.
© 2019 John Wiley & Sons Ltd. Published 2019 by John Wiley & Sons Ltd.

the Sustainable Development Goals (SDGs)? In other words, how can investors use the new SDGs as a framework for their investments and impact strategies?

If financial market participants are to switch to long-term investment horizons and other sustainable forms of investments, financial regulation and governance frameworks must provide the necessary incentives and the right policy mix to facilitate such a change. To this end, this chapter also discusses various examples of hard and soft financial regulation including the G20/OECD Principles of Corporate Governance and other frameworks. It discusses how these can be further amended and revised to reflect sustainability considerations. In doing so, the chapter aims to develop a sound policy and legal infrastructure – a global framework – that can underpin sustainable investing and enable this form of investment to grow in the future. The overarching theme of this chapter focuses on maximising the social utility of private capital and creating the necessary policies that can help move the financial system towards sustainability.

Although banks have an essential role to play in the transition towards a sustainable financial system, as well, and could indeed do much more to promote sustainability, their role will not be discussed in this chapter. This chapter therefore will mainly focus on sustainability disclosure and the role of financial intermediaries such as institutional investors[1] and asset managers[2] in delivering the SDGs. The key EU flagship directives that this chapter addresses are the Non-Financial Reporting Directive[3] and the revised Shareholders' Rights

---

1 The EU Shareholder Rights Directive defines 'institutional investor' as an undertaking carrying out activities of life assurance within the meaning of Article 2(3)(a), (b), and (c), and activities of reinsurance covering life insurance obligations and not excluded pursuant to Articles 3, 4, 9, 10, 11, or 12 of Directive 2009/138/EC of the European Parliament and of the Council and an institution for occupational retirement provision falling within the scope of Directive 2003/41/EC of the European Parliament and of the Council in accordance with Article 2 thereof, unless a Member State has chosen not to apply that Directive in whole or in part to that institution in accordance with Article 5 of that Directive (Article 2f).

2 'Asset manager' means an investment firm as defined in point (1) of Article 4(1) of Directive 2014/65/EU of the European Parliament and of the Council providing portfolio management services to institutional investors, an AIFM (alternative investment fund manager) as defined in Article 4(1)(b) of Directive 2011/61/EU of the European Parliament and of the Council that does not fulfil the conditions for an exemption in accordance with Article 3 of that Directive or a management company as defined in Article 2(1)(b) of Directive 2009/65/EC of the European Parliament and of the Council; or an investment company authorised in accordance with Directive 2009/65/EC, provided that it has not designated a management company authorised under that Directive for its management. See EU Shareholder Rights Directive

3 Directive 2014/95/EU amending Directive 2013/34/EU as regards disclosure of non-financial and diversity information by certain large undertakings and groups, 2014.

Directive 2017.[4] Furthermore, this chapter provides a discussion of fiduciary duties applying to financial intermediaries and considers whether fiduciary duties should be defined broadly so that they allow institutional investors and asset managers to consider environmental, social and governance (ESG) factors in the investment processes.[5]

Background

In 2015, the United Nations adopted the Agenda 2030 for Sustainable Development, consisting of 17 Sustainable Development Goals that holistically address the social, environmental, and economic dimensions of sustainable development.[6] The SDGs are intended to serve as a guide for both developed and developing countries and link concrete development goals such as poverty reduction and human rights to issues such as environmental and climate change, as well as economic prosperity. In the same year, the historic World Climate Change Agreement of Paris (COP 21) was signed. The latter Agreement contains legally binding provisions regarding the financing of climate-friendly investments. Among other things, the Agreement requires that flows of funds must be reconciled with a 'path to a low-emission and climate-resilient development of greenhouse gases.'[7]

Capital markets play an essential role in achieving the sustainability objectives set out in the 2030 Agenda and the Paris Climate Change Agreement and,

---

4 Directive (EU) 2017/828 of the European Parliament and of the Council of 17 May 2017 amending Directive 2007/36/EC as regards the encouragement of long-term shareholder engagement OJ L 132, 20.5.2017, 1–25. Directive 2007/36/EC was originally adopted to improve corporate governance by defining minimum rights for shareholders in listed companies across the EU. The Shareholder Rights Directive 2017 amends and modernises the latter Directive. By amending the Directive recently, the European Commission primarily sought to improve corporate governance of listed companies and strengthen shareholder engagement. In addition, as stated, it is envisaged that the amendments will contribute to the competitiveness and long-term sustainability of those companies. The new EU Shareholder Rights Directive therefore recognises that effective and sustainable shareholder engagement is one of the cornerstones of listed companies' corporate governance model.

5 See generally UK Law Commission, Fiduciary Duties of Investment Intermediaries (Consultation Paper No. 350, June 2014), 100. 'ESG factors can also be used in both passive and active strategies. For example, a passive mandate might track an index such as the FTSE4 Good series (managed by a policy committee using complex inclusion criteria) or one of the S&P DJSI Diversified indices (which adopt a "best of sector" approach). An active mandate might select an investment manager or fund on the basis of their stated policy on investment factors.'

6 United Nations, 'Sustainable Development Goals', A/RES/70/1 (September 2015), http://www .un.org/sustainabledevelopment/sustainable-development-goals/. For example, environmental factors could include climate change, carbon emissions, pollution, energy efficiency, waste management, biodiversity, deforestation, and water use related to water scarcity.

7 See Article 2, para. 1 of the Agreement.

more generally, in advancing sustainable development in the world. This has been recognised widely, including by the European Union, which is committed to promoting a vision of sustainable development 'that satisfies the needs of the present without compromising the ability of future generations to satisfy their own necessities.'[8] The European Union therefore attaches particular importance to ensuring that its financial system is in line with the premises of the 2030 Agenda and the Paris Agreement.[9] In fact, the European Union sees 'finance as an essential lever'[10] for achieving the ambitious goals for economic prosperity, social inclusion, and environmental regeneration. Moreover, the Union has expressly recognised in a review of its Capital Markets Union (CMU) that a 'deep re-engineering of the financial system is necessary for investments to become more sustainable and for the system to promote truly sustainable development from an economic, social, and environmental perspective.'[11]

To promote the achievement of the goals in the Agenda and the Climate Agreement, the Union recently implemented a first set of reforms including a directive that promotes the disclosure of nonfinancial and diversity information (including environmental, social, and governance matters, human rights, and anticorruption and board diversity issues, among others) and thus ensuring greater transparency in the capital market. Furthermore, the European Union has revised the Shareholder Rights Directive that applies to financial intermediaries requiring greater shareholder engagement. This is discussed in more detail in later sections of this chapter.

In December 2016, the European Commission established a High-Level Expert Group on Sustainable Finance to develop a proposal on how to best facilitate the transition towards a low-carbon, resource-efficient, and green economy. The group will provide recommendations on 'how to "hardwire" sustainability into the EU's regulatory and financial policy framework and how to mobilise more capital flows towards sustainable investment and lending.'[12] In its interim report of July 2017, the Group presented a first set of concrete recommendations for aligning the financial system with sustainability purposes.[13] The Commission now intends to review a number of these initial core

---

8 See definition contained in the Brundtland Commission, 'Report of the World Commission on Environment and Development: Our Common Future' (1987), 43.

9 E3G, 'A Sustainable Finance Plan for the European Union' (2016), https://www.e3g.org/docs/A_Sustainable_Finance_Plan_for_the_EU.pdf. See also 2 Degrees Investing Initiative, 'Building a Financial System in the European Union' (2016), https://europa.eu/capacity4dev/unep/document/building-sustainable-financial-system-european-union.

10 HLEG Interim Report on Sustainable Finance, 'Financing a Sustainable European Economy' (July 2017), 8, https://ec.europa.eu/info/publications/170713-sustainable-finance-report_en.

11 Ibid., 9.

12 Ibid.

13 Ibid., 24.

recommendations and has published a final report in February 2018 with the aim of developing further steps for legislative action.[14] In particular with regard to the Capital Markets Union, the aim is to develop a new and forward-looking, long-term strategic framework for sustainable finance. The SDGs and the Paris Agreement will provide the foundations for this transition.

The Legal and Regulatory Framework

To reorient market participants to sustainable investments and long-term investment horizons, policymakers will need to consider how to best align financial regulation and investment principles with sustainability. This, however, is an ongoing work in progress, with only a minority of countries currently taking concrete action to introduce measures to align their financial systems with aspects of sustainable development.[15] The upshot of this is that the bulk of finance today continues to flow towards unsustainable purposes, hindering the implementation of the sustainable development agenda.[16] Shifting the capital allocation from an unsustainable pathway to a sustainable one is therefore a global challenge.

There are several concrete initiatives, however, underway that provide a possible roadmap on how to reorient the global financial system towards greater sustainability and integrate sustainability into the regulatory and financial policy framework. The UNEP Inquiry into the Design of a Sustainable Financial System, for example, discusses how the regulation of key financial market participants – including banks, insurance companies, institutional investors, and capital markets – could be brought into alignment with sustainable development.[17] A key message of the UNEP Inquiry is that the financial system, as a whole, can be redesigned to support more sustainable development outcomes in the real economy.[18] The UNEP identifies five priority areas for action including: capital reallocation, risk-management, the responsibilities of the financial institutions, reporting and disclosure, and sustainable finance.[19]

---

14 HLEG, 'Final Report on Sustainable Finance, Financing a Sustainable European Economy' (31 January 2018), https://ec.europa.eu/info/sites/info/ files/180131-sustainable-finance-final-report_en.pdf.

15 See generally UNEP Inquiry, 'The Financial System We Need: Aligning the Financial System with Sustainable Development' (2015), http://unepinquiry.org/publication/inquiry-global-report-the-financial-system-we-need/. See also UN PRI, 'A Global Guide to Responsible Investment Regulation' (2016), https://www.unpri.org/download_report/22438.

16 See also G20, 'Green Finance Synthesis Report' (2016), http://unepinquiry.org/wp-content/ uploads/2016/09/Synthesis_Report_Full_EN.pdf.

17 See UNEP (note 12), 11.

18 Ibid., 14.

19 Ibid., 16.

To deliver systemic policy change and transition to sustainability, the core role and underlying purposes of the financial system will need to be re-framed, and new sustainability rules and practices developed. The latter can be incorporated into both hard and soft law instruments, including corporate governance codes, core indices, accounting standards, and credit ratings.[20] It will be equally important for national and international standard-setting bodies (SSBs) as well as relevant oversight bodies (such as the supervisory authorities) to embed sustainability aspects into common methods, financial reporting tools, and disclosure standards. This will necessarily entail developing common approaches, definitions, norms, and standards that provide a governing framework for the global financial system.

SSBs are likely to play a vital role in integrating sustainable development practices into financial standards, and providing the necessary governance, guidance, and regulatory framework to support a global shift to sustainability. At the international level, the Sustainable Banking Network, for example, brings together regulatory agencies and banking associations from developing countries committed to advancing sustainable finance.[21] The aim of the network is to facilitate collective learning and policy development initiatives to create the drivers for sustainable finance. A similar initiative for insurance supervisors is the Sustainable Insurance Forum.

Over recent years, there has also been a trend among SBBs towards integrating some SDG-related components into financial standards. For instance, the Financial Stability Board (FSB) has established a Taskforce on Climate-Related Financial Disclosure.[22] The latter is expected to help develop a framework for improving disclosure and transparency on climate-related risks. In addition, financial standards have evolved to consider financial inclusion, by promoting for example access to financial products and services.[23]

At the global level, efforts have also been pursued in the area of corporate governance. Thus, the G20/OECD Principles of Corporate Governance have been recently revised to place a greater emphasis on agency issues, the role of asset managers, and the importance of managing conflicts of interests

---

20 Corporate governance codes are self-regulatory in nature and have been adopted in all European jurisdictions. Ex post pressure to comply with corporate governance codes may be exercised by investors in the AGM (the Annual General Meeting), various pressure groups, corporate governance commissions, securities regulators, or institutional investors, for example. Over time, the law may absorb much of the content of the self-regulatory codes as certain provisions of the code may be transposed into strictly legally binding provisions via legislative action.

21 Sustainable Banking Network, https://www.ifc.org/wps/wcm/connect/topics_ext_content/ ifc_external_corporate_site/sustainability-at-ifc/company-resources/sustainable-finance/sbn.

22 Task Force on Climate-related Financial Disclosures, Recommendations (June 2017), https:// www.fsb-tcfd.org/.

23 Ibid.

between proxy advisors, analysts, brokers, and credit-rating agencies.[24] The Principles include a new chapter on institutional investors and contain recommendations with respect to 'active ownership' and disclosing investment policies and practices. The principles refer to the importance of 'engagement' and direct dialogue between institutional investors and investee companies, referencing national stewardship codes. Companies are also encouraged to disclose, in addition to their commercial objectives, their 'non-financial' policies about business ethics, the environment, human rights, and public policy commitments. However, the Principles do not contain an express reference to sustainability reporting practices or responsible investment policies.

At the national level, policymakers, central banks, and other relevant governing institutions responsible for stewarding the development of the financial system should reinterpret their institutional purposes and mandates to take account of the SDGs. This would signal an important policy shift towards sustainability among financial system policymakers.

Interestingly, some governments have already taken some steps to promote a sustainable finance approach and reform their financial market laws and regulations in line with the SDGs. One area in capital markets law in which some legislative action is visible is sustainability reporting (discussed in more detail further on). As we shall see, some countries have made significant progress in developing a more advanced sustainability disclosure regime and, alongside stock exchanges, are actively beginning to reformulate their disclosure requirements with the objective of conveying a better picture of issuers' financial and non-financial performance (by requiring disclosure, for example, on carbon emissions and other ESG factors). The fundamental purpose of sustainability-relevant information disclosure is to enable investors to receive more information on companies' exposure to climate-related and other sustainability risks and thus allow investors to engage in better-informed decision making. Disclosure is an essential instrument in re-orienting the capital markets towards sustainability. The legislative changes in this area of law are important as they reflect a growing demand amongst retail investors for sustainability disclosure. In fact, 'there is considerable evidence that most retail investors would like to invest in a sustainable manner, with over two thirds of retail investors considering environmental and social objectives as important for their investment decisions.'[25]

---

24 OECD, *G20/OECD Principles of Corporate Governance* (Paris: OECD Publishing, 2015), https://doi.org/10.1787/9789264236882-en.

25 HLEG, Final Report, 27.

Company Reporting: Sustainability Disclosure Requirements

A significant challenge for sustainability disclosure is the lack of common standards and practice in this area.[26] Currently, there is no standardised system for companies to report on their performance on the Sustainable Development Goals. It is impossible to compare and measure companies' sustainability performance against their peers, and, unlike international accounting standards, there are no internationally recognised sustainability performance standards or league tables that can be used for this purpose. Although companies increasingly report on their corporate sustainability, with 92% of the world's 250 largest companies reporting on sustainability, the diversity of internationally applicable standards on ESG performance makes comparison difficult, time consuming, and expensive.[27]

Companies have not only developed different approaches for reporting on ESG but also follow different guidelines, in the form of country-specific guidelines such as the UK's Connected Reporting, or international principles such as the UN Global Compact of the OECD's Guidelines for Multinational Enterprises.[28] ESG disclosure depends on the company's regulatory context, securities regulations or listing rules (which may require ESG disclosure as part of financial information disclosure), and the company's overall business and communication strategy. The lack of a standardised framework across different industries and geographies makes it not only harder for investors to use the ESG disclosures made by companies and monitor progress, but it also makes it more difficult to show empirically that companies with better sustainability often also achieve better financial returns.[29] Furthermore, neither policymakers nor companies can use the disclosures effectively to promote better corporate performance on sustainable development. It is critical to develop global sustainability benchmarks and reporting standards that will enable a greater sustainability performance cross-comparison between companies.

To improve the public availability of sustainability information, a number of countries have introduced so-called sustainability disclosure requirements for issuers. In France, for example, the Act on Energy Transition and Green Growth requires institutional investors to report on their sustainability and climate strategies in Article 173.[30] The Law Grenelle II de l'environnement also

---

26 Deloitte Touche Tohmatsu Limited, 'Navigating the Evolving Sustainability Disclosure Landscape' (September 2014), 2.
27 Business and Sustainable Development Commission, 'Better Business, Better World' (January 2017), 70, http://report.businesscommission.org/uploads/BetterBiz-BetterWorld.pdf.
28 See UN, Global Compact, https://www.unglobalcompact.org/what-is-gc/mission/principles.
29 See generally BNP Paribas Investment Partners, 'SRI Insights: Adding Value to Investments' (2012), 58, 60–61.
30 *La loi relative à la transition énergétique pour la croissance verte*, Article 173. UNEP French Energy Transition Law. Global Investor Briefing (2016), http://www.unepfi.org/fileadmin/documents/PRI-FrenchEnergyTransitionLaw.pdf.

obliges fund managers to report on how they incorporate ESG criteria into their investment strategies. In other countries, the prevalent approach has been to anchor sustainability disclosure obligations in company law or in corporate governance codes. In the United Kingdom, for example, the Companies Act of 2006 requires companies to comment on greenhouse gas emissions in their management report.[31] The report must enable readers of the emissions data to have a clear understanding of the operations for which emissions data has been reported, and if and how this differs from operations within the consolidated financial statement.[32] The regulation encourages assurance, but does not make it mandatory. In addition, in 1995, the United Kingdom introduced the Statement of Investment Principles, which obliges private, public, and occupational pension providers to report on how social, environmental, or ethical considerations influence their investment decisions.[33] In Australia, the Australian Securities Exchange revised its Corporate Governance Principles and Recommendations recently with the aim of encouraging listed companies to disclose significant environmental and social sustainability risks.[34]

Similarly, the European Union took a first step in 2014 and introduced disclosure requirements for certain large companies.[35] The reforms implemented at EU level reflect the policy view that the disclosure of sustainability information is essential in order to provide useful information to investors and other market participants in the capital market, and in the long term will contribute to promoting the functioning of the Union-wide capital market. The CSR Directive 2014/95/EU therefore provides that Member States are to require certain 'public interest entities', entities such as publicly listed companies, banks and insurers, to prepare a non-financial statement as part of their

---

31 The UK, for instance, has implemented the Companies Act 2006 (Strategic and Directors' Reports) Regulations 2013, which require publicly listed companies to report their annual greenhouse gas emissions in their directors' report.

32 UK Government (2012), 'Company Reporting on Green House Gas Emissions', https://www .gov.uk/government/uploads/system/uploads/attachment_data/file/69517/pb13718-company-reporting-ghg-emissions.pdf.

33 Pension Protection Fund, Statement of Investment Principles (November 2015). Principle 9.6: 'The Board will integrate the consideration of ESG issues across all asset classes and markets in which it invests. In particular the Board, or its agents on its behalf, will exercise its ownership rights, including voting rights, in order to safeguard sustainable returns in the long term.'

34 ASX Corporate Governance Council, Corporate Governance Principles and Recommendations (3rd edition, 2014), Principle 4 and Principle 7. See Recommendation 7.4: 'A listed entity should disclose whether it has any material exposure to economic, environmental and social sustainability risks and, if it does, how it manages or intends to manage those risks', https://www.asx.com.au/documents/asx-compliance/cgc-principles-and-recommendations-3rd-edn.pdf.

35 Directive 2014/95/EU of the European Parliament and of the Council of 22 October 2014 amending Directive 2013/34/EU as regards disclosure of nonfinancial and diversity information by certain large undertakings and groups OJ L 330, 15.11.2014, 1–9.

management report, and comment on how they address ESG issues, human rights, anticorruption, and bribery.[36]

In response to the Directive, several Member States have enacted specific acts to foster the disclosure of ESG-related issues. For example, Germany transposed the CSR Directive into national law in 2017 by passing the so-called Gesetz zur Stärkung der nichtfinanziellen Berichterstattung der Unternehmen in ihren Lage- und Konzernberichten (CSR-Richtlinien-Umsetzungsgesetz).[37] The *CSR Directive Transposition Act* applies to companies that are capital market-oriented, meet the requirements of a large corporation, and employ an annual average of more than 500 employees. Against this backdrop, Deutsche Börse also recently published a guide to sustainability in capital communications.[38] The recommendations in the guide are designed to help issuers integrate ESG criteria into their capital market communications and report on sustainability issues.

Other stock exchanges to publish ESG guides include, among others, the London Stock Exchange and the Toronto Stock Exchange.[39] The LSE has produced an ESG guide that contains important recommendations for sustainability reporting, while the Toronto Stock Exchange mandates sustainability disclosure in certain circumstances, expressly requiring listed companies to report on material changes with social or environmental implications immediately:

> If any environmental or social information is deemed 'material', it must be *immediately* disclosed by a news release as required by the Exchanges' Timely Disclosure Policies and the issuer must file a material change report on SEDAR if the material information is a material change. In addition, securities rules require issuers to disclose all material information including material environmental and social issues.[40]

As an intermediary between issuers and investors, stock exchanges are uniquely placed to enhance corporate transparency with respect to ESG issues. The United Nations Sustainable Stock Exchanges (SSE) initiative, which includes 58 stock exchanges across the world, launched a campaign in 2015 to close the gap on ESG reporting.[41] The Initiative developed the Model Reporting

---

36 Ibid.
37 The transposition occurred through §315 para. 3 of the German Commercial Code (Handelsgesetzbuch).
38 Deutsche Börse, Nachhaltigkeit in der Kapitalmarktkommunikation: Sieben Empfehlungen für Emittenten.
39 London Stock Exchange (LSE), Revealing the Full Picture: Your Guide to ESG Reporting (2017), https://www.lseg.com/esg.
40 http://www.sseinitiative.org/fact-sheet/tmx/.
41 http://www.sseinitiative.org/fact-sheet/tmx/.

Guidance for stock exchanges in September 2015 to assist them in providing voluntary guidance on sustainability reporting.[42] The latter campaign was launched in response to a widespread lack of ESG guidance by stock exchanges. As of 2014, less than one third of stock exchanges around the world provided any guidance to issuers on this matter.[43] However, by mid-2016 more than 50% of stock exchanges worldwide began providing guidance to issuers on ESG disclosure. Most recently, Nasdaq Nordic and the Baltic exchanges in Stockholm, Helsinki, Copenhagen, Iceland, Tallinn, Riga, and Vilnius launched a voluntary support programme on ESG disclosure to guide their listed companies.

In the United States, on the other hand, extensive transparency obligations have been established early on, which generally often go beyond the disclosure requirements in other countries. It is widely acknowledged that such duties form the decisive characteristic of US capital markets law. The Securities Exchange Commission (SEC) has continuously expanded these obligations, developing a well-defined set of legal requirements, mandatory regulations (Rules and Regulations) and Interpretive Releases.[44] With regard to ESG disclosure, the current position of the SEC is that disclosure of social and environmental factors is only required when it is essential, i.e. 'materially important' to the investment decision of a reasonable investor.

There are some indicators, however, that the SEC may introduce more extensive and binding transparency ESG-related obligations in the future. Thus, the SEC has recently published a concept paper – Concept Release on Business and Financial Disclosure Required by Regulation S-K – in which the SEC explores the importance of sustainability disclosure in connection with other disclosure obligations in the US capital market.[45] In the paper, the SEC considered whether existing disclosure requirements in Regulation S-K continue to ensure the disclosure of relevant information to investors. Although the SEC has not yet answered calls for more extensive regulation in the area of 'climate risk disclosure' and/or 'sustainability disclosure,'[46] it acknowledged in its concept release that it is seriously considering the introduction of ESG

---

42 http://www.sseinitiative.org/wp-content/uploads/2015/10/SSE-Model-Guidance-on-Reporting-ESG.pdf.

43 Ibid.v.

44 U.S. Securities Exchange Commission, 'Interpretive Guidance on Disclosure Related to Business or Legal Developments Regarding Climate Change', http://www.sec.gov/rules/interp/2010/33-9106.pdf.

45 U.S. Securities Exchange Commission, 'Concept Release on Business and Financial Disclosure Required by Regulation S-K' (2016), https://www.sec.gov/spotlight/disclosure-effectiveness.shtml.

46 The Dodd-Frank Act of 2010 §§1502, 1503, and 1504 required the SEC to adopt rules regulating conflict minerals, health and safety in mining-related facilities, as well as payments to governments for the commercial development of oil, natural gas, or minerals, respectively.

transparency obligations and assessing the associated costs and benefits of such disclosure. Furthermore, the Commission has expressly 'recognized that the task of identifying what information is material to an investment and voting decision is a continuing one in the field of securities regulation. The role of sustainability and public policy information in investors' voting and investment decisions may be evolving as some investors are increasingly engaging on certain ESG matters.'[47] Therefore, it remains to be seen whether the SEC will take a more proactive role in the area of sustainability disclosure.

The aforementioned legislative and policy developments therefore suggest that sustainability disclosure rules are likely to play an increasing role in securities regulation. As stated, a number of concrete legal requirements (such as the implementation obligations resulting from the CSR Reporting Guideline) and numerous voluntary self-regulatory measures have been already developed as part of nonbinding guidelines aimed at greater transparency. Examining these legislative measures is beyond the scope of this chapter; suffice to say, however, that further research should focus on investigating how disclosure requirements in this area of capital markets law could be further improved and designed more effectively. Especially, greater consideration needs to be given to the legal consequences of breaching a sustainability transparency obligation. In particular, it should be clarified when (i) a violation exists and which (ii) public sanctioning instruments or (iii) private liability instruments are available. Among other things, it will also be important to investigate in future which sanction mechanisms have already emerged for monitoring the transparency obligations and how the practical effect of these obligations could possibly be further developed or improved. Against this background, it will also be important to address problems such as the so-called 'greenwashing' phenomenon and problems stemming from the misstatements of disclosed ESG information.[48] It will be crucial to strengthen the credibility of nonfinancial reporting vis-a-vis financial reporting.

Institutional Investors: Responsible Investing and Investing for Impact

Impact investments are investment opportunities with a 'dual bottom line' – i.e. they generate both financial returns and positive societal returns to a wide group of potential stakeholders – including employees, customers, and society at large. Although there is no universal definition of impact investing, or responsible investment, a common approach is to define responsible investment as 'investment that explicitly acknowledges the relevance to the investor

---

47 U.S. Securities Exchange Commission, 'Concept Release on Business and Financial Disclosure Required by Regulation S-K' (2016), 210.
48 Bruce Watson, 'The Troubling Evolution of Corporate Greenwashing', *The Guardian* (20 August 2016), https://www.theguardian.com/sustainable-business/2016/aug/20/greenwashing-environmentalism-lies-companies.

of environmental, social, and governance factors, and of the long-term health and stability of the market as a whole.'[49] Hence, responsible investment is based on the notion that the 'generation of long-term sustainable returns is dependent on stable, well-functioning, and well-governed social, environmental, and economic systems.'[50]

By contrast, *impact investments* provide companies with capital that is supposed to achieve certain predefined sustainability goals. Impact investments are motivated by environment, social, and corporate governance (ESG) criteria. Such 'extra-financial' indicators often have an impact on the long-term success of a company and are thus increasingly not only perceived as important by a subset of investors interested in 'responsible investments' but also by 'mainstream' investors. Investors are increasingly interested in how corporate management addresses possible ESG risks as the latter can have a negative impact on corporate development. Furthermore, information on a company's sustainability profile is also of great importance to institutional investors who increasingly look at the sustainability performance of a company as part of pricing long-term risks and opportunities. Companies with better ESG performance often have better credit ratings and lower capital cost.

Investors may use the ESG criteria to filter out investments that cause social damage or are environmentally detrimental, for example (referred to as *negative screening* and the most commonly used strategy).[51] Alternatively, they may use ESG criteria to channel investments into important impact areas such as renewable energy or access to financial services, which align with the SDGs. The ESGs may therefore be used for positive screening purposes, integration, or engagement. In practice, so-called 'best in class' concepts are also used, whereby investors select investments which are superior to their competitors in terms of sustainability.

Sustainability ratings and rankings therefore play an increasingly important role in valuing companies in the capital market. They enable investors and other market participants (such as rating and research agencies, proxy advisors, analysts, and other service providers) to assess and compare companies' sustainability performance. This enables a diverse set of stakeholders to gain a better idea of the extent to which companies participate in sustainable value

---

49 See UN PRI, Principles of Responsible Investments, https://www.unpri.org/about/the-six-principles.

50 Ibid.

51 Negative ESG screening excludes companies that do not meet certain ESG criteria. In doing so, an investor explicitly decides against investing in certain products and companies and states that engage in human rights violations, environmental damage or corrupt behaviour. See BNP Paribas Investment Partners, 'SRI Insights: Adding Value to Investments' (2012), 58, 60–61.

creation.[52] In addition, special stock exchange sustainability indices[53] such as the Dow Jones Sustainability Index, the FTSE4Good Index Series,[54] or the Nasdaq Green Index[55] have emerged.

The market size of impact investing has grown significantly in recent years. Although impact investing is not yet mainstream, an increasing number of funds and asset managers are integrating ESG considerations in their investment processes. In fact, signatory firms to the UN Principles for Responsible Investment accounted for US$59 trillion of assets under management as of April 2015, a 29% year-on-year increase.[56] Similarly, a 2016 survey of 158 investors undertaken by the Global Impact Investing Network (GIIN) states impact investments have increased from US$10.3 billion in 2013 to US$77 billion.[57] The survey included a minimum deal size of US$10 million, and included investors who have engaged in at least five impact investing transactions.[58] The survey also indicates that over 60% of assets under management were allocated to emerging markets each year. Prominent investment managers including Bain Capital, BlackRock, Credit Suisse, Goldman Sachs, and JPMorgan Chase, among others, have added impact products to their portfolio.[59] Furthermore, some studies show that investors – particularly millennials and women – consider environmental and social impact an important factor in their investment decision making.

Other studies show regional variations in this context. The percentage of responsibly managed assets relative to total managed assets is highest in Europe (59%).[60] Impact investing is also on the rise in the United States. A report by the USSIF Foundation in fact, shows a significant rise in sustainable,

---

52 UK Law Commission, Fiduciary Duties of Investment Intermediaries (Consultation Paper No. 350, June 2014), p. 100. 'ESG factors can also be used in both passive and active strategies. For example, a passive mandate might track an index such as the FTSE4Good series (managed by a policy committee using complex inclusion criteria) or one of the S&P DJSI Diversified indices (which adopt a "best of sector" approach). An active mandate might select an investment manager or fund on the basis of their stated policy on investment factors.'
53 See http://www.sustainability-indices.com/.
54 See http://www.ftse.com/products/indices/FTSE4Good.
55 See http://business.nasdaq.com/intel/indexes/equity/green/index.html.
56 Business and Sustainable Development Commission, Better Business, Better World (January 2017), 70.
57 Ibid.,15.
58 Ibid.
59 Jonathan Godsall and Aditya Sanghvi, 'How Impact Investing Can Reach the Mainstream' (November 2016), https://www.mckinsey.com/business-functions/sustainability/our-insights/how-impact-investing-can-reach-the-mainstream.
60 PRI, Impact Evaluation (2016), 12.

responsible and impact (SRI) in the country, with SRI investing assets expanding from US$6.57 trillion in 2014 to US$8.72 trillion in 2016.[61]

This growth is primarily driven by asset managers who consider ESG criteria across $8.10 trillion in assets.[62] Asset managers report incorporating ESG factors primarily due to client demand (85%), mission (83%), risk (81%), returns (80%), social benefit (78%), fiduciary duty (64%) and regulatory compliance (22%).[63] Moreover, the USSIF Report shows that the number of investment vehicles and financial institutions incorporating ESG criteria continues to grow and includes mutual funds, variable annuities, ETFs, closed-end funds, hedge funds, VC/private equity, property/REIT, other pooled investment vehicles, and community investing institutions.[64] The two main ESG criteria that institutional investors consider are: (1) restrictions on investing in companies doing business in regions with conflict risk (particularly in countries with repressive regimes or sponsoring terrorism), and (2) climate change and carbon emissions considerations.[65]

What is the relevance of the SDGs for impact investors? First, the SDGs can be used by impact investors to provide a broader context or framework within which to develop their objectives and strategies. Given their investment orientations, impact investors have a unique role to play in furthering the SDGs and promoting alignment with the SDGs. For instance, impact outcomes – such as financial inclusion and promoting access to capital for women, job creation, and improved transparency in the financial sector – are captured by SDGs, such as SDG 5 that focuses on 'gender equality', SDG 8 that focuses on 'decent work and economic growth', and SDG 16 focusing on 'peace, justice, and strong institutions'. Second, the SDGs can be used as tools to explain to the wider investment community the impact of certain investments. As public awareness of the SDGs grows, investors are likely to place greater emphasis on investment opportunities that create impact, and render both financial returns, as well as social and environmental returns, a material factor in their decision making.

Moreover, a strand of literature has now emerged to show investment managers should be entitled to consider ESG factors, and long-term considerations, as part of their fiduciary duty obligations. Broadening the interpretation of fiduciary responsibilities to extend to long-term and ESG-considerations underscores the importance of the SDGs. In February 2016, the UNEP, PRI,

---

61 Eurosif, European SRI Study (2012) S.34, http://www.eurosif.org/wp-content/uploads/2014/05/eurosif-sri-study_low-res-v1.1.pdf.
62 Ibid.
63 Ibid.
64 Ibid.
65 Ibid.

and the Generation Foundation launched an initiative to harmonise asset owners, asset managers, and policymakers' understandings of fiduciary duties, and to extend fiduciary duties to incorporate sustainability aspects.

Fiduciary Duties of Institutional Investors and Other Financial Intermediaries

Fiduciary duties are central to the investment process and are relevant for various financial intermediaries across the investment and lending chain.[66] The term 'fiduciary duties' is used in different ways, however. In a broad sense, the term is used to encompass all the various duties owed by fiduciaries to their principals, including the duties of care and duties that arise from the exercise of a power. A narrower interpretation of the term – favoured by UK courts for instance – emphasises that the core of fiduciary duty is 'the obligation of loyalty', so that breach 'connotes disloyalty or infidelity'. Institutional investors such as pension funds and assets managers are generally obligated as part of their fiduciary duties to act in the best interests of their clients and beneficiaries – usually, retail investors, future pensioners, and other investors.

A key question in capital markets law concerns the scope and interpretation of fiduciary duties. More concretely, should fiduciary duties be defined broadly, so that they allow institutional investors and asset managers to consider environmental, social, and governance factors in the investment process and decision making? What is the responsibility of financial intermediaries to take account of long-term sustainability risks and manage these risks? Should intermediaries be obligated as part of their know-your-client assessments to proactively ask end investors and their beneficiaries about their views on sustainability and responsible investment preferences at the time of investing, and provide disclosure with regard to ESG factors in their investment mandates and strategies? Furthermore, should institutional investors encourage their investee companies and other entities in which they are invested to comply with high sustainability standards? An issue here is that fiduciary duties in some jurisdictions are not well defined. Furthermore, even in jurisdictions where fiduciary duties are long established, there appears to be a misconception that fiduciary duties require a focus solely on maximising short-term financial returns.

In the UK, the predominant interpretation appears to be that investment trustees (intermediaries) may take account of any factor which is financially material to the performance of an investment, including environmental, social,

---

66 Freshfields, Fiduciary Responsibility: Legal and Practical Aspects of Integrating Environmental, Social and Governance issues into Institutional Investment (2009), http://www .unepfi.org/publications/investment-publications/ fiduciary-responsibility-legal-and-practical-aspects-of-integrating-environmental-social-and-governance-issues-into-institutional-investment/.

and governance factors.[67] Hence, there is 'no impediment to trustees taking account of environmental, social or governance factors where they are, or may be, financially material.'[68]

In the European Union, different regulatory approaches have evolved with regard to fiduciary duties. Although fiduciary duties are originally derived from the common law, the underlying principles of loyalty, duty of care, transparency, and avoiding conflicts of interests, are also found in EU directives and regulations as well as the national laws of the Member States. At EU level, the fiduciary duty or related concepts are in part codified in several directives, such as the Directive on Markets in Financial Instruments (in relation to investment firms), the UCITS Directive (in relation to investment funds), and the AIFM Directive (in relation to Alternative Investment Funds). However, although the consideration of sustainability issues is permitted under these directives, the extent to which such considerations are mandatory and how potential conflicts of interests with other considerations are resolved is unclear. The UCITS and AIFM guidelines require asset managers to monitor short- and long-term risks that are relevant to their portfolio or investment strategy. However, at present, it is not necessary for asset managers to report how they integrate ESG factors into their risk management or investment strategy. The only exception is when the asset manager is expressly pursuing ESG-related investments. The HLEG comments on this problem as follows:

> The central problem relates to the lack of appropriate standards in some instances as well as a lack of clarity of legal rules on the overarching investment objective in case of trade-offs and potential conflicts of interest. Such trade-offs and conflicts can occur across beneficiaries or between beneficiaries and third parties, including the fiduciary institution itself. And even where there is no legal conflict, evidence suggests that some investors, directors and pension trustees still misinterpret their obligations.[69]

Commenting on the fiduciary duties of institutional investors and asset managers, more generally, the European HLEG made a recommendation to the European Commission to clarify that the fiduciary duties (which mainly consist of loyalty and due diligence obligations) of institutional investors and asset

---

67 P. Myners, 'Institutional Investment in the United Kingdom: A Review' (London: H.M. Treasury, 2001), 115.

68 The UK Law Commission, 'Fiduciary Duties of Investment Intermediaries' (2014), 112, https://assets.publishing.service.gov.uk/government/uploads/system/uploads/attachment_data/file/325509/41342_HC_368_LC350_Print_Ready.pdf.

69 HLEG Interim Report on Sustainable Finance, 'Financing a Sustainable European Economy' (July 2017), S.23. See further HLEG Final Report on Sustainable Finance (31 January 2018), 73.

managers also expressly mandate the consideration of significant ESG factors and long-term sustainability risks:

> The HLEG recommends clarifying the duties of institutional investors as well as their asset managers. [. . .] Clarified duties would encompass key investment activities, including investment strategy, risk management, asset allocation, governance and stewardship. Making it clear that sustainability factors must be incorporated in these activities can ensure that the clarified duty is effective. The clarified duty would also require that all participants in the investment chain pro-actively seek to understand the *sustainability interests* and preferences of their clients, members or beneficiaries (as applicable) and to provide clear disclosure of the effects, including the potential risks and benefits, of incorporating them into investment mandates and strategies. [. . .] By simultaneously clarifying investor duties at the highest level, benefits will cascade across the investment chain. This will require amendment of multiple EU directives to link investor duties to the investment horizon of the individual or institution they serve and to the ethical preferences on sustainability of members, clients and beneficiaries. *It will also require involving all participants in the investment chain, including pension funds and asset managers.* To maximise impact, these obligations should be clarified and captured in the revised directives . . ., so that expected adjustments across the investment chain and at all stages of the investment process are clear for everyone involved. If this proposal is implemented in a partial or voluntary way, the regulatory situation will not make sufficient progress on driving sustainability across the investment chain.[70]

The UK Law Commission has recently also commented on the incorporation of sustainability factors into fiduciary duties in its paper on 'Fiduciary Duties of Investment Intermediaries'.[71] The paper is based on the so-called Kay Review into the Short Termism of British Equity Markets.[72] It also refers to the possibility that investors may have conflicting views on nonfinancial, social, or ethical goals. Therefore, it is important to clarify which sustainability factors among the ESG factors should be considered as part of sustainable investment practices (e.g. factors mitigating the effects of climate change, other environmental factors, social factors, governance factors, or other relevant factors)?

---

70 Ibid., p. 21.
71 UK Law Commission, 'Fiduciary Duties of Investment Intermediaries' (Consultation Paper No. 350, June 2014).
72 John Kay, 'The Kay Review of UK Equity Markets and Long-Term Decision Making: Final Report' (July 2012), para 1.22, http://www.bis.gov.uk/assets/biscore/business-law/docs/k/12-917-kay-review-of-equity-markets-final-report.pdf.

Furthermore, in advancing sustainable investments practices, it is important to consider the interplay between soft law and hard measures. Sustainability considerations can thus be incorporated into various soft law instruments that supplement existing obligations enshrined in hard law. Such soft law instruments can be a powerful tool for alignment shareholders and investors' preferences with sustainability objectives and promoting greater transparency in this field. For example, it is possible to embed or, at the very least, more explicitly reference sustainability and long-term value creation as a concept in so-called stewardship and corporate governance codes which apply to institutional investors and other financial intermediaries.[73] The British Stewardship Code, for example, is intended to encourage institutional investors to actively and responsibly exercise their shareholding rights.[74] Furthermore, institutional investors could be encouraged as part of such codes to achieve greater transparency and greater sustainability.[75] In addition, asset managers could be required to disclose whether they incorporate ESG considerations into their decision making as part of their asset management mandates. Soft law measures, therefore, can potentially be used to involve all participants across the investment and lending chain into driving sustainability and, more generally, the SDG 2030 Agenda forward. The HLEG states as follows:

> Asset managers should ensure that their governance, expertise and stewardship practices take account of sustainability in order to deliver the best possible investment outcome for clients. As the institutions responsible for investing their clients' capital, asset managers play a crucial role in the investment chain. [. . .] Asset managers should be required to ask their institutional clients and their representatives whether there are any sustainability, governance or broader ethical concerns that the clients wish to have considered and reflected in the investment mandate. To ensure these preferences are properly reflected, asset managers should also seek informed consent from their clients on the strategy that they adopt for them.[76]

Accordingly, institutional investors, pension funds and asset managers should ensure that they have a proper understanding of the interests and preferences of their members and beneficiaries, which extends to their sustainability preferences.

---

73 See, for example, German Corporate Governance Code, http://www.dcgk.de/de/kodex.html.
74 Financial Reporting Council, UK Stewardship Code (September 2012), https://www.frc.org.uk/investors/uk-stewardship-code.
75 Ibid., p. 1. 'Stewardship aims to promote the long-term success of companies in such a way that the ultimate providers of capital also prosper. . . . Asset managers, with day-to-day responsibility for managing investments, are well positioned to influence companies' long-term performance through stewardship.'
76 HLEG Final Report on Sustainable Finance (31 January 2018), 73–74.

Finally, a key legal question requiring further examination in the future concerns the enforceability and legal nature of ESG-related fiduciary duties.[77] How should courts enforce any newly established fiduciary duties, and should investors be able to recover damages if the financial market intermediaries do not act in accordance with the fiduciary duties or their asset management mandates (e.g. by not investing in accordance with ESG criteria or not acting on financially material risks stemming from the ESG factors which they identify)? Which sanctioning mechanisms are appropriate here and should investors have recourse to so-called private rights of actions, which would entitle them under certain preconditions to sue institutional investors and other intermediaries in the event of a breach of the fiduciary duties? Furthermore, should such private rights of action be available in addition to any other supervisory sanction mechanisms available to the relevant supervisory authorities? The problem of the enforceability of loyalty obligations arises in particular if the noncompliance by the intermediaries does not lead to a financial loss for the concerned investors.

Here, regulators will need to consider the advantages and disadvantages of public vis-à-vis private law enforcement mechanisms. As Posner wrote in the context of US securities law, there is a 'choice between two methods of public control – the common law system of private enforced rights and the administrative law system of direct public control.'[78] The legal classification of newly introduced sustainability-oriented loyalty obligations in either the public or private law domain is thus not only of a purely dogmatic relevance but has significant practical effect and ultimately results in differing legal consequences. It will be crucial to determine in some jurisdictions whether aggrieved investors should be granted a special civil claim in accordance with well-established Anglo-American notions concerning private enforcement or whether the loyalty obligations are part of public law, with the result that they possibly only influence the interpretation of relevant standards applicable under private law.

Fostering Long-Term Sustainability

Policymakers also increasingly recognise that financial market participants need to be better incentivised to deal with long-term sustainability challenges.

---

77 See the U.S. case *Board of Trustees of Employee Retirement System of Baltimore (City) v. Baltimore (City)*. The Maryland Court of Appeal approved decisions requiring pension funds to divest from companies in apartheid South Africa. According to the Court, 'Thus, if . . . social investment yields economically competitive return at a comparable level of risk, the investment should not be deemed imprudent'. See further Benjamin J. Richardson, 'Do the Fiduciary Duties of Pension Funds Hinder Socially Responsible Investment?' 22 *Banking and Finance Law Review* 145 (2007): 179–80.
78 Richard A. Posner, *Economic Analysis of Law* (3rd ed, 1986), 343.

Sustainability requires a long-term perspective – both in terms of providing long-term funding for critical infrastructure and responding to long-term threats and opportunities such as climate change, for example.[79] The core challenge is not simply to improve access to finance but expand access to *better* finance that is more long-term oriented, attuned to sustainability risks and more efficient at delivering social, environmental, and governance returns for investors, as well as contributing to the achievement of the SDGs.[80] A key problem, however, is that many financial market participants appear to be biased towards short-term oriented results and a relatively narrow view of financial risk.

Policy regulators should aim to stretch the time horizon and broaden the conception of risk. In the European Union, the Shareholder Rights Directive was amended in 2017 with the aim of more comprehensively addressing short-termism and interest conflicts in the European equity markets. The Directive was implemented in response to a perceived lack of engagement on behalf of institutional investors and asset managers in the corporate governance of investee companies. Thus, the Preamble to the Directive notes that institutional investors and asset managers 'often exert pressure on companies to perform in the short term, which may jeopardise the long-term financial and nonfinancial performance of companies and may, among other negative consequences, lead to a suboptimal level of investments, for example, in research and development, to the detriment of the long-term performance of both the companies and the investors'.

The Revised EU Shareholder Rights Directive 2017 seeks to ensure that institutional investors and asset managers, as well as intermediaries such as proxy advisors are subject to appropriate transparency and engagement rules. The aim of the Directive is to increase shareholder engagement and give shareholders a greater say on various matters. The policy rationale behind the Directive is to contribute to the long-term sustainability of EU companies and create an attractive environment for shareholders. Greater involvement of shareholders in corporate governance is regarded as an important level that can help improve the financial and nonfinancial performance of companies.

Under the Revised Shareholder Rights Directive, institutional investors are thus to disclose how they take the long-term interests of their beneficiaries into account in their investment strategies and how they incentivise their asset managers to take these long-term interests into account. Asset managers, on the other hand, are required to report to the institutional investors for whom they manage funds, and how they have performed in relation to their mandate.

---

79 Ibid.
80 HLEG, Interim Report, 11.

The new requirements are intended to help institutional investors and asset managers be more transparent in their approach to shareholder engagement.

Article 3g(1)(a) of the Shareholder Rights Directive sets out the so-called 'Engagement Policy Requirements', providing that Member States shall ensure that institutional investors and asset managers shall develop and publicly disclose an engagement policy that describes how they integrate shareholder engagement in their investment strategy. In a nutshell, the policy shall describe how they monitor investee companies on relevant matters, including strategy, financial and nonfinancial performance and risk, capital structure, social and environmental impact, and corporate governance. Article 3g was specifically amended by the European Parliament to state that the engagement policy should also refer to nonfinancial performance and the reduction of social and environmental risks. The Article adopts a comply-or-explain approach, i.e. institutional investors should comply with the practice of developing an engagement policy as outlined in the Article, but if they choose not to, they should explain how the lack of an engagement policy would still enable them to achieve their objectives.

Conclusion

Achieving the SDGs will significantly depend on aligning the global financial system with sustainability and long-term outcomes. This will entail updating existing legislative and regulatory frameworks and creating new norms in the overall policy framework. It is especially important for policymakers to create incentives for financial intermediaries to allocate capital to sustainable purposes and consider long-term sustainability risk and opportunities. Furthermore, the use of clear metrics and benchmarks could increase the capital allocated to sustainable investments, and ESG-related investments.

Lastly, it is important to develop common standards and definitions concerning impact investment and enable more cross-comparison.

8

How Asset Managers Can Better Align Public Markets Investing with the SDGs

Emily Chew and Margaret Childe

Since the UN Sustainable Development Goals (SDGs) were adopted in September 2015, the values they espouse have caught the attention and imagination of the global investor community. As they provide a viable roadmap to sustainable development that promotes an active role for the private sector, the SDGs have become a regular focus topic for responsible and sustainable investment conferences, industry working groups, thought leadership, and, increasingly, thematic fund launches. Importantly, the SDGs have the potential to extend the concept and practice of 'impact investing' to public markets, which to date has remained mostly elusive for investors seeking to generate positive environmental and social impact by deploying capital in this area of the global investable markets.

In this chapter, we explore the reasons why the SDGs could prove to be a powerful framework with which to propel the next phase of responsible and sustainable investing. We also illustrate an approach developed by Manulife Investment Management that applies the SDGs to public markets investing (specifically, listed equities and corporate bonds) and share the results of applying this approach to a representative universe of US large-cap companies. Lastly, we offer our reflections on likely SDG-related developments and initiatives for public markets investing in coming years.

Why the SDGs Could Transform Sustainability Investing

The past decade has witnessed increasing sophistication of responsible and sustainable investment practices (or, 'environmental, social, and governance (ESG) investing') across the global asset management industry. This in turn has led to a growing awareness that many key sustainability issues are essentially long-term in nature and that long-term investors must understand how companies are positioned relative to the systemic nature of key sustainability

Sustainable Development Goals: Harnessing Business to Achieve the SDGs through Finance, Technology, and Law Reform, First Edition. Edited by Julia Walker, Alma Pekmezovic, and Gordon Walker.

trends. However, without a clear definition of what sustainable economic outcomes look like in global, absolute terms, there can be little discipline in or systematisation of the practice of investing for long-term sustainable impact.

In this context, the SDGs provide a language for defining and describing economic development outcomes that are sustainable, inclusive, stable, and desirable. The SDGs carry the weight of global consensus as convened by the United Nations and are applicable to all countries regardless of domestic stages of development. As the SDGs were developed in extensive consultation with both the private and public sectors, several of the sub-goals and targets defined under each of the 17 SDGs directly address the actions, operations, and opportunities of private business. They therefore allow the private sector, including investors, to intentionally focus on positive contributions to critical global issues. Further, the profit opportunity could itself be significant. The Business & Sustainable Development Commission asserts that the SDGs represent a US$12 trillion investment opportunity in four economic systems alone: food and agriculture, cities, energy and materials, and health and well-being, or 60% of the real economy.[1]

However, for investors, the challenge remains of how best to deploy capital across asset classes that will genuinely support the SDGs and enable access to this investment opportunity. Direct investing in real assets, private equity/small business, and 'blended finance instruments' that combine public or development finance with private finance has historically offered the primary avenues for sustainable impact investing because these have allowed investors to more easily select pure-play business models/projects with clear intentionality for and measurement of impact.[2] In contrast, the wide diffusion of ownership and the primacy of short-term investor profit over other stakeholder interests, which is germane to public markets, has made alignment and contribution to sustainable development more elusive for investors in these asset classes.

There are three ways that the SDGs can help solve this problem. First, they define the areas in which large investee companies can articulate a long-term sustainable development strategy; in other words, they offer a framework for defining investee intentionality or commitment. Second, they set global

---

1 Business & Sustainable Development Commission, 'Better Business, Better World' (January 2017), http://report.businesscommission.org/report.
2 For example, the signatories to the Dutch SDG Investing Agenda 'recognize that blended finance instruments provide an avenue for investors to increase capital allocation toward sustainable solutions in sectors such as energy, infrastructure, water, agriculture and food and healthcare. These are sectors that constitute a largely untapped potential in higher risk markets, where private investors would not venture alone, but will invest alongside development finance institutions and sovereign wealth funds.' See Dutch SDGI Report (December 2016), 'Signatories of the Dutch SDG Investing Agenda'.

sustainable development outcomes against which the private sector can begin to define relevant company-level reporting; that is, they help us establish standards around impact metrics. Third, they provide a framework for structured shareholder engagement with companies on sustainable development themes, thereby helping investors focus on desirable sustainability outcomes and demonstrate their own impact. A 2015 survey of 52 institutional investors indicated strong intentions among the group to engage on the SDGs, allocate capital in support of the SDGs, and support regulation that promotes the SDGs,[3] underlining the support that the SDGs have received from the investment community.

There is pent-up demand in the market for 'impact-oriented' investing options for public markets that do not sacrifice investment returns. Taking on this challenge, Manulife Investment Management aims to promote the relevance of SDG-aligned investing and has developed an analytical framework with reporting metrics that we hope will accelerate this movement among investors.

Implementing the SDGs as an Analytical Framework to Align Investing with the SDGs

Objectives of Manulife Investment Management's Approach to SDG-Aligned Investing

A spectrum of SDG investing approaches is available to investors (see Figure 8.1), supported by a growing range of resources and initiatives to explore them.[4] We tasked ourselves with developing a meaningful SDG-aligned framework and methodology applicable to returns-focused public markets investing that could enable thematic forms of SDG investing.

---

3 'In 2015 researchers from ShareAction interviewed 52 institutional investors, based in every region of the world, on their attitudes and intentions in relation to the SDGs and they found that:
- 95% of respondents plan to engage with investee companies about issues covered by the SDGs;
- 84% will allocate capital to investments supporting the SDGs;
- 89% will support regulatory reforms that promote the SDGs.'
UN PRI, 'Micro Opportunities: A Capital Allocation Guide' (12 October 2017), https://www.unpri.org/sdgs/the-sdgs-as-a-capital-allocation-guide/309.article.
4 For example, we found it helpful to refer to the guidance document 'SDG Impact Indicators: A Guide for Investors and Companies', which resulted from the joint effort of Dutch financial institutions and companies that formed a working group to focus on SDG Impact Measurement; see Initiative of the Dutch Sustainable Finance Platform, chaired by the Dutch Central Bank (DNB), https://tkpinvestments.com/wp-content/uploads/TKP-Investments-SDG-impact-indicators-brochure.pdf (accessed 28 January 2019).

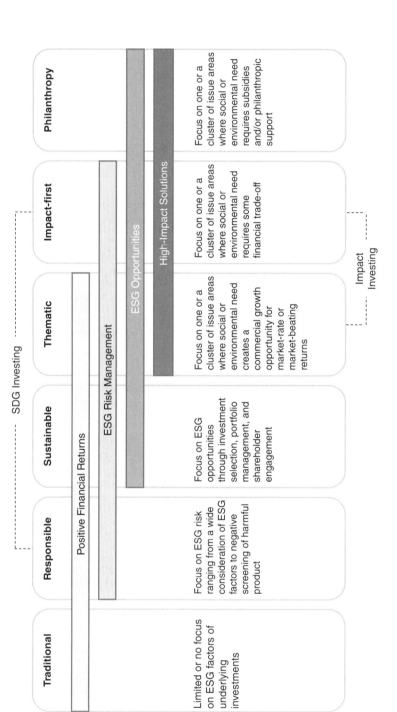

Figure 8.1 Spectrum of capital and the definition of SDG investing from the signatories of the Dutch SDG investing agenda. *Source:* C-Change analysis, Dutch SDGI Report (December 2016).

Manulife Investment Management has developed a Sustainable Development Goals Assessment Methodology (SDG Assessment Methodology) that provides a transparent and scalable process for assessing companies' commitments and contributions towards achieving the SDGs and comparing a broad universe of companies against one another. This enables investors to identify corporate leaders in a given universe based on the relative strength of their commitments and contributions, and in doing so, allows them to align with and contribute to achievement of the SDGs through their investments. We have chosen to conduct the research that underpins the SDG Assessment Methodology based on companies' publicly available information, with the aim of implicitly encouraging companies to improve their SDG-related disclosure. By applying the SDG Assessment Methodology to their investments, investors can signal their preference that companies measure and report on the social and environmental impact of their products and services, and explicitly state their intention to contribute to a sustainable development agenda.

We offer the SDG Assessment Methodology as a working model for applying the SDG framework to public markets investing. We recognise that industry best practice is to revisit and revise these models; as such, we expect our methodology will evolve as corporate disclosure improves and investment industry norms develop in this area.

SDG Assessment Methodology Overview

Investable Themes

The activities associated with achieving the SDGs are directly investable to greater and lesser degrees in the private sector. Indeed, many of the SDG goals and related targets are more relevant to actions or policies under the control of government and the public sector. There is also subject matter overlap between the SDGs. Therefore, to identify the realistic SDG investment opportunity set for the private sector, to set conceptual boundaries, and bring clarity to our SDG Assessment Methodology, we saw the need to aggregate the SDGs into broader investable themes that can be reasonably addressed by private sector business activities, with each theme tending towards an environmental or social impact focus (Investment Themes). Figure 8.2 outlines the Investment Themes available in our current iteration of the SDG Assessment Methodology, illustrating the clustering of certain SDGs into impact focus areas.[5]

---

5 At of the time of this publication, Investment Themes that address the remaining SDGs were under consideration.

Theme	SDGs	Impact aim	Key business themes
Shared Prosperity	SDG 1: No Poverty	End poverty in all its forms everywhere	Low-income access to products and services, access to quality essential health-care services and WASH (Water, Sanitation, and Hygiene), electricity availability and reliability, healthy and affordable food, access to financial services, economic inclusion and fair trade
	SDG 2: Zero Hunger	End hunger, achieve food security and improved nutrition, and promote sustainable agriculture	
	SDG 10: Reduced Inequalities	Reduce inequality within and among countries	
Better Health	SDG 3: Good Health and Well-Being	Ensure healthy lives and promote well-being for all at all ages	Health and safety; access to affordable medicines and quality essential health-care services, R&D on neglected diseases, drug donations, air quality, water quality
Safe and Quality Work	SDG 4: Quality Education	Ensure inclusive and equitable quality education and promote lifelong learning opportunities for all	Promotion of talent development and retention, high health and safety standards, non-discrimination, capacity building, elimination of forced or compulsory labor, educational and training services
	SDG 8: Decent Work and Economic Growth	Promote sustained, inclusive, and sustainable economic growth, full and productive employment and decent work for all	
Gender Equality and Diversity	SDG 5: Gender Equality	Achieve gender equality and empower all women and girls	Diversity and equal opportunity in company operations as well as for suppliers and partners, flexible work environment, equal remuneration for women and men, access to sexual and reproductive health-care services, elimination of workplace violence and harassment, diversity and inclusion initiatives, women in leadership, products/services that promote gender equality and diversity such as financial services for female entrepreneurs (e.g. microfinance) or specialized health insurance for women

Theme	SDGs	Impact aim	Key business themes
Clean Water	SDG 6: Clean Water and Sanitation	Ensure availability and sustainable management of water and sanitation for all	Sustainable water withdrawals, improved water quality and efficiency, affordable water access, sanitation, and hygiene for employees and communities, protection of water-related ecosystems and biodiversity, wastewater/water treatment and water-saving technologies or services, water-efficient appliances.
Climate Action	SDG 7: Affordable and Clean Energy	Ensure access to affordable, reliable, sustainable energy for all	Renewable energy, energy efficiency, GHG emissions reductions, focus on low-carbon vs. carbon-intensive business, such as products for renewable energy generation and LEDs
	SDG 13: Climate Action	Take urgent action to combat climate change and its impacts	
Modern Cities	SDG 9: Industry, Innovation, and Infrastructure	Build resilient infrastructure, promote inclusive and sustainable industrialization, and foster innovation	Infrastructure investments such as charging infrastructure for electric vehicles, environmental investments, research and development, sustainable transportation, sustainable buildings such as achieving LEED certification, IT security solutions and equipment that promote interconnectivity as well as data protection, insurance products to support general resilience to natural disasters, technologies that analyze air, water, and soil quality to support urban environmental issues stemming from population density.
	SDG 11: Sustainable Cities and Communities	Make cities and human settlements inclusive, safe, resilient, and sustainable	
Reduce, Reuse, Recycle	SDG 12: Responsible Consumption and Production	Ensure sustainable consumption and production patterns	Sustainable sourcing, resource efficiency of products and services, material recycling, procurement practices, products that use recovered materials or recycle waste into raw materials, cradle-to-cradle certified products, products and services that contribute to pollution reduction, and waste reduction/recycling services.

Figure 8.2 SDG Assessment Methodology Investment Themes. *Sources:* Manulife Investment Management, UN Sustainable Development Goals, SDG Compass.

Clustering the SDGs in this manner addressed two key concerns. First, the subject matter overlap or complementariness of certain issues suggested a natural clustering; for example, in practice, the corporate behaviours to support SDG 7 (Affordable and Clean Energy) are very similar to those in support of SDG 13 (Climate Action), and the intention of SDGs 1 (No Poverty), 2 (Zero Hunger), and 10 (Reduced Inequalities) were considered to be sufficiently analogous as to cluster into the Shared Prosperity Investment Theme.

Second, clustering enables the Investment Themes to be more broadly applicable to a greater number of industries than certain standalone SDGs, where broader applicability can enable diversification in the context of thematic investing. For example, whereas SDG 2 (Zero Hunger) would largely centre on consumer staples, agriculture, and food retailing companies – that is, a relatively narrow set of sectors is relevant, with likely very few companies in those sectors able to be assessed as 'aligned' or 'impactful' – the Investment Theme of Shared Prosperity has a broader conceptual focus on access to products/services for low-income populations, allowing companies in a greater range of sectors to be assessed as relevant. Therefore, using the Shared Prosperity Theme to construct an SDG-aligned portfolio results in a greater diversity of selected companies included than if SDGs 1 (No Poverty), 2 (Zero Hunger), and 10 (Reduced Inequalities) were used in a standalone manner.

In contrast, SDG 5 (Gender Equality) underpins an Investment Theme that is industry agnostic. SDG 3 (Good Health and Well-Being) underpins an Investment Theme that defines a relatively narrow set of relevant industries, and yet those industries run deep in most investment universes and are populated with companies with high direct impact.

SDG Alignment Assessment

The core of Manulife Investment Management's SDG Assessment Methodology is an evaluation of company performance against three weighted pillars that, when combined, generate an SDG Alignment Assessment for each Investment Theme (see Figure 8.3).

Figure 8.3 SDG Alignment Score Component Pillars.

The pillars are described as follows:

1. Goals, Targets, and Progress: This pillar assesses a company's level of commitment to the SDGs through the public communication of goals/targets and progress achieved. Our aim with this pillar is to capture the company's intention to generate future positive impact, and to hold them accountable to their ambitions through measurement of progress achieved. Therefore, goals that are time-bound, business-relevant, and for which progress is measurable and reported are more highly regarded by the SDG Assessment Methodology.

2. Business Opportunity: This pillar assesses companies' current capture of SDG-related business opportunities through identifying revenues derived from products and services contributing to absolute positive environmental or social impacts. Products and services that detract from the SDGs are counter-balanced against the positive impact, meaning that a company that is generating some positive impact could ultimately have a negative overall assessment for this pillar if the negative revenues are deemed to outweigh the positive revenues.[6]

3. Corporate Conduct: This pillar captures the degree to which a company's operations and corporate conduct are consistent with the SDGs overall, with a strong emphasis on operational alignment with the SDGs relevant to a given Investment Theme. This pillar recognises that beyond capturing absolute positive impact through products and services, companies' operations and supply chains also have a key role to play in achieving the SDGs, and that for some Investment Themes the main SDG-relevant impacts originate from corporate conduct (e.g., gender diversity, safe work).

The weighting assigned to each of the three pillars varies by Investment Theme. This recognises that the extent to which companies can demonstrate alignment to or progress towards achieving the SDGs can be more directly dependent on either (1) the services and products they offer or could potentially offer – for example, Climate Action and Better Health Investment Themes define a clear business opportunity set – or (2) their operations and corporate conduct – for example, the Gender Equality and Diversity and Safe and Quality Work Investment Themes – define limited business opportunities but are heavily influenced by corporate behaviour.

The resulting SDG Alignment Assessment can be used to construct portfolios, inform investment decisions, or to screen portfolios to identify company engagement targets.

---

6 Note that for certain Investable Themes, there may not be both positive and negative products/services relevant to include in the assessment. In these situations, only the revenue generated from either the negative or the positive products/services is included in the assessment.

Through our analysis and research, we noted that the ability to measure and quantify impact varies significantly across companies and Investment Themes, and that despite the early stage of corporate reporting on the SDGs, we can identify proxy key performance indicators (KPIs) that address many of the sub-goals of the SDGs to support the assessment. Our efforts also focused on defining the KPIs that support measurement and reporting of impact. These KPIs are often industry-specific and address a selected number of the SDGs. Through our evaluation of a comprehensive set of potential KPIs, we have identified the most significant and relevant ones per Investment Theme. For example, assessment of business opportunity capture for the Modern Cities Investment Theme included green building revenues for real estate companies (addressing the green, low-carbon infrastructure opportunity) as well as privacy and data security revenues for technology and information security companies (addressing the opportunity to ensure that connected, smart cities also remain safe). Further, assessment of corporate conduct for the Reduce, Reuse, Recycle Investment Theme encompassed a wide range of indicators, from sustainable forestry certifications for raw material use (relevant to paper products and household products companies) to use of eco-design principles in product design (relevant to semiconductors, technology hardware, textiles, consumer durables, homebuilders, etc.).

Our research supported the value of an industry-relative approach to the SDGs, and that seeking to assess companies on SDG alignment 'overall' or across all 17 of the SDGs has dangers of over-simplifying real-world complexity and reducing the SDGs to a set of compliance-oriented reporting objectives rather than a strategic business-planning framework.

Exclusions

In our view, certain business activities are not compatible with the SDGs (such as involvement in manufacturing controversial weapons or tobacco), and some corporate track records have violated global business and human rights norms in conflict with the ideals of the SDGs (such as evidence of child labour). Our SDG Assessment Methodology renders such companies ineligible for an SDG-aligned portfolio. In our analysis of the constituents of the S&P 500 index, this exclusion rule applies to roughly 4% of the companies.[7]

Applying the SDG Analytical Framework to the S&P 500 Index

We applied the SDG Assessment Methodology to the constituents of the S&P 500 index because this is a highly liquid, commonly invested universe for both

---

7 Index data as of 31 October 2018. See S&P Dow Jones Indices, https://us.spindices.com/ (accessed 28 January 2019).

institutional and retail investors. In doing so, we sought to understand what kinds of SDG alignment can be achieved through investing in this asset class. From this work, we conclude that the current nascent state of corporate SDG practice and disclosure means no single analytical pillar (goals, business opportunity, or corporate conduct) is sufficient to construct concentrated and thematic SDG-aligned portfolios, and that using more than one lens of analysis is necessary to identify SDG-aligned companies within a country-based universe of large-cap companies.

The Current State of Corporate Goals with Respect to SDG Impact

Corporate goal disclosure is key for investors to be able to hold companies accountable to their sustainability commitments and branding, and to parse out those companies with 'genuine' sustainability strategies versus those that are potentially 'greenwashing'. Our findings with respect to SDG-aligned goal disclosure among the S&P 500 constituents have suggested several potential focus areas for future shareholder engagement, including:

- Sectors that lag in the rate of goal disclosure;
- Sectors in which disclosed goals appear to be less relevant to the typical business model;
- SDG areas for which there is less goal adoption; and
- SDG areas for which goals tend to be weaker (i.e. not measurable, time-bound, or business relevant).

In this universe, the proportion of companies disclosing at least one goal in alignment with the SDGs is a clear majority, standing at around 74% (see Figure 8.4). This means that within three years of the SDGs being adopted by the international community, only a quarter of companies had not publicly disclosed any commitments that were relevant to achieving the SDGs. We believe that the SDG framework will prompt more corporate disclosure and target-setting aligned with the 17 SDGs, as well as the re-mapping of existing sustainability goals to explicitly link to the SDGs.

Thirty percent of companies disclosed goals in alignment with 5 or more SDGs and only 3% disclosed goals that aligned with 10 or more SDGs. Together these findings highlight that the vast majority of companies are not attempting to pursue and report against all SDG impact areas, and that the minority of companies that adopt more than one SDG-related goal are likely doing so in a way that is strategically relevant to their business model and operations.

The proportion of companies adopting primarily environmental-focused and social-focused goals is 58% and 56% respectively, signifying that the spread of sustainable impact focus is relatively even across the universe.

Sectors with the most universal rate of at least one SDG-related goal adoption were Utilities (97%), Materials (92%), and Consumer Staples (91%). This perhaps reflects the direct nature of negative sustainable impact traditionally

GICS Sector	At least 1 SDG-aligned goal disclosed	At least 5 SDG-aligned goals disclosed	At least 10 SDG-aligned goals disclosed	At least 1 Environment-aligned goal disclosed	At least 1 Social-aligned goal disclosed
Utilities	97%	52%	3%	79%	79%
Materials	92%	52%	0%	80%	76%
Consumer Staples	91%	64%	9%	91%	76%
Health Care	79%	33%	5%	52%	65%
Real Estate	76%	30%	0%	61%	48%
Industrials	76%	29%	1%	61%	60%
Energy	75%	0%	0%	28%	63%
Information Technology	72%	28%	3%	58%	48%
Communication Services	65%	26%	0%	52%	35%
Consumer Discretionary	63%	27%	7%	58%	39%
Financials	60%	16%	0%	43%	45%
Total (n=506)	**74%**	**30%**	**3%**	**58%**	**56%**

Figure 8.4 Disclosure of rates of SDG-aligned corporate goals/targets by the S&P 500 constituents. *Sources:* Manulife Investment Management, public company disclosures and filings.

associated with these sectors, spurring in recent years the adoption of ESG-related risk management goals, which can now be re-mapped to the SDGs (e.g. carbon efficiency or reduction goals). The lowest rate was among Financials, with around 60% of companies in this sector having disclosed at least one SDG-related goal or target, closely followed by Consumer Discretionary (63%) and Communication Services (65%). The lagging sectors may reflect a historical perception among stakeholders and corporate boards that these sectors were less impactful on sustainability issues, and therefore there is less of a base of sustainability-related goals already adopted or publicly communicated as the SDG framework has taken hold. Again, this seems likely to change given the consumer focus of many companies in these sectors, as the SDGs become better understood by the public.

We noted that some sectors appeared less focused on impact areas considered more intuitive. For example, the Energy sector showed a relatively lower adoption of environmental-related goals (28%) in favour of social-related goals (63%), despite the high contribution of the sector to global greenhouse gas emissions;[8] the Information Technology, Communication Services, and Consumer Discretionary sectors all favoured environmental-related goals over social, despite their primary impacts broadly centring on customers, employees, and supply chain stakeholders.

The universe showed a strong focus on climate- and energy-related goals (those linked to SDG 7 and SDG 13), perhaps reflecting greater attention from the corporate sector to climate change and energy efficiency issues, and greater shareholder engagement on these issues to date (see Figure 8.5). The second highest rate of adoption was SDG 12 (Responsible Consumption and Production), perhaps reflecting greater moves among product manufacturers to leverage sustainability principles for operational efficiencies and improved input costs (e.g., targets around zero-landfill and use of recycled/recovered content), and pressure from stakeholders around product lifecycles (e.g., green certifications for supply chains and for product use).

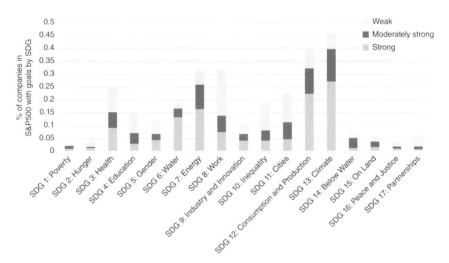

Figure 8.5 Strength of SDG-corporate goal adoption by SDG (506 large-cap US companies). *Sources:* Manulife Investment Management, public company disclosures and filings.

Our specific universe in focus may also explain the goal areas showing very low rates of adoption, with possibly few companies perceiving meaningful business exposure to bottom-of-the-pyramid populations regarding SDGs 1 (No Poverty) and 2 (Zero Hunger), and few companies operating in the

---

8 MSCI research demonstrates that the three most carbon-intensive sectors based on direct/indirect carbon emissions are (in order) Utilities, Materials, and Energy; and that the sectors with the most potential future carbon emissions (based on Mt reserves) are (in order) Energy, Materials, and Utilities: MSCI, 'Beyond Divestment: Using Low Carbon Indexes' (April 2015), p. 11.

agricultural sectors that directly address SDGs 14 (Life below Water) and 15 (Life on Land).

It is surprising to note the low goal adoption related to SDG 5 (Gender Equality) despite a strong discourse on gender equality in the corporate sphere, perhaps reflecting political sensitivities and ambivalence about explicit goal-setting on gender for this universe.

Stronger goal-setting – i.e. measurable, time-bound, and business-relevant – was evident for SDGs 6 (Clean Water and Sanitation), 7 (Affordable and Clean Energy), 12 (Responsible Consumption and Production) and 13 (Climate Action) – the clearly environmental-focused SDGs. For all other areas, less than half of the goals adopted were considered 'strong' according to the SDG Assessment Methodology. Our goals research on the S&P 500 constituents underlines that there is clearly a need for more US large-cap listed companies to step up their level of ambition in relation to the SDGs.

The Current Opportunity Capture of SDG-Related Profit Opportunities

Many current approaches to SDG-aligned investing are focused on identifying companies earning revenues that are aligned with positive impact. This involves mapping companies' disclosed revenue segments to various SDG impact areas based on a qualitative assessment of what counts as a positive contribution.[9] This has generally been feasible when applied to a large, global universe of companies that provides access to a range of geographies and company sizes, given that some SDG impacts can be more available in different regions, and some impactful and innovative business models are found among smaller-cap companies (e.g. pure-play waste management, micro-finance, etc.). However, revenue analysis when applied to the S&P 500 universe only yields a small minority of companies that are substantively leveraging the revenue-related opportunities defined by the SDGs.

Using ISS-ESG's Sustainability Solutions Assessment (oSSA) data, Figure 8.6 illustrates the distribution of positive impact revenues across the universe, with a clustering of positive impact revenues around two environmental themes (mitigating climate change and sustainable energy use), and two social themes (ensuring health and providing basic services). Counter-balancing net negative impact revenues against net positive revenues, only the two social issues remain as an ultimate net positive impact revenue opportunity represented by this universe. The positive revenues associated with mitigating

---

9 Refer to, for example, MSCI, 'MSCI ESG Sustainable Impact Metrics' (https://www.msci.com/esg-sustainable-impact-metrics), and ISS-ESG, 'Sustainability Solutions Assessment' (https://www.issgovernance.com/esg/impact-un-sdg/sustainability-solutions-assessment/) (both accessed 28 January 2019).

	oSSS Achieving sustainable agriculture and forestry	oSSS Conserving water	oSSS Contributing to sustainable energy use	oSSS Promoting sustainable buildings	oSSS Optimising material use	oSSS Mitigating climate change	oSSS Preserving marine ecosystems	oSSS Preserving terrestrial ecosystems	oSSSOther (Environmental)
% Positive Impact of Total Revenues	0.8%	0.1%	2.5%	0.2%	0.2%	3.2%	0.0%	0.2%	0.0%
% Negative Impact of Total Revenues	−0.2%	−1.5%	−15.5%	0.0%	0.0%	−15.1%	−0.8%	−2.1%	0.0%
Net Impact	**0.6%**	**−1.4%**	**−13.0%**	**0.2%**	**0.2%**	**−11.9%**	**−0.7%**	**−1.9%**	**0.0%**

	oSSS Alleviating poverty	oSSS Combating hunger and malnutrition	oSSS Ensuring health	oSSS Delivering education	oSSS Attaining gender equality	oSSS Providing basic services	oSSS Safeguarding peace	oSSSOther (Social)
% Positive Impact of Total Revenues	0.7%	0.2%	15.6%	0.2%	0.2%	8.2%	0.1%	0.0%
% Negative Impact of Total Revenues	−0.1%	0.0%	−4.7%	0.0%	0.0%	0.0%	−1.5%	0.0%
Net Impact	**0.6%**	**0.2%**	**10.9%**	**0.2%**	**0.2%**	**8.2%**	**−1.4%**	**0.0%**

Figure 8.6 Net positive/negative revenue activity by ISS-ESG impact area: S&P 500 constituents' one-year annual revenue as of 31 October 2018.
Sources: Manulife Investment Management, ISS-ESG.

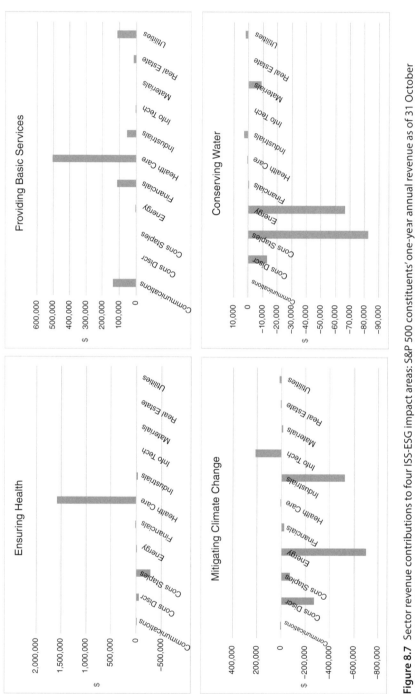

Figure 8.7 Sector revenue contributions to four ISS-ESG impact areas: S&P 500 constituents' one-year annual revenue as of 31 October 2018. *Sources:* Manulife Investment Management, ISS-ESG.

climate change and sustainable energy use are ultimately outweighed by revenues with negative climate/energy impact (e.g. fossil fuel energy systems, combustion-based vehicles, etc.). The data highlights several potentially under-exploited business models and revenue opportunities by US large-cap companies, from water conservation and sustainable buildings to combating hunger, improving nutrition, and delivering education solutions.

Figure 8.7 illustrates that the net positive impact revenues can be quite concentrated into certain sectors, depending on the SDG impact area. Health care dominates both the impact areas of ensuring health and providing basic services. Perhaps less intuitive is that most of the positive contributions to the mitigating climate change impact area centre on the Information Technology sector. The state of play for the conserving water impact area seems dismal, with negatively impactful business models common to the Consumer Staples and Energy sectors in particular.

Such business opportunities and revenue analysis allow both companies and investors to examine whether management teams have truly identified the addressable markets defined by the SDGs. To apply our SDG Assessment Methodology to the S&P 500 universe, we categorised revenues in terms of positive and negative impacts across the Investment Themes. The results demonstrated that, other than the Better Health theme, there are very few 'pureplay' companies available in this universe (i.e. positive impact revenues greater than or equal to 50%), and that meaningful levels of positive impact revenue (greater than or equal to 10% of annual reported revenues) is highly concentrated with a handful of companies for most Investment Themes (see Figure 8.8). These results informed our view that SDG-alignment methodologies for public markets investing must look beyond revenue generation to goals adoption and corporate conduct, so that these methodologies can produce a more holistic view of company SDG alignment and have broad application and relevance for a variety of investors.

Areas in which Corporate Operational Conduct Is Most Strongly Aligned with SDG Impact

Using extensive data sets of corporate sustainability performance metrics, our SDG Assessment Methodology defines the selected metrics that we believe can indicate, either directly or by proxy, the strength of a company's operational alignment with the various Investment Themes. Figure 8.9 highlights that 'very strong' alignment also remains quite concentrated among a high-performing minority in the universe.

The marginally stronger levels of corporate operational conduct for the Reduce, Reuse, Recycle; Climate Action; and Clean Water Investment Themes (20%, 30%, and 31% of strong/moderately strong performance, respectively) seems consistent with the trend noted earlier that goals adopted pertaining to these themes tend to be stronger (where goals are adopted) – suggesting a

	Shared Prosperity	Better Health	Safe and Quality Work	Gender Equality and Diversity	Clean Water	Climate Action	Modern Cities	Reduce, Reuse, Recycle
>=50% positive impact revenue (n)	7	56	0	0	1	4	4	0
% of universe	1.4%	11.1%	0.0%	0.0%	0.2%	0.8%	0.8%	0.0%
>=10% positive impact revenue (n)	28	79	4	0	5	28	24	4
% of universe	5.5%	15.6%	0.8%	0.0%	1.0%	5.5%	4.7%	0.8%

Figure 8.8 Companies with high positive impact revenues, S&P 500 constituents. *Source:* Manulife Investment Management.

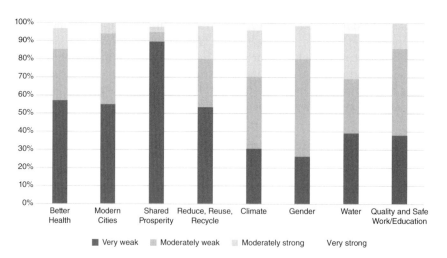

Figure 8.9 Strength of corporate conduct alignment by Investment Theme for S&P 500 constituents as of 5 October 2018. *Source:* Manulife Investment Management.

correlation between stronger goal adoption and actual company follow-through with performance metrics and reporting. This relationship does not appear to hold for the Gender Equality and Diversity Investment Theme, where we observe around 20% of companies had 'very strong' or 'strong' practices on issues such as gender diversity in boards, management teams, anti-discrimination, and diversity policies. This suggests that corporate attention in this impact area has not been entirely lacking, despite the lower rates of explicit gender-related goal adoption noted previously.

The lower levels of 'very strong' or 'strong' corporate conduct alignment for the Better Health, Modern Cities, and Shared Prosperity Investment Themes may be explained by strong industry tilts for these themes, with SDG impacts and opportunities being directly geared towards certain clusters of industries, meaning that fewer companies in the universe are likely to have strategic interests or disclosure for the relevant corporate conduct metrics (e.g. among other things, the Better Health Investment Theme looks at initiatives around health care and medicines access, drug pricing and donations, and organic products).

Across this universe, it is possible to find companies with strong goals, substantial revenue alignment, and strongly aligned corporate performance, but the overall quantity is relatively few and the results can be mixed. Some companies may show strong corporate operational conduct but may not have an explicitly stated goal or intention; other companies may have strong revenue generation in an impact area but not match this with evidence of corporate operational alignment. We believe this is an expected outcome for this type of universe, and that expanding scope to a global universe of stocks would produce quite differentiated results. We posit that universe selection is crucial in determining the degree of SDG alignment that it is possible for an investor to achieve. In universes where not very much strong or direct alignment is currently available, the emphasis of an investment solution for that universe should be on tilting towards SDG impact or on company engagement. To support engagement efforts, the framework allows an investor to measure, monitor, and track company and universe progress over time.

What SDG Developments Can We Expect in the Public Markets Investor Community in 2020 and Beyond?

Looking forward, we see continued growth opportunity for SDG-aligned investing; indeed, many reports already cite the growing demand for impact investing opportunities more broadly.[10] The primary obstacles to increased SDG-aligned investing include risk concerns, performance worries, and a

---

10 For example, the 2016 Canadian Impact Investment Trends Report, which surveyed 87 organisations, reported that there were CAD$9.2 billion in assets under management (AUM) in impact investments at the end of 2015. This represents a more than doubling in AUM from 2013, when assets were measured at $4.1 billion. In the UK, the Implementation Taskforce has been charged with bringing recommendations from 'Growing a Culture of Social Impact Investing in the UK' to life; see Implementation Taskforce, 'Growing a Culture of Impact Investing in the UK', https://www.grow-impact-investing.org/ (28 January 2019).

shortage of viable products/investment vehicles. However, we propose that the market will rise to these challenges and offer tailored solutions that respond to these concerns, thereby allowing SDG-aligned investing to flourish.

SDG-aligned Investing Is Expected to Become Easier

Large financial firms are signalling their intention to enter the field of SDG-aligned investing. Generally, this can be seen as a positive development, as their participation in this space is likely to lead to the development of credible and scalable SDG-aligned frameworks to help measure corporate impact, a wider breadth of investment solutions that align with a sustainable future, and potentially a new influx of capital into SDG-aligned investing – particularly in the public markets.

We envisage increased effort and coordination among financial market partici-pants to measure and incentivise corporate behaviour that promotes a sustainable future. For example, the World Benchmarking Alliance, in which Manulife Investment Management is participating, has set out to develop benchmarks to compare company performance on the SDGs, which are designed to further empower investors to allocate capital towards the SDGs. The benchmarks will be free to use and will be based on input from a multi-stakeholder dialogue. In addition to this, other initiatives related to SDG impact measurement have emerged as resources for investors to use, including the Sustainable Development Goals Investment Initiative (SDGI)[11] and the PRI SDG Advisory Committee.[12]

As the investment industry attempts to make SDG-aligned investing scala-ble, there will be different approaches and solutions made available to inves-tors. Investors in turn will want assurance that the solutions are credible, and that the market has maintained integrity in these offerings. It is important for investors to recognise that there will be varying levels of positive impact embedded in the investment solutions depending on asset class, investable universe, and the framework chosen for SDG-alignment or impact measure-ment. To properly navigate the various SDG-aligned investing solutions, investors will need to assess the methodology and approach taken to measure SDG alignment to determine if there is sufficient impact or SDG-alignment achieved for their purposes. The challenges around identifying corporate SDG-related intentions and conducting impact measurement will persist for investors, especially those focused on liquid investments delivering market-rate returns.

---

11 SDGI, 'SDGI Launch at GIIN Investor Forum', https://www.sdgi-nl.org/ (accessed 28 January 2019).

12 UN PRI, 'SDG Advisory Committee Terms of Reference', https://www.unpri.org/Uploads/u/i/o/Sustainable-Development-Goals-advisory-committee---Terms-of-Reference.pdf (accessed 28 January 2019).

Some questions that may help make this determination of whether an SDG- or impact-oriented investment solution is sufficient include:

- Does the methodology anchor the analysis beyond the interests of the company's shareholders/bondholders, to those of a wider stakeholder group?
- Does the solution aim to deliver purist intentional impact (e.g. only pure-play companies can be included), or is the focus on impact tilting (e.g. moving incrementally towards companies that show relatively strong SDG alignment)?

Corporate Reporting on the SDGs Will Improve

Another emerging trend is improved corporate reporting on the SDGs. Many companies are just beginning to think about their approach to these global issues. As such, corporate reporting of goals/targets that are relevant to the SDGs remains at an early stage. The goals we researched for the S&P 500 constituents went beyond those explicitly linked to SDGs, and much of the data collected related to goals already disclosed as part of an existing ESG/sustainability corporate strategy. Over the course of 2018 we observed a marked increase in the rate of company reporting on the SDGs among the S&P 500 constituents, and expect this trend to continue in coming years, as well as the conscious mapping of pre-existing corporate sustainability goals to the SDG framework.

The entrance of large asset managers into the SDG-aligned investing space is expected to help spur improved corporate disclosure and measurement of key metrics related to the SDGs. In this regard, we note the potential impact of Climate Action 100+, a five-year global collaborative engagement initiative that as of year-end 2018 had convened more than 310 investors managing over US\$32 trillion in AUM to focus on engaging with the world's largest greenhouse gas emitters about the Paris Agreement goals.[13] The first year of the initiative showed that the most common ask of companies from this investor group was the adoption of carbon reduction targets, underlining the importance that investors place on corporate goal-setting.

Constructive Dialogue or Engagement with Companies Is Necessary to Achieve the SDGs

Large institutional investors are engaging with companies on important sustainability issues at a volume and scale not seen previously in the investment industry. Accordingly, as this trend continues to gain momentum, engagement

---

13 Refer to Climate Action 100+, 'Global Investors Driving Business Transition', http://www .climateaction100.org/ (accessed 28 January 2019).

with companies on the SDGs will become a key area of sustainable impact for the asset management industry itself.

At Manulife Investment Management, we leverage engagement as a constructive exercise to help promote positive change among companies and to enhance the long-term value of our clients' investments. Rather than divesting a company in the first instance due to sustainability concerns, we believe we can help achieve these objectives as an active owner, working on behalf of our clients. Further, as an active, long-term-oriented investment manager, we are motivated to ensure that systemic risks are addressed and that the opportunities of a global economy undergoing tremendous change are captured. We recognise that large asset managers need to provide the long-term capital that enables companies to address and adapt to these systemic risks and opportunities.

In this context, we believe the SDGs will increasingly be adopted by long-term, active investment managers as an engagement framework for influencing corporates towards a more systemically stable, sustainable economy.

A Call to Action

The SDGs provide a roadmap for the role that investors can play in moving capital markets towards sustainable development outcomes. Manulife Investment Management's SDG Assessment Methodology is one of our contributions to this movement, which aims to facilitate SDG-aligned investing to take its place on the ever-increasing spectrum of responsible and sustainable investing styles. By basing our research on corporate public disclosure, we aim to encourage greater corporate disclosure of the goals, business opportunity capture, and corporate operational conduct in alignment with the SDGs.

As our research has demonstrated, SDG-aligned investing is in its early days for public markets. However, we expect to see increased scale and efficiency as both public companies and investors pay more attention to the SDGs. We are encouraged by the efforts made towards SDG impact measurement by the investor community and foresee that more thematic and impact funds will be made available to both institutional and retail investors who wish to consciously allocate their capital towards SDG achievement.

We believe employing our SDG Assessment Methodology will lead to different outcomes when applied to global versus country-specific investable universes, or large-cap versus small-cap strategies. A global strategy may be able to achieve more direct and measurable impact, whereas a country-specific strategy may achieve more of a tilt towards impact. Regardless of the strategy employed, investors need to continue to push for improved corporate disclosure and action that promotes the attainment of the SDGs and focus on building their own capabilities to channel investments appropriately towards alignment with the SDGs.

Our call to action is two-fold: firstly, we urge companies to consider the opportunities embedded in the SDGs for their own strategic growth plan and value proposition over the long term. Sustainability is often seen through the lens of achieving efficiencies, for example reducing water and energy consumption. While these are important operational metrics on which to focus that can yield financial benefit, we encourage companies to broaden their vision on the business opportunities that a focus on sustainability can bring. Companies should set and disclose clear goals that communicate how their business will address these long-term opportunities. They should consistently look at the products and services they offer to determine how these may deliver positive social and environmental impact.

Similarly, we encourage investors to broaden their investment time horizon and scope of vision. Typically, investors take a risk-based approach to using ESG (environmental, social, and governance) factors in their analysis and decision making. By broadening the lens of ESG-investing to include an analysis of SDG-alignment in creating investment products, determining asset allocation strategies, and measuring performance, investors can support public companies to address the strategic SDG-related opportunities available and align the investment management industry itself with a long-term sustainable future.

Acknowledgements

The contributors wish to acknowledge the assistance of Hideki Suzuki of Manulife Investment Management in preparing this chapter.

Disclaimer

The opinions expressed herein represent the current, good faith views of the author(s) at the time of publication and are provided for limited purposes, are not definitive investment advice, and should not be relied on as such. The information presented in this material has been developed internally and/or obtained from sources believed to be reliable; however, Manulife Investment Management does not guarantee the accuracy, adequacy, or completeness of such information. Predictions, opinions, and other information contained in this material are subject to change continually and without notice of any kind and may no longer be true after the date indicated. Any forward-looking statements speak only as of the date they are made, and Manulife Investment

Management assumes no duty to and does not undertake to update forward-looking statements. Forward-looking statements are subject to numerous assumptions, risks, and uncertainties, which change over time. Actual results could differ materially from those anticipated in forward-looking statements. Individual portfolio management teams may have different views and opinions that are subject to change without notice. The historical success or Manulife Investment Management's belief in the future success of any of the strategies is not indicative of, and has no bearing on, future results.

9

The Significance of Sustainable Development Goals for Government Credit Quality

Alastair Wilson

Market participants are increasingly paying attention to the potential impact of their investments on society at large. In part, this is based on a view that 'sustainability' and 'responsibility' should play a more important role, with decisions linked to environmental, social, and governance (ESG) factors.

But there is also a growing body of research exploring the impact of such issues on economic and financial returns. In particular, the assumption that social responsibility comes at the price of lower nominal financial return is challenged by evidence that ESG considerations affect the level and variability of returns over the full investment term, not just at some point in the distant future.

In its analysis of government credit, Moody's Investors Service takes into account a wide range of ESG considerations, many of which directly relate to the sustainable development goals (SDGs).

Our global sovereign rating methodology is based on four key factors: a country's economic strength, institutional strength, government fiscal strength, and susceptibility to event risk. While it is rarely possible to identify the precise impact of a single SDG or ESG element on a particular sovereign's rating, the considerations behind both are embedded in our analysis, as they influence the factors that drive government credit quality.

Our sovereign ratings incorporate the foreseeable credit implications of progress towards the SDGs, or the absence thereof. When SDG-related risks will materialise over long time periods, and uncertainty surrounding their credit effects and the potential mitigating actions that governments may take is particularly high, their credit implications will not be fully captured in Moody's current ratings.

In this chapter, we explain how, in Moody's view, the SDGs and the ESG factors to which they are linked underscore sovereign credit quality, including by fostering sustained growth, reducing income inequality, supporting social stability, promoting stronger governance, and mitigating environmental risk. We also illustrate the observed quantitative relationship between ESG

Sustainable Development Goals: Harnessing Business to Achieve the SDGs through Finance, Technology, and Law Reform, First Edition. Edited by Julia Walker, Alma Pekmezovic, and Gordon Walker.

considerations and rating factors. There will be cases where an ESG factor exerts a material influence on a particular government's rating, although its overall impact on sovereign credit quality may be modest.

At the outset, it is important to take into account the relationships between individual ESG factors. The quality of a country's governance encompasses a broad range of matters, including management of its natural resources and environmental risks. The strength and resilience of an economy can bolster the ability of policymakers to pursue social objectives, and changes in society can influence economic strength over time. Meanwhile, social factors partly determine and can constrain governance choices and outcomes.

Environmental Preservation Influences Credit Quality, Including Through the Impact of Climate Change on Growth and Institutions' Resilience to It

Environmental considerations reflect the physical conditions in which societies operate both now and, to the extent it can be foreseen, in the future. The latter draws in the impact of climate change, as well as the global transition to less carbon-intensive economic development. From a credit perspective, environmental risks primarily relate to the economic and fiscal impact of shocks specific to each sovereign's environment, and stem from overall environmental living conditions such as access to clean water and pollution. Shocks could include either predictable or unforeseen natural disasters, or other phenomena that threaten the availability of resources. Planned policies by various governments that would allow progress towards the SDGs on climate action, life below water and life on land, sustainable cities, and consumption, amongst others, can mitigate climate change and a related deterioration in credit quality for those sovereigns.

Weather-related shocks such as climate change – induced natural disasters can push up government debt in the short term and result in lower growth in the long term, as we have seen in small island economies across the world. Frequent natural disasters lead to heightened volatility in growth, which is a sign of low shock absorption by the economy, a negative feature for sovereign creditworthiness. Long-term climate trends such as rising sea levels place coastal areas at risk; increasing pollution and deteriorating urban living conditions can also curb growth potential and lead to structurally higher government expenditure. Changes in energy and food availability can exacerbate growing social demands.

In general, economies concentrated in sectors reliant on favourable weather conditions, like agriculture or tourism, are particularly exposed to environmental risks. Cambodia, Ethiopia, Kenya, and Rwanda are examples of countries where agriculture accounts for more than 30% of gross domestic product (GDP).

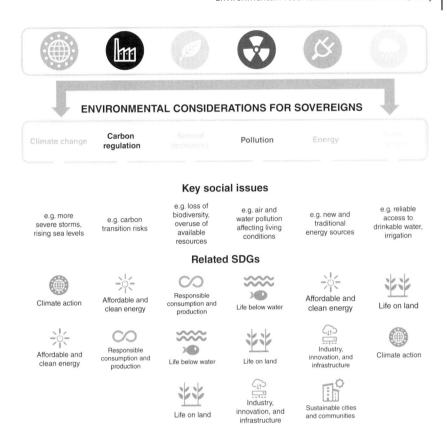

Environmental Considerations for Sovereigns. *Note:* Listed examples of social issues and related SDGs are illustrative rather than exhaustive.

The Maldives and the Seychelles have weather-dependent tourism industries, representing over 25% of GDP.

There are numerous examples of sovereign credit profiles that are influenced by environmental considerations. The economic and fiscal impact of droughts and other natural disasters resulting from shifting weather phenomena such as El Niño and La Niña can be seen all over the globe, from Papua New Guinea, to Peru, to South Africa. India's growth potential is hampered by the variability of monsoons, exacerbated by poor irrigation in large parts of the agricultural sector. In 2016, a cyclone hit Fiji, resulting in losses of close to 20% of GDP. And hurricanes regularly result in lost economic output in many Caribbean islands. In each case, the impact on medium-term growth to some extent influences Moody's assessment of economic strength.

Governments that are highly exposed to climate change tend to have lower ratings and less robust institutions, but the quantitative correlation is weak. Some relatively exposed sovereigns, such as Japan and Singapore, are also highly rated, whereas some little exposed sovereigns, such as Jordan, have lower ratings for different reasons.

The correlation between Moody's assessment of a sovereign's economic strength and measures of environmental exposure, such as the Notre Dame Global Adaptation Initiative (ND-GAIN) exposure index, is very loose, illustrating that low or very low economic strength may reflect a variety of factors unrelated to exposure to climate change. That said, while the correlation is low it is not negligible: amongst the 20% of sovereigns with the highest exposure to climate change according to Moody's, more than two-fifths have low or very low economic strength in our assessment, on a 15-rung scale from 'Very High (+)' to 'Very Low (–)' compared with under 35% amongst all rated sovereigns. (The credit ratings and factor scores referenced in this chapter are as of 7 March 2019.)

By contrast, we have found a stronger correlation between measures of environmental vulnerability, which consider not just exposure but also capacity to respond to climate change, as well as our assessment of sovereigns' institutional strength. This observed link likely reflects the fact that countries with stronger institutions also tend to have greater adaptive capacity. For example, Japan is highly exposed to environmental risk but has greater adaptive capacity than many other nations, which reduces its overall vulnerability.

Environmental vulnerability is also negatively correlated with economic strength. The more vulnerable sovereigns have relatively weak capacity to absorb economic shocks generally, and climate change-related shocks in particular. These sovereigns tend to have small economies, low incomes, and low and/or volatile growth. Rwanda, for instance, is reliant on weather-dependent subsistence agriculture. And while Cambodia has a large textile sector that is not particularly vulnerable to climate change, half the labour force is employed in agriculture and susceptible to large fluctuations in incomes depending on weather conditions.

Overall, environmentally vulnerable sovereigns have lower ratings from Moody's. The median rating of the 20% of sovereigns with the highest environmental vulnerability is B2, four notches below the median rating of all rated sovereigns.

Social Risks Such as Poverty and Inequality Feed into Economic and Institutional Strength

Social considerations encompass threats to sovereigns' credit profiles that derive from society's characteristics and structure. That may be because of the direct impact of those characteristics on economic, fiscal, or institutional strength, or because of the effect of social changes on those key credit features.

Social considerations include fiscal, economic, and political implications of social conditions, such as poverty, inequality, or violence and crime; the quality of education and the extent to which it supports an economy's competitiveness and flexibility; the availability of adequate housing to support working populations; and the mainly policy-related credit implications of societal tensions resulting from lack of political freedom and representation.

Low female labour participation and/or a lack of schooling and training can limit a country's economic growth potential. Government policies to increase

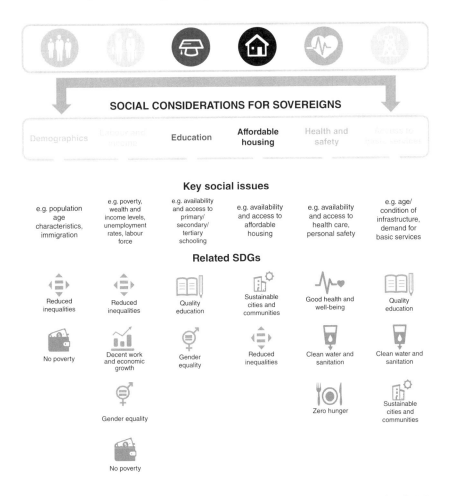

Social Considerations for Sovereigns. *Note:* Listed examples of social issues and related SDGs are illustrative rather than exhaustive.

female skills have had success in boosting productivity growth, while measures to raise female mobility and change attitudes to female education have helped to create broader access to education. Higher education amongst women may be associated with reduced fecundity, curbing labour supply growth, while also supporting female productivity.

Beside gender-focused policies, higher quality of education tends to boost workers' ability to build and use more innovative capital equipment and operational techniques, and to adjust to changing work demands, raising productivity growth rates. Simply boosting the number of years spent in education does not in itself lift worker capabilities. Higher incomes, reflecting more advanced levels of education and productivity, also give workers the capacity to move geographically to emerging sectors and between sectors, potentially improving the allocation of human capital in the economy.

Rising income inequality can damage sovereign credit quality by weighing on the strength and sustainability of economic growth, spurring higher fiscal expenditure to support lower-income households, weakening government institutions, and encouraging corruption or law breaking at either extreme of the income scale. In combination with increased wealth, it can also lead to demands for new types of policies, governments, and political parties, with implications, positive or negative, for policy effectiveness and potential growth. In Chile, for example, the emergence of an affluent middle class with higher expectations for public services has put strains on official finances. At lower levels of economic development, the Kenyan government's desire to broaden health care coverage and to provide housing to an increasingly urbanised population is contributing to fiscal pressures. In South Africa, the longstanding social aim of redistributing land risks undermining investment in the near to medium term, set against longer-run benefits of higher, more inclusive growth if implemented effectively.

Where politicians are perceived to be unresponsive to emerging social demands, lack of representation can result in sudden and, at times, violent pushes for greater freedom, increasing political turmoil and cooling economic growth. Meanwhile, chronically high levels of violence may reduce investment and drag on output. When it results in sharp and sustained increases in government spending on security, violence can also hurt a sovereign's fiscal strength.

Pent-up social demands may take years, sometimes decades, to crystallise as credit risks. Poverty and lack of political representation had long been concerns in the Middle East and North Africa, but it was not until 2010 that these social issues came to the fore in most of the region. Starting in Tunisia, political unrest and turmoil spread to several other countries, including Bahrain, Egypt, Libya, and Syria, almost simultaneously. This unrest led to regime change in several of the affected countries, increasing political risk and denting economic growth. In Moody's view, the measures taken by several of the governments, in part to address some of the social demands – including very large increases in the public sector wage bill in Oman and Tunisia – have weakened the fiscal strength of these sovereigns.

Quantitatively, we have found that poverty – measured by the percentage of the population living on less than $3.20 a day, in 2011 prices, adjusted for living cost differentials – is negatively correlated with sovereign ratings and factor scores. Countries with higher levels of poverty tend to have lower ratings. The correlation is not very strong, in part because the measure of incomes in Moody's sovereign rating methodology is purchasing power parity (PPP) GDP per capita – an average metric rather than a distributional one. That said, the average and distributional measures are correlated. And there is a growing body of literature demonstrating the link between income equality and long-run growth, and, as a result, economic resilience.

The sovereigns with a high prevalence of poverty are all low-rated by Moody's: amongst the 10 with the most elevated poverty rate, Côte d'Ivoire and Bangladesh have the highest rating (Ba3) and the median rating is B2. Indonesia and the Philippines are two sovereigns with relatively high ratings (both Baa2) but also relatively widespread poverty. These two countries' credit strengths include large economies, strong growth potential, and moderate debt burdens. Nonetheless, that large shares of their populations have very low incomes is a long-term credit constraint for both.

While poverty is negatively correlated with our assessment of overall economic strength, it is positively correlated with growth potential – one element of economic strength. Poorer nations tend to expand more rapidly than richer ones, in part because they are likely to have younger, faster-growing populations and lower productivity levels with scope to catch up. Still, and despite faster growth potential, the capacity of poorer sovereigns to absorb economic shocks tends to be lower. Ethiopia is one of the poorest countries rated by Moody's, with a PPP GDP per capita in 2017 of just above $2,000. Its economic strength largely stems from its high growth potential: it was expected that annual real GDP growth will average 9% in 2012–2018, amongst the highest of all rated sovereigns.

Poorer countries tend to have weaker institutions, partly because a higher share of the population being in extreme poverty is likely to hamper policy effectiveness. Poverty can also reflect a high prevalence of corruption, an indication of weak institutions. Further, weak institutions raise the risk of conflict, which lowers the chances of a country escaping poverty. Moody's assessment of institutional strength for the median sovereign amongst the 20% poorest is in the low range.

Strong Institutions Are Closely Related to Ratings and Ratings Factors

Strong governance is part of strong institutions. Governance relates to the quality, predictability, transparency, and effectiveness of a sovereign's institutions. Moody's looks at both the political institutions responsible for developing and implementing social, economic, and fiscal policy and the broader institutional framework that determines important credit features such as control of corruption, respect for the rule of law, and transparency of public actions and data. Respect for the rule of law is a key indicator of willingness to pay debt obligations, and weak legal institutions, in our view, will generally result in lower investment and growth. The quality, availability, and transparency of public data influence the quality of policymaking and the accountability and credibility of policymakers.

Since weak governance raises the risk that political tensions or conflict have an impact on a country's economy or public finances, governance risks are also relevant to our assessment of political risk.

Argentina highlights the relevance of weak governance to sovereign ratings. A history of unsustainable macro- and micro-economic policies and a highly contentious political process led to a sovereign bond default in 2014, after the country's unwillingness to abide by certain US court rulings impeded disbursements to bondholders. After a new administration came to power in 2015 and began to address many of those institutional shortcomings, the default was remedied and the country's credit profile – and its ratings – strengthened.

At a higher rating level, robust governance supports Thailand's sovereign credit quality. Despite repeated coups and sudden changes in political regimes, Thailand's institutions are, in Moody's opinion, relatively strong and consistently deliver transparent, predictable, and effective policies.

Strong governance and strong credit profiles are closely related. The highest-rated sovereign issuers – for example, those in western Europe – tend also to have the most developed, transparent, and effective institutional frameworks.

The Worldwide Governance Indicator of government effectiveness is part of Moody's assessment of a sovereign's institutional strength and, as a result, highly correlated with it. It is also highly correlated with ratings and economic strength. The latter relationship suggests that effective governance increases an economy's shock absorption capacity; it may also be that high incomes, strong growth potential, and high competitiveness – all features of high economic strength – bolster government effectiveness.

Higher government effectiveness is also relatively closely related to lower susceptibility to event risk. Effective governance is generally associated with

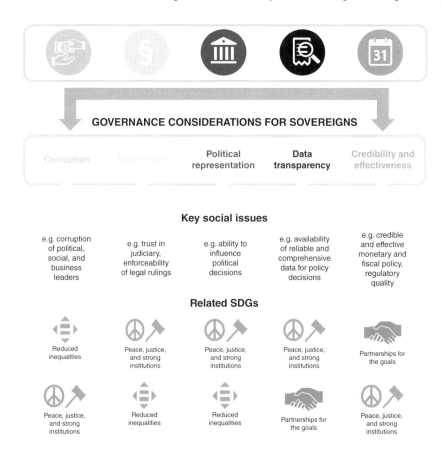

Governance Considerations for Sovereigns. *Note:* Listed examples of social issues and related SDGs are illustrative rather than exhaustive.

low political risk, contributes to low government liquidity risk, and suggests strong supervision and regulation of the banking sector, reducing related risks for sovereigns. To the extent that effective governance involves the build-up of external buffers and because perceptions of effective governance reduce the risk of capital flight, it is also likely to be associated with lower external vulnerability. Singapore, the sovereign with the highest government effectiveness score, demonstrates all of these features. For those sovereigns with very low government effectiveness, event risk is often high, as is the case for the Republic of the Congo and Venezuela.

Looking at data transparency as one indicator of governance, we see a moderate correlation between sovereign ratings and budget transparency (as measured by the Open Budget Index, produced by the International Budget

Partnership), indicating that countries with open budget processes tend to be rated higher.

Brazil has one of the most transparent budget processes worldwide, but Moody's assesses its fiscal strength to be 'Low', based on the country's comparatively high debt burden and low debt affordability. We have looked at fiscal transparency based on a range of surveys and similarly found that sovereigns with low fiscal transparency typically have low ratings. There are a few outliers with low budget transparency and relatively high ratings, such as Botswana and China. To the extent that low transparency impedes policymakers' accountability and, as a result, policy effectiveness, we take it into account in our assessment of China's institutional strength and rating. We adjust our assessment of China's institutional strength downwards to reflect the size of the challenge that the authorities face in managing high debt levels, in particular amongst state-owned enterprises, while maintaining their targets for robust growth. Conversely, we take South Africa's very high budget transparency into account in our assessment of institutional strength.

SDGs Influence Government Credit Quality Through Different Channels, to Varying Degrees

In conclusion, there are many influences on sovereign ratings, some – but not all – of which are closely related to SDG and ESG considerations.

Of the three ESG themes, governance has the strongest relationship with both sovereign ratings and our four credit factors. Besides having an SDG devoted to it, it is also a pivotal driver of the ability of national authorities to implement the other 16 SDGs.

Environmental and social factors can also influence Moody's assessment of economic, institutional, and, to a lesser extent, fiscal strength. In that context, progress towards each of the SDGs has the potential to shape credit quality through different credit channels, to varying degrees. Gender equality can support economic strength if it boosts workforce participation. Provision of affordable and clean energy could initially carry a fiscal cost for governments, but also promote more sustainable growth.

The quantitative relationship of environmental and social factors with susceptibility to event risk is weaker, reflecting the fact that the events that may weigh on a government's credit profile are wide-ranging. Still, in some instances, ESG factors may drive particular risk events that affect a sovereign's credit fundamentals.

ESG considerations are being embedded into financial asset prices. Sovereign ratings already factor in these important influences and governments' credit profiles will continue to be shaped by changes in the significance of ESG factors.

Part III

Technology, Innovation, and Entrepreneurship

10

FinTech for Financial Inclusion: Driving Sustainable Growth

Dirk A. Zetzsche, Ross P. Buckley, and Douglas W. Arner

Introduction

Between 2010 and 2017, 1.2 billion people gained a financial or mobile money account for the first time, with most located in developing countries. But much remains to be done: as of 2017, 1.7 billion adults still lacked access to an account – some 31% of the world's people.[1]

From 2010 to 2017, much of this progress came from the impact of technology in finance. For example, mobile money has played a significant role in increasing financial inclusion in Kenya and East Africa.[2] China has also moved in recent years from an essentially traditional financial system to perhaps the world's most digitised financial system.[3] India has similarly dramatically increased financial access by building the infrastructure for a new digital economy ('India Stack'), which has led to approximately 350 million people gaining accounts. Along with similar developments in Russia, these four economies account for the vast majority of the increases in financial inclusion since 2010.

---

1 A. Demirguc-Kunt, L. Klapper, D. Singer, S. Ansar, and J. Hess, 'The Global Findex Database 2017: Measuring Financial Inclusion and the Fintech Revolution', World Bank (April 2018).

2 F. Pasti, 'Mobile Money as a Driver of Financial Inclusion in Sub-Saharan Africa', GSMA (June 7, 2017), https://www.gsma.com/mobilefordevelopment/programme/mobile-money/mobile-money-driver-financial-inclusion-sub-saharan-africa/; A. Beyene Fanta, et al., 'The Role of Mobile Money in Financial Inclusion in the SADC Region' (Policy Research Paper No. 03/2016, FinMark Trust), https://www.finmark.org.za/wp-content/uploads/2016/12/mobile-money-and-financial-inclusion-in-sadc.pdf; The World Bank, '2012 Information and Communications for Development: Maximizing Mobile' (2012), ch. 4.

3 J. Chien, 'Key Lessons for Policymakers from China's Financial Inclusion Experience', World Bank (15 February 2018), http://blogs.worldbank.org/psd/key-lessons-policymakers-china-s-financial-inclusion-experience; see also on the regulatory approaches that delivered this transformation: W. Zhou, D. Arner, and R. P. Buckley, 'Regulation of Digital Financial Services in China: Last Mover Advantage' *Tsinghua China Law Review* 8, no. 1 (2015): 25.

Sustainable Development Goals: Harnessing Business to Achieve the SDGs through Finance, Technology, and Law Reform, First Edition. Edited by Julia Walker, Alma Pekmezovic, and Gordon Walker.

These developments are part of a global phenomenon encapsulated under the term *FinTech* – financial technology. In fact, FinTech is a new term for a long-standing phenomenon – the application of technology to financial services.[4] This chapter examines why FinTech is important for sustainable development and which steps regulators and governments need to undertake to develop a comprehensive strategy to support digital financial transformation, underpinning both financial inclusion and sustainable balanced growth more broadly.

Financial Inclusion and Sustainability: Introducing the Long-Term Perspective

This part will examine the following questions: why focus on FinTech; how does it relate to financial inclusion, and how does FinTech for financial inclusion relate to sustainability, the key criterion of the United Nations' Sustainable Development Goals[5] (UNSDGs)?

Financial Inclusion: Why It Matters

Financial inclusion involves the delivery of financial services at affordable cost to all sections of society.[6] It improves individuals' livelihoods by enabling them to manage their financial obligations efficiently, reduces poverty, and supports wider economic growth.[7] It does so, first, by increasing the efficiency of daily life: electronic payments allow people to pay bills without taking time off work to physically do so. Second, it reduces individuals' vulnerability. For instance, facilitating saving allows people to invest in their education, health, and micro-businesses. Third, financial inclusion allows peoples' financial risks to be shifted into the financial system, where they can be socialised and diversified. For instance, breadwinner insurance can prevent people from falling back into poverty. Fourth, financial inclusion supports economic growth through increasing the financial resources to support real economic activity, particularly for individuals and small and medium-sized businesses (SMEs).

---

4 D. W. Arner, J. Barberis, and R. P. Buckley, 'The Evolution of FinTech: A New Post-Crisis Paradigm?' *Georgetown Journal of International Law* 47, no. 4 (2016): 1271.
5 See the United Nations Sustainable Development Goals, online https://www.un.org/sustainabledevelopment.
6 FATF, 'FATF Guidance: Anti-Money Laundering and Terrorist Financing Measures and Financial Inclusion' (February 2013), 12.
7 Center for Financial Inclusion, 'About Financial Inclusion 2020', http://www.centerforfinancialinclusion.org/fi2020/about-fi-2020; A. Dermish, C. Kneiding, P. Leishman, P., and I. Mas, 'Branchless and Mobile Banking Solutions for the Poor: A Survey of the Literature' *Innovations* 6, no. 4 (2012): 81, 93.

Two Sides of the Same Coin

Financial inclusion is a crucial element to address today's global challenges, including poverty, inequality, climate, environmental degradation, prosperity, peace, and justice. FinTech is central to this process. Financial access is one way to escape or reduce the burden of the challenges of life, including sickness, crime, poverty, unemployment, age, and others.[8] Individuals excluded from the financial system lack tools to manage and prepare for such risks. For instance, farmers selling goods without access to electronic payment systems need to worry about theft; many will seek to consume what they can on the spot rather than taking the risks. Health insurance covers medical costs crucial to secure one's long-term working capacity. Savings could fund the kids' educations and function as provisions for old age. All of these are long-term goals. If we exclude individuals from the financial system, we take from those individuals the opportunity to think, plan, and *act* long-term. Where risks that could be avoided, hedged, transformed, or socialised through the financial system materialise for financial exclusion, we force the excluded to think and act *short-term*, often in an unsustainable manner. Hence, financial inclusion and sustainability are two sides of the same coin and both aim at the same goal: promoting prosperity while balancing risks.[9]

FinTech as a Tool for the SDGs

In light of the inherent connection between the financial inclusion agenda and the UNSDGs, at first one would expect to find financial inclusion listed as a UNSDG. However, FinTech is not an objective in itself. Nor is financial inclusion. Rather, both are *tools* in an effort to build a sustainable future. Table 10.1[10] lays out in which way FinTech for financial inclusion could contribute directly or indirectly to the 17 UNSDGs. If financial markets have achieved a sufficient degree of maturity, providing payment services, long-term (project and firm) financing, insurance services and savings/investment products, supporting financial inclusion – in particular through FinTech – could indeed contribute to *all* of the 17 UNSDGs.

It becomes evident from Table 10.1 that financial inclusion is probably one of, if not the most, important of the intermediate steps that economies must

---

8 These are listed as key challenges in the United Nations Sustainable Development Goals, online https://www.un.org/sustainabledevelopment (last accessed December 3, 2018).
9 This is the UNSDG's core objective, see idem.
10 Table 10.1 draws on the authors' own research and experience with FinTech projects. The insight that digital financial services are consistent with the UNSDGs is unanimously accepted. See, for instance, United Nations, 'Digital Finance and the SDGs', http://www.uncdf.org/mm4p/dfs-and-the-sdgs (detailing how UNCDF contributes to the SDGs with digital finance).

Table 10.1 How FT4FI Could Further the UNSDGs.

Nr	Goals	Impact Direct=D Indirect=I	How FT4FI Can Further Goal
1	No poverty	I	Allow for online financing, including credit and crowdfunding; create new income opportunities through online markets and payments; reduce impact of disasters with local impact
2	Zero hunger	I	Enhance financial stability; stabilise cash flows through saving and lending
3	Good health and well-being	I	Provide health insurance and financial stability
4	Quality education	I	Provide financial planning and savings for school fees
5	Gender equality	D	Strengthening female entrepreneurship and financial controls
6	Clean water and sanitation	I	Provide financing for development and maintenance of infrastructure; further education for local sustainability expertise
7	Affordable and clean energy	I	Provide financing for development and maintenance of infrastructure; further education for local sustainability expertise
8	Decent work and economic growth	D	Allow for online financing, including credit and crowdfunding; create new (online) income opportunities; ensure funding and use symmetry (long-term for long-term projects, short-term for short-term projects)
9	Industry, Innovation and Infrastructure	D	Provide financing for development and maintenance of infrastructure
10	Reduced inequalities	D	See on gender at UNSDG5. Regional, economic, and educational equality, education, and savings provide the best opportunity for greater participation for most societies; both are furthered by FT4FI
11	Sustainable cities and communities	I	FT4FI assists the development of and investment in sustainable technology and transformation
12	Responsible production and consumption	I	FT4FI assists the development of and investment in sustainable technology and transformation

(Continued)

Table 10.1 (Continued)

Nr	Goals	Impact Direct=D Indirect=I	How FT4FI Can Further Goal
13	Climate action	I	FT4FI assists the development of and investment in sustainable technology and transformation
14	Life below water	I	FT4FI assists the development of and investment in sustainable technology and transformation
15	Life on land	I	FT4FI assists the development of and investment in sustainable technology and transformation
16	Peace, justice, and strong institutions	I	Robust economic development strengthens peace and civil institutions
17	Partnerships	D	FT4FI allows for engagement of private actors, multiplying assistance by public or state-supported actors

take on their (long) way towards the UNSDGs, and FinTech is the best way to achieve financial inclusion. Economies are best advised to focus on developing strategies for digital financial transformation, focusing on the role of FinTech in financial inclusion, as one important potential solution to the most important and most difficult question which is: how shall economies approach achieving the SDGs.

FT4FI Initiatives

An ever-increasing range of international development organisations are focusing on FinTech and financial inclusion, including the prominent initiative of the Alliance for Financial Inclusion (in which the authors of this chapter were involved),[11] as well as the World Bank, together with the Consultative Group to Assist the Poor (CGAP),[12] the United Nations Development Programme (with its Task Force on Digital Financing[13]), and many regional

---

11 AFI, 'FinTech for Financial Inclusion: A Framework for Digital Financial Transformation' (September 2018), https://www.afi-global.org/publications/2844/ FinTech-for-Financial-Inclusion-A-Framework-for-Digital-Financial-Transformation.
12 See Worldbank, 'Fintech and Financial Inclusion', see online http://pubdocs.worldbank.org/ en/877721478111918039/breakout-DigiFinance-McConaghy-Fintech.pdf.
13 See UNDCF, 'Digital Finance and the SDGs', http://www.uncdf.org/mm4p/dfs-and-the-sdgs.

development banks.[14] All are focusing on furthering digital financial services. These initiatives on the global and regional level are all evidence of the importance of strategies for digital financial transformation.

Four Pillars of Digital Financial Transformation

Given the many partly competing, partly complementary initiatives, it is crucial to avoid the mistakes of the past. Thus, this part addresses two questions: what lessons have we learned, and what types of FinTech are most likely to advance balanced sustainable growth and financial inclusion?[15]

Experiences and Lessons

Financial Inclusion Initiatives Since 2008: G20

The 2008 financial crisis prompted sweeping regulatory responses coordinated by the G20 aimed at building a resilient global financial system.[16] At the 2009 Pittsburgh Summit, G20 leaders committed to improving access to financial services for the poor[17] and established the Financial Inclusion Experts Group (FIEG).[18] In 2010, the Global Partnership for Financial Inclusion (GPFI) was also established, and the G20 leaders endorsed the first Financial Inclusion Action Plan (FIAP).[19]

The GPFI formally recognised digital financial solutions as critical tools for facilitating global financial inclusion in 2016[20] and the G20 High Level Principles for Digital Financial Inclusion (HLPs) were also introduced.[21] Together with two accompanying initiatives – the Recommendations for

---

14 The authors are aware of FinTech initiatives sponsored by the Asian Development Bank, the Islamic Development Bank, the European Investment Bank, and the Financial Development Corporation.

15 G20 Global Partnership for Financial Inclusion, 'Digital Financial Inclusion: Emerging Policy Approaches' (2017), https://www.gpfi.org/publications/ g20-report-digital-financial-inclusion-emerging-policy-approaches.

16 R. P. Buckley, 'The G20's Performance in Global Financial Regulation', *University of New South Wales Law Journal* 37, no. 1 (2014): 63.

17 G20, 'Pittsburgh Summit: Leaders' Statement' (25 September 2009), 41.

18 G20 Financial Inclusion Experts Group, 'Innovative Financial Inclusion' (ATISG Report, 25 May 2010); GPFI, 'Principles and Report on Innovative Financial Inclusion', http://www.gpfi.org/ publications/principles-and-report-innovative-financial-inclusion.

19 G20, 'Financial Inclusion Action Plan' (2010), 3.

20 GPFI, Launch of the G20 Basic Set of Financial Inclusion Indicators (22 April 2013) http:// www.gpfi.org/featured/launch-g20-basic-set-financial-inclusion-indicators.

21 GPFI, see note 15.

Responsible Finance[22] and the ID4D[23] – the HLPs aim to encourage and guide governments to embrace digital approaches to financial inclusion.[24] In 2017, the FIAP was updated to reflect the pivotal role of digitisation.[25]

Financial Inclusion Initiatives Since 2008: AFI

In parallel with these G20 processes, the Alliance for Financial Inclusion (AFI) was established in 2008 by a group of developing country central banks to focus exclusively on financial inclusion. In 2012, its members signed the historic Maya Declaration on Financial Inclusion, by which developing countries committed to financial inclusion targets and national policy changes.[26] A number of other agreements have followed, including the Sharm El Sheikh Accord, which recognised the relationship between climate change and financial exclusion.[27]

FinTech and Financial Inclusion: The Foundation of Digital Financial Transformation

FinTech today encompasses a number of technologies such as the application of artificial intelligence to big data. Which among these innovations are most likely to facilitate financial inclusion?

The immediate answer is mobile money – the provision of e-money on mobile phones – of which the paradigmatic example is the story of M-Pesa in Kenya. The longer-term answer is more complex. The real opportunity FinTech affords is the development of an entire infrastructure for a digital financial ecosystem.

Lessons on how to proceed can be taken from India where a FinTech strategy dubbed the 'India Stack' has been implemented over the past decade. India

---

22 See Responsible Finance Forum, 'Best Practices and Recommendations on Financial Consumer Protection' (April 2011), https://responsiblefinanceforum.org/publications/best-practices-recommendations-financial-consumer-protection/.

23 See World Bank, 'Identification for Development', http://www.worldbank.org/en/programs/id4d.

24 R. Grady, 'G20 High-Level Principles for Digital Financial Inclusion' (2016), https://rosgrady.com/project/g20-high-level-principles-for-digital-financial-inclusion-2016/.

25 B. Timmermann and P. Gmehling, 'Financial Inclusion and the G20 Agenda' (Paper presented at the International Statistical Institute Regional Statistics Conference, Bali, March 22–24 (2017), https://www.bis.org/ifc/events/ifc_isi_2017/06_timmermann_paper.pdf.

26 AFI, 'Maya Declaration', https://www.afi-global.org/maya-declaration.

27 AFI, 'Maya Declaration Continues to Evolve with Financial Inclusion Commitments from 66 Countries' (6 November 2017), https://www.afi-global.org/news/2017/11/maya-declaration-continues-evolve-financial-inclusion-commitments-66-countries/.

Stack is a set of APIs that forms a digital infrastructure to be used by the government, businesses, and other entities to provide paperless and cashless services.[28] India Stack involves four main levels.[29] First is a national system of biometric identification. Second is the establishment of bank accounts to deliver national services, such as pension, health, and other welfare payments. Third is a common payment API to enable payments to be made. Fourth is a series of electronic KYC initiatives that allow individuals to provide their financial details to financial services and other providers to meet KYC requirements. These eKYC utility platforms show how RegTech – regulatory technology – can improve integrity of financial markets and reduce counterparty risks.

Based on the Indian experiences, we argue that economies must focus on four pillars of digital financial infrastructure to support digital financial transformation, maximising financial inclusion and sustainable balanced growth from FinTech while likewise supporting the core financial policy objectives of financial stability, consumer protection, and financial integrity:

- Pillar I: Digital ID and eKYC (section III);
- Pillar II: Open electronic payment systems (section IV);
- Pillar III: Account opening and electronic government services (section V);
- Pillar IV: Design of digital financial market infrastructure and systems.

Each of these four pillars is examined separately next.

Pillar I: Digital ID and eKYC: Establishing the Foundation

Experience indicates that identity and in particular digital identity is central to the transformation process. This is a particular challenge in developing countries where often substantial portions of the population lack formal identification documents. At the same time, this shows the potential transformative impact of digital identity, e.g. as with India's Aadhaar system. A digital ID allows a person or SME to open an account without having to be present themselves.

Example: The Indian Aadhaar System

India's Aadhaar system is the first level of India Stack and involves issuing a 12-digit randomised number to all residents to be used to access government and other services.[30]

---

28 What Is IndiaStack? IndiaStack, http://indiastack.org/about/.
29 A. Bose, 'India's Fintech Revolution Is Primed to Put Banks Out of Business', *TechCrunch* (14 June 2016), https://techcrunch.com/2016/06/14/indias-fintech-revolution-is-primed-to-put-banks-out-of-business/; To learn more about India Stack, visit its official website at http://www.indiastack.org/about/.
30 About Aadhaar, Unique Identification Authority of India, https://uidai.gov.in/.

Aspects of the Aadhaar system have been strongly criticised, including it being described as 'mass surveillance technology'.[31] However, it has also proven beneficial in minimising 'leakage' of welfare payments through fraud and corruption. The Indian government claims this alone has saved an estimated US$5 billion.[32]

Difficulties in implementation should not detract from the potential of a national biometrically based identification system to underpin a digital financial ecosystem. Digital ID is necessary if the subsequent parts of the digital financial ecosystem are to rest upon a solid foundation.

Such a comprehensive digital financial ecosystem will transform government tax collection and thereby better fund government investments into education, health, roads, and other infrastructure, as well as enable the allocation of credit such that SMEs can thrive.

The experiences of the UN and Jordan with developing a digital identity solution for refugees provide an illustration of both system design and synergistic development.

IrisGuard

IrisGuard is an iris recognition technology that converts an image of the iris into a unique code which is then used to identify the individual.[33] Since 2016, IrisGuard's EyePay platform has been used by the UN to deliver financial aid. The technology provides sufficient digital identity for beneficiaries to receive food vouchers, withdraw cash, and transfer funds without requiring a credit card or bank account.

EyePay, in conjunction with the Ethereum blockchain, is now used to promote financial inclusion of Syrian refugees in Jordan by processing supermarket and ATM transactions in real time.[34] As of April 2018, the platform had been rolled out to five supermarkets in Jordanian refugee camps and serves over 120,000 Syrian refugees.[35]

Secure technology is important for vulnerable individuals to protect themselves and their money from corruption and identity theft. Iris recognition and distributed ledger technology work towards this goal by providing an immutable form of digital identity and rendering physical cash unnecessary.

---

31 S. Abraham, R. S. Sharma, and B. J. Panda, 'Is Aadhaar a Breach of Privacy?' *The Hindu* (31 March 2017), http://bit.ly/2BpbVyx.

32 'Indian Business Prepares to Tap into Aadhaar, a State-Owned Fingerprint-Identification System', *The Economist* (24 December 2016), http://econ.st/2FyB0hb.

33 'About IrisGuard', IrisGuard, https://www.irisguard.com/node/29.

34 'IFC and IrisGuard to Support Financial Inclusion and Syrian Refugees in Jordan', IrisGuard (14 February 2018), http://www.irisguard.com/index.php/news/index/2018/112.

35 Ibid.; 'Iris-Secured Blockchain Project Officially Recognised as Leading International Innovation', IrisGuard (13 April 2018), http://www.irisguard.com/index.php/news/index/2018/114.

Regional Approaches: eIDAS in the EU

The eIDAS Regulation was adopted in 2014 to provide mutually recognised digital identity for cross-border electronic interactions between European citizens, companies, and government institutions. Member States notify the European Commission of their eID, and other Member States are required to recognise it. Once the eID is recognised, an individual is able to use it in any Member State.[36]

Regardless of structure, it is central to consider how base digital ID can extend to as much of the population as possible to maximise efficiencies. Base identity provides the fundamental element of the KYC process. Particularly when linked electronically with other golden source data (such as tax information), it provides the basis of a simple eKYC system. The core objective is to make it as simple and inexpensive as possible to open accounts for most people and entities, thereby allowing resources to be focused on higher-risk customers and protecting market integrity.

eKYC and KYC Utilities

Verifying customer identity and carrying out KYC due diligence are fundamental to maintaining market integrity and underpin understanding customer needs. Technology presents opportunities to reconsider existing systems and build the infrastructure necessary to balance market integrity, financial inclusion, and economic growth, while meeting international financial standards.

Example 1: South Africa Web-Based KYC Database

In South Africa, three major financial institutions and Refinitiv (formerly Thomson Reuters) have partnered to create a web-based database of KYC information. The service collects the KYC information from the customer, verifies it, and then distributes it to all the customer's chosen institutions. The centralised database streamlines account opening procedures for the customer at no cost.[37] The benefits of this system are not yet fully apparent as not all financial institutions have chosen to participate, but as adoption levels increase, so should the efficiency benefits.

Example 2: India's e-KYC System

In another example, India has developed a paperless eKYC service, based on its Aadhaar system, to instantly establish the identity of prospective customers.[38]

---

36 R. Bastin, I. Hedea, and I. Cisse, 'A Big Step Toward the European Digital Single Market', Deloitte (October 2016), 70–77, https://www2.deloitte.com/lu/en/pages/about-deloitte/articles/inside/inside-issue13.html.

37 The South African KYC Service, Thomson Reuters Africa, https://africa.thomsonreuters.com/en/products-services/risk-management-solutions/kyc-as-a-service.html.

38 S. Desai and N. Jasuja, 'India Stack: The Bedrock of a Digital India', *Medium* (27 October 2016), https://medium.com/wharton-fintech/the-bedrock-of-a-digital-india-3e96240b3718.

The digitisation of identity authentication streamlines account opening and allows easy access to both digital and traditional financial services.

Axis Bank was the first in India to offer an eKYC facility in 2013. This reduced the turnaround time for opening a bank account from 7–10 days to just one day.[39] Today, many traditional banks and licensed payments banks in India offer bank accounts that can be opened and used instantly with eKYC.[40]

Example 3: eIDAS and eKYC

In the regional context, in the EU, eIDAS is intended to be the starting point for a similar system, making it 'possible to open a bank account online while meeting the strong requirements for customer identity', which is enhanced by eSignatures and operates across borders.[41] First steps in that direction have been undertaken by the European 4th Anti-Money Laundering Directive by accepting electronic identification for meeting CDD requirements.

Synthesising the Lessons

Such systems – while technically feasible – may not be politically feasible in many countries. In these cases, systems of optional digital identity separate from sovereign identification systems hold the greatest transformative potential.

Pillar II: Open Electronic Payment Systems: Building Connectivity

Payments systems provide the fundamental infrastructure for money to flow through any economy. They are thus foundational to financial inclusion as well as financial development and the functioning of the real economy. A flourishing mobile money ecosystem is only one element of how FinTech may enhance financial inclusion. Technology can enable many developing countries to leapfrog the construction of bricks-and-mortar bank branches and instead deliver a seamless financial system digitally. In turn, even the poorer members of society can have accounts that meet their financial needs and SMEs can have access to the services they need to flourish.

---

39 'Axis Bank Introduces a Paperless eKYC Based A/c Opening', *India Infoline News Service*, https://www.indiainfoline.com/article/news/axis-5875391291_1.html.
40 For example, AXIS Bank (https://www.axisbank.com/accounts/savings-account/axis-asap/axis_ASAP.html) and RBL Bank (https://abacus.rblbank.com/).
41 European Commission, 'Consumer Financial Services Action Plan: Better Products, More Choice' (March 2017), 13–14, https://ec.europa.eu/info/publications/consumer-financial-services-action-plan_en.

Mobile Money

Mobile money enables mobile phones to be used to pay bills, remit funds, deposit cash, make withdrawals, and save, using e-money, sometimes issued by banks but mostly by telecommunication companies ('telcos'). The service currently exists in over 89 developing countries and is growing rapidly.[42] E-money is typically defined as a stored value instrument or product that: (i) is issued on receipt of funds; (ii) consists of electronically recorded value stored on a device such as a mobile phone; (iii) may be accepted as a means of payment by parties other than the issuer; and (iv) is convertible back into cash.[43]

Today, M-Pesa is a major success providing financial services to a sizable proportion of the Kenyan population.[44] However, mobile money success has by no means been consistent. This has to do with the differing needs of consumers in different countries, the inability of service providers to adapt their offerings to different markets,[45] a tendency of central banks to over-regulate these services,[46] and a lack of trained payments professionals in many markets.[47] Other aspects of why cash remains king in so many poorer countries doubtless reside in matters cultural and anthropological.

Mobile money services, especially those offered by telcos, are a key part of the solution to financial exclusion in poorer countries; however, these pose real regulatory challenges. Such services do not initially pose systemic stability concerns and cannot afford, and do not require, the level of regulation generally applied to traditional banks. However, service providers need a central bank that encourages innovation and understands the needs of customers in their country: a major shift from the traditional role of central banks.

---

42 GSMA, 'State of the Industry 2014 – Mobile Financial Services for the Unbanked' (March 2015), https://www.gsma.com/mobilefordevelopment/wp-content/uploads/2015/03/SOTIR_2014.pdf.

43 Mobile Financial Services Working Group, 'Mobile Financial Services: Basic Terminology, Alliance for Financial Inclusion' (1 August 2014), http://www.afi-global.org/library/publications/mobile-financial-services-basic-terminology-2013.

44 In 2016, through embracing M-Pesa and similar digital payment networks, over 75% of adults in Kenya had access to formal financial services, a 26.7% increase from a decade earlier, N. Ndung'u, 'M-Pesa – A Success Story of Digital Financial Inclusion' (Blavatnik School of Government, July 2017), https://www.bsg.ox.ac.uk/research/publications/m-pesa-success-story-digital-financial-inclusion.

45 R. P. Buckley and S. Webster, 'FinTech in Developing Countries: Charting New Customer Journeys', *Journal of Financial Transformation* 44 (2016): 151.

46 For example, the Central Bank of Kenya applied a 'light-touch' approach from the outset, which many believe assisted the provision of these services. See also E. Gibson, F. Lupo Pasini, and R. P. Buckley, 'Regulating Digital Financial Services Agents in Developing Countries to Promote Financial Inclusion', *Singapore Journal of Legal Studies* 26 (2015).

47 R. P. Buckley and I. Mas, 'Coming of Age of Digital Payments as a Field of Expertise', *Journal of Law, Technology & Policy* 2016 (1): 71.

Designing Regulatory Infrastructure for an Open Electronic Payments System

While mobile money has been very powerful, it nonetheless is constrained by the limitations of simple mobile devices.

In this context, the Gates Foundation's Level One Project[48] provides an important example of how such systems should be designed. The Level One Project seeks to address unequal access to financial systems by developing 'new national shared financial systems', which are 'enabled by shared, open, standards-based components' such that payment services 'are integrated at a national (or even regional) level'.[49]

In China, Alipay and WeChat Pay likewise show the power of facilitating new entrants and the digitisation of the traditional payments system among banks.

Alibaba established Alipay in 2004 as a payment method for its ecommerce business. It is now the second largest mobile wallet provider in the world, behind only PayPal.[50] The Yu'e Bao money market fund was integrated with the Alipay mobile wallet in 2013, and provides the opportunity to make small investments, and is now the world's largest money market fund.[51]

WeChat was established as a messaging platform by Tencent in 2011. In 2013, the WeChat Wallet was introduced to allow users to make mobile payments in WeChat social games. Cash transfers and in-store cashless payments in stores became possible in 2014.[52] By 2017, 92% of survey respondents were using mobile payment systems like this for retail payments.[53]

The People's Bank of China (PBoC) has since 2017 subjected these mobile wallet services to increasing regulation. Mobile payment institutions are now required to channel payments through a new centralised clearing house, the China Nets Union Clearing Corporation.[54] This change gives the PBoC further

---

48 Bill & Melinda Gates; The Level One Project Guide – Designing a New System for Financial Inclusion', https://btca-prod.s3.amazonaws.com/documents/231/english_attachments/ The-Level-One-Project-Guide-Designing-a-New-System-for-Financial-Inclusion1. pdf?1470437926.

49 Ibid., 2, 7.

50 D. Bushell-Embling, 'Alipay Is World's Second Largest Mobile Wallet', *ComputerWorld Hong Kong* (9 April 2018).

51 E. Mu, 'Yu'ebao: A Brief History of the Chinese Internet Financing Upstart', *Forbes* (18 May 2014), https://www.forbes.com/sites/ericxlmu/2014/05/18/ yuebao-a-brief-history-of-the-chinese-internet-financing-upstart/#25c898583c0e.

52 S. Millward, '7 Years of WeChat', *Tech In Asia* (21 January 2018). https://www.techinasia.com/ history-of-wechat.

53 China Tech Insights, WeChat User & Business Ecosystem Report 2017 (2017), https:// technode.com/2017/04/24/wechat-user-business-ecosystem-report-2017/.

54 J. Hong, 'How China's Central Bank Is Clamping Down on the Mobile Payment Industry', *Forbes* (18 August 2017), https://www.forbes.com/sites/jinshanhong/2017/08/18/ how-chinas-central-bank-is-clamping-down-on-the-mobile-payment-industry/#5fa0a13b50be.

control. The PBoC has also raised payment platforms' reserve funds ratio to 50% from 20%, with the ratio to gradually increase to 100% over time, in order to further protect consumers.[55] Payment institutions must now also obtain permits to offer barcode payments, a method proving increasingly popular in China.[56]

The experiences of WeChat Pay and Alipay highlight that payments providers should be subject to appropriate proportional regulation, both to address risks and provide a level playing field.

The combination of digital ID/eKYC with open electronic payments provides the fundamental infrastructure to support a wide range of transactions. However, it is when combined with Pillar III that the greatest potential transformation can be achieved.

Pillar III: Account Opening and Electronic Government Provision of Services: Expanding Usage

While a wide range of governments have experimented with electronic provision of government services and mandatory account approaches, these tend to be of limited effectiveness unless combined with Pillar I and Pillar II infrastructure. It is this combination which has underpinned the third element of the India Stack strategy, namely providing government salaries and services electronically through bank accounts. A similar approach can be seen in the UN's approach in Jordan, whereby benefits are transferred electronically to accounts established on the basis of biometric digital identification.

Such systems not only support financial inclusion, empowerment, and savings but also have the potential to dramatically reduce leakage. Over time, such systems also have the potential to improve tax collection, as SMEs grow within the formal financial system instead of outside. In addition to simple savings, the Pillar I-II-III infrastructure can also support national pension systems, which not only enhance the financial safety net but also can provide additional financial resources to support economic growth.

---

55 Y. Wang, 'China Tightens Regulations over Mobile Payment Apps – What's Next for Tencent and Ant Financial?' *Forbes* (3 January 2018), https://www.forbes.com/sites/ywang/2018/01/03/china-tightens-regulation-over-mobile-payment-apps-whats-next-for-tencent-and-ant-financial/#47e526ae7f1d.
56 Xinhua, 'China Looks for Right Balance between Financial Innovation, Risk', *China Daily* (30 December 2017), http://www.chinadaily.com.cn/a/201712/30/WS5a46fd55a31008cf16da4599.html.

Electronic Payment: Government Salaries and Transfers

For the poor in many countries, state or state-backed support payments are important. Financial inclusion polices focused on government payments to the poor achieve two beneficial outcomes. First, digital payments enable governments to shift from in-kind assistance (food, water supply) to inexpensive cash transfers. This reduces administrative costs, better controls leakage and increases transparency.[57] Second, accounts used for support payments, once established, can be used for nongovernment payments. Once the unbanked gain access to digital financial services due to government support payments, they can over time learn to trust, and deal in, electronic payments generally instead of cash.

There are many notable examples of government-to-person (G2P) payment programmes aiming at financially including the unbanked. At least 19 G2P programmes operate in developing countries.[58] Probably the most prominent is the Bolsa Familia card programme in Brazil.[59] However, most of these projects are at best half-digital. For instance, in the case of Bolsa Familia in Brazil, Familias in Colombia, and Benazir in Pakistan, a debit card is provided to the recipients who may then withdraw cash. Further digitalising these projects does, however, face real challenges. According to CGAP, '31% of accounts in low-income countries ... [are] used for only one or two withdrawals per month'.[60] CGAP has identified a range of reasons for this, including use limitations of the accounts and insufficient recipient and agent training about their use.[61]

The Center for Financial Inclusion highlights the need for payment processes to 'align with customer life patterns'.[62] For instance, in a Pakistani G2P women's programme, a mere 53% of the transactions were actually initiated by women; the rest were initiated by male representatives.[63] In response, the Pakistan government adopted biometric technology to ensure women received the cash

---

57 CGAP, Govt. to Person Payments, http://www.cgap.org/topics/gov-person-payments;
G. Stewart, 'Government to Person Transfers – On-Ramp to Financial Inclusion?' (2016), https://www.centerforfinancialinclusion.org/storage/documents/Government_to_Person_Transfers.pdf.
58 Stewart, see note 57, 29 (citing policy reports from PFIP, CGAP, Gates Foundation, and others).
59 T. Campello and M. Côrtes Neri, 'Programa Bolsa Familia: Uma Década de Inclusão e Cidadania' (2014), 9, http://www.ipea.gov.br/portal/images/stories/PDFs/140321_pbf_sumex_portugues.pdf.
60 CGAP, see note 57.
61 Ibid.
62 Stewart, see note 57, 2.
63 Ibid., 19.

transfers directly, thereby hopefully empowering them to decide how to use the money.[64]

G2P payments have the potential to further financial inclusion, *if properly designed*. However, G2P payments frequently do not underpin a flourishing digital financial ecosystem. In particular, the three following features need to be addressed:

1) Government-designed account procedures should facilitate later unrestricted payments. For instance, the Kenyan Uduma card can be used at government counters, at least four major banks, at ATMs and by merchants that accept a major global credit card.[65]
2) The digital-to-real gap must be bridged well. When digital transaction partners are few, individuals will prefer cash. While most people interpret this as a problem of agent efficiency, the logic behind this is odd. In a fully digital system there will be no agents. If merchants cannot do business without accepting e-money, they will provide the devices to accept e-money efficiently, with or without incentives. Hence, *it all starts with e-liquidity on the customers' side*. Disenabling the exchange of significant amounts of e-money into cash and slowly calibrating the amount depending on availability and acceptance of G2P systems could provide a viable strategy.
3) Functionality must be simple.[66] What needs to be learned to receive government support must enable one to make and receive other transfers. A *customised set-up* of the system could assist, for instance by providing customers with the account information of their most important recipients, such as schools and electricity providers.

Electronic Payment and Provision: Other Core Services

The combination of Pillars I, II, and III – in addition to core government services – supports a range of service payments, particularly for utilities and telecommunications services, that fundamentally improve the lives of individuals. The infrastructure for Pillars I, II, and III also supports ecommerce, carrying significant benefits for SMEs.

Governments can support digital transformation by highlighting the advantages of e-money, setting limits for cash transactions in the real economy, or

---

64 Government of Pakistan/BISP, 'Women Empowerment: Status and Challenges' (2017), 12, http://bisp.gov.pk/wp-content/uploads/2017/05/BISP-Women-empower-forum-24-05-2017-latest.pdf.
65 Center for Financial Inclusion, 'Kenyan Government Expands Insurance and Social Security via Digital Finance' (15 February 2017), https://www.centerforfinancialinclusion.org/kenyan-government-expands-insurance-and-social-security-via-digital-finance/.
66 For instance, Pakistani women often had difficulties using the debit card granted to them at ATMs: Stewart, see note 57, 19.

requiring merchants to offer the means of digital payments at low or no cost to customers. An example of the former is in Fiji, where the G2P programme has led to greater inclusion, with G2P accounts functioning as saving devices.[67]

From the mutually reinforcing foundations of Pillars I–III, Pillar IV focuses on other forms of infrastructure to support access to finance more broadly.

Pillar IV: Design of Financial Market Infrastructure and Systems: Enabling New Wider Development

A range of additional digital infrastructure supports increases in access to finance, financial stability, and market integrity, including digitised systems for securities trading, clearing, and settlement, both for debt and equity. Combined with the foundational infrastructure of Pillars I–III, these systems can dramatically increase access to a range of financial services, including credit, investment, and insurance. In terms of credit, perhaps the most potentially transformative changes can arise from automated cash flow-based lending for SMEs. The addition of Pillar IV allows for the provision of investment opportunities at much lower cost. The experiences of China, Kenya, and India among others highlight how such systems can be used to provide greater access to investment products (particularly government bonds), as well as support financial sector development more broadly.

Transforming Credit Provision: From Collateral and Microfinance to Cash Flow

Credit provision traditionally suffers from problems of information asymmetry, with banks specialising in analysing credit risk. Credit risk analysis however has traditionally been costly, making it uncommercial in the context of many individuals and SMEs. Traditional reliance on collateral as a cheaper alternative has been difficult in developing countries where property rights and other institutional frameworks may be weak or nonexistent. The traditional answer to that challenge is the creation of credit bureaux that aggregate credit data and in turn reduce overall costs.[68]

Digitalisation is changing all this. The provider with the most accurate, detailed, and extensive digitalised information about a customer is best placed to price credit (and other financial services, such as insurance) through

---

67 Ibid., 29.
68 D. Zetzsche and T. Ratna Dewi, 'The Paradoxical Case Against Interest Rate Caps for Microfinance' (University of Luxembourg Faculty of Law, Economics and Finance Working Paper No. 2018-008), 25.

datafication, i.e. the process of analysing and using data. Superior, comprehensive customer data may be generated from:

- Software companies aggregating information about users' activities;
- Hardware companies and Internet-of-things (IoT) companies utilising sensors that monitor usage behaviour and location;
- Social media services (Facebook, Tencent) and search engines (Google, Baidu), providing insight into social preferences and activities;
- E-commerce, providing insight into consumer demand and payment history; and
- Telecommunications services providers (Safaricom, Vodafone), providing data on mobile activities.[69]

The big data approach applied by these firms (referred to as 'TechFins') should improve business decisions as their *data sets are typically of far better quality* than traditional financial institutions. This enables a TechFin to form a far truer picture, in close to real-time, of the customer's financial position.

From a financial inclusion perspective, these TechFins (while creating other reasons for concern) are helpful in that they replace the need for interpersonal relations. TechFins can better adjust credit rates to the risk (i.e. the client) at hand, and *'re-personalise' the financial relationship* via algorithms. Data-based finance could be simultaneously more attuned to individuals' real risk profiles (if the data-based methodology is sound) and more inclusive as it could provide 'personalised' financial services at a much lower cost per client. Real-world examples include Amazon's lending programme to small businesses and Alipay's consumer loan offerings.

The use of technology to provide cash flow-based lending for individuals and SMEs on a cost-effective and risk-prudent basis is exciting, but requires the necessary foundational support.

Adding Insurance and Investments to Savings and Credit

While online payments and lending are at the heart of most financial inclusion strategies, extensions into the investment sector are necessary. This is particularly true if payments infrastructure is designed nationally, with participants being subject to the same systemic risks. For instance, in a case of serious drought not only will farmers suffer, but also the financial institutions that service those farmers and other members of society due to reduced demand and economic downturn.

---

69 D. A. Zetzsche, R. P. Buckley, D. W. Arner, and J. N. Barberis, 'From FinTech to TechFin: The Regulatory Challenges of Data-Driven Finance', 14 *New York University Journal of Law and Business* 101 (2018).

In the Global North, insurance and investment products reduce risks for customers and ensure risk diversification. Both are a necessary addition to payments. For instance, crop insurance helps farmers restart after droughts.

Digitalisation could address the two major barriers to financial inclusion in these areas: access and transaction costs. As a third advantage, online providers may reduce human biases which are particularly serious in long-term investments and pooled money management (such as insurance). This has been widely discussed in the context of robo-advisors, but is also true for other financial services that rely on long-term cash flow plans. At the same time, an enhanced savings rate could strengthen local capital markets.

From a client protection perspective, adding online insurance and investments is not only an opportunity, but also a challenge. Financial markets risks never go away, but are simply transformed into other types of risk. For instance, exposure to insurance and investments enhances the risk of volatility and fraud, since the exposure is long term. Insurance and investment require providers that will be solid over many years.

Another major issue is the complexity of long-term investments. Savings in nominated currency (i.e. interest-based savings) do not fare well over very long savings cycles. But investments come with a great degree of uncertainty and complexity, which could further misselling and Ponzi schemes.

Bridging the trust divide – because investors cannot control the risk, they must trust the intermediary – is at the heart of developing liquid financial markets. There are multiple global online (micro-) insurance[70] and investment schemes[71] that commit to financial inclusion principles.

M-Akiba

For instance, Kenyan government bonds can be acquired through mobile accounts relying on the M-Akiba scheme. M-Akiba enables digital savings in, and trading of, Kenyan government bonds. Money raised is earmarked for infrastructural development projects to further support FinTech in Kenya.

M-Akiba avoids the investment risks associated with (regional or global) market access. However, M-Akiba does not further diversification of regional risk and rests on public sector involvement. Both aspects may prove a disadvantage if the Kenyan political system is hit by a shock and the state's ability to service its loans becomes uncertain. Regardless, it could serve as a good starting point for investors unequipped to deal with more sophisticated financial products.

---

70 See e.g. the online crop insurance project, IBISA, which is building a globally diversified insurance pool based on satellite screening and blockchain technology: BitValley, www.bitbank.lu.
71 See e.g. Advicement in South Africa: Advicement, https://advicement.co.za/.

Building Better Financial Infrastructure

Today cloud, IoT, blockchain, and other digital technologies are being used to redesign markets and infrastructure, particularly in the context of payment systems, securities clearing, and settlement systems, early stage financing, and trade and agricultural finance. Maximising this potential requires a foundation of Pillars I–III.

The EU Example: GDPR, PSD2, MiFID2

European digitalisation at the regional level developed from the bottom up following the financial crisis, starting with extensive reporting requirements which created the need for intermediaries and supervisors to digitalise. Kickstarted by the introduction of extensive digital reporting to regulators and the imposition of 'open banking' where incumbent intermediaries must share client data with competitors, Europe's digitalisation strategy is multidimensional.

As compared to India, the European approach is characterised by a *lack of a centralised agenda*. Rather, sectoral needs such as those of financial regulators to better control systemic risks or ensuring privacy in a world dominated by data-driven firms (BigTech) determined the path.

As compared to the US, EU law's distinctive factor is its *restrictive approach to the use of data*. Data protection laws and protected factors have the same consequence. Both require the partial exclusion of protected data from algorithmic analysis. Data and factor protection laws differ, however, based on who has jurisdiction over the decision to exclude data. Data privacy privatises the data – i.e. data users need qualified consent from the data owners to use the data – while protected factors are not subject to private transactions.

Developing a Comprehensive Strategy

What broader lessons can we draw from experience to date?

Strategic Approach

The starting point is that the power of these pillars is greatest when they are all pursued and become mutually reinforcing. This is the core lesson from India Stack.

The Challenge of Technology

Any FinTech/RegTech-based financial inclusion approach must accept that technology is not perfect. This has three consequences.

First, technology may do things other than what its developers anticipate. For instance, self-learning algorithms may enhance rather than mitigate biases existing in the data.[72] Perfect technologies to check on the limits of technologies do not yet exist. In the meantime, providers need to constantly test the outcomes of algorithmic interpretation of data.

Second, technology may do exactly what the developers anticipate, but the problem is the developers. Financial history is replete with fraud. Every new technology will be abused by some. Recent examples include the use of virtual currencies for drug trafficking and money laundering[73] and the use of initial coin offerings for defrauding investors/participants.[74]

Third, technology is ever-accelerating and facilitating ever more new entrants, making the role of the regulator ever more challenging. In many cases, this will require regulators to use technology in response. This is one aspect of RegTech. RegTech includes automation and data-driven analysis of internal control systems and internal and external reporting.

Regulatory Sandboxes, Piloting, and Test-and-Learn Approaches

One recent development with real potential to assist financial inclusion is regulatory sandboxes. At a basic level, the sandbox creates an environment for businesses to test products without having to meet the full panoply of regulation. In return, regulators require applicants to incorporate appropriate safeguards.[75]

The number of entities typically in a regulator's sandbox at any one time is very small and it follows that the actual exemption from regulation afforded by the sandbox is not its most important impact. Our research suggests sandboxes play two far more important roles, and both should appeal to

---

72 See e.g. Uber's use of machine learning: H. Reese, 'How Data and Machine Learning Are "Part of Uber's DNA", *TechRepublic* (Oct. 21, 2016), https://www.techrepublic.com/article/how-data-and-machine-learning-are-part-of-ubers-dna/.

73 *United States v. Ulbricht*, 31 F. Supp. 3d 540, 569 (S.D.N.Y. 2014); *United States v. Faiella*, 39 F. Supp. 3d 544 (S.D.N.Y. 2014); M. I. Raskin, 'Realm of the Coin: Bitcoin and Civil Procedure', (2015) 20 *Fordham Journal of Corporate & Financial Law* 970 (2015): 980–83; M. Tsukerman, 'The Block Is Hot: A Survey of the State of Bitcoin Regulation and Suggestions for the Future', 30 *Berkeley Technology Law Journal* (2015): 1127, 1146–59, 1166–67.

74 D. A. Zetzsche, R. P. Buckley, and D. W. Arner, 'The ICO Gold Rush', Harvard Law School Forum on Corporate Governance and Financial Regulation (1 December 2017), https://corpgov.law.harvard.edu/2017/12/01/the-ico-gold-rush/.

75 FinTech Supervisory Sandbox (FSS), Hong Kong Monetary Authority (6 September 2016), 2, http://www.hkma.gov.hk/media/eng/doc/key-information/guidelines-and-circular/2016/20160906e1.pdf; Monetary Authority of Singapore, MAS FinTech Regulatory Sandbox Guidelines, marginal nos 2.2, 6.2, 6.2.g (16 November 2016), See also Bank Negara Malaysia, Financial Technology Regulatory Sandbox Framework, marginal no 6.1 ff (18 October 2016), http://www.bnm.gov.my/index.php?ch=57&pg=137&ac=533&bb=file.

developing country regulators.[76] Firstly, instituting a sandbox sends a strong message to FinTechs that the regulator is open to innovation. Secondly, the sandbox provides an important learning opportunity for regulators, especially when coupled with an 'innovation hub'. The Australian Securities and Investment Commission has managed to engineer a slow cultural shift towards it being seen as a regulator that can be approached for assistance by a combination of its Innovation Hub, regulatory sandbox, and Digital Finance Advisory Panel.[77]

However, sandboxes come with significant risks. If the sandbox is too generous it may jeopardise regulatory priorities, such as customer protection. Further, sandboxes may undermine the rule of law and the objective of facilitating fair competition. In particular, in countries with high corruption levels, the sandbox may facilitate illicit supervisory 'friendliness' serving the entrepreneurs. With or without undue influence on regulators, the sandbox creates costs and risks, and perhaps potential liability if a sandboxed firm harms its customers. Finally, sandboxed firms are not 'equivalently' regulated and supervised and thus may find it difficult to do business with regulated firms, in particular on a cross-border basis.

All in all, a sandbox is unlikely to be the best way to support financial transformation through digital financial infrastructure. It is likely to assist to a very limited extent, and is most useful when a jurisdiction exhibits the following characteristics:

- The jurisdiction has strong rule of law and transparency;
- Regulation or time to market is the main barrier for innovation;
- Risk of corruption is low;
- The ecosystem furthers social business models; and
- Functional substitutes for the sandbox are not available.

Functional substitutes include balanced reform of financial regulation, such as removing red tape legislation and establishing a waiver practice. Importantly, innovation hubs, where knowledge exchange takes place,[78] are not conditional on the existence of a sandbox, and represent a parallel regulatory response with more potential to enhance innovation, while correspondingly making larger demands on regulator resources.

---

76 D. Zetzsche, R. Buckley, D. Arner, and J. Barberis, 'Regulating a Revolution: From Regulatory Sandboxes to Smart Regulation', 23 *Fordham Journal of Corporate & Financial Law* (2017), 31–103.

77 ASIC, Digital Finance Advisory Committee, http://asic.gov.au/for-business/your-business/innovation-hub/digital-finance-advisory-committee/; ASIC, 15-21MR Innovation Hub: ASIC Update (5 August 2015), http://asic.gov.au/about-asic/media-centre/find-a-media-release/2015-releases/15-211mr-innovation-hub-asic-update/.

78 See Zetzsche et al., see note 76, 38–47.

Balancing Inclusion with Other Regulatory Objectives

Client protection is key for digital financial inclusion. One promising option is for regulatory restrictions to be embedded technologically in the product. These restrictions would be based on client exposure and ability to bear risks and would substitute for today's restrictions on access to financial services.

A reasonable approach will never aim at full access for all parts of society to all kinds of financial services. In order to protect clients adequately and proportionately, any policy must be partially exclusive: restricting access to products too risky for people with low financial literacy. Examples include certain derivatives, currency trading, and extensive leverage. The result will be an asymmetric paternalistic system in which people with a greater degree of financial sophistication have access to a wider range of financial products. We envisage that clients will be assessed by income, education, experience, and wealth and categorised in classes. Depending on the class, access to risky products will be controlled. This approach will also allow ethical restrictions in line with clients' preferences. For instance, clients that qualify for risky products but who wish to avoid leverage for religious reasons (e.g. Islamic finance) will be able to do so.

The FinTech aspect of this new, legal rather than factual, segregation is that the criteria can be set, reviewed, and adjusted on a day-to-day basis, as its application follows data-driven rules, and its outcome can be supervised by means of RegTech.

Designing Regulatory Systems: The Example of Mexico

An increasing number of jurisdictions are developing specific regulatory approaches to FinTech. Given the speed of change, laws and regulations should be based on principles, not rules. Mexico provides a very good example of a comprehensive approach focused on general principles.

Mexico's Financial Technology Law came into effect in March 2018 and regulates the registration and operation of nonbanks offering access to finance or investment, digital money, and cryptocurrencies. The law also deals with related issues such as crowdfunding, regulatory sandboxes, robo-advisory services, and APIs. A number of authorities have been given supervisory powers, and the Committee on Financial Technology Institutions was established to grant authorisations to prospective institutions.[79] Mexico's sandbox allows

---

79 R. Arce Lozano, F. de Noriego Olea, M. Salazar, M. Aldonza Sakar, 'Mexico's Fintech Law Initiative: What You Need to Know', Hogan Lovells (Summer 2017), https://www.hoganlovells.com/~/media/hogan-lovells/pdf/debt-capital-markets-global-insights/mexicos-fintech-law-initiative.pdf?la=en.

companies to apply for a temporary authorisation for up to two years to trial their services to a small number of customers.[80]

Mexico's law is comprehensive, with a balance of regulations protecting consumers, such as supervisory powers and authorisation requirements, and promoting innovation, such as the regulatory sandbox.

Significantly, it takes an approach based on regulatory principles, rather than one tied to specific technologies, business forms, or product types. Going forward, such principles-based approaches are key to successful regulatory development.

Towards Inclusive *and* Sustainable Growth

Digital financial inclusion is one of the most important answers to the question of how regulators and government should achieve the UN Sustainable Development Goals. In that regard, aiming at a comprehensive FT4FI policy based on four pillars, including Digital ID, open payment platforms, public FinTech use, and long-term development for sophisticated financial market infrastructure, is key.

Besides the opportunities, the FinTech transformation in China and India highlights new challenges including the risk of a permanent digital divide within, and between, economies, and the challenges of cybersecurity and data protection. This strategy of digital financial infrastructure development rests fundamentally on availability of communications' infrastructure. It offers the greatest potential in countries with high smart phone penetration rates and inefficient old-fashioned financial systems. While financial inclusion remains a challenge in many countries, the cost of smart phones is falling rapidly, while construction of related infrastructure is proceeding apace in most markets, at least in urban and semiurban areas.

Nonetheless, a key risk going forward remains the potential emergence of an insurmountable digital divide between economies which manage to put in place the necessary conditions to support smart phone access and couple this to a digital financial infrastructure development strategy, and those which do not, as well as the analogous divide within countries between access for more affluent urban dwellers and poor, rural residents and the elderly.

While our four pillars strategy will not solve all financial inclusion challenges, it is designed to address the vast majority efficiently, enabling digital financial transformation and supporting the achievement of the SDG agenda.

---

80 Ibid.

Acknowledgements

We are grateful for the financial support for this research provided by the Alliance for Financial Inclusion (AFI); the Luxembourg National Research Fund project 'A New Lane for FinTechs – SMART Regulation', INTER/MOBILITY/16/11406511; and the Australian Research Council Linkage project 'Regulating a Revolution: A New Regulatory Model for Digital Finance'. We also owe a real debt, for her superb research assistance, to Jessica Chapman. All responsibility is the authors'. This research relies heavily upon our earlier, extended report for AFI: 'FinTech for Financial Inclusion: A Framework for Digital Financial Transformation', September 2018; available at https://www.afi-global.org/publications/2844/FinTech-for-Financial-Inclusion-A-Framework-for-Digital-Financial-Transformation.

11

Financing and Self-Financing of SDGs through Financial Technology, Legal, and Fiscal Tools
Jon Truby

Introduction

The question of solutions to help achieve and finance the United Nations Development Programme's (UNDP) Sustainable Development Goals is one with no single answer; rather there are a range of answers that differ depending on national circumstances. The focus of this chapter is upon two imperatives for the developing world: first, the need to develop innovative Sustainable Development Goals (SDGs) financing solutions that can be designed to simultaneously produce benefits going towards the achievement of related SDGs; and second, the need to develop clean energy and low emissions solutions to achieve sustainability in the developing world. The chapter provides a selection of innovative legal and policy solutions designed to offer policymakers realistic choices for achieving and financing SDGs. The focus throughout is on the developing world. The chapter is divided into three sections based upon the type of policy tool or solution and the purpose behind it, with each section subdivided into differing thematic solutions.

Vast sums of money in developing countries are lost to corruption, tax avoidance, and tax evasion, erosion of the tax base, theft, inefficiency, and mismanagement. By providing innovative technological solutions and fiscal policy options, these funds can be better allocated towards the achievement of SDGs such as economic development and poverty reduction.

The first two sections of the chapter focus on how developing countries can finance SDGs in a self-sufficient manner, without (or with limited) dependence on foreign contributions. The aim here is the empowerment of developing countries to take full control of the policy and programme that best fits the national circumstances without reliance upon foreign aid or investment. As well as reducing corruption, this enables institutions to meet SDG 16 target to 'develop effective, accountable and transparent institutions at all levels' which has the double dividend of strengthening institutions and promoting self-reliance. Reducing leakage and having strong and transparent administrative bodies provides wider

Sustainable Development Goals: Harnessing Business to Achieve the SDGs through Finance, Technology, and Law Reform, First Edition. Edited by Julia Walker, Alma Pekmezovic, and Gordon Walker.

benefits to the economy, the rule of law, and trust in government. It also gives more certainty and confidence to both donor states and business investors that inward investment will be managed responsibly.

The first section of the chapter studies the choices available to reform taxation and the administration of taxation to self-finance and achieve the SDGs. It first considers how shifting the tax burden from productive activities to negativities can provide the revenue-neutral achievement of SDGs. It is important not to increase the overall burden on taxpayers which can be economically detrimental, as noted in the Pearce Report.[1] We then examine the problem of the tax base in developing countries being eroded through the generation of revenues in the virtual economy that see profits flowing outside the jurisdiction with limited benefits to the local economy. Although this problem is not specific to technology firms and is commonly attributed to multinational enterprises generally, a realistic solution is a digital services tax such as the UK's proposed Digital Services Tax Bill. The first section next considers how digitalisation of tax administration can achieve efficiencies including lowering leakage through enhanced transparency and accuracy, which can add revenue for achievement of SDGs generally.

Possibly controversially, this section moots a novel proposal to bring jet fuel within the taxation system to produce revenues, achieve lower emissions, and benefit the economy. Such a measure may have the potential of going towards achieving multiple SDGs, and bringing an antiquated subsidy on fossil fuels in line with the global environmental programme.

The second part continues on the subject of realising means of self-financing, by considering how both the digitisation of money and the formation of digital identities, can benefit the developing world and go towards the achievement of SDGs. In particular this demonstrates how digitisation can prevent revenues being lost to corruption, theft, and accounting mistakes. The second part of this section points to a number of studies to show how digital identities can both improve efficiency generally but – importantly – enable financial inclusion for many in the developing world, which can open up financial opportunities and entrepreneurship in line with SDG 8. On both subjects it is indicated that digitisation can not only help open up the necessary finance but also contribute to achievement of other SDGs at the same time.

The third section of the chapter focuses on financial technology solutions to achieving and financing SDG 7 and related SDGs. The United Nations Development Programme recognises that 60% of greenhouse gas emissions globally are caused by energy.[2] Its 2030 energy sustainability targets involve

---

1 D.W. Pearce, A. Markandya, and E. Barbier, *Blueprint for a Green Economy* (Earthscan, 1989).
2 United Nations Development Programme, 'Goal 7: Affordable and Clean Energy,' Sustainable Development Goals (n.d.).

increasing renewable energy's share of global energy, but also promoting 'investment in energy infrastructure and clean energy technology' and enhancing 'international cooperation to facilitate access to clean energy research and technology'. These targets explicitly focus upon the provision of sustainable energy for LDCs (least developed countries),[3] which is necessary to achieve other SDGs related to economic development, financial inclusion, education, hygiene, and modernising infrastructure.

The third section identifies multiple options available to policymakers to fund the clean energy objective of SDG 7 while providing ancillary benefits related to economic growth (SDG 8), climate action (SDG 13), and responsible consumption (SDG 12). This involves an examination of technology-centric market-based policy measures, fiscal and legal tools, and financial technology solutions to provide a comprehensive study of available options.

The options highlighted throughout are legal and policy concepts, either novel or based on existing proposals, and do require additional study prior to implementation. Importantly, they provide a basis for further research as well as initial options for policymakers.

Self-Sufficient Financing and Achievement of SDGs through Tax Reform

Shifting the Tax Burden to Create a Double Dividend

Tax reform can offer relatively achievable solutions for developing countries seeking to self-sufficiently achieve and finance SDG 7. This requires examination of what the tax base should be and how it is taxed. Developing countries may be able to ease taxation on productive activities that benefit the local economy and promote innovation in line with SDG 7. The European Commission, for example, encourages Member States to 'shift taxes away from labor to other tax bases that are less detrimental to growth' in order to promote both welfare and economic growth.[4] Over-reliance on taxation of labour and other productive activities can also be economically detrimental.[5] Shifting the tax burden to an unproductive activity or an activity that causes negative externalities, in a revenue-neutral manner, can provide economic benefits and labour opportunities without increasing the overall tax burden in an economy. It can also lower welfare costs for the government through added employment, freeing up money that can be targeted towards the achievement of

---

3 United Nations Development Programme, 'Goal 16: Promote Just, Peaceful and Inclusive Societies', Sustainable Development Goals (n.d.).
4 M. Mathé, G. Nicodeme, and S. Rua, 'Tax Shifts', Taxation Papers, 2015.
5 Å. Johansson et al., 'Taxation and Economic Growth', *European Economy* 1, no. 620 (2009): 71.

SDGs. In terms of the environment, it has been found to be feasible that a double dividend can 'improve the environmental quality without any cost in terms of non-environmental economic welfare.'[6] A double dividend can also apply to non-environmental SDGs, producing benefits through costless reforms.

Previous replacements of taxes on productive activities to environmental taxation have shown that labour taxes and small business taxes[7] can be minimised, which can boost the economy and innovation in line with SDG 8. For example, the Institute for Public Policy Research found new 'polluter-pays' taxes on landfill to be capable of reducing employers' tax contributions without increasing the overall tax burden on the economy.[8]

Base Erosion and Digital Services Taxation

In the digital economy, replacement streams of national tax revenue could further be generated from taxation of multinational online technology companies who generate revenue domestically but declare minimal taxable profit in the jurisdiction, via a group company structure.[9] This is a modern tax loophole that can be closed to generate additional revenue for funding SDGs. Such firms may provide benefits to local businesses, but revenues leave the jurisdiction and flow to the parent company, which can outstrip the benefits. Income and corporation tax rules are commonly antiquated in that they are designed for companies with significant physical presence in a jurisdiction. This no longer makes sense when multinational enterprises are able to virtually generate revenue from the sales of goods and services in nations without such a presence[10] and declare the profits in a lower tax jurisdiction, a procedure known as 'profit shifting'.

As developing countries tend to be 'net digital importers', their tax base is threatened by the digital economy through 'tax base cyberisation', generally known as 'base erosion'.[11] Arnold further explains that 'developing countries have become increasingly concerned about the erosion of their domestic tax

---

6 F. J. André, M. A. Cardenete, and E. Velázquez, 'Performing an Environmental Tax Reform in a Regional Economy. A Computable General Equilibrium Approach', *The Annals of Regional Science* 39, no. 2 (2005): 375–92.

7 M. Carnahan, 'Taxation Challenges in Developing Countries', *Asia and the Pacific Policy Studies* 2, no. 1 (2015): 169–82.

8 S. Tindale and G. Holtham, 'Green Tax Reform: Pollution Payments and Labour Tax Cuts' (Institute for Public Policy Research, 1996).

9 M. L. Schippers and C. E. Verhaeren, 'Taxation in a Digitizing World: Solutions for Corporate Income Tax and Value Added Tax', *EC Tax Review* 27, no. 1 (2018): 61–66.

10 J. Li, 'Protecting the Tax Base in the Digital Economy' (2014), https://www.un.org/esa/ffd/wp-content/uploads/2014/10/20140604_Paper9_Li.pdf.

11 Ibid.

bases by multinational enterprises ...' in relation to services.[12] The Organization for Economic Cooperation and Development's (OECD) 'base erosion and profit shifting plan' and the UN's updated Model Double Taxation Convention[13] both endorse solutions for developing countries in this regard.[14]

Developing countries may be able to learn from the UK's current unilateral action, taken after OECD countries failed to take coordinated international measures to mitigate the problem of base erosion and profit shifting. The UK's public consultation on charging a digital services tax under Finance Bill 2019–2020 is intended as a 'narrowly targeted 2% tax on the UK revenues of digital businesses that are considered to derive significant value from the participation of their users.'[15] This noncreditable tax under the Corporation Act would target technology giants generating annual revenues of over £500 million or otherwise, generating over £25 million annually from business activity linked to UK users. As such, it is intended to bring in revenue from 'big tech' firms who have commonly demonstrated an ability to declare minimal taxable profits in the UK despite substantial revenue.

It is likely that the UK would seek to increase such a tax over time if the scheme is successful in the initial pilot. The taxation can be designed so that it does not discourage multinational enterprises and disruptive multinational technology firms from establishing a physical presence in the jurisdiction – something that would be attractive to host countries – as the taxes would apply on the goods and services sold in the country regardless of such a presence. This would mean developing countries would not have the incentive to undertake tax competition.

Digitisation of Tax Administration

Technology can also be an effective means of ensuring increased compliance with existing, rather than new, tax rules. Closing the gap on noncompliance with tax requirements or poor tax administration can be achieved through digitisation. Digitisation of tax administration is a measure developing countries can implement to enhance enforcement, while tools such as blockchain can be adopted to improve monitoring and lower auditing costs. The additional revenue can go towards the achievement of SDGs. Compliance has rule

---

12 B. J. Arnold, 'The Taxation of Income from Services' (2014), https://www.un.org/esa/ffd/wp-content/uploads/2014/10/20140604_Paper2_Arnold.pdf.

13 United Nations, *United Nations Model Double Taxation Convention between Developed and Developing Countries* (2017), 213.

14 Yansheng Zhu, 'Proposed Changes to the UN Model Tax Convention Dealing with the Cyber-Based Services' (Geneva: Committee of Experts on International Cooperation in Tax Matters, 27–31 October 2014).

15 HM Treasury, 'Digital Services Tax: Consultation' (HM Revenue & Customs, November 2018).

of law benefits in ensuring that taxpayers are more confident they are not overly bearing the tax burden when others are avoiding their liability. Lawmakers are also careful not to implement taxes that have high administration costs and so with digitisation and automated tax collection lowering such costs, it would be more straightforward to bring a wider range of taxpayers into the tax base.

Increased information on economic activity has been advocated by IMF economists to be able to reduce tax evasion and tax fraud, and help divide tax revenue into calendar cycles for improved financial planning.[16] Improved compliance with rules such as consumption taxes can also reduce the need for labour taxes.

On an international level, digitisation can also enable improved sharing of tax information which can improve cross-border tax compliance as well as ensuring multinational enterprises and high value taxpayers bear their required tax burden.[17] It can also better handle taxation of electronic commerce[18] with a possibility of automation.

Amendment of the Chicago Convention

Dating back to 1944, the Chicago Convention (Convention on International Civil Aviation, Chicago, 7/12/1944; TS 8 [1953]; Cmd. 8742) exempts aircraft from fuel charges (Article 24[a]). Since greenhouse gases from aviation contribute 3% of emissions in the European Union[19] and there has been an absence of coordinated global action to tackle it, the European Commission has managed to include aviation emissions in its emission-trading scheme as an environmental measure[20] in a unilateral attempt to mitigate climate change from aviation.[21]

Seventy-five years on from the Chicago Convention, it may be prudent for developing countries to consider withdrawing from Article 24(a) in the pursuit

---

16 S. Gupta, M. Keen, A. Shah, and G. Verdier, *Digital Revolutions in Public Finance* (Washington, DC: International Monetary Fund 2017).

17 S. K. McCracken, 'Going, Going, Gone . . . Global: A Canadian Perspective on International Tax Administration Issues in the 'Exchange-of-Information Age', *Canadian Tax Journal* 50, no. 6 (2002): 1869–1912.

18 C. E. McLure, 'The Value Added Tax on Electronic Commerce in the European Union', *International Tax and Public Finance* 10, no. 6 (2003): 753–62; R. Jones and S. Basu, 'Taxation of Electronic Commerce: A Developing Problem', *International Review of Law, Computers & Technology* 16, no. 1 (2002): 35–51, https://doi.org/10.1080/13600860220136093.

19 European Commission, 'Reducing Emissions from Aviation' (2018), https://ec.europa.eu/clima/policies/transport/aviation_en.

20 J. Truby, 'Extraterritoriality or an Illegal Tax? A Challenge to the Inclusion of Aviation in the EU Emissions Trading Scheme' *Environmental Law Review* 14, no. 4 (2012): 301–6.

21 J. Scott and L. Rajamani, 'EU Climate Change Unilateralism', *European Journal of International Law* 23, no. 2 (2012): 469–94, https://doi.org/10.1093/ejil/chs020.

of the SDGs. The European Federation for Transport and Environment's Roadmap to Decarbonising European Aviation is one recent policy study examining means of reducing the harm of aviation and discusses measures such as the tax exemption of jet fuels.

Subjecting aviation fuel to taxation or charges would primarily raise revenue for developing countries to self-finance SDGs generally. Furthermore, it would encourage airlines to adapt their choice of aircraft engine to achieve a switch to lower emissions aviation fuel which could be exempt from tax, and thus encourage responsible consumption (SDG 12). It may raise the cost of airline tickets for aircraft dependent on energy inefficient fuelling, and make flights on more efficient aircraft comparably less expensive and therefore raise demand for more efficient aircraft. This could lead to the retirement of more inefficient aircraft, as well as a boost to local industry if the tax revenue raised could be used towards research and development of efficient aircraft or fuel sources.

Importantly, the tax revenues could be hypothecated towards funding low carbon technologies and renewable energy for the achievement of SDGs 7 and 13. Such funding could include helping to manufacture or at least finance low-emissions aircraft with alternative sustainable fuel sources. Once such an investment is made, aircraft operators' costs could potentially fall since they would not have to rely on older, less efficient aircraft requiring substantial purchases of non-renewable fuel sources. This would reduce hydrocarbon importation costs, which would have a positive impact on the national balance of payments, lower emissions to help the nation achieve its SDG targets and Paris Agreement commitments, and provide an advanced technology industry for the local economy.

Such a move may be considered internationally as negative, going against the Convention. Alternatively, it may be understood in the context of both climate change and international development, neither of which goals align with the exemption of aviation fuels from duties.[22] The taxation exemption is effectively a subsidy[23] for airline companies, whose environmental costs are socialised for private benefit.[24] This focus on airlines would go towards achieving the UNDP Goal 7 of doubling energy efficiency, increasing the proportion of renewable energy in overall energy consumption, introducing cleaner technology, and promoting investment in clean energy technology.[25]

---

22 Transport & Environment, 'Roadmap to Decarbonising European Aviation' (22 October 2018), https://www.transportenvironment.org/publications/ roadmap-decarbonising-european-aviation.

23 OECD, *Environmentally Harmful Subsidies: Challenges for Reform* (2005).

24 J. Stiglitz, 'A New Agenda for Global Warming', *The Economists' Voice* 3, no. 7 (2006): 1–4.

25 United Nations Development Programme, 'Goal 7: Affordable and Clean Energy', https:// www.undp.org/content/undp/en/home/sustainable-development-goals/goal-7-affordable-and-clean-energy.html.

Part IV of the Chicago Convention makes it legally troublesome to withdraw from any specific Article of the Convention without withdrawing from the entire agreement. Full withdrawal would be impractical for a state given the other parts of the agreement related to air navigation and travel rights. In practice, it may be more prudent for a nation to either lobby for amendment of the Convention within a regional group concerned about the environment, or alternatively, to introduce an emissions trading scheme including aviation that can raise revenues on emissions without infringing the agreement, as the European Commission succeeded in doing. The International Civil Aviation Organisation is itself working to reduce airlines' emissions levels and improve environmental protection practices through resolutions and policies, and has itself determined to introduce global market-based measures.

Self-Sufficient Financing of SDGs through Financial Technology

Digitisation of Money

SDG 16 indicates that 'Corruption, bribery, theft and tax evasion cost some US$1.26 trillion for developing countries per year'[26] and indicates that the saved losses could be used towards poverty reduction in line with SDG 1. Switching physical sovereign currency to digitised versions to enable digital payments, storage and finance offer significant benefits for self-financing SDGs in developing countries. Indeed, the IMF has encouraged central banks to introduce digital currencies to promote financial inclusion, to lower the cost of payments by preventing the monopolisation of payments services that result in higher costs, and provide an alternative to cash due to its limitations.[27]

Encouraging widespread and ultimately universal digitalisation through digital payments[28] provides the opportunity for more efficient and accurate tax collection, while real-time information on payments can vastly improve tax enforcement[29] including reducing tax avoidance by multinational enterprises and globally mobile taxpayers. With tax avoidance and evasion hitting developing countries the most and costing US$500 billion in lost revenue

---

26 United Nations Development Programme, 'Goal 16: Promote Just, Peaceful, and Inclusive Societies', https://www.undp.org/content/undp/en/home/sustainable-development-goals/goal-16-peace-justice-and-strong-institutions.html.

27 D. Strauss, 'Look at Issuing Digital Currency, IMF Head Tells Central Banks', *Financial Times* (November 2018).

28 K. S. Rogoff, *The Curse of Cash: How Large-Denomination Bills Aid Crime and Tax Evasion and Constrain Monetary Policy* (Princeton: Princeton University Press, 2017).

29 See note 16.

annually,[30] closing the gap can go a long way towards funding achievements of SDGs through self-sufficiency rather than charitable overseas donations, which frequently see high levels of leakage.

Digitising payments makes it simpler to monitor payments to ensure workers are paid on time, and provide a safer and more efficient infrastructure for customers to bank. Digital payments provide instant and cost-effective means of doing business and receiving payments, and an opportunity for entrepreneurs in developing countries to make and receive cross-border payments for selling goods and providing services. Cross-border remittances from overseas workers have previously been subject to relatively high transaction fees, which can be lowered through access to financial technology, providing much needed savings and additional funding directed to developing countries.

The process of connecting customers who may have either been without access to banking or depended on high cost banking to the banked economy, can provide employment and business opportunities as well as savings that go towards the achievement of SDG 8. Further benefits have been found to be increased financial inclusion for the poor, and financial empowerment of women, key to achievement of SDG 5; in particular the goal of fully including women in economic life and ensuring women have equal access to financial services.[31]

Social welfare payments from government to individuals are also found to benefit from digitisation. Writing in the World Bank Research Observer, Klapper and Singer cited numerous advantages including lower administrative costs, faster and more timely delivery of payments, reduced fraud and more accurate delivery though improved transparency, more secure and less risk of crime, all of which provide direct benefits towards achievement of SDGs particularly in DCs and LDCs. The World Food Programme has utilised blockchain to make cash payments in Jordan and Pakistan, which considerably saved administration costs and made such transfers more 'efficient, transparent and secure'.[32]

These same benefits were highlighted in a World Bank report, which additionally found that financial inclusion through digitisation increased the incentive for those in developing countries to save and manage economic risks. Importantly, the digitised records can provide verified information to credit assessors to enable those previously unbanked customers in developing

---

30 A. Cobham and P. Jansky, 'Global Distribution of Revenue Loss from Corporate Tax Avoidance: Re-estimation and Country Results', WIDER Working Paper (2017).

31 Leora Klapper and Dorothe Singer, 'The Opportunities and Challenges of Digitizing Government-to-Person Payments', *World Bank Observer* 32, no. 2 (2017), 211–26, https://doi.org/10.1093/wbro/lkx003.

32 World Food Programme, 'Building Blocks' (2016), https://innovation.wfp.org/project/building-blocks.

countries greater access to finance, helping to finance business opportunities[33] to promote economic growth in line with SDG 8. An IMF study shows how India's governmental programmes have managed to utilise digitalisation and digital identification to provide access to banking for over half a billion people.[34] Lower fees and even rewards were offered to customers to encourage the utilisation of digital payments particularly for governmental payments.

Digitising payments can help reduce corruption in developing countries which limits their progress towards sustainable development and discourages foreign investment. One billion of the $8 billion donated to Afghanistan in recent years has been lost to corruption, showing how progress towards the sustainable development goals is hindered despite money being available.[35] A World Bank study showed that increased transparency in payments through digitisation meant fewer bribe demands in India.[36] World Economic Forum studies showed how digitisation of payments considerably reduced leakage in both developed and developing countries, making public funds available elsewhere.[37] India was able to save $9 billion by digitising social protection payments, where previously this was lost through leakage to corruption and false claims.

Digital Identity

Development of digital identity can facilitate access to the financial system to the unbanked by providing a trusted verifiable identity. It removes the need to rely on physical documentation and removes outdated and burdensome procedures particularly for 'Know Your Customer/KYC' requirements.[38] In the developing world, over a billion people do not have any type of official identification, which prevents them from accessing basic services.[39] Access to innovative banking services can enable individuals to make sales and purchases, save money, access credit needed for entrepreneurialism and have the opportunity to develop a business or receive education. A report by US Aid shows that

---

33 World Bank Development Research Group, the Better Than Cash Alliance, and Bill & Melinda Gates Foundation, 'The Opportunities of Digitizing Payments' (28 August 2014).
34 See note 16.
35 Transparency International UK, 'Corruption: Cost for Developing Countries,' n.d.
36 World Bank Development Research Group, the Better Than Cash Alliance, and Bill & Melinda Gates Foundation, 'The Opportunities of Digitizing Payments'.
37 T. Wald, 'Governments Can Fight Corruption by Joining the Digital Payment Revolution,' World Economic Forum, 2018.
38 J. Truby, 'FinTech and the City: Sandbox 2.0 Policy and Regulatory Reform Proposals,' *International Review of Law, Computers & Technology* (2018).
39 World Economic Forum, 'Digital Identity: On the Threshold of a Digital Identity Revolution' no. (January 2018).

blockchain can be utilised to develop a digital identity infrastructure,[40] which would provide security benefits and importantly create a verifiable history of transactions and actions. Arner further studies the legal issues surrounding digital identity.[41] As well as removing barriers to access banking, a digital identity can also enable access to other government and private services, providing citizenship rights, travel rights, property rights and more. Such measures can bring social inclusion, equality of opportunity, and economic benefits.

Financing SDG 7 and Related Goals through Financial Technology

Offsetting Investments in Energy-Intensive Digital Currencies

Identifying that some digital currencies require greater computational power and subsequently depend upon higher levels of electricity consumption than others, this writer recommends fiscal and policy tools to incentivise behavioural change including a type of 'sin tax' to encourage technology developers to rely upon low-consumption versions of Blockchain over high-energy consumption versions.[42] The fiscal tool recommendations therein are intended to differentiate charges between low- and high-energy-dependent digital currencies, so that digital currencies depending upon high-energy-dependent technology would be charged a higher rate of tax (or other charge). Charging lower or zero rates on less energy-dependent technology would make them more attractive to purchasers and accordingly affect demand. Ultimately, such intervention would be intended to motivate developers to factor in environmental impact in the designs of their technology and ultimately to design blockchain consensus protocols built on less resource-dependent techniques. The tax or charge attributed to digital currencies would differentiate based upon the CO_2 transaction. It would be charged to the purchaser at the point of sale, collected by the broker – the coin exchange – and paid to the revenue authorities.

Building on such ideas, an alternative solution may be proposed here for the purpose of financing SDG 7. Rather than a CO_2/transaction tax, the additional sum charged to buyers of energy-intensive digital coins would not be transferred directly to the tax authorities. Instead, at the point of purchase at the

---

40 Center for Digital Development, 'Identity in a Digital Age: Infrastructure for Inclusive Development' (2017), https://www.usaid.gov/sites/default/files/documents/15396/IDENTITY_IN_A_DIGITAL_AGE.pdf.

41 D. W. Arner, D. A. Zetzsche, R. P. Buckley, and J. N. Barberis, 'The Identity Challenge in Finance: From Analogue Identity to Digitized Identification to Digital KYC Utilities', European Banking Institute Working Paper Series 2018 (2018).

42 J. Truby, 'Using Bitcoin Technology to Combat Climate Change', *Nature Middle East* (September 2018), https://doi.org/10.1038/nmiddleeast.2018.111.

exchange, it would be mandated that any purchase of a carbon-intensive digital currency could only be sold as a package with a mandatory additional purchase. The automatic additional purchase would be a share in a renewable energy plant or carbon offset project in a LDC, or a share of a fund owning such projects. The collective revenues would provide the necessary infrastructure investment.

Financing such sustainable energy development would create foreign direct investment into LDCs which would have the double-dividend of contributing to the achievement of both SDG 7 and SDG 8, helping to meet the targeted 7% of gross domestic product growth in LDCs, through the diversification and technological upgrading mandated. It would serve the principle of ensuring that the polluter pays and desocialises the environmental cost of energy-intensive digital currencies, which would otherwise be borne by the taxpayer. It would also create a market-based, nonregulatory incentive for both decarbonising digital currencies and facilitating technological investments in renewable energy production or carbon offset projects in LDCs. The advantage to purchasers of digital currencies is that they would not be simply losing money; their investment, although forced, could prove profitable. The infrastructure project would continue to be owned (at least in part) by the investors who could generate profits from the enterprise.

To be effective, this solution would require either implementation in a jurisdiction with a high usage of digital currencies such as South Korea, Japan, or Switzerland. For the most effective and less distortionary results, international cooperation would be required so that multiple nations make similar requirements to prevent cost competition, where jurisdictions not requiring the additional purchase would benefit through additional sales.

It would also be advantageous to prohibit immediate sale of the mandatory-purchased shares in the project, to prevent it becoming insolvent through low valuation of the shares. A restricted buy-in would enable the project to prove its success before shareholders could decide to sell or not.

Digital Token Investments

An alternative to mandatory share purchases (as proposed above) connected with energy-intensive digital currencies would be mandatory supplemental purchases of a digital token that could only be used to invest or trade with renewable energy projects or carbon offset projects in developing countries. A similar concept was proposed partially[43] regarding the reform of the EU Emissions Trading Scheme, though it was not connected specifically with SDG 7.

---

43 J. Truby, 'Decarbonizing Bitcoin: Law and Policy Choices for Reducing the Energy Consumption of Blockchain Technologies and Digital Currencies', *Energy Research & Social Science* 44 (2018): 399–410.

Rather than mandating a specific project, it would enable the token holders the choice of a variety of projects supported by the digital token. The token holder would be able to research and ascertain the most financially attractive project, which would also be intended to increase interest in, and exposure of, such projects, raising awareness of climate change in line with SDG target 13.3. Furthermore, it would create competition among the various projects to attract investment that could improve their efficiencies. Finally, it would create a market for the tradeable token that would be based upon profitability and values of the projects. This would be most attractive for many purchasers over other tokens and digital coins, which are frequently not backed by any notional or physical value.

The options sketched out above would each provide several benefits. They would help achieve the target in SDG 7.A, to 'promote investment in energy infrastructure and clean energy technology', providing financing towards the SDG 7.A.1 and SDG 13.A.1 indicators of mobilising $100 billion for clean energy and climate change mitigation. Such projects would help diversify the economies of developing countries and promote 'decent job creation' as per SDG targets 8.2 and 8.3, respectively.

Conclusion

In summary, the three sections of this chapter have proposed a variety of feasible innovative solutions to achieving and financing SDGs. Each requires further analysis but can form the basis of both further research, and, importantly, options for policymakers. Legal and economic studies ought to be carried out as an analytical tool to ascertain the correct approach. The ideas presented here are intended to add to the discourse in this field.

Importantly, it should be noted that the technology is available to implement the types of proposals highlighted. With modest initial investment, the types of digitisation techniques can be introduced that would have a highly beneficial reformative impact upon the collection of revenues and the supplementary benefits of transforming and advancing the economy and society's utility of such tools. The findings in the second section showed the considerable benefits attributed with digitisation of money and the formation of digital identities, which can go towards achieving multiple SDGs and generally creating a fairer society that is more equipped to protect rights and improve business opportunities.

Similarly, the tax and fiscal tools proposed in the first and third sections are within the reach of countries and can be introduced without detriment to the economy. Indeed, the instruments highlighted in both parts show how the introduction of such measures can have benefits for multiple SDGs and should be considered by policymakers. It will be most interesting to follow the UK's Financial Services Taxation Bill as this is a measure that could be introduced by further jurisdictions if no international action is taken. Furthermore, similar types of financial technology and blockchain solutions as indicated in the third section for creating clean energy and improving the climate are being implemented, such as through the 'Green Digital Finance Alliance', which seeks to 'align the global FinTech system with sustainable development.'[44] Such disruptive technological solutions may ultimately help facilitate the low-carbon financing needed to achieve the SDGs.

Acknowledgements

This publication was made possible by the NPRP award NPRP 11S-1119-170016 from the Qatar National Research Fund (a member of The Qatar Foundation). The statements made herein are solely the responsibility of the author.

---

44 UN Environmental Programme; Switch Asia, 'Show Me the Money: Innovative Finance', Issue Brief 2 (2018).

12

SDG Challenges in G20 Countries
Guillaume Lafortune and Guido Schmidt-Traub

Introduction

In their December 2018 declaration 'Building Consensus for Fair and Sustainable Development,'[1] the G20 leaders reaffirmed their commitment to supporting the 2030 Agenda and related Sustainable Development Goals (SDGs), which were adopted by all Member States of the United Nations in 2015. This declaration is very timely. On the one hand, no country is fully on track for achieving the SDGs.[2] On the other hand, not achieving the goals, for instance on climate mitigation, will generate major risks for all G20 economies and the rest of the world.[3]

Altogether, G20 countries represent two-thirds of the world's population, 85% of global gross domestic product and over 75% of global trade. They also account for about 80% of global energy-related carbon dioxide emissions. As such, their leadership in the context of Agenda 2030 and the SDGs is crucial for success.

Recoupling economic growth with social gains and environmental sustainability requires deep transformations of education, health, energy systems, land-use, urban development, and many other dimensions. Each transformation requires long-term changes involving large numbers of stakeholders from government, business, and civil society. At a global scale, it also requires

---

1 https://sdg.iisd.org/news/g20-declaration-focuses-on-fair-sustainable-development/.

2 J. D. Sachs, G. Schmidt-Traub, C. Kroll, G. Lafortune, and G. Fuller, *SDG Index and Dashboards Report 2018* (New York: Bertelsmann Stiftung and Sustainable Development Solutions Network (SDSN), 2018); IEA et al., *Tracking SDG7: The Energy Progress Report* (Washington, DC: World Bank Group, May 2018).

3 V. Masson-Delmotte et al., eds., 'Summary for Policymakers,' in *Global Warming of 1.5°C. An IPCC Special Report on the Impacts of Global Warming of 1.5°C above Pre-Industrial Levels and Related Global Greenhouse Gas Emission Pathways, in the Context of Strengthening the Global Response to the Threat of Climate Change, Sustainable Development, and Efforts to Eradicate Poverty* (Geneva: World Meterological Organization, 2018).

Sustainable Development Goals: Harnessing Business to Achieve the SDGs through Finance, Technology, and Law Reform, First Edition. Edited by Julia Walker, Alma Pekmezovic, and Gordon Walker.

a better understanding of how financial and trade flows can benefit (or hamper) sustainable development.

This chapter sheds light on G20 countries' performance gaps on the SDGs and discusses how the SDGs can be used more extensively as problem-solving tools for transformative actions and policies. Using the results from the latest SDG Index and Dashboards Report prepared by the Bertelsmann Stiftung and the Sustainable Development Solutions Network (SDSN), the first and second sections discuss the performance of G20 countries on the SDGs and identify three major transformations and one cross-cutting challenge that require further actions. The third section discusses how the SDGs can be used to inform policies and investments for sustainable development. It focuses on four major levers that can support the needed transformations: (1) long-term planning and back-casting; (2) data and monitoring; (3) financing strategies (including PPPs); and (4) technological change.

The performance of G20 countries on the SDGs varies greatly; but all of them need to accelerate progress to achieve the goals by 2030.

Every G20 member is behind in achieving at least one or more SDG.[4] In the latest SDG Index and Dashboards Report 2018, which measures every year countries' distance to achieving the SDGs, G20 countries rank from number 4 (Germany) to 113 (India) out of 157 countries. The best-performing countries are from the Nordic region (Sweden, Denmark, and Finland), but even these countries face major challenges in meeting the environment goals. Half of the G20 countries are not among the top 50 global performers (Argentina, Brazil, China, India, Indonesia, Mexico, Russian Federation, Saudi Arabia, South Africa, and Turkey). Even the best-performing G20 countries – Germany, France, the United Kingdom, Japan, and the European Union – have significant distance to travel to achieve the SDGs (Figure 12.1).

Based on the most recent trend data available, G20 countries are not on track for achieving the SDGs by 2030. Despite some improvements over the past five years on socioeconomic goals (Goals 1–10) the pace of progress remains too slow in many countries to fully achieve the SDGs. On Goals 12–15 – related to sustainable consumption and production, climate action, and the protection and restoration of nature – trends are going in the wrong direction due to rising energy-related CO_2 emissions in many countries and rapid biodiversity loss. Germany, the best performer among G20 countries, will not meet the SDGs by 2030 based on current trends and will fall considerably short on SDG 13 (Climate Action) and 14 (Life Below Water). The United States is currently on track for achieving only one of the 17 Goals – SDG 9 (Industry, Innovation, and Infrastructure). On the rest of the Goals, the United States would need significant acceleration of progress on SDG 4 (Quality Education), SDG 13

---

4 Sachs et al., *SDG Index and Dashboards Report 2018.*

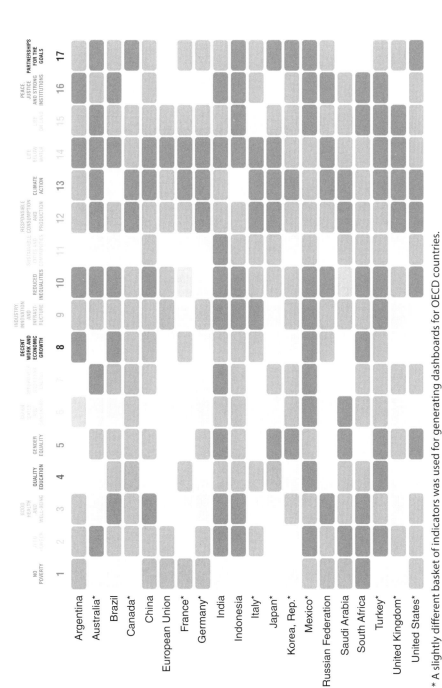

Figure 12.1 G20 Dashboards, 2018. *Sources*: J. Sachs, G. Schmidt-Traub, C. Kroll, G. Lafortune, and G. Fuller, *SDG Index and Dashboards Report 2018* (New York: Bertelsmann Stiftung and Sustainable Development Solutions Network (SDSN), 2018).

* A slightly different basket of indicators was used for generating dashboards for OECD countries.

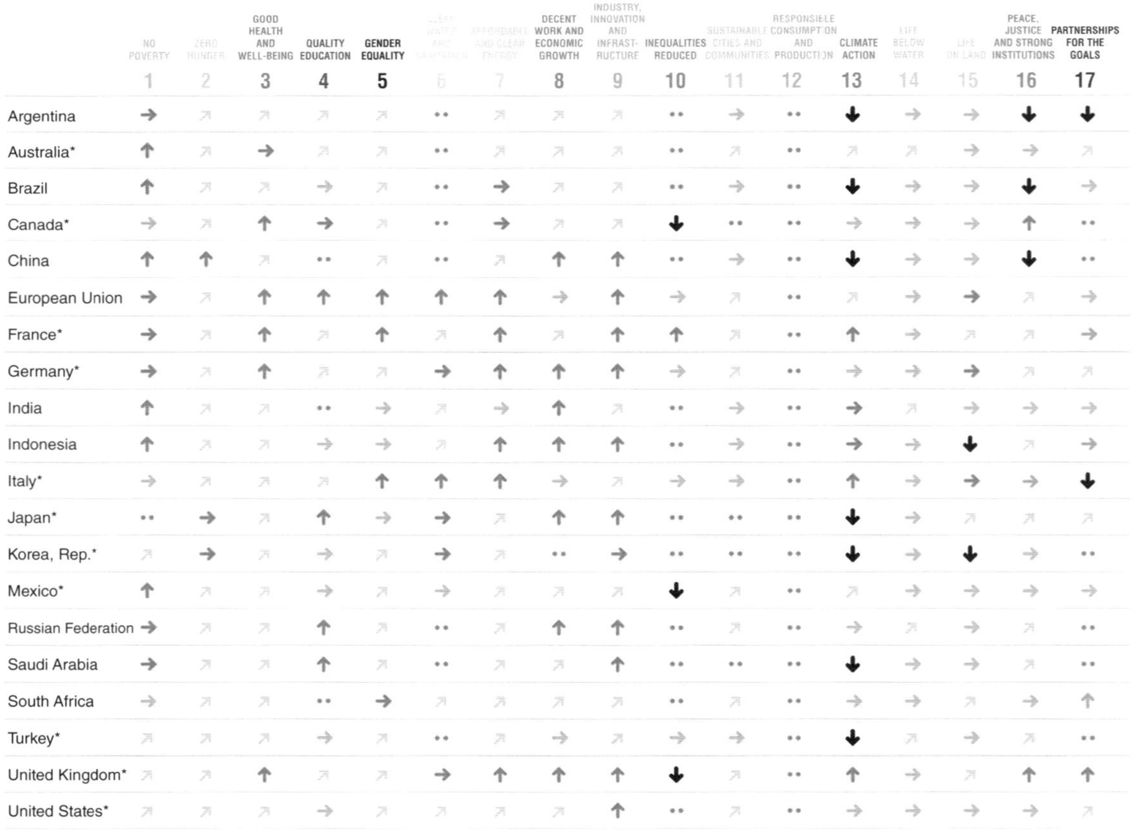

Figure 12.2 G20 Trend Dashboards, 2018. *Sources: J. Sachs, G. Schmidt-Traub, C. Kroll, G. Lafortune, and G. Fuller, SDG Index and Dashboards Report 2018 (New York: Bertelsmann Stiftung and Sustainable Development Solutions Network (SDSN), 2018).*

* A slightly different basket of indicators was used for generating dashboards for OECD countries.

Column headers (SDGs):

1 NO POVERTY · 2 ZERO HUNGER · 3 GOOD HEALTH AND WELL-BEING · 4 QUALITY EDUCATION · 5 GENDER EQUALITY · 6 CLEAN WATER AND SANITATION · 7 AFFORDABLE AND CLEAN ENERGY · 8 DECENT WORK AND ECONOMIC GROWTH · 9 INDUSTRY INNOVATION AND INFRASTRUCTURE · 10 REDUCED INEQUALITIES · 11 SUSTAINABLE CITIES AND COMMUNITIES · 12 RESPONSIBLE CONSUMPTION AND PRODUCTION · 13 CLIMATE ACTION · 14 LIFE BELOW WATER · 15 LIFE ON LAND · 16 PEACE JUSTICE AND STRONG INSTITUTIONS · 17 PARTNERSHIPS FOR THE GOALS

Countries (rows):

Argentina · Australia* · Brazil · Canada* · China · European Union · France* · Germany* · India · Indonesia · Italy* · Japan* · Korea, Rep.* · Mexico* · Russian Federation · Saudi Arabia · South Africa · Turkey* · United Kingdom* · United States*

(Climate Action), SDG 14 and 15 (Life on Land and Life below Water), and SDG 16 (Peace, Justice, and Strong Institutions).

These findings are supported by other reports.[5] For instance, the Climate Action Tracker (CAT) and Climate Transparency have analysed both the content of Intended Nationally Determined Contribution (INDCs) (*what governments propose*) to do and current policies (*what governments are actually doing*) on climate mitigation in G20 countries.[6] These independent reviews of SDG 13 (Climate Action) show that, with the exception of India, NDCs and current climate policies pursued by G20 countries are insufficient and, in some cases, critically insufficient to achieve the 'well below 2°C rise in global temperature' objective of the Paris Climate Agreement. Some countries have set insufficient targets, which they can reach without implementing new policies. Others have implemented policies that will not even allow insufficient targets to be met.

Assessments of individual countries also showcase large performance gaps. For example, Biggs and McArthur identify several areas where Canada drastically needs to change trajectories to meet the goals.[7] According to the audit conducted by Canada's Office of the Auditor General in 2018, the country 'has not done enough to prepare to implement the United Nations' 2030 Agenda for Sustainable Development'.[8] Similarly, a report by the European Think Tanks Group concludes that the European Union 'has made only limited progress in implementing the SDGs, and has invested more in "stocktaking" than in transformative reforms'.[9]

G20 countries need to prioritise three broad transformations and address one major cross-cutting challenge.

---

5 Eurostat, 'Sustainable Development in the European Union: Monitoring Report on Progress towards the SDGs in an EU Context (2018 Edition)' (Brussels, Belgium, October 2018), https://ec.europa.eu/eurostat/documents/3217494/9237449/KS-01-18-656-EN-N.pdf/2b2a096b-3bd6-4939-8ef3-11cfc14b9329; OECD, *Measuring Distance to the SDGs Targets: A Pilot Assessment of Where OECD Countries Stand* (Paris: OECD, 2016), http://www.oecd.org/std/measuring-distance-to-the-sdgs-targets.htm; Climate Action Tracker, 'Improvement in Warming Outlook as China and India Move Ahead, but Paris Agreement Gap Still Looms Large', 2017, https://climateactiontracker.org/documents/61/CAT_2017-11-15_ImprovementInWarmingOutlook_BriefingPaper.pdf.

6 Climate Action Tracker, 'Improvement in Warming Outlook as China and India Move Ahead, but Paris Agreement Gap Still Looms Large'.

7 Margaret Biggs and John W. McArthur, 'A Canadian North Star: Crafting an Advanced Economy Approach to the Sustainable Development Goals'. Brookings Global Economy and Development Working Paper No. 111. March 2018.

8 Office of the Auditor General of Canada, *Report 2 – Canada's Preparedness to Implement the United Nations' Sustainable Development Goals* (Federal Government of Canada, 2018).

9 European Think Tanks Group, 'Steering the EU towards a Sustainability Transformation' (April 2018).

The pursuit of sustainable development requires deep transformations that go beyond marginal progress or adaptation.[10] The term transformations comprises deep changes in policies, institutions, behaviour, and social norms that are needed to achieve the SDGs by 2030. Without long-term transformations of key sectors and industries, especially in G20 countries, the world will considerably fail in achieving the Agenda 2030, the SDGs, and Paris Climate Agreement. Figure 12.3 illustrates the importance of G20 countries by estimating *absolute*[11] performance gaps (in %) for achieving each of the goals. Apart from Goal 1 (No Poverty), where the bulk of the performance gap is located in sub-Saharan African countries, altogether G20 countries represent close to or more than 50% of the total performance gap for each of the goals. Brazil, China, India, Indonesia, and the United States each represent more than 2% of the global achievement gaps for the majority of the goals. Therefore, a lack of action and commitment from G20 countries would deprive large shares of the world population from sustainable development and improved living conditions.

China and India account for the largest shares of global SDG performance gaps. For example, China alone represents close to a third (30.1%) of the global performance gap on Goal 13 (Climate Action).[12] Using one of the underlying metrics, energy-related CO_2 emissions,[13] if China was to reduce emissions to 2 tonnes of CO_2 per capita per year (equivalent to a total reduction in CO_2 emissions equivalent to 73.5% compared to current levels of emissions) the world would be 34.5% closer to having achieved the SDG target on CO_2 emissions. Similarly, India alone represents 24.4% of the total achievement gap on SDG 2 (Zero Hunger).[14] If India eradicates undernourishment (currently 14.5% of the

---

10 TWI2050, 'Transformations to Achieve the Sustainable Development Goals. Report Prepared by The World in 2050 Initiative'. (Laxenburg, Austria: International Institute for Applied Systems Analysis, 2018), www.twi2050.org.

11 In the SDG Index and Dashboards, values are reported in most cases on a per capita basis (divided by total number of people). Absolute values represent the total raw value of each indicator (total CO_2 emissions, total number of poor people, total number of people with access to water, electricity, sewage etc.) without any transformations to account for differences in population sizes across countries.

12 In the SDSN/Bertelsmann Report, Goal 13 (Climate Action) is measured using four indicators: energy-related CO_2 emissions per capita; imported CO_2 emissions, technology adjusted; Climate Change Vulnerability Index; and CO_2 emissions embodied in fossil fuel exports.

13 Emissions of carbon dioxide that arise from the consumption of energy. This includes emissions due to the consumption of petroleum, natural gas, coal, and also from natural gas flaring (Source: Oak Ridge National Laboratory, 2018).

14 In the SDSN/Bertelsmann Report, SDG 2 (Zero Hunger) is measured by 6 indicators: prevalence of undernourishment, prevalence of stunting, prevalence of wasting, prevalence of obesity, cereal yield, and sustainable nitrogen management. The full title of SDG 2 is : 'End Hunger, Achieve Food Security and Improved Nutrition and Promote Sustainable Agriculture'.

	SDG1	SDG2	SDG3	SDG4	SDG5	SDG6	SDG7	SDG8	SDG9	SDG10	SDG11	SDG12	SDG13	SDG14	SDG15	SDG16	SDG17
Argentina	0.0	0.4	0.4	0.2	0.2	0.2	0.2	0.7	0.6	0.8	0.7	0.3	0.6	0.7	0.7	0.6	0.6
Australia	0.0	0.3	0.1	0.0	0.2	0.2	0.2	0.1	0.1	0.2	0.6	1.3	0.3	0.5	0.5	0.2	0.3
Brazil	1.0	2.0	2.0	2.2	2.3	0.2	0.8	2.9	2.6	4.5	3.0	1.4	2.1	2.8	4.3		2.1
Canada	0.0	0.4	0.1	0.0	0.2	0.6	0.1	0.2	0.2	1.7	0.6	0.9	0.4	0.5	0.3	0.2	0.4
China	0.7	12.1	12.4	16.9	11.7	8.9	16.7	10.1	13.3	16.4	17.5	18.5	30.1	23.8	17.9	15.1	19.9
European Union	0.6	4.3	1.8	1.9	3.5	4.0	2.3	4.0	3.6	3.7	10.5	5.3	6.4	4.3	4.7		6.2
France	0.0	0.5	0.2	0.3	0.3	0.4	0.1	0.5	0.4	0.3	1.4	0.7	0.6	0.6	0.6	0.5	0.6
Germany	0.0	0.5	0.2	0.5	0.5	0.7	0.4	0.3	0.3	0.4	1.8	0.7	1.2	0.6	0.5	0.4	0.6
India	7.8	24.4	24.2	21.5	29.1	25.0	23.7	22.0	20.5	19.6	23.7	12.1	18.0	16.0	22.1	14.6	19.8
Indonesia	1.5	4.0	4.5	2.8	3.4	2.3	3.6	3.2	4.6	4.9	3.8	2.7	2.0	3.6	4.7	2.7	4.4
Italy	0.1	0.5	0.2	0.2	0.5	0.6	0.3	0.7	0.5	0.7	1.3	0.7	0.9	0.8	0.8	0.7	
Japan	0.1	0.9	0.3	0.3	1.7	0.7	0.6	0.5	0.8	1.3	2.8	1.3	1.4	0.6	1.3	0.5	1.7
Korea. Rep.	0.1	0.3	0.2	0.2	0.6	0.6	0.2	0.4	0.4	0.4	0.9	0.5	0.6	0.7	0.6	0.6	0.8
Mexico	0.6	1.7	1.0	1.1	1.0	1.0	1.0	1.9	3.2	1.0	1.6	1.1	1.4	2.3	2.4	1.5	
Russian Federation	0.0	2.2	1.4	0.4	1.4	0.6	0.8	2.1	1.8	0.9	2.1	2.0	1.8	1.8	3.6		2.0
Saudi Arabia	0.0	0.5	0.2	0.2	0.6	1.2	0.2	0.3	0.4	0.8	0.7	1.0	0.4	0.5	0.3	1.2	0.4
South Africa	3.0	0.8	1.1	3.6	0.3	0.9	0.7	1.2	0.7	1.6	0.4	0.7	0.6	1.0	1.2	0.3	
Turkey	0.0	1.1	0.6	0.7	1.3	1.6	0.6	1.3	0.9	1.4	0.9	0.7	1.3	1.3	1.3	1.1	0.9
United Kingdom	0.0	0.5	0.2	0.0	0.4	0.3	0.3	0.3	0.3	0.5	0.2	1.5	0.9	0.8	0.8	0.4	1.2
United States	0.4	2.4	1.5	1.2	2.7	1.9	1.5	1.7	1.1	4.9	1.7	10.0	7.8	4.2	5.5	3.8	4.2
Total G20	15.5%	55.6%	50.9%	48.9%	58.4%	47.9%	52.1%	50.7%	50.9%	62.6%	56.3%	64.5%	72.1%	61.9%	65.8%	53.5%	62.3%

Legend

Less than 2%	10% to < 20%
2% to < 10%	20% or more

Figure 12.3 Absolute performance gaps for achieving the SDGs, 2018. *Source:* Author's analysis based on Sachs et al. (2018).

Indian population) the world will be 24.8% closer to having achieved the SDG target on undernourishment.

G20 countries are grappling with common challenges, even if the specifics vary. The need for three broad transformations and for addressing one cross-cutting challenge stands out. The first major transformation is related to *inequalities, education, and innovation*. The SDGs call on all countries to tackle income and other inequalities and achieve universal secondary school completion by 2030. Many G20 countries have high levels of inequality, and inequality is rising in most G20 countries. Unequal access to public services and opportunities among certain population groups are major impediments for achieving SDG 4 (Quality Education), SDG 5 (Gender Equality), and SDG 10 (Reduced Inequalities) in most G20 countries. They also lower people's confidence in public institutions and are a major cause of social unrest and major discontent among parts of the population – including in Europe.

Even some of the top-performing G20 countries face major challenges in improving equity and in ensuring decent living conditions for all. For instance, in their assessment of Canada's domestic status on the SDGs, McArthur and Rasmussen[15] find that Canada has been moving backward recently on 18 indicators, including on adolescent numeracy, access to safe drinking water, access to affordable housing, and reported crimes against females. Persisting shortfalls in access to water and sanitation and to health care and education services among first nations and indigenous communities must be addressed in order to leave no one behind, as called for by Agenda 2030.[16]

Fiscal and policy levers can help address some of these complex challenges.[17] Improving access to schools and quality of education, investing in preschool programmes, strengthening the transition from school to work (including through apprenticeship programmes or vocational training), expanding social safety nets, introducing anti-discrimination measures, and improving labour standards are important measures to address persisting performance gaps on SDG 4 (Quality Education), SDG 5 (Gender Equality), and SDG 10 (Reduced Inequalities). G20 countries should also consider further investments and measures to boost R&D, promote innovation (SDG 9), and accelerate the adoption of new technologies, which together form a basis for long-term economic growth (SDG 8).

The second major priority for G20 countries is the transformation to *clean energy and sustainable industries*. As emphasised by the IPCC's Special Report

---

15 John McArthur and Krista Rasmussen, 'Who and What Gets Left Behind? Assessing Canada's Domestic Status on the Sustainable Development Goals' (Brookings, October 2017).
16 United Nations, 'Transforming Our World: The 2030 Agenda for Sustainable Development', A/RES/70/1 (New York: United Nations, 2015), https://sustainabledevelopment.un.org/post2015/transformingourworld.
17 TWI2050, 'Transformations to Achieve the Sustainable Development Goals'. Report Prepared by The World in 2050 Initiative.

on 1.5°C,[18] countries need to fully decarbonise their energy systems by the middle of this century. The transformation to zero-carbon power systems is technically feasible and economically affordable, but it touches on virtually every aspect of a country's economy: power generation and transmission, transport, industry, and buildings.[19]

As the SDG Dashboard (Figure 12.1) and the trend analysis (Figure 12.2) show, all G20 countries are far from decarbonising their energy systems. Indeed, the Climate Action Tracker[20] shows that current policies and most targets are insufficient for meeting the goals of the Paris Climate Agreement. G20 countries should pursue three broad pillars for decarbonising their energy systems.[21] First, they need to decarbonise power generation by replacing fossil fuels, such as coal, oil, and gas, with renewable sources (e.g. solar, hydro, wind) and other zero-carbon technologies. Second, countries need to vastly increase the efficiency of energy use through improved appliances and industrial processes, smart grid management, thermal insulation of buildings, shift to public transport, demand management, and other techniques. Finally, the decarbonisation of power systems requires that point emission sources, such as vehicles, industrial plants, and heating systems in buildings, are electrified or replaced with zero-carbon fuels.

The third broad transformation is related to sustainable land-use and food systems, which includes moving to net-negative greenhouse gas emissions for land use. As described above, G20 countries are losing biodiversity at unprecedented rates – driven largely by the expansion of agriculture and the widespread use of chemicals. Agriculture is also driving widespread loss of topsoil and falling groundwater tables in many countries, particularly parts of China, India, and the United States. While overall food production in G20 countries is sufficient to meet caloric needs, countries do not produce healthy foods. Obesity is spreading in all G20 countries, and micronutrient deficiencies remain high.[22]

To address these challenges, countries need to transform their land-use and food systems by focusing on three pillars.[23] First, agricultural, livestock, and

---

18 IPCC, 'Summary for Policymakers'. In T. F. Stocker et al. (eds), *Climate Change 2013 (2013): The Physical Science Basis* (Cambridge, UK and New York: Cambridge University Press) https://www.ipcc.ch/report/ar5/wg1/.

19 Steven J. Davis et al., 'Net-Zero Emissions Energy Systems', *Science* 360, no. 6396 (2018): eaas9793 https://science.sciencemag.org/content/360/6396/eaas9793.editor-summary.

20 'Improvement in Warming Outlook as China and India Move Ahead, but Paris Agreement Gap Still Looms Large.'

21 SDSN and IDDRI, 'Pathways to Deep Decarbonization 2015 Report,' Deep Decarbonization Pathways (DDPP) Project, 2015.

22 Walter Willett et al., 'Food in the Anthropocene: The EAT–Lancet Commission on Healthy Diets from Sustainable Food Systems,' *The Lancet* 393, no. 10170 (February 2019): 447–92, https://doi.org/10.1016/S0140-6736(18)31788-4.

23 Guido Schmidt-Traub and Michael Obersteiner, 'Fixing Our Broken Food System: A Crucial SDG Challenge,' *Horizons*, no. 12 (2018): 160–73.

forestry production systems must become vastly more efficient in resource use to increase productivity and reduce their environmental impact, including greenhouse gas emissions. This also includes investments to make agriculture more climate resilient, for example through better water resource management and the introduction of heat-tolerant varieties. Second, countries need to protect and restore terrestrial and marine biodiversity and ecosystem services. And, third, they need to support a shift towards healthy diets that are also environmentally sustainable. Implementing these three pillars will require concerted action across all branches of government.

Finally, one major cross-cutting SDG challenge relates to *international spillover effects* caused by G20 countries. International spillover effects occur when one country's actions generate benefits or impose costs on another country that are not reflected in market prices, and therefore are not 'internalised' by the actions of consumers and producers.[24] These include notably environmental spillovers (such as CO_2 emissions or groundwater depletion embodied in trade). In the SDG context, it is no longer acceptable or possible for countries to reduce their national environmental footprint by outsourcing environmental impacts to other countries. Beyond environmental spillovers, there can be security spillovers (such as weapons exports) or spillovers related to the economy, finance, and governance (such as international tax evasion). Positive spillovers also matter, for instance official development assistance (ODA).

The 2018 SDG Index and Dashboards Report shows that most G20 countries generate larger negative spillover effects than the rest of the countries included in the report (Figure 12.4). These spillover effects undermine other countries' efforts to achieve the SDGs. Yet, there is high variation in spillovers among G20 countries with the United Kingdom and the United States generating the largest negative spillover effects, and India on balance generating very low per capita spillover effects on other countries. There is high variation in spillovers among countries with a similar per capita income. This suggests that countries can reduce their negative spillover effects without reducing their per capita incomes.

These high negative spillover effects call for changes in G20 countries' trade policies but also for special attention to human rights and international cooperation. A fair, rules-based trade system supports economic development in rich and poor countries alike. It promotes export-led development, which has driven unprecedented poverty reduction over the last several decades, particularly in much of Asia. International diplomacy and law to promote peace, human rights, and secure the benefits of cross-border cooperation is also an area where G20 countries can play a major role. They depend on the legitimacy

---

24 J. D. Sachs et al., 'SDG Index and Dashboards Report 2017. Global Responsibilities: International Spillovers in Achieving the Goals' (Gütersloh and New York: Bertelsmann Stiftung and Sustainable Development Solutions Network, 2017), http://sdgindex.org/.

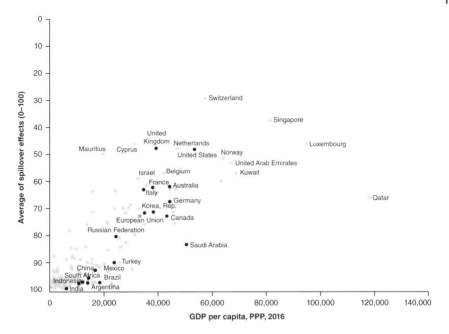

Figure 12.4 International spillover effects by level of GDP, 2018. *Source:* Authors' analysis based on Sachs et al., 2018.
Note: The darkest dots denote G20 countries. Spillover effects include environmental spillovers (such as CO_2 emissions or groundwater depletion embodied into trade), security spillovers (such as weapons exports) or spillovers related to the economy, finance, and governance (such as international tax evasion). The total score was generated using a simple average of all spillover indicators used in Sachs et al., 2018.

of and participation in regional and global institutions to set norms, resolve conflicts, and promote collaboration. As the largest economies in the world, G20 countries bear a special responsibility to ensure that critical global systems are consistent with the SDGs.

The SDGs as Problem-Solving Tools for Transformative Actions and Policies

Unlike other great transformations of the past, sustainable development requires long-term directed change. This section discusses the role of (a) long-term planning and back-casting; (b) data and monitoring; (c) financing strategies; and (d) technological innovation as key enablers of long-term change in G20 countries and other countries.

Long-Term Planning and Back-Casting

The SDGs call for target-based and time-bound policies and action plans. Long-term pathways need to be developed in many areas to capture synergies and trade-offs across policy options, but also to support coherent actions and interventions from various stakeholders, including investors, businesses, industries, and the research community. This requires working backwards from the goals ('back-casting') to identify the investments and policies required to build infrastructure, strengthen human resources, deliver services, and undertake other interventions to achieve the SDGs.[25] Such long-term planning can help lay our potential operational pathways that demonstrate the feasibility of achieving complex, ambitious goals. Projects such as the Deep Decarbonization Pathways Project (DDPP)[26] or the Food, Agriculture, Biodiversity, Land, and Energy (FABLE) Consortium[27] aim to generate the necessary knowledge to support policymakers in designing and implementing such trajectories for decarbonisation and land-use.

Results from the 2018 survey on national SDG implementation mechanisms conducted by the SDSN and the Bertelsmann Stiftung show large variations among G20 countries in how the SDGs are embraced by the political leadership and translated into long-term action plans and dedicated institutional mechanisms.[28] All G20 countries have presented a Voluntary National Review (VNR) at the United Nations – except the Russian Federation (planned for 2020), South Africa (planned for 2019), and the United States. Some countries have established dedicated coordination units, strategies and action plans, and accountability systems, while others lag behind on some or all of these dimensions. Yet, over one-quarter of G20 members – Australia, Canada, South Korea, Russia, Saudi Arabia, and the United States – have not yet identified key national priorities regarding the implementation of the SDGs. This is a critical shortcoming since the SDGs do not themselves offer a roadmap to sustainable development. Rather, stakeholders within each country – including civil society, business leaders, and financial regulators – convened by national governments, are supposed to formulate their own strategic priorities, national plans, and implementation strategies to attain the goals in accordance with their domestic contexts.[29]

---

25 Jessica Espey, Guillaume Lafortune, and Guido Schmidt-Traub, 'Delivering the Sustainable Development Goals for All: Policy Priorities for Leaving No One Behind,' in *Development Co-operation Report 2018. Joining Forces to Leave No One Behind* (Paris: OECD, 2018).

26 SDSN and IDDRI, 'Pathways to Deep Decarbonization 2015 Report.'

27 Schmidt-Traub and Obersteiner, 'Fixing Our Broken Food System: A Crucial SDG Challenge.'

28 Sachs et al., *SDG Index and Dashboards Report 2018. New York: Bertelsmann Stiftung and Sustainable Development Solutions Network (SDSN).*

29 Homi Kharas et al., 'Advancing the G20's Commitment to the 2030 Agenda' (CARI and CIPPEC, T20 Argentina, September 2019).

Data and Monitoring

To support these long-term plans and institutional processes, it is essential that governments invest in and have access to timely, disaggregated data. Under SDG 17.19 all countries have committed to 'build on existing initiatives to develop measurements of progress on sustainable development that complement gross domestic product [. . .]'. A majority of G20 countries, via their National Statistical Institute, have developed or are in the process of developing national indicators of progress on the SDGs (Figure 12.5). There is no common approach across G20 countries for identifying the nature and number of national indicators to monitor progress on the SDGs, which range from 63 in Germany to 201 in Italy. The European Union, via Eurostat, has identified 100 indicators to monitor the implementation of the SDGs in the EU.[30]

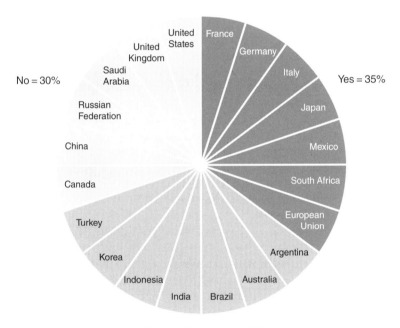

Figure 12.5 Did the National Statistical Institute or any mandated central/federal institutions identify official key national indicators to monitor the implementation of the SDGs? (2018). *Source:* J. Sachs, G. Schmidt-Traub, C. Kroll, G. Lafortune, and G. Fuller, *SDG Index and Dashboards Report 2018*. New York: Bertelsmann Stiftung and Sustainable Development Solutions Network (SDSN) (2018).

---

30 Eurostat, 'Sustainable Development in the European Union: Monitoring Report on Progress toward the SDGs in an EU Context', 20 November 2017; Eurostat, 'Sustainable Development in the European Union: Monitoring Report on Progress towards the SDGs in an EU Context (2018 edition)'; Sachs et al., *SDG Index and Dashboards Report 2018*. New York: Bertelsmann Stiftung and Sustainable Development Solutions Network (SDSN).

Governments, international organisations, business, and civil society should continue to increase their investments in more and better data for SDG implementation.[31] New sources of data, including for instance big data, censors, and satellite imagery, can help bridge data gaps in official statistics and support evidence-based policymaking. TReNDs, the SDSN's thematic network on data and statistics provides guidance on how to improve the quality of available data and ensure adequate data governance. For instance, POPGRID, a consortium of research organisations looking to standardise and expand new innovative methodologies, has catalogued a huge array of high-resolution population estimation techniques drawing on satellite imagery, mobile telecommunications data, and much more.[32]

Performance audits, using a mix of quantitative and qualitative data, are also being used to inform the implementation of the SDGs. In particular, Supreme Audit Institutions (SAIs), play a growing role in promoting effective implementation and accountability in the SDG context.[33] Traditionally SAIs have focused on financial and compliance audits, but they are increasingly incorporating other aspects, such as performance and value for money audits.[34] The International Organization of Supreme Audit Institutions (INTOSAI) has issued guidelines for how SAIs can contribute to the success of the 2030 Agenda and the SDGs in their countries.[35] As of 2019, SAIs in four G20 countries – Argentina, Brazil, Canada, and Germany – have produced audit reports on the SDGs. These reports, and audit reports produced in other countries, demonstrate the positive role that performance auditing can play in promoting a whole of government approach to implementing the SDGs and in highlighting shortfalls, including in addressing issues related to access to and quality of public services across population groups and regions.

Financing

Financing the long-term transformations needed to achieve the SDGs requires large-scale increased financing. At some 2–3% of world gross product, the incremental resources needs from public and private actors are substantial

---

31 OECD, *Development Co-Operation Report 2018: Joining Forces to Leave No One Behind* (Paris: OECD Publishing, 2018).

32 Espey, Lafortune, and Schmidt-Traub, 'Delivering the Sustainable Development Goals for All: Policy Priorities for Leaving No One Behind.'

33 Vries, G.d., 'How National Audit Offices Can Support Implementation of the SDGs', 2016, http://blog-pfm.imf.org/pfmblog/2016/06/national-audit-offices-should-support-implementation-of-the-sdgs.html.

34 OECD and OCDE, *Government at a Glance 2017* (OECD Publishing; Éditions OCDE, 2017).

35 INTOSAI, 'SDGs: SAIs and Regions', 2018, http://www.intosai.org/about-us/sdgs-sais-and-regions.html.

but manageable.[36] However, meeting the SDGs in the poorest countries does represent a major financing challenge, and these countries will need to greatly increase domestic resource mobilisation in the context of increased international development finance flows.[37]

Given the tight fiscal environment in many G20 countries, these governments will need to find more effective and efficient ways to raise, leverage, and direct their investments.[38] Public-private partnerships (PPP) – in which a formal partnership is formed between government agencies (often serving as funders) and private business (often serving as implementers) – can serve as powerful tools to leverage each partner's comparative advantage. Public-private partnerships are pervasive in sustainable development, typically because the private sector is the exclusive holder of the requisite technologies and large-scale management capacities, while the public sector is needed to mobilise resources for public goods that would otherwise be underprovided by the market.

Yet, PPPs have proven difficult to implement in many areas. In particular, the challenges of balancing social and private interests through efficient contracting and results-based payments have proven challenging to implement. Given the scale of the SDG financing challenge, we need greater innovation in the sector. Long-term pathways for the transformations can help provide a framework for coherent action on leveraging finance around long-term policy frameworks by standardizing project types, ensuring system-based design and implementation, and by reducing the transaction costs for project design and monitoring.

Technology Missions

Finally, many SDG transformations are constrained by the high cost or unavailability of sustainable technologies. As the world's major hubs for innovation, G20 countries need to accelerate innovation, technology development, and

---

36 UNCTAD, 'World Investment Report 2014. Investing in the SDGs: An Action Plan' (Geneva: United Nations Conference on Trade and Development, 2014), http://unctad.org/en/pages/PublicationWebflyer.aspx?publicationid=937; Guido Schmidt-Traub, 'Investment Needs to Achieve the Sustainable Development Goals', SDSN Working Paper (Paris: Sustainable Development Solutions Network, 2015), http://unsdsn.org/resources/publications/sdg-investment-needs/.

37 Vitor Gaspar et al., 'Fiscal Policy and Development: Human, Social, and Physical Investment for the SDGs', IMF Staff Discussion Note SDN/19/3 (Washington DC: International Monetary Fund, 2019).

38 Blended Finance Task Force, 'Blended Finance Better World. Consultation Paper of the Blended Finance Task Force' (London: Blended Finance Task Force, 2018), https://static1.squarespace.com/static/59562732f7e0ab94574ba86a/t/5a70981d24a6940ca887c5fa/1517328443557/BFT_BetterFinance_FINAL_18012018.pdf.

deployment. Mission-oriented public policies, which mobilise resources and knowledge in the direction of the desired technological objectives and over-arching societal goals provide a useful operating framework[39] that is being operationalised in the European Union.[40]

Technology missions can mobilise public and private actors across a broad range of sectors. They comprise making strategic decisions on how to allow general purpose technologies (e.g. Internet-based applications, battery storage for intermittent renewable energy) to create opportunities across sectors. Similarly, attention must be placed on the type of long-term finance that is needed by innovative firms; innovation systems; regulations and common standards to create a more certain and cohesive investment environment; the innovative use of government purchasing/procurement to allow small firms to scale up; and a tax system that rewards long-termism and investments towards targeted technological changes, while always nurturing bottom-up experimentation.

Conclusion

Like the rest of the world nations, G20 countries signed up to Agenda 2030, including the Sustainable Development Goals, in 2015. These goals provide a useful framework for collective problem solving in G20 countries and enhanced international cooperation around shared goals within the G20 and beyond.

Almost all G20 leaders have taken some steps towards implementing the SDGs and have presented a Voluntary National Review at the UN High-Level Political Forum since 2016. Yet, this chapter shows that G20 countries are not on track to meeting the goals. Major transformations are needed to address inequalities, decarbonise energy systems, and make land-use and food systems sustainable. Marginal changes will not be enough to deliver on the SDGs.

Time is short to launch the transformations needed to achieve the SDGs, as described in this chapter. Yet, these transformations are feasible and affordable. As the largest economies in the world, G20 countries bear a special responsibility to lead on implementation. They need to undertake back-castings to chart strategies for achieving the goals, strengthen their data and monitoring systems, develop sound financing strategies, and launch technology missions to support directed changes that can help achieve the goals. G20 countries must also help the world's poorest countries escape extreme forms of deprivation, including by curbing negative international spillovers and by providing more generous international development finance, such as official development assistance.

---

39 Mariana Mazzucato, 'Mission-Oriented Innovation Policy: Challenges and Opportunities', UCL Institute for Innovation and Public Purpose Working Paper (London: UCL, 2017), https://www.ucl.ac.uk/bartlett/public-purpose/wp2017-01.
40 Mariana Mazzucato, 'Mission-Oriented Research & Innovation in the European Union: A Problem-Solving Approach to Fuel Innovation-Led Growth', Report for the European Commission (Brussels, 2018), https://publications.europa.eu/en/publication-detail/-/publication/5b2811d1-16be-11e8-9253-01aa75ed71a1/language-en.

13

The Future-Fit Business Benchmark

Flourishing Business in a Truly Sustainable Future

Geoff Kendall and Martin Rich

Introduction

Our global economy is not fit for purpose: we are degrading the environment, failing to meet the basic needs of billions of people, and not adequately incentivising business to tackle these problems. The SDGs are a global response to these challenges, and a call for rapid and radical collective action. Representing a $12 trillion market opportunity by 2030, the SDGs have been hailed as a 'purchase order from the future' for businesses willing to step up. However, being 'least bad' among peers is not going to be good enough: to thrive, business must find new ways to create value that deliver environmental, social, and financial success. Hundreds of resources exist to help business respond, but a critical question has gone unanswered: what's the destination?

This chapter explores the Future-Fit Business Benchmark – a free business tool designed to guide real progress towards a flourishing future, and to make the SDGs a reality. Built upon more than 30 years of scientific research, the Benchmark consists of 23 social and environmental goals which together identify the extra-financial breakeven point every business must eventually reach to ensure it protects people and the planet. The Benchmark also shows how all businesses can make credible positive contributions to the SDGs, while simultaneously working to ensure that they are not inadvertently undermining progress elsewhere. Furthermore, businesses are able to convey their journey towards future-fitness through consistent, comparable, forward-looking data, enabling investors to identify which ones are on the right trajectory and increasingly direct their capital accordingly.

Sustainable Development Goals: Harnessing Business to Achieve the SDGs through Finance, Technology, and Law Reform, First Edition. Edited by Julia Walker, Alma Pekmezovic, and Gordon Walker.

The Journey Ahead

The World We Want

Imagine a future in which business is truly, unquestionably a force for good; a future where no company, intentionally or otherwise, undermines the well-being of people or the planet.

In this future, the global economy works in harmony with nature: today's take-make-waste approach to meeting human needs has been supplanted by a borrow-use-return approach. The more profitable a company is, the more it is celebrated – not just by its shareholders, but by everyone – because every dollar earned is creating value for society as a whole.

In this future, the concept of 'growth' is synonymous not with higher GDP, but with increasing trust, greater equity, healthier lives, and richer ecosystems. And in their pursuit of growth, all companies strive to ensure that every person contributing to their success is afforded the opportunity to learn, grow, and lead fulfilling lives.

In this future, society becomes ever more environmentally restorative, socially just, and economically inclusive, because all key actors are working collaboratively, consciously, and continuously to the same end: the removal of barriers to our collective progress.

This is a vision of a Future-Fit Society: one serviced by an economy of Future-Fit Businesses, each playing its part to create the conditions required for humanity to flourish on our finite planet. This is no utopia – people will still get sick, crimes will occur, accidents will happen – but it is a compelling, plausible, and achievable vision.

Unfortunately, however, we are a long way from realising this vision.

The World We Have (and How We Got Here)

Since the start of the industrial revolution, humanity has made astonishing progress. The proportion of people living in extreme poverty, for example, was cut in half between 1990 and 2010.[1] Early in the nineteenth century only 12% of the world could read and write, whereas today over 83% of people across the globe are literate.[2] And while in 1870 life expectancy at birth was only around 30, the average life expectancy around the world today is closer to 72.[3]

Yet this great progress has come at a cost.

---

1 World Bank, Progress on the Millennium Development Goals, www.worldbank.org/en/topic/poverty/overview.
2 Our World in Data, *Literacy by Max Roser and Esteban Ortiz-Ospina*, www.ourworldindata.org/literacy.
3 Our World in Data, *Life Expectancy by Max Roser*, www.ourworldindata.org/life-expectancy.

Roughly 250 years ago, there were fewer than a billion people on Earth. Back then, the planet's resources – and its resilience in the face of our demand for them – must have seemed limitless. So it should come as no surprise that classical economics, which dates from that period, did not consider the fact that we live in a finite, resource-constrained world. In fact, it was widely believed that 'growth' is intrinsically good, and that infinite growth is both possible and desirable.

This thinking set the tone for the way we have done business for generations: producing, consuming, and disposing of ever more stuff, without weighing the long-term consequences. Nature provides us with a vast range of essential resources, but we are using them up around 1.7 times faster than the Earth can regenerate them.[4] Indeed, the scale of our consumption and impact is astonishing.

Consider, for instance, that the world lost the equivalent of one football pitch of forest every second in 2017.[5] Chemical-intensive farming techniques, deforestation, and global warming have been destroying our soil for decades, meaning that at current rates all of the world's top soil could be gone within 60 years.[6] That would mean no more harvests, which is a sobering thought given that 95% of our food comes from the soil. Diseases caused by pollution were responsible for around 9 million premature deaths in 2015,[7] representing 16% of all deaths worldwide, and three times more than from AIDS, TB, and malaria combined. And each year around 8 million tons of plastic ends up in our oceans,[8] which, given that plastic waste doesn't biodegrade but just breaks down into ever-smaller pieces, will find its way back into our food and water systems. Indeed, a recent study across five continents found plastic particles in 83% of tap water.[9]

Of course, no one deliberately caused these issues. These examples are just symptomatic of the way our global economy has evolved to value financial performance ahead of societal and planetary well-being. As a result, the basic needs of billions of people around the world are not being met, while the gap between the haves and have-nots grows. And we are disrupting and degrading Earth's natural processes, which humanity and all other life depend upon.

---

4 Ecological Footprint, 'Global Ecological Overshoot', www.footprintnetwork.org/our-work/ecological-footprint.

5 Global Forest Watch, www.globalforestwatch.org.

6 Food and Agriculture Organization of the United Nations, www.fao.org/soils-2015/events/detail/en/c/338738/.

7 The Lancet Commission on Pollution and Health (19 October 2017), www.thelancet.com/commissions/pollution-and-health.

8 J. R. Jambeck et al., 'Plastic Waste Inputs from Land into the Ocean' (13 February 2015), http://science.sciencemag.org/content/347/6223/768.

9 C. Tyree and D. Morrison, 'Invisibles: The Plastic Inside Us', www.orbmedia.org/stories/Invisibles_plastics/.

These problems are so big and so complex that they are undermining the viability of civilisation as we know it – making it impossible for *any* company to thrive. To neutralise these threats, we need to start favouring economic activity that *enriches* our social fabric and Earth's natural systems – what we might call *extra-financial performance.*

There are currently 7.5 billion people on the planet, and 2 billion more are set to join us by 2050. So if we're going to usher in a Future-Fit Society, we need to act fast. One thing is for sure, though: we will only get things back on track if everyone – companies, governments, investors, and so on – work together. Recognising this, world governments came together in 2015 under the auspices of the United Nations to launch the Sustainable Development Goals – a rallying call for everyone, from nation states to corporations. They offer all economic actors something that has been sorely lacking: a shared vision for the problems we must solve, and a common vocabulary for directing and describing progress. If everyone plays their part, and all of the underlying 169 targets are reached, we won't have completely eradicated poverty or climate change by 2030, but we will be on a trajectory to doing so.

The World We Can Create

At their heart, the SDGs are really about fixing how our economy operates – which means changing how we do business. Governments must put in place the rules and incentives necessary to foster effective market-based solutions. But as the engines of our economy, it is the tens of thousands of companies around the world that have the biggest part to play.

The SDGs represent an urgent call to action for business and have been described as a 'crowd-sourced purchase order from the future'. This purchase-order analogy is instructive for two reasons. First, it acknowledges that the SDGs identify what society needs – and therefore what the global economy must deliver. And second, it reflects the fact that the SDGs offer a tremendous financial opportunity. Indeed, research estimates that the market for SDG-related goods and services will reach $12 trillion per year by 2030.[10]

So how should business leaders respond to this call to action?

The first option is to defend the status quo: to tell a story about what the company is already doing on topics relating to the SDGs, rather than seeking out opportunities to change. For example, a company with an existing target to reduce its greenhouse gas emissions may claim it is aligned with SDG 13 – Climate Action. But most of today's greenhouse gas targets are nowhere near ambitious enough to deliver what's required.

---

10 Better Business, Better World, *The Business and Sustainable Development Commission,* http://report.businesscommission.org/report.

Emphasising storytelling over action merely justifies 'business as usual' – which is what got us into this mess in the first place. A defensive approach to the SDGs may appeal to CEOs who still believe in the primacy of shareholder value – in other words, that companies exist only to deliver financial returns – but claims that lack ambition and authenticity only leave companies open to accusations of SDG-washing. Any company taking such a defensive route is unlikely to attract and retain great employees, loyal customers, and increasingly concerned investors.

The second option open to business leaders is to be selective and focus on just one or a few of the SDGs. This selective approach is akin to the notion of Creating Shared Value, whereby a company looks for opportunities where its current business model happens to overlap with societal needs. For example, a pharmaceutical company may choose to focus on SDG 3 – Good Health and Well-being – by making medicines that help people to live productive lives. Such efforts may indeed make a genuine contribution to SDG 3, if the medicines are affordable and accessible to those who need them most. But what if manufacturing the medicines uses huge amounts of fresh water, and the production takes place in a water-stressed area? For local communities in that region, the company may actually be *undermining* SDG 6 – Clean Water and Sanitation.

The reality is that today's companies exist only as part of a complex value web that touches multiple, interlinked systems: markets, communities, ecosystems, and so on. In this sea of complexity, linear notions of cause and effect start to evaporate – and without careful consideration, any action in one area can lead to undesirable consequences elsewhere. Hence a selective approach to the SDGs can be counterproductive: even the most well-meaning company might seek to solve one problem while inadvertently exacerbating another. Are such trade-offs acceptable? Possibly, but how can we decide if we don't know what they are?

All of which brings us to the third option for business leaders: taking a holistic approach, to consider all of a company's SDG impacts, both positive and negative, across the company's value web. No business decision is ever free of trade-offs. But if we take a systems approach – by looking at all interactions between the company and its suppliers, its customers, other socioeconomic actors, and the environment – it is possible to identify otherwise unforeseen issues. Negative trade-offs across the company's value web can then be anticipated, avoided, or at the very least mitigated.

This kind of systems approach to managing extra-financial performance is crucial, because we will only make the SDGs a reality if we start to eliminate – and eventually reverse – damage to our natural systems and social fabric. We can think of this as striving to create not just *shareholder* value, or even *shared* value, but *system* value. That means responding to the SDGs in a holistic way, to maximise the good while working consciously, continuously, and collectively to eliminate the bad.

Why a Systems View Is Good for Business

How should this notion of creating system value change how we think about business performance? The SDGs were introduced in 2015, but there is nothing new about the idea that business performance is not just about profit, but about people and the planet, too. Indeed, the term 'Triple Bottom Line' was coined to describe this concept 25 years ago.

Unfortunately, the Triple Bottom Line has often been portrayed as three overlapping circles. This visual framing is unhelpful, because it suggests that business touches society and the environment to some degree, while being largely independent of them. Looking at this diagram, it should perhaps be no surprise that social and environmental issues are often missing from discussions about core business strategy.

But taking a systems view, the Triple Bottom Line is more accurately represented as three nested circles (see Figure 13.1). Now the true context becomes apparent: business can only thrive if society flourishes, and society can only flourish if the environment is capable of supporting its needs. Yet as we've already discussed, neither of these conditions for success can be taken for granted today. In fact, as we move further into the twenty-first century, every company's financial performance will become ever-more dependent on how well it manages its extra-financial performance.

The good news however is that many CEOs already 'think in systems' to some extent. Figure 13.2a shows Porter's Five Forces Model, which has been taught in MBA programmes since the 1970s. It's a tool that business leaders use to understand the various forces operating in and around their industries, and to identify the risks and opportunities they pose.

We can think of this as a *systems intelligence* tool: the Five Forces help business leaders 'see' the context within which their company is operating, so they can create better strategic responses to it. But in today's ever-more complex world, companies must improve the quality of their systems intelligence by looking *beyond* their immediate industries. When we extend our view outwards, we see that entire industries are being buffeted by a further three, macro-level forces (see Figure 13.2b).

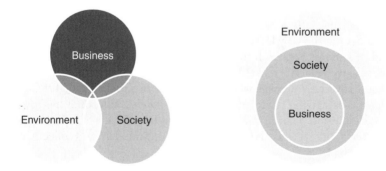

Figure 13.1 From Shared Value to System Value

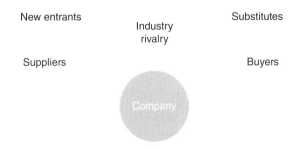

Figure 13.2a Porter's Five Forces Model.

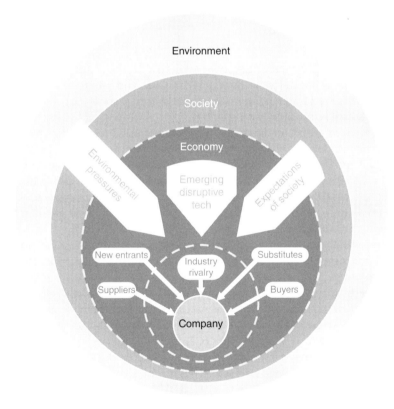

Figure 13.2b Future-Fit's Eight Forces Model. *Source:* © 2018 Future-Fit Foundation. Reproduced with permission.

1) Societal Expectations: Social norms and people's needs are shifting, in response to factors as diverse as growing inequality, mass economic migration, and workforce automation – all exacerbated by a rapidly growing and aging population.

2) Environmental Pressures: These range from more intense and frequent droughts and flooding brought on by climate change, to the build-up of pollutants in nature, and increasing competition for natural resources.
3) Disruptive Technology: A wide range of emerging technologies – from artificial intelligence to gene therapy – have the potential to disrupt entire industries, by making it possible to meet societal needs in completely new ways.

It is, of course, a simplification to talk about three separate forces, because they affect each other in complex ways. For example, economic migration into cities from rural areas may be driven by extreme weather events, which wipe out the livelihoods of smallholder farmers. Such an influx of people may in turn increase competition for low-paying jobs, at a time when workforce automation is making such jobs harder to come by.

The Automotive Sector

Artificial intelligence, advances in battery technology, and progressive emissions regulations are combining to make a rapid shift to autonomous, electric road vehicles not just possible, but inevitable.

The implications of this are immense. A network of self-driving cars, which can be summoned in minutes from any smartphone, will mean that many people will never need to buy a car. And smart routing will enable near-100% utilisation: there will be no need for cars to sit idle on driveways for 23 hours a day just in case people need them. What's more, electric vehicles contain far fewer moving parts than gasoline cars, extending the life while reducing their need for costly ongoing maintenance.

Combine all of these factors together, and any company that relies on selling more and more new cars every year should already be fundamentally rethinking its business model.

The benefits of this transformation in road-based transport are likely to include less congestion on our roads, fewer accidents, near-zero emissions, and more affordable access to mobility. But there will be downsides too: it's projected that within 10 to 15 years, the jobs of every bus, truck, and taxi driver in the developed world may be in jeopardy. When you consider that there are 3 million truckers in the United States alone, this is a massive challenge.

Any business can increase its chances of success by enriching its systems intelligence. We just need to extend our horizons – from Porter's Five Forces to what we might call Future-Fit's Eight Forces. This is a message all twenty-first-century CEOs would be wise to embrace. Every business decision should take account of the systems context, if companies are to successfully anticipate and adapt to what's coming in the years ahead.

A Star to Steer By

Current Assessment Methods Are Flawed

The SDGs serve as an urgent call to action for companies to pay as much attention to their extra-financial performance as to their financial performance. We've already seen that a defensive response to the SDGs achieves nothing, and a selective response risks causing negative trade-offs that undermine any gains. Hence a holistic approach is required: while any company may seek to contribute positively to some SDGs, it must also strive to eliminate any negative contributions caused by activities across its value web.

So how can a company assess its positive and negative contributions? Unfortunately, it's not straightforward. The Global Reporting Initiative and others have worked for years to standardise how nonfinancial data are reported, usually in sustainability reports. But the reality is that no two companies are assessing and communicating their performance in exactly the same way today. As a result, sustainability reports don't really help readers to compare and contrast companies, or to identify who the real leaders are.

More than a hundred sustainability ratings, rankings, and indices have appeared over the past decade or so, claiming to identify exactly who the leaders are – and to encourage companies to improve year-on-year. Yet while the idea of 'scoring' a company's environmental and social performance may seem sound, it just isn't working for three main reasons.

First, today's ratings usually focus on *relative* performance *within* each industry, so they are blind to wider systemic risks. Even a company with a fundamentally unsustainable business model is called a 'leader' as long as it is doing slightly better than its peers. This can lull business leaders and investors into a false sense of security about how well a company is doing, when in fact its entire industry may be facing existential threats.

The second reason is that the scoring is done by third-party raters, not the companies themselves. Once a year, companies typically have to complete a long questionnaire – often demanding commercially sensitive information – and the rater then takes two or three months to calculate their scores. Even when companies find out their scores, they often struggle to interpret them because most raters don't publish exactly how their scores are calculated. Which all means that the companies don't gain much, if any, actionable insight from being rated.

And the third reason today's ratings don't work is that they emphasise current performance and governance, rather than real commitments and progress towards a flourishing future. Hence companies that really *are* taking transformative steps aren't being recognised for doing so.

So all in all, today's sustainability reports and ratings aren't really driving the progress we need. Instead, a new kind of tool is required. It must be a self-assessment tool – one which enables companies to calculate their own performance, so they don't have to share commercially sensitive information with third parties, and so that they can see exactly where action is most needed. It must be forward-looking – supporting decisions in pursuit of a necessary future state, rather than just rewarding gradual improvements to the unsustainable status quo. And it must equip companies to communicate on their commitments and progress in a concise, comparable way – so investors and others can spot the true game-changers.

The Future-Fit Business Benchmark was created to address these needs. And to build it, we had to start with the end in mind.

Starting with the End in Mind

A clear vision for society could be summarised as follows:

> A Future-Fit Society protects the possibility that humans and other life will flourish on Earth forever, by being environmentally restorative, socially just, and economically inclusive.

For society as a whole to become Future-Fit therefore, all socioeconomic actors – and companies in particular – will have to play their part. But it is important to recognise that some may do more than others.

Many types of business – movie studios, fashion houses, and ice cream vendors, to take a few examples – do not sell products that seek to solve society's biggest challenges. This doesn't in any sense make them 'bad' or incompatible with a Future-Fit Society. On the contrary, many might say life would be a bit dull without great films, fine clothes, and the occasional delicious treat! And such companies may benefit society in other ways, e.g. by actively helping their suppliers to eliminate their negative impacts.

In contrast, some companies have business models that specifically seek to address societal needs – such as pharmaceutical companies or food producers – but this doesn't mean they are inherently 'good' either. Even if their products are beneficial, such companies could be exacerbating all sorts of environmental and social problems across their operations and supply chains. So how can we tell what is 'good' and what is 'bad'?

How Much Is Enough?

What matters from a systems perspective is that every company, irrespective of its size or sector, does nothing to undermine society's transition to future-fitness. And we must also recognise that any company working to solve a societal problem may help to speed up our collective transition.

We can capture both aspects with a clear definition of what it means to be a Future-Fit Business:

> A Future-Fit Business in no way undermines – and ideally increases –
> the possibility that humans and other life will flourish on Earth forever.

So what is the minimum all companies must aim for? In terms of financial performance, the goal has always been clear. A company might get away with making a loss for a while, but to survive in the long-term it must make at least as much money as it spends. The more profit it produces the better, but the minimum threshold of performance necessary for the business to remain viable is to break even.

Yet when it comes to the environmental and social dimensions of the Triple Bottom Line, the business world has been lacking a clear understanding of what it means to break even. *What is the extra-financial break-even point for business?* In other words, what are the minimum thresholds of social and environmental performance every company must strive to reach, to eliminate its negative impacts?

The Future-Fit Business Benchmark offers an answer, in the form of 23 Break-Even Goals. These goals are grounded in a deep understanding of systems science, and cover all crucial issues: from worker well-being to water use, from procurement practices to product performance. Collectively the goals also span all parts of the company's value web – from the supplies it purchases, through to the products it sells. The same set of 23 Break-Even Goals apply to all companies, so the destination is the same. But since every business is unique, the journey to future-fitness will be different for everyone. Goals that are easy for some companies to reach might prove incredibly difficult for others.

Nonetheless, if a business has not yet reached a particular Break-Even Goal, it is in some way slowing down society's transition to future-fitness. Bold actions to correct such shortfalls should of course be encouraged, but it would be misguided to claim that efforts to be 'less bad' are creating a positive impact.

However, there are many things a business may do to improve the well-being of people or the planet, even if it has not yet reached every Break-Even Goal. Removing waste from the environment, for example, or providing essential services – such as sanitation or clean energy – to underserved customers. Such actions have the potential to take a business beyond break-even, so they should be encouraged; any company working to become part of the solution should be recognised for doing so. That's why the Benchmark also identifies a full range of Positive Pursuits: activities where the outcomes can actually speed up society's transition to future-fitness. And just as with the Break-Even Goals, the Future-Fit Positive Pursuits span activities across the full value web.

A Holistic View of Future-Fitness

Between them, the Future-Fit Break-Even Goals and Positive Pursuits characterise all of the ways a company can contribute – positively and negatively – to our collective progress. But as we have already seen, we must look at impacts in a holistic way. That's because no attempt to 'do good' must counteract progress elsewhere, and positive and negative impacts almost never cancel each other out.

It is helpful therefore to consider side-by-side what companies must do as a minimum, and what they may do beyond that. We can do this by grouping the Break-Even Goals and Positive Pursuits into eight categories, as follows:

- Energy is renewable and available to all
- Water is responsibly sourced and available to all
- Natural resources are managed to benefit local communities, ensure animal welfare, and maintain the health of ecosystems
- The environment is free from pollution
- Our physical presence protects the health of ecosystems and communities
- Waste does not exist
- Everyone has the capacity and opportunity to lead a fulfilling life
- Social, political, and economic systems value nature, well-being, and inclusion.

On the Break-Even side, for example, every company *must* ensure that its energy is from renewable sources, whilst on the Positive Pursuits side a company *may* also help more people to have access to energy or others to depend less on nonrenewable energy.

This holistic framing can be used to look at what a business is doing to maximise its positive impact while striving to eliminate its negative impact. At this point we can start to see how the Future-Fit Business Benchmark can offer companies both a clear destination to aim for, and a way to articulate their progress towards it. When a company reaches all 23 of the Break-Even Goals, it can say with confidence that it is truly creating system value – and that its contribution to the SDGs is unequivocally positive. That day could well be a long way off: some Break-Even Goals may take many years to reach, given the problems facing our economy today. But it is surely a vision worth striving for.

A Practical Tool

The Benchmark supports a holistic approach to managing extra-financial performance. It helps companies set authentic and business-relevant ambitions with respect to their environmental and social impacts, it provides detailed guidance on how to make and measure meaningful progress in pursuit of those ambitions, and it offers a way to engage stakeholders more effectively by shifting the narrative to focus on the future – where the company is going, how it's working to get there, and why that is good for both the business and society as a whole.

Future-Fit Break-Even Goals

The Break-Even Goals collectively represent the line in the sand that every business has to reach. Each goal is expressed as a single sentence, which anyone in business should be able to grasp at a high level, without any expert knowledge. And each goal represents the minimum level of performance to aim for, in one part of the value web – such as products or operations – and with respect to one issue – such as wages or waste.

Table 13.1 lists the 23 Break-Even Goals aligned with the aforementioned eight categories.

Table 13.1 Future-Fit Break-Even Goals

In a Future-Fit Society . . .	Future-Fit Break-Even Goal
Energy is renewable and available to all	• Energy is from renewable sources
Water is responsibly sourced and available to all	• Water use is environmentally responsible and socially equitable
Natural resources are managed to benefit local communities, ensure animal welfare and maintain the health of ecosystems	• Natural resources are managed to respect the welfare of ecosystems, people and animals
The environment is free from pollution	• Operations emit no greenhouse gases • Products emit no greenhouse gases • Operational emissions do not harm people or the environment
Our physical presence protects the health of ecosystems and communities	• Operations do not encroach on ecosystems or communities
Waste does not exist	• Operational waste is eliminated • Products can be repurposed
Everyone has the capacity and opportunity to lead a fulfilling life	• Community health is safeguarded • Employee health is safeguarded • Employees are paid at least a living wage • Product communications are honest, ethical, and promote responsible use • Employees are subject to fair employment terms • Employees are not subject to discrimination • Employee concerns are actively solicited, impartially judged and transparently addressed • Product concerns are actively solicited, impartially judged and transparently addressed • Products do not harm people or the environment

(Continued)

Table 13.1 (Continued)

In a Future-Fit Society . . .	Future-Fit Break-Even Goal
Social, political, and economic systems value nature, well-being, and inclusion	• Procurement safeguards the pursuit of future-fitness • Financial assets safeguard the pursuit of future-fitness • Lobbying and corporate influence safeguard the pursuit of future-fitness • Tax is paid in the right amount, in the right place, at the right time • Business is conducted ethically

If 23 goals seem like a lot, it's worth bearing in mind two things. First, when we hear the term 'business goal' we often think no more than two or three years ahead. But the Break-Even Goals represent the ultimate destination of a journey that may take much longer. To reach some goals, a company may have to fundamentally change how it operates, and that can't happen overnight. So a company shouldn't be put off if at first glance a goal seems 'impossible'. This kind of transformation may involve a series of multiyear targets, each one a stepping-stone towards future fitness. And that's okay. The important thing is not how far away the destination is, but whether or not you have a credible plan in place to reach it.

Second, it is likely that only some of the 23 goals will require rapid and radical action. Every company is different, so every company's impacts on people and the planet are different. While all 23 goals eventually need to be reached, some will require a more urgent and concerted response than others.

Future-Fit Positive Pursuits

Many companies actively seek to be a force for good in the world, even if they have not yet addressed all of their negative externalities. But the challenge lies in identifying what 'doing good' really means. Almost any action can be framed positively if the full context is not considered, such as opening up the Arctic for oil exploration to create new jobs, or cigarette manufacturers paying tobacco farmers a living wage to help bring them out of poverty. The downsides of these particular examples may be obvious, but that is not always the case. Unless decisions are informed by a systems perspective, even the most well-meaning projects or products may solve one problem only to exacerbate another.

Table 13.2 shows the Future-Fit Positive Pursuits aligned again with the eight over-arching categories.

Table 13.2 Future-Fit Positive Pursuits

In a Future-Fit Society...	Future-Fit Break-Even Goal
Energy is renewable and available to all	• Others depend less on nonrenewable energy • More people have access to energy
Water is responsibly sourced and available to all	• Others contribute less to water stress • More people have access to clean water
Natural resources are managed to benefit local communities, ensure animal welfare, and maintain the health of ecosystems	• Others depend less on inadequately managed natural resources
The environment is free from pollution	• Others generate fewer greenhouse gas emissions • Greenhouse gases are removed from the atmosphere • Others generate fewer harmful emissions • Harmful emissions are removed from the environment
Our physical presence protects the health of ecosystems and communities	• Others cause less ecosystem degradation • Ecosystems are regenerated • Others cause less damage to areas of high social or cultural value • Areas of high social or cultural value are restored
Waste does not exist	• Others generate less waste • Waste is reclaimed and repurposed
Everyone has the capacity and opportunity to lead a fulfilling life	• More people are healthy and safe from harm • People's capabilities are strengthened • More people have access to economic opportunity • Individual freedoms are upheld for more people • Social cohesion is strengthened

(Continued)

Table 13.2 (Continued)

In a Future-Fit Society. . .	Future-Fit Break-Even Goal
Social, political, and economic systems value nature, well-being, and inclusion	• Infrastructure is strengthened in pursuit of future-fitness • Governance is strengthened in pursuit of future-fitness • Market mechanisms more effectively signal and reward the pursuit of future-fitness • Social norms increasingly align to support the pursuit of future-fitness

There is a very real difference between a good intention and a meaningful outcome – and that's the distinction the Future-Fit Positive Pursuits seek to make. Positive Pursuits encompass only a *subset* of outcomes that might be described as 'good' on some level. Handing out free ice cream to customers might bring them joy, and supporting local sports tournaments may foster community goodwill, but neither action makes society more economically inclusive, socially just, or environmentally restorative. Likewise, Positive Pursuits do not include actions which serve only to reduce the business's own negative impacts. A company's efforts to be 'less bad' are of course important – and their effects are captured as progress towards the Break-Even Goals.

Positive Pursuits therefore refer only to those outcomes that can *speed up* society's progress towards future-fitness. Each one identifies a way to either *reverse* the effect of a negative impact that occurred in the past, or to *help others avoid* contributing to a negative impact in the future. And as with the Break-Even Goals, each Positive Pursuit is expressed as a single sentence, which anyone in business should be able to grasp without any expert knowledge.

Engaging Stakeholders More Effectively

Even the most passionate and committed CEO can't transform a business without securing the support of key stakeholders, from employees to investors. The Future-Fit approach can enhance such engagement efforts, in three ways.

First of all, Future-Fit enables companies to exhibit true leadership. There is a very real difference between a company that is *in the lead* at a moment in time, and one that is a *true leader*. To be in the lead one need only do better than one's peers, and perhaps receive the occasional award or appear in best-in-sector rankings. But to be a true leader, one must chart a path towards the destination we seek, and light that path for others to follow. The SDGs define this shared destination, and Future-Fit translates the SDGs into something business can pursue. By acknowledging the need to reach extra-financial break-even, a business can send a clear message that it is leading the charge to the future we need. And that commitment will appeal to anyone with an interest in the company's success.

Second, Future-Fit can help the business to get the best from its employees. Nothing is more dispiriting for an employee who wants to make a difference in the world than to see a disconnect between their day-to-day role and what the company's sustainability report says. And nothing is more valuable than an employee who is passionate about where the business is heading, and understands exactly how they are contributing to it. The Future-Fit guidance documents are designed specifically to bridge the gap between boardroom ambitions and shop-floor actions. They also help to reframe the conversation: it is no longer about demanding ever-more data from colleagues who can't fathom its value, but rather it is about empowering people to make better day-to-day decisions for themselves and see how these contribute to the organisation's overall ambitions.

And third, Future-Fit can help to increase support among investors, partners, and other external stakeholders. In today's ever-more volatile, uncertain, complex, and ambiguous world, companies should focus their external communications on what they are doing to become part of the solution. This is about making clear how the company's extra-financial ambitions are the right ones – for both society and the business's ongoing success.

Some companies may be put off by the idea of talking publicly about goals that they don't know how to achieve, or that will take them many years to reach. But true leaders don't shy from the challenge. They understand that no one will expect them to become Future-Fit overnight. True leaders state bold ambitions, and explain what actions they are taking to make those ambitions a reality. This means talking openly about the gaps between where the business is now and where it needs to be, and explaining what is being done to close those gaps. And in some cases it means being willing to say *'we don't know how to do that'*. Some barriers to progress are so complex that nothing short of a technological or regulatory breakthrough will knock them down. True leaders see such obstacles as a way to rally others – to foster collaborative solutions to problems that no one organisation can address alone. Future-Fit provides an authentic foundation for having such conversations.

Conclusion

The Future-Fit Business Benchmark takes the form of a suite of open-source documents, with over 400 pages of advice and links to useful third-party resources in the public domain. All of this can be downloaded for free from the foundation's website: www.futurefitbusiness.org.

The 23 Break-Even Goals together mark the line in the sand that all companies must strive to reach, to protect people and planet across their value web. Positive Pursuits offer a way to look at 'doing good' through a systems lens, to maximise positive outcomes for society while minimising the chances of harmful side effects.

Bringing all of this together, companies can use the Benchmark to set more authentic and business-relevant goals, to take better day-to-day decisions in pursuit of those goals, and to engage people more effectively on their progress. We all need to play our part in the transition to a Future-Fit Society, and we can speed up and scale up our progress if we work together.

14

Financing for Youth Entrepreneurship in Sustainable Development

Inna Amesheva, Alex Clark, and Julian Payne

The Role of Young Entrepreneurs in Sustainable Development

Young people currently represent approximately two-fifths (more than 40%) of the world's population[1] and constitute a primary source of untapped potential for the implementation of the Sustainable Development Goals (SDGs). The majority of young people live in developing countries, where they tend to constitute a larger proportion of the population. Nearly all projected population growth will occur in less-developed countries with high fertility rates, primarily in Africa. These countries, the major focus of this chapter, typically already have large youth cohorts that will continue to grow as the world races towards a projected population of 9.6 billion by 2050.[2]

The 2030 Sustainable Development Agenda emphasises the role of young people as 'critical agents of change.'[3] Young people are the workers and entrepreneurs who hold the responsibility of building a brighter future for their countries and the planet. Providing them with education, employment, and entrepreneurial opportunities, particularly in the poorest countries and communities, will prove critical to leveraging the demographic dividend and the unique potential of an ever-increasing youth demographic to deliver on the SDGs.

---

1 The World Bank, 'How Is the World's Youth Population Changing?' (17 April 2017), http://blogs.worldbank.org/opendata/chart-how-worlds-youth-population-changing.
2 United Nations, Department of Economic and Social Affairs (UN DESA), Population Division, 'World Population Prospects: The 2015 Revision, Key Findings and Advance Tables', Working Paper No. ESA/P/WP.241, 2015.
3 United Nations General Assembly, 'Transforming Our World: The 2030 Agenda for Sustainable Development', United Nations General Assembly (UNGA) Resolution 70/1, 25 September 2015, http://www.un.org/en/development/desa/population/migration/generalassembly/docs/globalcompact/A_RES_70_1_E.pdf.

Sustainable Development Goals: Harnessing Business to Achieve the SDGs through Finance, Technology, and Law Reform, First Edition. Edited by Julia Walker, Alma Pekmezovic, and Gordon Walker.

In parallel, sustainable development is becoming a mainstream element of the investment landscape. Corporate and financial actors across sectoral and geographic boundaries are beginning to grasp the importance of sustainable products and policies, and the emergence of robust public policy measures to support them, from local to global levels.[4] The SDGs are more than a mere political declaration. The economic opportunities sustainable business offers are clear – from sustainable transportation to clean energy, and from health-care technology to reducing food waste.

In the short term, this means understanding the skill profiles of the future, incorporating the SDGs into high-level strategy, and appreciating the financing requirements of an economic opportunity worth an estimated $25–35 trillion by 2030.[5] Simultaneously, if societies and businesses are to reap the rewards of the shift towards a sustainable economy, the next generation of entrepreneurs and innovators will need tangible support such as access to networks, access to affordable financing, and multi-faceted expert guidance.

This chapter looks first at the needs of young entrepreneurs working on the SDGs and the barriers faced in scaling their projects. It then surveys financing options for young entrepreneurs and identifies the gaps between what is needed and what is available. The chapter closes with an exploration of alternative financing mechanisms and of the need to develop robust investment pipelines to attract capital on more traditional terms.

The Needs of Young Entrepreneurs Working on the SDGs

Barriers to Innovation and Scale

There is no shortage of creativity and innovation among young people in developing countries – but a lack of entrepreneurial opportunities can stifle these qualities, increasing the risk of leading a life of poverty. Without avenues for the acquisition and development of entrepreneurial skill sets, young leaders and their communities will struggle to adapt to globalisation and environmental change in market economies. Providing young people with such opportunities, especially in the realm of sustainability, requires an understanding of the barriers faced by young entrepreneurs in scaling their solutions.

---

4 Volans and Business and Sustainable Development Commission, 'Breakthrough Business Models: Exponentially More Social, Lean, Integrated and Circular' (September 2016), 3, https://volans.com/wp-content/uploads/2016/09/Volans_Breakthrough-Business-Models_Report_Sep2016.pdf.
5 Business and Sustainable Development Commission, 'Better Business, Better World: The Report of the Business and Sustainable Development Commission' (January 2017), 15–17, http://report.businesscommission.org/report.

Based on a series of interviews and a literature review, SDSN Youth identified five categories of barriers facing young entrepreneurs working on the SDGs, displayed in Table 14.1.[6] The extent to which entrepreneurs encounter these barriers depends on several variables, including but not limited to: (i) the nature of their business, (ii) the stage/level of progress in developing the business, (iii) the geography of operation, and (iv) their social and economic status.

The 2018 Youth Solutions Report (YSR)[7] surveyed 207 youth entrepreneurs' perceptions of the main hurdles they faced in scaling sustainability-oriented ideas (see Figure 14.1, cross-referenced with the taxonomy in Table 14.1). Access to finance was identified as the main barrier impeding the scaling of solutions, closely followed by awareness and networking possibilities. The emphasis on access to finance is closely aligned with a survey conducted by the Foundation for Social Entrepreneurs,[8] which identified access to finance and a lack of financial resources as the main issue facing social entrepreneurs – receiving almost twice as many votes as the next-highest-ranked barrier.

The need for access to finance was further underlined in interviews with entrepreneurs and ventures featured in the first iteration of the YSR, including Bean Voyage, the Educate! Experience, and Pixis. Access to finance has had a significant impact on the viability and structure of these ventures and many others. In the early stages, financial constraints place significant pressure on meeting operating costs as well as the administrative expenses of registering a non-profit or for-profit business. In later stages, growing expenditures for on-the-ground resources and staffing budgets mean that many solutions rely heavily on grants, family support, or volunteers to continue their work. Finally, the administrative burden of continuously applying for grant funding

6 United Nations Conference on Trade and Development, *Policy Guide on Youth Entrepreneurship* (2015), http://unctad.org/en/PublicationsLibrary/webdiaeed2015d1_en.pdf; J. Kempner, N. Nielsen, D. Maingot, D. Piselli, and S. Rajagopalan, 'Supporting Youth-Led Innovation to Achieve the SDGs', *SDSN Youth & The Social Investment Consultancy* (July 2017); F. Green, *Youth Entrepreneurship: A Background Paper for the OECD Centre for Entrepreneurship, SMEs and Local Development*, (Organisation for Economic Co-operation and Development (OECD), 2013), https://www.oecd.org/cfe/leed/youth_bp_finalt.pdf; G. Ahaibwe and I. Kasirye, 'Creating Youth Employment Through Entrepreneurship Financing: The Uganda Youth Venture Capital Fund', (Economic Policy Research Centre, 2015); Child and Youth Finance International, 'CYFI and UNCDF Launch the "Bank the Youth" Campaign in 7 African Countries' (27 March 2017), https://childfinanceinternational.org/news-and-events/news-blog/entry/cyfi-and-uncdf-launch-the-bank-the-youth-campaign-in-7-african-countries.html; S. R. Ramirez, *More Inclusive Finance for Youth: Scalable and Sustainable Delivery Models for Financial and Non-Financial Services*, European Dialogue Number 8, European Microfinance Platform (2015), http://www.e-mfp.eu/sites/default/files/resources/2015/05/European_Dialogue_No_8_web.pdf.
7 Sustainable Development Solutions Network – Youth, *Youth Solutions Report* (2018), https://drive.google.com/file/d/1CoMNN9gUOcDpKWpmqBmn52hvAXJAZ7IW/view.
8 The Geneva Foundation for Social Entrepreneurs, *European Learning for Youth in Social Entrepreneurship (ELYSE) Final Report* (July 2016), http://www.gsen.global/wp-content/uploads/GSEN-Report-Design-5-forweb-2.pdf.

Table 14.1 Taxonomy of barriers facing young entrepreneurs working on the SDGs.

Barrier type	Description
(A) Legal and Regulatory	• High business registration costs, complex regulatory procedures, and distrust in regulatory environments • Limited knowledge of regulatory issues, in particular of copyright, patent, or trademark regulations
(B) Access to Finance	• A shortage of appropriate youth- and social venture–focused financial products and excessive restrictions on engagement in the financial sector • Low financial literacy levels and high credit, age, and collateral requirements for obtaining loans
(C) Education and Skills	• A lack of entrepreneurship education and limited practical or experiential opportunities restricting young people from becoming successful entrepreneurs • Limited and poor-quality business development and incubation services
(D) Awareness and Networking	• Negative social attitudes towards entrepreneurship in sustainability, especially among potential financiers (including domestic commercial banks and venture capital investors) • Underdeveloped young entrepreneurship networks • Insufficient promotion of role models and/or entrepreneurship networks, including linkages between youth-led start-ups and investors
(E) Data and Technology	• Knowledge gaps regarding geographical contexts in which youth-led innovation occurs, including regulatory and financial contexts, as well as supporting mechanisms • Insufficient digital infrastructure, access to reliable/cheap electricity, and workspace

Source: Adapted from UNCTAD (2015).

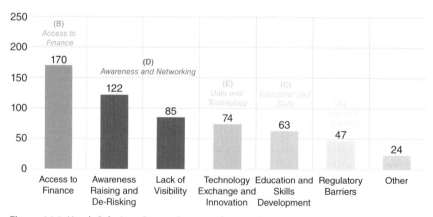

Figure 14.1 Youth Solutions Report Survey: What are the main challenges your organisation faces in scaling? (*n* = 207)

consumes resources more productively employed in product design, development, and testing. The instability associated with reliance on grants also leads to high turnover rates and time lost in retraining.

Supporting Young Entrepreneurs Working on the SDGs

There are a variety of activities and interventions that can encourage the contribution of youth-led solutions to sustainable development. An indicative and non-exhaustive list of interventions mapped to the barriers in Table 14.1 is presented in Table 14.2.

The YSR survey also asked entrepreneurs what they needed to overcome the barriers they identified in Figure 14.1 (see Figure 14.2). While many entrepreneurs indicated that they required technical assistance (for example, on legal, regulatory, or technological issues) or support in marketing and

Table 14.2 Mapping interventions to barriers facing young entrepreneurs.

Barrier type	Potential interventions
(A) Legal and Regulatory	• Advise countries on using legal and regulatory frameworks to support youth entrepreneurship most effectively • Provide technical assistance to assist young entrepreneurs in complying with and navigating regulation
(B) Access to Finance	• Develop additional investment opportunities for youth solutions • Establish innovation grants, awards, and prizes with links to follow-on financing and access to investor networks • Develop a pipeline of viable youth solutions for investors to fund
(C) Education and Skills	• Develop innovation incubators, acceleration programmes, and mentorship programmes to provide a combination of training and hands-on experience to develop idea generation, market research, business planning, pitching, value proposition, financial sustainability, marketing and communications, monitoring • Promote education on SDG-oriented impact assessment to comply with the reporting requirements of many investors
(D) Awareness and Networking	• Develop mapping tools to connect social ventures with large organisations and funders • Encourage cooperation with community groups, NGOs, and other local stakeholders to develop meaningful partnerships at the local level • Develop media campaigns and public showcasing of youth entrepreneurship research
(E) Data and Technology	• Provide technical assistance to ventures to develop digital infrastructure and plug knowledge gaps

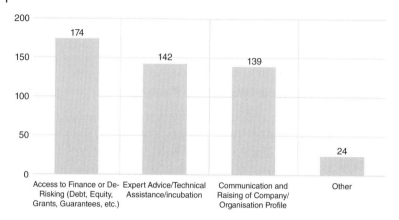

Figure 14.2 Youth Solutions Report Survey: What are your needs to overcome the barriers identified above? (*n* = 207)

communications, the majority identified access to finance as the key bottleneck to growth and the area requiring most support. Some entrepreneurs indicated that they required support in multiple areas. Separately, in a series of 98 interviews conducted by the Foundation for Social Entrepreneurs, 22% of practitioners working with young and social entrepreneurs identified their primary support need as 'business training and business experience', while 17% prioritised 'business support and pro-bono advice', and 14% 'financial support'.[9] These percentages are comparatively low, as interviewees were asked to identify only one priority area.

There is a clear need to develop additional investment opportunities for youth solutions. SDSN Youth is already actively engaged in raising company profiles via the YSR, as well as providing technical assistance and incubation activities through the newly inaugurated Investment Readiness Program (IRP). There is immense catalytic potential in providing appropriate financial support to the strongest Youth Solutions emerging from this process.

The Financing Options Available to Young Entrepreneurs Working on the SDGs

There are numerous examples of corporate leaders, international networks, and national governments highlighting the work of youth entrepreneurs, but these remain isolated exceptions. In general, very little work is currently being done to support young entrepreneurs in systematic ways. Corporations

---

9 The Geneva Foundation for Social Entrepreneurs *European Learning for Youth in Social Entrepreneurship (ELYSE) Final Report* (July 2016), http://www.gsen.global/wp-content/uploads/GSEN-Report-Design-5-forweb-2.pdf.

with funds available for providing risk capital are more often inclined to pay high dividends to shareholders and engage in share buybacks than put their capital to work.[10] Public-private blended finance vehicles are gaining traction in the agricultural, clean energy, and urban development sectors, but currently have little to offer to first-time young entrepreneurs amid persistent structural barriers to obtaining financing from such vehicles.[11] Although technical assistance and business support form a major focus of youth entrepreneurship programmes globally, additional support is needed and there remains a need for follow-on financing that is rarely met. Opportunities to push for youth-driven evolution in existing business practices and models are being missed as a result.

Sources and Instruments of Finance for Young Entrepreneurs

Lack of access to financial services is an urgent and chronic problem, especially in developing countries, where 62% of 18- to 25-year-olds have no access to formal financial services[12] and only 6% source start-up capital from financial institutions as opposed to family savings or similar sources.[13] There are three main sources of finance relevant to youth-focused social impact entrepreneurship, namely:

1. **Public and blended finance** – Bilateral aid agencies, development finance institutions, foundations, and so forth. The use of blended finance (using public capital to de-risk an investment enough to attract private investors) is a trend of growing size and sophistication in the context of financing the SDGs.
2. **Private finance** – Commercial banks, impact investors, venture capital, and private equity. Institutional and other mainstream investors' role is limited due to the insufficient scale and high risk of usually early-stage youth sustainability ventures.

---

10 Business and Sustainable Development Commission, *Better Business, Better World: The Report of the Business and Sustainable Development Commission* (January 2017), 10, http://report.businesscommission.org/report.

11 Ibid., 13. Examples include the &Green Fund for sustainable agricultural intensification, supported by the Norwegian government; the Terra Bella Fund with first-loss and technical assistance support from USAID; and affordable housing and mortgages in Honduras, supported by concessional loans from OPIC.

12 S. R. Ramirez, *More Inclusive Finance for Youth: Scalable and Sustainable Delivery Models for Financial and Non-Financial Services,* European Dialogue Number 8, European Microfinance Platform (2015), 6–7, http://www.e-mfp.eu/sites/default/files/resources/2015/05/European_Dialogue_No_8_web.pdf.

13 United Nations Capital Development Fund, *YouthStart Global: Inception Phase – Youth Economic Opportunities Ecosystem Analysis – Uganda Country Report* (2016).

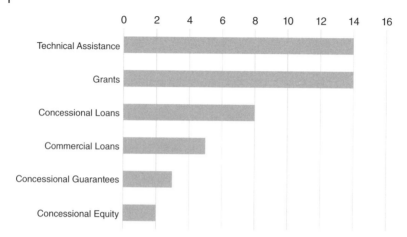

Figure 14.3 Summary of youth finance-focused initiatives, by instrument type offered.

3. **Alternative finance** – Crowdfunding and other technology-underpinned financing sources such as microfinance institutions and financial technology (FinTech) start-ups provide a promising venue for raising capital to young social impact entrepreneurs. However, entrepreneurs should also be wary of the potential drawbacks and increasingly cumbersome regulatory and compliance implications associated with using alternative finance options.

Of the youth finance initiatives examined in this chapter, a substantial majority (14) provide grants and technical assistance to recipients (see Figure 14.3). Concessional loans (e.g. with low interest rates and delayed repayments) are provided by only eight initiatives, whereas five provide loans on commercial terms. Concessional guarantees (3) and equity (2) are offered least of all.

Venture capital and private equity markets are underdeveloped in many emerging economies, but even in developed economies, entrepreneurs frequently raise initial funds through family and friends. In emerging economies, this typically means that start-up capital volumes are meagre and insufficient, owing to the relatively low savings volumes from which they are sourced.

Financial institutions in developing countries are not meeting the needs of young borrowers, either. Banks typically see youth as commercially unattractive, with a lack of collateral, no credit history, limited ability to pay, low employment stability, low average balances, and high customer retention costs counting against them. A USAID survey found that although savings products are the most widely accessed by young people, loans are the most commonly offered products.[14] Loans are inherently more profitable to banks, but difficult to scale due to the perceived risks of lending to youth.

---

14 M. McNulty and G. Nagarajan (eds), *Serving Youth with Microfinance: Perspectives of Microfinance Institutions and Youth Serving Organizations*, USAID, September 2005, https://www.marketlinks.org/sites/marketlinks.org/files/resource/files/ML3350_mr_30_serving_youth_with_microfinance.pdf.

The potential for mobile banking and FinTech (including peer-to-peer lending, investment, and wealth management services not necessarily connected to the formal banking system) in promoting and monitoring youth financial activity remains largely untapped in many of these markets and can compensate for the riskier profile of young people by driving down customer acquisition costs, vastly improving data collection, and reaching scale by reducing customer acquisition and retention costs. From a regulatory perspective, relaxing age restrictions on banking down to 16 have proven helpful in rapidly scaling youth savings in Rwanda. Elsewhere, most financial institutions still require account holders to be 18 years old.[15]

The relative paucity of commercial loans to youth entrepreneurs underlines the importance of improving commercial banks' ability to extend financing to youth. Low-income or otherwise vulnerable youth face challenges in accumulating assets due to high interest rates, a low ability to save, and small loan amounts. For more far-sighted banks, initiatives tackling these barriers can translate into long-term profit by increasing credit lines and loan sizes over time, as young clients mature into more lucrative customers, even if youth lending cannot generate short-term returns.[16] Achieving the right balance between commercial viability and meeting youth needs, however, requires greater tailoring of products (longer loan tenors and preferential interest rates), supported by risk mitigation measures (formal training and mentorship) that can help generate short-term returns for less flexible banks and reduce collateral requirements.

Existing pilot schemes in El Salvador and Uganda have yet to turn a commercial profit, but have established several avenues for lenders to control costs and achieve scale, notably mobile banking technology, aggregation of multiple small deposits through cooperatives and savings groups, and youth-specific training for bank staff.[17] The East African Youth Entrepreneurship Facility, Root Capital, and Saudi Arabia's Centennial Fund have seen considerable success in linking formal training programmes with commercial banks and market actors to facilitate access to financing.[18]

Non-profit organisations do offer grants or interest-free debt financing to emerging youth-led ventures – including the various branches of Youth Business International, SAJE in Portugal, and Imprenditorialità Giovanile in Italy – but they are generally restricted to OECD countries and frequently come with onerous documentation and reporting requirements that can dissuade inexperienced youth. Microfinance, interest-free microloans, and

---

15 S. R. Ramirez, *More Inclusive Finance for Youth: Scalable and Sustainable Delivery Models for Financial and Non-Financial Services*, European Dialogue Number 8, European Microfinance Platform (2015), http://www.e-mfp.eu/sites/default/files/resources/2015/05/European_Dialogue_No_8_web.pdf.

16 V. I. Rivas SchurerR. Magala Lule, FINCA Uganda, and A. Lubwama, *Sustainable Business Models for Youth Financial Services: Case Study*, The SEEP Network (2011), 6.

17 The Prince's Youth Business International, *Youth Entrepreneurship Beyond Collateral: How to Increase Access to Capital for Young Entrepreneurs* (August 2012), 8, https://www.youthbusiness.org/wp-content/uploads/2012/08/BeyondCollateral.pdf.

18 Ibid., 10.

delayed interest payments are all tools that have been applied in developing markets, but reliance on donor funds greatly restricts their scalability. Fully private venture capital is even thinner on the ground outside developed markets and is available only to the well-connected, well-resourced few, even in sectors like IT, medical tech, biotech, and commercial research and development (R&D) that are beginning to attract greater investor interest.[19]

The UN-led SDG Fund, focused on poverty alleviation, runs grant-driven pilot programmes in Fiji, Vanuatu, and Samoa designed specifically to help youth find viable economic opportunities in agricultural harvesting and production.[20] In general, sustainable development projects like these tend to focus on matching youth skill profiles to resilience-building needs, rather than financing entrepreneurship per se. The SDG Fund has generated private sector interest from firms looking to coordinate more closely with the UN, suggesting a greater potential role for private capital in its future activities.[21] Research from Youth Business International (YBI) shows that simply increasing financial access for youth is pro-poor and pro-growth, and non-intervention carries real costs by precluding these opportunities.[22]

Bridging the Gap Between Young Entrepreneurs and the SDGs

Sectoral Coverage

Financing for youth entrepreneurship has a limited track record from which to draw reliable data and replicable insights. This paucity of data is an even greater problem for assessing youth entrepreneurship in sustainable development, with only 17% of youth financing initiatives examined in the Youth Solutions Report including a sustainability focus and very few institutions reporting sustainability and youth indicators in combination.

Moreover, the sustainability-focused youth financing initiatives that do exist are typically grant-dependent, with no clear pathway to financial independence. With respect to the sectoral focus, from the sample of existing initiatives targeting young people, it appears that most existing youth-focused instruments revolve around youth entrepreneurship in a broad sense, followed by programmes

19 P. Juneja, 'Youth Entrepreneurship: An Overview', *Management Study Guide* (2017), https://www.managementstudyguide.com/youth-entrepreneurship.htm.
20 P. Duran, 'SDG Fund Launches New Programs in Pacific Islands to Support Youth', Office of the Secretary-General's Envoy on Youth (19 April 2016), http://www.un.org/youthenvoy/2016/04/sdg-fund-launches-new-programs-in-pacific-islands-to-support-youth/.
21 United Nations Development Group, *2016 Annual Progress Report of the Sustainable Development Goals Fund* (2016), 49–51. https://undg.org/wp-content/uploads/2016/12/SDGs-are-Coming-to-Life-UNDG-1.pdf.
22 The Prince's Youth Business International, *Youth Entrepreneurship Beyond Collateral: How to Increase Access to Capital for Young Entrepreneurs* (2012), 7, https://www.youthbusiness.org/wp-content/uploads/2012/08/BeyondCollateral.pdf.

specific to agriculture and financial services. A lack of reliable data on the size and impact of each initiative places limits on the conclusions that can be drawn, but Figure 14.4 summarises the current landscape in approximate terms.

Even so, the currently available data suggests a number of sectors within the SDGs that could benefit from a greater supply of youth-focused financing, including climate change, clean energy, energy access, biodiversity protection, responsible consumption and production, and universal education, among others. On the demand side, a large proportion of youth-led sustainability initiatives target fulfilling SDGs relating to economic growth, education, health, eradicating poverty, achieving gender equality, and tackling climate change (see Figure 14.5).

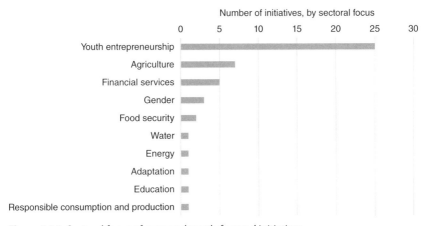

Figure 14.4 Sectoral focus of surveyed youth-focused initiatives.

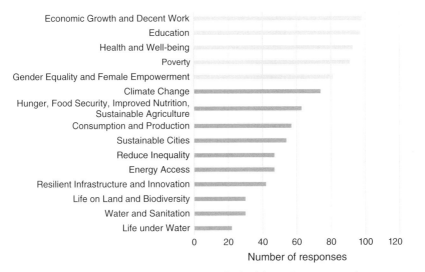

Figure 14.5 Youth Solutions Report Survey: Which of the SDGs are most relevant to your project? *Source:* Youth Solutions Report Innovator Submissions. Reproduced with permission from SDSN Youth.

These insights help us draw out tentative insights on the gaps in existing support provision. Youth entrepreneurs active in sectors that are most in need of sustainability-driven financing and resources are not receiving the attention and tools required to secure their financing needs and achieve scalability. There is a substantial market opportunity in tackling sustainability challenges – up to $12 trillion of the $25–35 trillion total expected economic benefits from realising the SDGs will go to the private sector, by UNDP estimates.[23] Drawing on the YSR survey results and interviews, a much greater deployment of funds towards youth-led ventures may be warranted in the fields of economic growth and decent work, health, and gender equality, as well as food security and nutrition. Progress on each of these SDGs will in most cases spill over to other goals, with strong synergies expected with respect to clean energy, energy efficiency, smart mobility, urban housing, and urban infrastructure. Establishing a funding mechanism focused on providing resources and capacity-building to young entrepreneurs targeting these focus areas would result in considerable economic benefits, as well as reduced inequality and health-related and environmental co-benefits.

Geographical Coverage

Drawing on YSR submissions data, one can discern a substantial level of overlap in the geography-specific demand and supply patterns of SDG innovators and funding providers. A large proportion of both SDG entrepreneurs and existing funds are oriented towards tackling problems in Africa and Asia (see Figure 14.6).

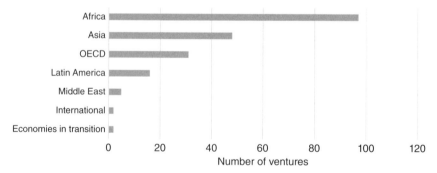

Figure 14.6 Geographic focus of youth-led sustainability ventures. *Source:* Youth Solutions Report Innovator Submissions. Reproduced with permission from SDSN Youth.

---

23 N. Vali, 'More Than Philanthropy: SDGs Are a $12 Trillion Opportunity for the Private Sector', United Nations Development Programme (25 August 2017), http://www.undp.org/content/undp/en/home/blog/2017/8/25/More-than-philanthropy-SDGs-present-an-estimated-US-12-trillion-in-market-opportunities-for-private-sector-through-inclusive-business.html.

While the greatest proportion of supply-side youth financing initiatives target less wealthy regions of the world (see Figure 14.7), this is partly a reflection of the barriers that generate the needs for such facilities in the first place, although funding demand in developing regions is clearly high and support needs are larger and more diverse than the current environment is able to support. Emmanuel Noah of BenBen, a blockchain land transaction firm, comments, 'All the support is at one side of the world whereas a majority of the youth SDG entrepreneurs are at the opposite side – there's a gap that needs to be bridged', alluding to the chronic insufficiency of capital aimed at developing regions.

The SDG opportunity in OECD countries is perhaps more significant in monetary terms, given their established technical capacity, well-developed markets, more advanced regulatory frameworks, and financial resources – but the SDG needs are greater, and growing, in the developing world. Focusing on financing OECD-based ventures as a pathway to developing world SDG solutions would depend heavily on rapid, smooth technology transfer – by no means a given in a global trade environment dominated by powerful market players with privileged access to intellectual property rights. Developing on-the-ground capacity in developing countries will be critical in supporting the longer-term success of youth entrepreneurship for sustainability.

Summary data from our survey of existing youth financing initiatives shows the majority targeting the African, OECD, and Latin American markets, all of which feature significantly in the YSR survey. While the focus on Africa does seem to align with the YSR results, there is a suggestion that insufficient attention is being paid to Asia relative to needs, while the Middle East and small island developing states (SIDS) also receive little attention, despite their greater exposure to environmental change and more urgent need for youth solutions.

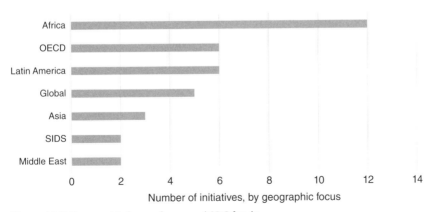

Figure 14.7 Geographic focus of surveyed SDG funds.

A delicate balance must be found that promotes sustainability innovation by global youth while at the same time maintaining an equitable and financially viable geographic representation in key regions according to their future expected potential and development needs. This requires effective financing mechanisms that reach the right targets on reasonable terms but also lay down the building blocks that young entrepreneurs need to make financing work – including access to networks, expert advice, and communication tools.

Beyond Banks: Alternative Financial Structures for Youth-oriented Sustainable Development Initiatives

Nearly 30% of entrepreneurs in YSR submissions identified access to finance as one of the chief barriers they faced in scaling their organisation. Finance was also identified as the leading requirement for sustainability-focused youth-led organisations to achieve scalability, closely followed by the need for technical assistance, expert advice, and venture incubation programmes. While the ways in which commercial banks can increase youth access to financial services have already been discussed, a step change towards more innovative financing structures is required that most banks are unwilling, or unable, to provide without external guarantees protecting them from losses.

The mobilisation of existing latent funding sources for young SDG innovators is critical. To succeed, however, it must be complemented by providing targeted capacity-building, ranging from technical assistance, expert-led mentorship and advice programmes, and the establishment of channels for networking, marketing, and dissemination of youth-driven sustainability solutions. In this respect, 'alternative' funding instruments, such as crowdfunding and reliance on decentralised FinTech solutions, as well as the provision of greater early-stage financing, could bridge the funding gap between youth-led innovations and project implementation and scale-up in a way that most effectively blends financial and non-financial services.

The gaps in access to finance and relevant support services are clear. With an SDG investment gap of US$5–7 trillion globally, with $2.5 trillion in developing countries alone, there is a clear opening to provide youth-led innovation with the financial and practical tools needed to achieve scale.[24] Further, the long-term importance of moving steadily away from grant-based, public sector-led SDG funding programmes towards scalable, financially viable, and commercially underpinned projects cannot be understated. This would be essential in ensuring a long-lasting and commercially viable transition towards

---

24 M. Niculescu, 'Impact Investment to Close the SDG Funding Gap', United Nations Development Programme (13 July 2017), http://www.undp.org/content/undp/en/home/blog/2017/7/13/What-kind-of-blender-do-we-need-to-finance-the-SDGs-.html.

a more sustainable economy, with youth empowerment at its heart, and build entrepreneurial ecosystems in developing countries that will help retain talent and use domestic financial resources more effectively.

Prioritising Financial Interventions for Youth Entrepreneurs and the SDGs

A consistent complaint of the financial services industry is not a lack of funding, but a lack of ambitious, bankable projects. The traditional catalysts of such projects – public investors like development banks, development finance institutions, and aid agencies – are proving unable to develop them and unable to link them effectively to a cash-rich private sector. 2016 saw $23 trillion in socially responsible investments, while private equity markets have up to $1 trillion available seeking early-stage investment opportunities.[25] On the institutional investor end of the scale, insurers, banks, and pension funds alike are struggling to meet 'alternative' investment targets due to a lack of projects. There is no lack of capital, but a perceived dearth of suitable investments, in part due to the limited capacity of both investors and financial institutions to accurately and cost-effectively assess the risk profiles of innovative sustainable ventures.

Most youth entrepreneurship ventures are too small to attract commercial venture capital funding – and in most developing countries, venture capital is in short supply anyway. Governments in Uganda, South Africa, Tanzania, Botswana, and Kenya have been active in establishing youth-focused venture capital funds, primarily to combat youth unemployment, rather than in harnessing innovation. In Uganda, the government was involved in partnerships with three commercial banks to provide debt funding at fixed below-market rates to viable projects, accompanied by bank-led mentorship services and guarantees in the form of assets of the borrowing enterprise. In Botswana, public sector involvement acted as a check on profiteering tendencies that tend to further marginalise youth who already struggle to meet banks' requirements, but was also linked to higher default rates and a lack of fund sustainability stemming from insufficient interest earnings. Tanzania's potentially more resource-efficient approach was to provide a credit guarantee fund to banks to encourage youth lending by removing the need for other forms of collateral.[26]

---

25 D. Beal, J. Fetherston, and D. Young, *Narrowing the SDG Investment Gap*, Boston Consulting Group (12 February 2018), https://www.bcg.com/en-us/publications/2018/narrowing-sdg-investment-gap-imperative-development-finance-institutions.aspx.
26 G. Ahaibwe and I. Kasirye, 'Creating Youth Employment Through Entrepreneurship Financing: The Uganda Youth Venture Capital Fund', Economic Policy Research Centre (2015), 4, 7–8, 12–15.

Excessive public involvement in youth entrepreneurship can be distortionary if it stifles innovation and misdirects resources inefficiently.[27] This is not to say policy support is not needed: startup capital that cannot yet be provided by commercial actors is in short supply.[28] However, relatively light-touch instruments like government credit guarantee facilities can remove barriers to financing for high-risk youth borrowers, whilst allowing the private sector to allocate greater capital resources to youth entrepreneurs on more favourable terms.

While the exact structure of funds or financial instruments targeting young entrepreneurs is highly context-dependent, there are several initial conclusions that can be drawn. First, instruments ought to be married to pipeline-building activities to ensure that there are effective, sustainable disbursement mechanisms to channel public and private funds effectively. Second, while non-repayable grants have historically been used to support youth-led ventures, they should be deployed more strategically and with the explicit aim of being phased out over time, to be gradually replaced by financing on commercial or concessional terms as appropriate. In countries with poor regulatory environments and shallow financial markets, the need for early-stage grants is unlikely to diminish rapidly. However, grant funding should be prioritised for meeting one-off project preparation activities (i.e. non-operational expenses like legal and advisory costs), rather than directly subsidising project revenues. Concessional loans, convertible equity, and guarantees are likely to be better candidates for encouraging long-term financial sustainability and resilience.

Non-financial Services

While young entrepreneurs typically perceive access to finance as their largest hurdle, non-financial services also play a key role. Young people are often perceived as lacking an understanding of debt financing, working capital management, and overall fiduciary responsibility. Non-monetary support in the form of technical, legal or regulatory advice, and access to networks can be extremely valuable in addressing these concerns and improving the likelihood of success once financing is obtained.

In the long run, non-financial services can address the stigma around lending to youth and drive down risk perceptions of banking and risk capital providers.

---

27 Business and Sustainable Development Commission and Convergence, 'The State of Blended Finance' (July 2017), http://s3.amazonaws.com/aws-bsdc/BSDC_and_Convergence__The_State_of_Blended_Finance__July_2017.pdf.
28 The Prince's Youth Business International, 'Youth Entrepreneurship Beyond Collateral: How to increase access to capital for young entrepreneurs' (August 2012), 4, https://www.youthbusiness.org/wp-content/uploads/2012/08/BeyondCollateral.pdf.

Spotlight: Crowdfunding

Crowdfunding is emerging as a fast-growing alternative financing model, particularly relevant for earlier-stage ventures that have limited access to traditional funding sources. The *Oxford English Dictionary* (2018) defines crowdfunding as 'the practice of funding a project or venture by raising many small amounts of money from a large number of people, typically via the Internet'.

In 2015 alone, US$34 billion was raised globally through the crowdfunding model (Cambridge Centre for Alternative Finance 2015). There are an increasing number of crowdfunding platforms specifically aimed at sustainability-focused enterprises and social impact ventures. One advantage of crowdfunding for early-stage ventures is market validation, in effect providing a free marketing channel to entrepreneurs and creating early adopters and champions of the business. A crowdfunding campaign can drive audience engagement and provide instant feedback and market testing to young businesses. This is especially pertinent for youth-founded ventures with otherwise limited networks and resources to devote to costly marketing and user acquisition channels. Crowdfunding campaigns can also strengthen the case for subsequent venture capital funding, thus reducing the time spent on capital-raising and instead allowing entrepreneurs to focus on building and scaling their ventures.

Based on the 2018 YSR submissions data, crowdfunding emerged as the second-most-cited source of funding for young sustainability innovators, after grants (see Figure 14.8).

Notable is the prevalence of 'Other' sources of funding, which may denote the importance of more informal financing sources – such as 'friends and family' sources of capital – that could potentially be bolstered or supplanted by crowdfunding.

The potential of crowdfunding for social impact projects established by young entrepreneurs is immense due to the greater accessibility and lower barriers to entry compared to conventional forms of finance. For instance,

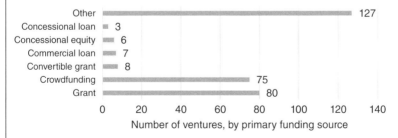

Figure 14.8 Sources of funding for youth-founded sustainability ventures. *Source:* Youth Solutions Report Innovator Submissions. Reproduced with permission from SDSN Youth.

(Continued)

Crowdfunding (Continued)

platforms such as GlobalGiving allow backers to select from many small projects led by non-profit organisations globally, donating funds to projects of their choice. There are also microcredit crowdfunding platforms, such as Kiva, which facilitate the crowdfunding of loans managed by microfinance organisations in developing countries. These examples demonstrate the high impact alternative finance can have in the race towards sustainable development, not only in industrialised economies, but also in developing countries.

Despite the various advantages offered by crowdfunding platforms in terms of flexibility and raising project awareness, entrepreneurs should also be wary of the costs of capital associated with crowdfunding, which can vary between 2 and 9% of the total amount raised (Crowdfunding 2018) – although this is a comparatively low figure in most developing countries, and lower than interest rates for most microfinance transactions.

There may also be increased levels of risk, uncertainty, and asymmetric information associated with crowdfunding for both investors and entrepreneurs (Agrawal, Catalini, and Goldfarb 2013). There might be reputational and intellectual property implications in running an unsuccessful crowdfunding campaign. Moreover, while it does provide a substantial investor base, crowdfunding does not supply the advice and mentorship that an angel investor or venture capital firm might provide. Entrepreneurs who are considering crowdfunding should thus be aware of not only the benefits, but also the potential drawbacks this form of fundraising may entail.

Developing a Robust Investment Pipeline

Delivering the SDGs will require increased investment in socially, economically, and environmentally sustainable businesses. Meeting these goals will in turn require action and support from young people to develop innovative solutions to sustainable development challenges.

Access to finance and how it pertains to young entrepreneurs has been discussed extensively here. However, many investors working in developing countries alongside experts interviewed in the process of developing the 2018 Youth Solutions Report commented on the need to develop well-prepared and investment-ready solutions to fund.[29] This is critical in order to effectively match the access to finance needs of young entrepreneurs with the capital that investors have at their disposal.

---

29 D. Nassiry, S. Nakhooda, and S. Barnard, 'Finding the Pipeline: Project Preparation for Sustainable Infrastructure', *Overseas Development Institute* (ODI) (November 2016), http://newclimateeconomy.report/workingpapers/wp-content/uploads/sites/5/2016/11/Finding-the-Pipeline.pdf; A. Mudaliar, R. Bass, and H. Dithrich, *Annual Impact Investor Survey*, 8th ed. (June 2018), Global Impact Investing Network (GIIN), https://thegiin.org/assets/2018_GIIN_Annual_Impact_Investor_Survey_webfile.pdf.

The metrics investors assess when determining the risk-and-return profiles of investments are many and extend beyond the perceived merits of business, including the regulatory and policy environment, local currency challenges, and the broader financial ecosystem. Greater support is needed at the project preparation stage in order to develop a pipeline of viable sustainable businesses for investors to fund. Of 219 impact investors interviewed regarding the growth of the impact investing industry by the Global Impact Investing Network (GIIN), 32% indicated that sourcing high-quality investment opportunities with a track record was a significant challenge – and a further 43% indicated it was a moderate challenge.[30]

As different investors use different metrics to assess investment opportunities, sourcing a pipeline is about finding ways to access a set of high-quality potential deals that suit a given investment strategy. Key activities for developing an investment pipeline include:[31]

- Developing or joining a value-aligned network of investors and impact investing funds;
- Attending business plan competitions and 'pitch' events for entrepreneurs;
- Employing impact intermediaries and investment advisory firms;
- Collaborating with incubators, accelerators, academic institutions, and non-profits;
- Tracking online databases and global crowdsourcing sites; and
- Attending key events and conferences.

Designing Youth-focused Funding Vehicles for the SDGs

There is immense catalytic potential in providing appropriate financial support to youth-oriented sustainable development initiatives, including the Youth Solutions emerging from the YSR. The development of an investment pipeline for youth solutions will need to be integrated into a broader investment strategy that assesses investment priorities, goals, and assets, alongside other variables.

Critically, a step change towards more innovative financing structures is required that most financial institutions are unwilling, or unable, to provide without external guarantees protecting them from losses. Opportunities to push for youth-driven evolution in sustainable development and business practices are being missed as a result.

Targeted financial mechanisms and capacity-building activities will need to be married to an appropriate youth-adjusted risk assessment. An indicative framework for setting up funding vehicles for youth solutions is presented in Table 14.3.

---

30 Ibid.
31 Toniic, The 7-Step Framework (29 May 2018), https://www.toniic.com/7-step-framework/.

Table 14.3 Indicative framework for design of youth-focused funding vehicles.

Step	Title	Description
I	Investment Strategy	• Set and identify **investment priorities**, including (i) the balance between finance-first and impact-first investments; and (ii) the portion of the portfolio devoted to early-stage impact investments.
		• Define impact and determine alignment across **investment themes**, including: (i) articulating mission and values; (ii) deciding on industry, impact goals, and investment themes; and (iii) the geographical breadth.
		• **Evaluate assets**, including: (i) portfolio size, as well as the diversification of risk, time commitment, and follow-on reserves for equity investments; (ii) define the appropriate investment vehicle (e.g. private family foundations, public charities, donor-advised funds (DAFs), private trusts, private capital, special purpose vehicles (SPVs)); and (iii) consider non-monetary assets, such as knowledge of and access to networks and investment style preferences.
II	Investment Pipeline	• Find **trusted partners** through: (i) incubators and accelerators; (ii) business plan competitions; (iii) impact investing funds; (iv) networking groups; (v) deal flow and investor networks; (vi) events and conferences; (vi) impact intermediaries; and (vii) crowdfunding.
III	Due Diligence	• Assess appropriate **due diligence** processes, ensuring that the investor (i) shares a set of values and enterprise objectives with the entrepreneur; (ii) knows the environment of prospective investments; (iii) takes a portfolio approach; and (vi) evaluates the legal constraints and opportunities before diving into a new geography (onsite visit and eco-system analysis).
		• Develop a **management and engagement framework**, focusing on (i) establishing the path to decision and listing deal-breakers, (ii) staging questions and requests to the entrepreneur, (iii) treating due diligence as capacity building, (iv) becoming acquainted with other investors in an enterprise, and (v) leading or empowering leadership.
IV	Deal Terms	• Determine appropriate **capital and deal terms**, including (i) return expectations, size and type of investments (e.g. grants, loan guarantees, debt and demand dividend, convertible debt, subordinated debt, revenue share, profit sharing, equity); (ii) syndication preferences to match investment styles; and (iii) using appropriate legal council.
V	Management	• Establish a regular **financial and impact reporting process** that balances need and time, as well as determine shortcuts, benchmarking, and portfolio-wide reporting.
		• Determine **technical assistance and capacity building** needs, potentially working directly with the enterprise.

Step	Title	Description
VI	Assess Performance	• Assess **performance goals through the investment lifecycle**, including (i) setting clear targets for social and financial performance; (ii) managing financial returns; and (iii) managing impact.
VII	Cultivating Lessons	• **Develop lessons** from existing investments and experienced practitioners to develop new models and norms to re-assess and improve steps I to VI.

Source: Adapted from Toniic, 'The 7-Step Framework' (29 May 2018), https://www.toniic.com/7-step-framework/.

15

Transparency in the Supply Chain
Julia Walker

Introduction

As 193 governments have now agreed to deliver 17 goals tackling major global issues by 2030, the private sector and businesses across the globe will need to rethink their roles in achieving the SDGs. This will likely require a reexamination of strategy, risk management, and business behaviour. They will need to understand their impact towards to SDGs, ways to report against them and what actions they could take in accelerating their achievement.

Nearly every country has now submitted their first Voluntary National Review (VNR) against the SDGs and are starting to define policy, regulations and align budgets to enable their achievement. So too are some forward looking businesses. Understanding the SDGs will help business achieve their own aims in parallel with the countries that they operate in and the governments that regulate them. Climate change, as an example, represents a material and cascading risk to the private sector, with implications across the supply chain.

Most companies have not yet analysed the full impact of climate risk on business risk factors, including financial, operational, human resources, compliance, and legal risks. They have struggled to map the full spectrum of risks across their business and supply chains and in the ways environmental and social risks intersects with other trends and issues that affect business and society.

Engaging with the SDGs at a core strategy level should be expected. In particular, the impacts of the supply chain will need to be better understood and become increasingly transparent. The supply chain and the private sector's impact on SDG 8, Decent Work, and SDG 12, Responsible Production and

Sustainable Development Goals: Harnessing Business to Achieve the SDGs through Finance, Technology, and Law Reform, First Edition. Edited by Julia Walker, Alma Pekmezovic, and Gordon Walker.

Consumption, are a key lever for business in helping to achieve the SDGs. In committing to SDG 12.6, national governments have agreed 'to encourage companies, especially large and transnational companies, to adopt sustainable practices and integrate sustainability information into their reporting cycles'.

Supply chains or ecosystems also have wide-reaching implications and can impact and support other goals, such as Goal 1 (End Poverty), Goal 5 (Achieve Gender Equality), Goal 10 (Reduce Inequalities), Goal 14 (Conserve Marine Resources), and Goal 16 (Promote Peace and Justice). Consider, for example:

SDG 8.7 Take immediate and effective measures to eradicate forced labour, end modern slavery and human trafficking, and secure the prohibition and elimination of the worst forms of child labour, including recruitment and use of child soldiers, and by 2025 end child labour in all its forms.

Child labour is one of several areas of concern in global supply chains that will need to be reviewed to ensure achievement of SDG 8.7. Research by the International Labour Organization (ILO) and the Walk Free Foundation shows that more than 40 million people around the world are victims of modern-day slavery. It is estimated that the human exploitation industry is worth around US$150 billion per year.[1]

The ILO states that around 152 million children between the ages of 5 and 17 years old are in child labour, of which 73 million are in hazardous work. Forty-eight percent are between 5 and 11 years old.[2] This accounts for almost one in 10 children worldwide. The business-as-usual scenario would leave 121 million children in child labour in 2025, of which 52 million would be involved in hazardous work.

Environmental crimes can also thrive in unchecked supply chains. These include illegal trade in wildlife; smuggling of ozone-depleting substances (ODSs); illicit trade in hazardous waste; illegal, unregulated, and unreported fishing and illegal logging and the associated trade in stolen timber. Illegal logging contributes to deforestation, causes ecological problems like flooding, and is a major contributor to climate change – up to one-fifth of greenhouse gas emissions stem from deforestation. Significant global threats, including the challenges addressed in the SDGs, are connected to and exacerbated by environmental crimes.

Transparency, therefore is a key foundation of any solution to the SDG's. Once businesses know where their key impacts, risks, and opportunities lie, they can focus their resources effectively. As Peter Drucker has commented, what gets measured gets managed.

---

1 *Global Estimates of Modern Slavery: Forced Labour and Forced Marriage* (Geneva: International Labour Organization, 2017).

2 *Global Estimates of Child Labour: Results and Trends, 2012–2016* (Geneva: International Labour Organization, 2017).

As the supply chain involves the product from initial processing of raw materials to delivery to the customer, a focus on supply chains has an impact on the achievement of many of the SDGs. Companies will need to embrace the growth potential of responsible environmental and societal polices and drive sustainable business practices through the value chain.

Globalisation and outsourcing has led to businesses regularly going beyond geographical borders and establishing their manufacturing and/or operations in developing countries such as Thailand, Bangladesh, India, China, the Philippines, and Malaysia.[3] This has led to supply chains becoming more complex and risks difficult to manage. Technology, regulations, and operations have struggled to keep up with providing the transparency and information required to ensure that environmental crimes, child labour and modern-day slavery are not operating in businesses' supply chains.

In a 2019 report by Refinitiv on over 3,000 businesses globally, 51% of survey respondents reported that they had never screened or done appropriate due diligence on their third-party vendors, suppliers, or partners when onboarded. These firms have on average over 4,000 external relationships and 15% of those surveyed had over one million relationships. Four % of turnover is spent on average by companies on customer and third-party due diligence checks. Over 61% of respondents agreed that their company is not using innovative solutions to keep on top of supplier/customer relationships. This is concerning, as a lack of information, transparency, and data can allow illicit acts to continue in supply chains unnoticed. Fortunately, 60% are prioritising automation and digitisation for investment.[4]

On a positive note, regulation, policy, and disclosure requirements have played a critical role in driving transparency in supply chains and businesses' reporting requirements. The UK's Modern Slavery Act 2015 brought in tougher laws and sanctions against slavery and encourages businesses to ensure that they are not participating in labour abuse in their supply chain. As a result of the act businesses in the UK with a turnover excess of GBP36 million need to publish an annual statement explaining the steps they have taken to ensure that their business and supply chains are not tainted by slavery and human trafficking. The Chartered Institute of Procurement and Supply Chains (CIPS), however recently published a report on progress since the act was put in place; Cath Hill, group director at the CIPS, said: 'The true cost of modern slavery is

3 Ambika Zutshi, Andrew Creed, and Amrik Sohal, 'Child Labour and Supply Chain: Profitability or (mis)management', *European Business Review* 21 (2009): 42–63. 10.1108/09555340910925175.
4 Innovation and the Fight against Financial Crime, Refinitiv, https://www.refinitiv.com/en/resources/special-report/innovation-and-the-fight-against-financial-crime.

buried deep within global supply chains. The unfortunate truth is that slaves from around the world are involved in every part of our lives, making the clothes we wear and the food we eat. Ignorance is no longer an excuse'. She went on to say, 'Businesses are left to police their own supply chains but too many of them do not know how best to tackle modern slavery and are seeking more guidance. The Modern Slavery Act has made great strides in raising awareness but businesses face no consequences if they fail to implement even the most basic checks to prevent modern-day slavery.'[5] Australia also recently introduced a Modern Day Slavery act, but a lack of penalisation, will likely bring the same result.

The Freedom Seal was recently set up by Rani Hong, a survivor of child slavery. The aim here is to provide companies with 'pre-vetted' and 'trusted' companies. However, to be able to provide a seal – significant transparency, due diligence, and reporting will be required.

In regard to climate risks, the world's 500 largest companies face $1 trillion potential financial risks, such as asset write-offs from climate change. The Financial Stability Board's Task Force of Climate–related Financial Disclosures (TCFD) has helped drive the mainstreaming of corporate transparency on environmental risks. It was noted by the chairman that 'increasing transparency makes markets more efficient, and economies more stable and resilient'.[6] Overall however finance chiefs are underestimating how climate-related risks could affect their companies' bottom lines.

Increasing client demand for sustainable products also raises the need to review transparency initiatives. Sales of sustainable products are estimated to hit US$150 billion by 2020; therefore, as demand grows, supply needs to grow as well. The ability to prove that an item has been sustainably and ethically made will grow in importance to consumers and with businesses as they focus more on the risks in their supply chains.

As we have seen, regulation, disclosure, and demand are important levers in driving corporate action; however, specialised workflow solutions, data collection, and emerging technology will need to play a larger role in enabling transparency and governance.

An initial step in preventing child labour or questionable practices is knowing which suppliers are involved in the sourcing and production of your products. Traceability, supplier assessment, audit management, and reporting are some of the processes that can also assist.

---

5 CIPS, Supply Management https://www.cips.org/en/supply-management/news/2019/may/government-should-lead-by-example-to-tackle-slavery/.
6 TCFD, https://www.fsb-tcfd.org/.

Supplier prequalification tools

Multi-national companies may have thousands of suppliers and their supply chains can be multi-leveled. Walmart, for example, has over 100,000 suppliers and Procter & Gamble over 75,000. Deals can be executed across the enterprise in various business units and geographies.

The general assumption is that suppliers are selected via a tender or Request for Proposal (RFP) process that includes questions to assess a supplier. This may be true for the larger-spend areas, but it is not true across all suppliers and requires a large investment in supply chain and procurement teams to provide that coverage.

Most companies will have a manual process to collect the supplier information required to onboard a supplier into their finance applications for payment of invoices. These will have varying degrees of approvals and often supplier risk management activities are done after this process. Some companies (mainly financial institutions) will regularly 'sanction screen' to ensure they avoid payments to blacklisted entities and avoid incurring penalties for sanction breaches. For example, payments in US dollars are automatically subject to US sanction legislation.

A few of the finance, purchasing, and invoicing technology players such as SAP, Oracle, and Coupa are starting to include prequalification question sets that can be used during the onboarding process and by creating databases of suppliers that run across multiple clients. There are also specialist companies such as Avetta, Achilles, ISNetworld, and EcoVadis that focus on providing audit and assurance of health, safety, and environment (HSE), financial, and sustainability status. Suppliers need to pay for registration on these platforms and are audited to varying degrees and hence often still rely on accurate inputting.

The data challenge

The challenge of data connectivity and the ability to derive deeper insights from data analysis have several dimensions. Firstly, the lack of digitisation is an issue in certain areas such as supply chain finance, which is still running as a fairly traditional, non-digital operation in many financial institutions and is therefore leaving large gaps that criminals can infiltrate. Data protection laws pose an additional challenge, given the fact that firms often have challenges to get a global view of customers within their own organisation and across organisations or regulators.

(Continued)

Supplier prequalification tools (continued)

As supply chains regionalise due to geopolitical trends and regulations, they will increasingly require greater transparency; more data will be digitalised and can be shared via platforms and open (or public) application programming interfaces (APIs).

Some companies are developing their own prequalification platforms with open-source providers, bringing together a Decision Manager application (for condition-based questions) with a database of supplier information. This also allows APIs to start connecting data sources from financial, HSE, social, forced labour, legal, risk, and media sources to provide a fuller picture of the supplier. The data needed to pull in often simply does not exist in a database or platform.

While few would question the benefit of having financial, HSE, legal, and other assessments in the pre-qualification of a company's supply chain, including a sustainability assessment provides a great addition in understanding overall company risk. This was highlighted by recent research that positively linked the level of sustainability programmes companies had with their processes and performance.[7]

If this benefit helps companies identify all the suppliers they want to work with, then looking down another level into the products and services they provide requires another strategy. Here, we need Procure to Pay (P2P) platforms to provide transparency on the products and services sustainability levels.

Maintaining data records and providing ongoing monitoring and updated service and product information also requires a large investment, either by the company or by the supplier updating the numerous platforms used by their different clients.

The growing demand for transparency and reporting obligations of suppliers on HSE, social, forced labour, governance, data privacy, Codes of Conduct, and so on is being matched with an increasing supply of prequalification platforms and standardisation of open APIs. This will allow companies to develop supplier assessments using externally validated data for a broad range of requirements, from modern-day slavery to emission targets to safety records.

---

7 Robert G. Eccles, Ioannis Ioannou, and George Serafeim, 'The Impact of Corporate Sustainability on Organizational Processes and Performance', *Management Science* 60, no. 11 (2014): 2835–2857, https://doi.org/10.1287/mnsc.2014.1984.

Emerging Technology in Supply Chains

Technology is key for traceability and transparency. Several technologies, including big data and analytics, the Internet of Things (IoT), and robotics, are being used today. 3D printing, artificial intelligence, and blockchain are newer emerging technologies being looked at in relation to sustainable development. Blockchain has captured hearts and minds for its ability to transform current practices and provide more transparency in the supply chain. While blockchain is still new and experimental, there is interest in the technology and how it might be used to facilitate transactions between participating organisations without a central authority.

Adding transparency, traceability, and security to the supply chain could help to achieve the SDGs by increasing information and oversight, potentially preventing questionable practices and easing friction in the process. In a recent report by R3, Brexit has been used as a case study to look at how the technology could be used to reduce frictions in exchanging data across entities in a trade transaction. The report highlights the stages along the trade process where blockchain can be potentially applied to increase resilience to future trade uncertainty and highlights key legal questions surrounding blockchain applications in different parts of the trade process.

A pilot has also been launched by the Banking Environment Initiative Fintech Taskforce in the UK to test whether blockchain can help unlock financial incentives that reward sustainability in supply chains. If successful, the outcome could ultimately benefit the 1.5 billion families whose lives depend on small-scale agriculture.[8]

Blockchain is a method of recording data – a digital ledger of contracts, agreements, and transactions. It can be used for anything that needs to be independently recorded and verified as having happened. While many users may access it, inspect it, or add data, they can't change or delete it. Every time a product changes hands, the exchange could be documented and a permanent history created. When data is added to the ledger, the participating organisations that hold copies of the blockchain must agree that the transaction is valid before the new transaction is approved and the block of data associated with the transaction is added to the ledger.

Blockchain has the capability of creating and validating provenance by holding an immutable digital record of an item and following the life cycle of this item through a chain of custody. Once items are registered, the records are permanent and cannot be changed, thus providing an audit trail to be used by multiple parties throughout the supply chain to verify authenticity.

---

8 University of Cambridge Institute for Sustainability Leadership (CISL), *Catalysing Fintech for Sustainability: Lessons from Multi-sector Innovation* (Cambridge, UK: Cambridge Institute for Sustainability Leadership, October 2017).

The application of the blockchain could replace industry-wide paper-based processes that are fragmented, susceptible to tampering, and often unavailable as an item changes ownership or location throughout its lifetime journey. Blockchain can act as the infrastructure for registering and authenticating asset ownership between untrusting parties with common interests. It also has the ability to prove sourcing in a sustainable manner and verify that there was no slavery or exploitation involved.

Diamond supply chains in particular are tainted by gross human rights violations, including those committed against children. Although prohibited by law, thousands of children appear to work in diamond mines. Girls and women are at particular risk to harm and sexual abuse. According to the ILO, 'the dangers are so obvious and extreme that there are no conditions – poverty included – under which child work in mining can be tolerated'.[9] Nevertheless, an estimated one million children aged 5–17 work in small-scale mining globally, and the number is said to be increasing.[10] This industry is a good example of how this technology could be applied as self-regulation but has not worked to date.

The diamond industry

There have been efforts to drive transparency in the diamond industry and end the trade in 'blood diamonds' for over two decades, but progress has been slow. The Kimberley Process Certification Scheme (KPSC) was established by the UN General Assembly Resolution in 2003 to increase transparency in the diamond trade and keep conflict diamonds out of the market. Self-regulation via the System of Warranties was introduced by the World Diamond Council in 2002 in order to comply with, support, and strengthen the KPSC. This voluntary system of industry self-regulation threatened expulsion from industry organisations for failure to abide by its practices.

Companies also have a responsibility to not contribute to human rights violations. To do this they need to have due diligence safeguards in place to identify and respond to human rights risks throughout their supply chain. Yet many companies do not achieve these standards.

Diamonds rely on records of origin, identity, and custody to prove authenticity and provenance. The KPCS imposes extensive requirements on its members to enable them to certify shipments of rough diamonds as conflict-free and prevent conflict diamonds from entering legitimate trade. Participants can only legally trade with other participants who have also met the minimum requirements of

---

9 International Labour Organization (ILO), 'Mining and Quarrying', http://www.ilo.org/ipec/areas/Miningandquarrying/lang--en/index.htm, retrieved 4 November 2016.

10 Dylan O'Driscoll, 'Overview of Child Labour in the Artisanal and Small-scale Mining Sector in Asia and Africa', K4D Helpdesk Report (Brighton, UK: Institute of Development Studies, 4 October 2017), https://assets.publishing.service.gov.uk/media/5a5f34feed915d7dfb57d02f/209-213-Child-labour-in-mining.pdf.

the scheme, and a KPCS certificate guaranteeing that they are conflict-free must accompany international shipments of rough diamonds.

In the past 10 years, a number of non-governmental organisations (NGOs) have pulled out of the scheme. Global Witness argued that 'most consumers still cannot be sure where their diamonds come from' and IMPACT, the Canadian NGO, advised, 'we have come to the conclusion that the Kimberley Process has lost its will to be an effective mechanism for responsible diamond governance. The Kimberley Process – and its certificate – has lost its legitimacy. The internal controls that governments conform to do not provide the evidence of traceability and due diligence needed to ensure a clean, conflict-free, and legal diamond supply chain'.

Transparency is important, as child labour in the diamond industry is a widely reported and criticised issue.

Faced with this issue, entrepreneurs like Leanne Kemp of Everledger and now the industry's largest players like De Beers Group have started to collaborate on blockchain-based platforms to introduce solutions for responsible and ethical diamonds.

Leanne Kemp advised 'This technology is being used to capture the complete life cycle of a diamond, thus enabling transparency at every stage of a diamond's journey and ensuring that the journey from mine to jeweler is ethical and conflict-free. It can also ensure that the ownership and authenticity of a diamond is securely recorded on the digital ledger. This enables companies to track the provenance of diamonds and allows buyers to screen for stones mined in regions where forced labour is common or where proceeds from previous sales were used to fund violence'.

Beyond document tampering, issues with fraudulent claims continue to plague the industry, resulting in the retreat of major banks from financing the diamond supply chain. A number of banks believed the risk was too high and de-risked their exposure to this sector. Standard Chartered, for example, lost $400 million on diamond debt. Therefore, transparency could also help with financing and funding.

Blockchain's decentralised and secure environment for joint record-keeping provides a foundation for building a global, digital ledger for high-value assets, creating a permanent record that can be used by the industry as a clear audit trail to the asset that proves authenticity.

For industries like insurance, there are extensive opportunities for ledgers to be used to secure assets and process claims. The potential of blockchain applicability goes beyond diamonds into most luxury markets where provenance matters – for example, fine wine.

This application ensures that the ownership and authenticity of an item is securely recorded on a digitised ledger, which, unlike the paper records that can be enhanced, cannot be altered to fraudulently copy. From blood diamonds mined out of Africa to the movement of counterfeit goods over borders internationally, the addition of a global verification system ensures transparency at every stage of the supply chain process and encourages ethical sourcing.

Summary

Transparency of business conduct and processes has long been a primary engine of improvement and will remain critical as stakeholders across the world continue to advance the shared goals of the 2030 Agenda for Sustainable Development.

The SDGs will need to be studied and understood by business and strategies aligned to help achieve, not hinder, their realisation of the goals. There is also a great opportunity to be realised – it is anticipated that the SDGs will generate at least $12 trillion worth of market opportunities by 2030. Transparency and traceability will become increasingly critical as the economy digitises and we get closer to 2030. Supply ecosystems are vast, unwieldy, and often impact citizens and the environment in a negative and unintended way. It is often difficult to understand who we are doing business with or the implications of what we are buying without investing in due diligence, risk intelligence, and technology. However, mitigating risk to citizens and the environment and by providing new products and services that support sustainable development, businesses can capture new market opportunities.

Innovation, digitisation, and emerging technology channeled towards the achievement of the SDGs can have impactful consequences. Technology can provide a platform to reduce middlemen and differentiate value based on sustainability. There are many ways to use technology to provide trust and transparency. Many exist today, but are not used as widely as they could, while others are emerging and in an experimental phase. Demand is also critical; as consumers demand more ethical products, companies will have an extra driver to respond.

Regarding technology like blockchain, it is crucial to look at the issues around the asset to see whether it really requires the immutability, security, and scalability that blockchain provides. Success is being found when the technology is being applied to the problems that need it most.

Currently we are not on track to achieve SDG 8.7 or indeed many of the SDGs. Innovation, technology, and change will be needed for us to have any chance of achieving them. Luckily, as this book proves, there are people in the private sector that are focused on this happening. We just need more.

Acknowledgements

Acknowledged and appreciated are the supply chain transformation insights from Mat Langley, Head of Supply Chain Operations and Technology, CBRE and Leanne Kemp, CEO and Founder of Everledger.

Part IV

Facilitating the SDGs by Legal Infrastructure Reform

16

Facilitating Sustainable Development Goal 8 by Legal Reform Measures
Gordon Walker

Introduction

The SDG Resolution adopted by the General Assembly of the United Nations on 25 September 2015 and reproduced in the Appendix to this book is entitled 'Transforming Our World: The 2030 Agenda for Sustainable Development'. It contains 17 Sustainable Development Goals (SDGs) and 169 targets. Goal 8 (SDG 8) states:

> Goal 8. Promote sustained, inclusive and sustainable economic growth, full and productive employment and decent work for all.

The targets of SDG 8 include the following:

> 8.3 Promote development-oriented policies that support productive activities, decent job creation, entrepreneurship, creativity and innovation, and encourage the formalization and growth of micro-, small- and medium-sized enterprises, including through access to financial services.
>
> …
>
> 8.10 Strengthen the capacity of domestic financial institutions to encourage and expand access to banking, insurance and financial services for all.

This chapter considers how legal reform in support of financial technologies (FinTech) and small business fundraising can facilitate SDG 8. The targets aimed at are: entrepreneurship, creativity, and innovation (8.3); the growth of micro-, small-, and medium-sized enterprises (MSMEs) through access to financial

Sustainable Development Goals: Harnessing Business to Achieve the SDGs through Finance, Technology, and Law Reform, First Edition. Edited by Julia Walker, Alma Pekmezovic, and Gordon Walker.

services especially capital raising services (8.3); and financial inclusion (8.10). All of these targets can be pursued by legal reform, especially by enabling alternative financing platforms (AFPs).[1] This is because the traditional method of fundraising by means of a prospectus is costly and time-consuming for MSMEs, and AFPs provide an attractive and speedy solution. AFPs have grown rapidly in recent years; one report listed the peer-to-peer lending (P2PL) marketplace and consumer lending market in Asia-Pacific excluding China at a total size of US$484.86 million and equity crowdfunding (ECF) at US$98.56 million.[2]

This chapter begins by discussing some overarching contextual issues (legal traditions, regulators, policymakers, and implementation) and the key existing constraint (the funding problem universally faced by small businesses). It then highlights the 'digital nation' strategy of e-government exemplified by Estonia as a means of supplying the infrastructure for FinTech innovation before considering two candidates for FinTech and MSME law reform: Hong Kong and Papua New Guinea.

Contextual Issues

Legal Traditions

This chapter considers legal reform in countries with a common law heritage. The form and content of legal systems vary according to the legal traditions from which they are derived, with different traditions dealing with legal reforms in different ways.[3] The term *common law* refers to the form of legal system in the UK and those jurisdictions that adopted English law.[4] In common law

---

1 According to the methodology developed by the Cambridge Centre for Alternative Finance, the key AFPs are characterised as technology-enabled online channels or models that act as intermediaries in the demand or supply of funding (capital formation and allocation activities). Here, two mechanisms predominate: equity-based models such as equity crowdfunding (ECF) and debt-based models (marketplace/peer-to-peer business lending or consumer lending). ECF and peer-to-peer lending (P2PL) are two of the earliest examples of FinTech – new and disruptive business models enabled by technology.

2 Cambridge Centre for Alternative Finance and the Australian Centre for Financial Studies, *Cultivating Growth: The 2nd Asia-Pacific Region Alternative Finance Industry Report* (November 2017).

3 See H. Patrick Glenn, *Legal Traditions of the World: Sustainable Diversity in Law*, 5th ed. (Oxford: Oxford University Press, 2014).

4 The common law tradition is one of the dominant legal traditions in the world, distinguished from the civil law tradition of the European continent by the binding application of judge-made law. During the period from 1607, when the colony of Virginia introduced English law to the American continents, to 1997, when Hong Kong again became part of mainland China, the common law spread to cover one-third of the world. In the Asia-Pacific region, five major commercial jurisdictions with a common law heritage are Hong Kong, Singapore, Malaysia, Australia, and New Zealand. Most South Pacific island nations, including Papua New Guinea, have a common law heritage.

countries, the usual and most well-known means by which legal change occurs is by an Act of Parliament or by legislative amendment to an existing Act. In addition, an Act or other legislation sometimes delegates power to regulatory bodies (such as a Securities Commission) to amend schedules to an Act or issue Guidelines on the application of particular provisions in legislation.

Why is consideration of the means of change important? Here is one answer: in times of rapid technological change, the ability of nations to respond quickly assumes importance as a matter of competitive advantage. So, for example, a 'socialist legality' country might be able to respond quickly to change by issuing a decree but in a common law country amending legislation means finding a place in the legislative 'queue' before the legislature. Suppose a small Pacific island nation has a bill dealing with its economically significant fisheries. The Fisheries Bill might be placed high in the legislative queue because of its economic importance. By contrast, a bill amending the Companies Act may not be deemed as urgent, nor given corresponding priority. If, however, the relevant changes to the Companies Act could be made by the promulgation of new regulations, then the legislative queue could be bypassed.

Regulators and Policymakers

In discussions about law reform and legal change, a careful distinction should be made between 'regulators' and 'policymakers'.[5] Policymakers are the persons or bodies tasked with making and amending laws, such as Members of Parliament, or in some governmental systems, persons within the executive who are invested with legislative power. Regulators, by contrast, are persons given delegated authority under a specific piece of legislation to administer that legislation. So, for example, securities regulation legislation might be administered by a Securities Commission comprised of a chairperson and commissioners. The powers of the commission are spelt out in the relevant legislation and might include administrative power to make exemptions, amend schedules, and issue guidelines on aspects of the legislation. The relevance of the distinction between regulators and policymakers is that regulators do not have a legislative, or law-making, function except in the narrow sense mentioned above, and so, generally speaking, criticism of 'the regulators' regarding perceived deficiencies in legislation is often misplaced.[6] Instead, that criticism should be aimed at policymakers, who are the persons with the authority to make and amend laws.

---

5 This is especially true of commentary regarding the regulation of cryptocurrencies.
6 For example, there is much discussion of the attitude of 'regulators' towards initial coin offerings. Most of this discussion misses the obvious point that regulators are charged with administering and applying existing law not creating new law.

New laws are usually the expression of the policy agenda of the political party in government. For example, a majority political party in government with a business growth agenda might adopt policies that assist MSMEs by permitting alternative financing platforms such as P2PL and ECF, dropping the tax rate for companies with a turnover of no more than 50 million dollars, and allowing for an immediate tax deduction for business expenditure up to 20 thousand dollars. In such cases, the relevant governmental department charged with drafting legislation would be tasked with producing amendments or new legislation. In developed countries, these departments are well resourced, but this is not the case in some countries, such as Small Island Developing States (SIDS). In these countries, two problems typically arise: the lack of knowledge as to what type of policies might best promote MSMEs, and the inadequate methods of implementation. In such cases, international financial institutions (IFIs) such as the Asian Development Bank can play an important role in addressing this 'knowledge and means' gap by providing technical assistance.[7]

Implementation Problems

SDG 17 calls for strengthening the means of implementation, which has presented particular difficulties to many SIDS, including Pacific Island nation states. The SDG Resolution supports customised strategies and programmes of action for SIDS including the so-called SAMOA Pathway.[8] Here, IFIs can go a long way towards addressing the gap in knowledge and means and, in some cases, have a strong track record for driving through meaningful reform.[9] However, success turns on many factors and cannot be assumed.[10] For example, in some SIDS, corruption, ignorance, and the actions of interest groups can effectively stymie reform. In others, the public sector is seen as the prime avenue for personal advancement, leading to a drainage of human capital into government that 'crowds out' the private sector. As a result, in such countries,

---

7 Gordon Walker and Alma Pekmezovic, 'Legal Transplanting: International Financial Organisations and Secured Transactions Law Reform in South Pacific Island Nations', *New Zealand Universities Law Review* 25 (2013): 560.
8 Small Island Developing States Accelerated Modalities of Action (SAMOA) Pathway. This document was a result of the Third International Conference on Small Island Developing States held in Apia, 1–4 September 2014. Available at https://sustainabledevelopment.un.org/samoapathway.html.
9 Ibid, n.7.
10 See Wade Channell, 'Lessons Not Learned about Law Reform', in Thomas Carothers, ed., *Promoting the Rule of Law Abroad: In Search of Knowledge* (Washington, DC: Carnegie Endowment for International Peace, 2006), 137.

there is little interest in reforms that promote MSMEs, notwithstanding that such businesses comprise the overwhelming majority of all enterprises. This problem may be exacerbated by domestic laws intended to reserve certain opportunities for citizens but which have the perverse consequence of discouraging foreign investment and other forms of international involvement.[11]

Capital Formation for Micro-, Small-, and Medium-Sized Enterprises

The international literature on the funding of small and medium-sized enterprises (SMEs) is extensive and amply demonstrates that SMEs face special financing hurdles. They make up a large part of the private sector and account for a significant share of employment in most countries but are more constrained in their access to capital than larger companies. The Hong Kong data is to the same effect. One report found that SMEs in Hong Kong accounted for 98% of enterprises and employed about 60% of private sector employees.[12] As for MSMEs, more than 200 million worldwide lack access to traditional finance.[13]

Meta-Strategy: The Promise of e-Government

In considering the following two specific examples of how law reform can facilitate SDG 8, it is pertinent to mention the 'digital nation' meta-strategy pursued by Estonia, a country often described as the global model for e-government.[14] In Estonia, many public services have been digitally linked across a government platform, producing massive productivity gains and the key infrastructure for digital innovation.[15] While numerous OECD countries are considering this example, the benefits of the Estonian strategy to SIDS, in particular those in the Asia-Pacific region seem more obvious. Assuming good internet capabilities, it would be a relatively straightforward matter to install a version of the Estonian e-government strategy in small SIDS such as the Solomon Islands, the Republic of Vanuatu, and the Kingdom of Tonga; ideally, that task should precede or run parallel with more targeted solutions.

---

11 For example, a SIDS seeking to cultivate its tourism industry may have a foreign investment law that restricts ownership and operation of taxi services to citizens of the country. At the same time, however, lack of development of domestic capital markets results in domestic operators only being able to afford taxis of inferior quality. The resulting quality of taxi services has an adverse impact on tourism, at cross-purposes with the country's economic agenda.

12 Hong Kong SAR, Department of Trade and Industry Development, *A Report on Support Measures for Small and Medium Enterprises* (2001), www.tid.gov.hk.

13 See United Nations, *Report of the Committee of Experts on Sustainable Development Financing* (2014), 25.

14 The Estonian government website has details and is accessible at www.https://e-estonia.com.

15 Nathan Heller, 'Estonia, The Digital Republic', *The New Yorker* (18 December 2017), www.https://newyorker.com/magazine/2017/12/18/estonia-the-digital-republic.

The SDGs and Domestic Policy Formation

At the national level, the familiar political pattern is one of political parties setting out a policy agenda and, when in power, legislating to achieve those policies. In fact, most OECD countries have national policies that purport to support such SDG targets as 'innovation' and the 'growth of micro-, small-, and medium-sized enterprises' and have legislated accordingly. For example, France has initiated the so-called PACTE Bill ('plan d'action pour la croissance et la transformation des enterprises'), the main goal of which is to strengthen French SMEs so they can grow and expand internationally.[16] Again, the EU issued a new Prospectus Regulation in July 2018 aimed at increasing SME access to finance.[17] Another example is provided by changes introduced into financial markets law in New Zealand in the Financial Markets Conduct Act 2014, which provided for ECF and P2PL via licensed intermediaries. As a result, the disclosure obligations imposed on these providers are less onerous than those that apply to issuers on a registered exchange. For example, a company issuing securities through ECF services is subject to less disclosure than a company listed on the New Zealand Exchange thereby reducing compliance costs. The policy rationale for these initiatives derives from the Business Growth Agenda of a former New Zealand government, which was designed to make it easier for SMEs to raise capital.[18] In implementing an ECF regulatory framework, the New Zealand government stated:

> The Government's updated securities legislation provides explicit mechanisms for regulating new forms of intermediated capital raising, such as 'peer-to-peer lending' and 'crowd funding'. These enable funds for small businesses and individuals to be raised in internet-based market places, potentially more efficiently than through traditional public or private offerings.[19]

---

16 J. D. Alois, 'French Enlightenment: Comments Provide Insight into France's ICO Aspirations', *Crowdfund Insider* (12 June 2018), www.crowdfundinsider.com.

17 Dechert LLP, 'New EU Rules Ease Access to Capital for SMEs', *Lexology* (2 July 2018), www.lexology.com.

18 In June 2017, 97% of enterprises in New Zealand had fewer than 20 employees: see Statistics New Zealand, 'Small Businesses in New Zealand' (June 2017). The SME funding problem in New Zealand is well known and is consistent with the international position. Historically, fundraising regulation in New Zealand did not address the problem and there was hence a mismatch between the needs of the majority of New Zealand businesses and fundraising legislation. The problem (and the solution) was well known in the 1990s: see G. Walker and M. Fox, 'Closing the Loop: SMEs and Securities Regulation in New Zealand' (1999) NZLJ 275 and G. Walker and M. Fox, 'An Internet Solution to the SME Funding Problem' (1999) NZLJ 318.

These alternative financing platforms have proven successful. In November 2017, the Financial Market Authority in New Zealand published a report on P2PL and ECF that indicated that $259.9 million was currently loaned to individuals and $29.5 million loaned to businesses via P2PL in the year ending 30 June 2017. An additional total of $74.2 million was raised from investors via ECF.[20]

Facilitating SDG 8 by Law Reform

This section examines how two jurisdictions could facilitate SDG 8 by law reform measures. The two countries considered are Hong Kong and Papua New Guinea (PNG), a South Pacific island nation.

Hong Kong

As stated, the International Organization of Securities Commissions (IOSCO) defines FinTech as comprising innovative business models and emerging technologies, such as distributed ledger technologies (DLT) including blockchain.[21] ECF and P2PL are two of the earliest examples of FinTech, and these innovative business models can help meet targets 8.3 and 8.10 of SDG 8. So how can law reform assist FinTech, other start-ups, and MSMEs in Hong Kong? One answer is the enactment of legislation enabling ECF and P2PL and relaxing present caps on small-scale fundraising.

FinTech is a priority for the Hong Kong Special Administrative Region (HKSAR or Hong Kong). As one report noted, the city's four priorities are biotechnology, financial technology, AI, and smart cities.[22] To be sure, there has been progress.[23] In the public sector, the Securities and Futures Commission (SFC) of Hong Kong established the FinTech Advisory Group in 2016 and became one of the first prominent national regulators to launch a dedicated FinTech Contact point.[24] In September 2017, the SFC Regulatory Sandbox

---

19 See New Zealand Government, *Building Capital Markets Report,* which formed part of the *Business Growth Agenda.*

20 FMA Media Release No. 2017-53, 'FMA Published First Peer-to-Peer/Crowdfunding Statistical Returns' (27 November 2017).

21 IOSCO, *Research Report on Financial Technologies* (February 2017).

22 Tony Cheung and Su Xinqi, 'Beijing Recruits HK Start-Up to Lead Tech Drive', *South China Morning Post* (21 September 2018). See also, Alice Shen, 'Innovation and Trade: Top Priorities for Closer HK and Britain Ties', *South China Morning Post,* 22 March 2018 (both economies to develop clear regulatory environments so FinTech firms can operate easily and simplify procedures for small business).

23 J. D. Alois, 'Hong Kong is Rocking FinTech', *Crowdfund Insider,* 14 October 2018, www .crowdfundinsider.com.

24 Benedicte Nolens, 'Update on SFC FinTech Initiatives' (23 May 2017), available at the SFC website.

initiative was announced to provide a confined regulatory environment for qualified firms to operate regulated activities before being used on a larger scale.[25] In May 2017, the Hong Kong Financial Services Development Council issued a report on the subject area.[26] The FinTech Association of Hong Kong promotes FinTech[27] and there is widespread private sector interest in the application of the technology.[28]

Despite these initiatives, public and private sector enthusiasm for FinTech in Hong Kong has not been matched by corresponding fundraising law reform. There is no specific or 'tailored' legislation for ECF or P2PL, and there are relatively few concessions for small-scale fundraising. In order to better understand the present position, we now briefly review the fundraising regime in Hong Kong.

Fundraising Law in Hong Kong: A Brief Overview

The Securities and Futures Ordinance Cap. 571 (SFO) came into effect on 1 April 2003. The term 'securities' is broadly defined in the SFO, Schedule 1, and includes a collective investment scheme (CIS). The SFO does not contain prospectus requirements; at the time of its passage, these provisions appeared in the former version of the Companies Ordinance. However, section 103 of the SFO makes it an offence to issue an advertisement, invitation, or document that contains an invitation to the public without SFC authorisation. Hong Kong company law subsequently underwent a major overhaul with the Companies Ordinance Cap. 622, which came into force on 3 March 2014. Surprisingly, that revision did not extend to the prospectus provisions. In the context of fundraising by the issuance of securities, section 6 of the current Companies Ordinance confines the meaning of regulated 'securities' to shares and debentures while preserving the concept of an 'offering . . . to a section the public' – a concept abandoned in other common law jurisdictions. So-called 'private offers' are permitted: see section 6(5). Section 11 states that a 'private' company is a company with articles that provide for share transfer restrictions, no more than 50 members and a restriction on making an invitation 'to the public.'[29]

25   Julia Leung, 'New Technologies and Asset Management: A Time of Great Promise and Great Peril?' (13 April 2018), available at the SFC website.
26   Hong Kong Financial Services Development Council, *The Future of FinTech in Hong Kong* (May 2017).
27   See www.Fintech.org.hk.
28   Georgina Lee, 'Life Beyond Cryptocurrencies: Hong Kong and China FinTech Firms Show There Is More to Blockchain', *South China Morning Post* (24 February 2018); Kathy Zhang, 'Experts See Future Fintech Role for HK, Shenzhen', *China Daily* (3 August 2018), www.chinadailyhk.com/index.html.
29   These aspects of a private company were common in jurisdictions that adopted the Companies Act 1948 (UK).

Thus, a private company can make offers to 50 persons. By contrast, public companies can make offers to the public only pursuant to the prospectus provisions.

As stated, the prospectus provisions do not appear in the Companies Ordinance or the SFO but instead appear in the former Companies Ordinance, parts of which remained active after the enactment of the new Companies Ordinance. The former Companies Ordinance was renamed the Companies (Winding Up and Miscellaneous Provisions) Ordinance Cap. 32 (CWUMPO). Part II, Div.1 provides the operative provisions most relevant to prospectus offerings. Section 2 of CWUMPO gives the term 'prospectus' a wide definition. Section 38 imposes the key prohibition: the requirement of a prospectus for an offer to the public subject to the exemption power granted to the SFC appearing in section 38A. Section 38B contains a prohibition on advertisements in relation to a proposed prospectus. Provisions as to civil and criminal liability for misstatements appear in sections 40 and 40A. Section 48A deals with the construction of references to offering shares to the public.

Safe Harbours in the 17th Schedule of CWUMPO
The 17th Schedule to CWUMPO is addressed to offers of securities that are deemed to fall outside the definition of a prospectus. These excluded or exempted offers (which also fall outside section 103 of the SFO) provide a set of safe harbours from the prospectus requirements. They are:

- Offers to professional investors (institutional investors and persons holding an investment portfolio of at least HKD8 million);
- Offers to no more than 50 persons;
- Offers where the total consideration is no more than HKD5 million or equivalent in foreign currency; and
- Offers where the minimum subscription payable for shares or the minimum principal amount to be subscribed for debentures is HKD500,000 (the so-called gold card exemption).

The effect of the first of these exclusions is that such raisings are confined to institutions and high-net-worth persons (HNWs). The policy rationale for the exclusion of institutions and HNWs is that such persons have the means to protect themselves and hence the investor protection desideratum is relaxed.[30] The '50 offers' exclusion flows from the private/public company distinction but must be carefully managed since each offer, whether accepted or not, is counted

---

30 See generally, Gordon Walker, 'Securities Regulation, Efficient Markets and Behavioural Finance: Reclaiming the Legal Genealogy', *Hong Kong Law Journal* 481 (2006): 36.

towards the limit of 50 offers. As for the 'small offers' exclusion: the cap of HKD5 million (approximately US$637,000) is too low for anything but seed money. In the result, these exclusions are not especially helpful for FinTech or any form of SME fundraising.

ECF and P2PL in Hong Kong

Unlike Malaysia, Australia, New Zealand, and elsewhere, Hong Kong has no legislation making specific provision for ECF or P2PL. At first glance, any form of ECF or P2PL activity in Hong Kong would have to comply with the prospectus provisions or qualify for the exclusionary provisions of the 17th Schedule to CWUMPO. This was confirmed in a 'Notice on Potential Regulations Applicable to, and Risks of, Crowd-funding Activities', issued by the SFC on 7 May 2014.[31] The Notice stated that any form of crowdfunding that involved an issue of securities (equity or debt securities or interests in a CIS) would result in the application section 103 of the SFO, which makes it an offence to issue an advertisement, invitation, or document which contains an invitation to the public without SFO authorisation. The provisions of sections 38, 38B, and 38D of CWUMPO would also apply.

As for crowdfunding platform operators, the SFC stated that, even if an exemption applied (for example, the exemption of an offer to professional investors), the platform might still be subject to licensing obligations for carrying on a 'regulated activity' (such as dealing in securities). In any event, it appears that the exemption for dealing with professional investors in Schedule 5 of the SFO might be unavailable, since the exemption is only available where a person acts as principal, which would not cover some crowdfunding platforms.

In the case of P2PL, the prohibition on carrying on a money-lending business without a licence as required under section 7 of the Money Lenders Ordinance Cap. 163 (MLO) might apply. For this reason, platforms operating in Hong Kong are not 'pure' P2PL platforms where the platform matches borrowers and loans are entered directly between borrowers and lenders. If they were, then the MLO would apply.

The SFC's interpretation of these provisions has not been tested in court, but the issuance of the SFC's Notice, despite not carrying any force of law, appears to have pre-emptively discouraged breaches. The conclusion is that despite supportive rhetoric, existing fundraising laws do not support ECF or P2PL or other forms of SME fundraising. Are there fast and effective means of addressing the problem without amending legislation? The answer is yes. First, the SFC has the power to prepare and publish Guidelines in relation to the provisions of the 17th Schedule, perhaps providing an immediate means to enable a

---

31 The Notice can be viewed on the SFC website.

more permissive application of the Schedule.[32] Second, and most pertinently, section 360(6) of CWUMPO gives the Commission the power, by means of an order published in the Gazette, to amend the 17th Schedule, and hence this discretionary power could be used to relax the existing exclusions (for example, by increasing the small offers cap) and creating new exclusions such as a 'bounded' or circumscribed exclusion for ECF and P2PL.[33] Here, there are ample international precedents; New Zealand, for example, provides a good model of a bounded exclusion for ECF and P2PL.[34]

Supporting FinTech and MSME Fundraising Solutions in Papua New Guinea

No South Pacific island nation has enabled ECF or P2PL or introduced any type of tailored legislation to assist MSMEs in fundraising. All of these nations could facilitate SDG 8 by introducing these AFPs and other means of small-scale fundraising. This section considers how ECF and P2PL might be accomplished in PNG.

Survey of Papua New Guinea Legislation

The Companies Act 1997 is based on the Companies Act 1993 (NZ) and provides the framework for the formation and operation of limited liability companies in PNG. There is nothing in this legislation that might pose a constraint upon the use of AFPs.

The Securities Commission Act 2015 (SCA) contains various grants of power to the Securities Commission of PNG (SC), including those that can be used to enable any required change. The objectives and functions of the SC appear in sections 7 and 8. One objective of the SC contained in section 7 is to study new avenues for development in the securities market services sector, to respond to new challenges and to take full advantage of new opportunities for achieving economic sustainability and job creation.

---

32 See Clause 7, Part 4, 17th Schedule of CWUMPO. There is a Singapore precedent for such action: see Monetary Authority of Singapore, Media Release, 'MAS to Improve Access to Crowd-funding for Start-Ups and SMEs' (8 June 2016), accessible at the MAS website.

33 The amendment power is qualified by section 360 (7) which states that the Commission shall publish a draft of the proposed order for the purpose of inviting representations from the public. Where an order is made after a draft is published, section 360 (8) applies. However, section 360 (7) and (8) do not apply if the Commission considers it is inappropriate or unnecessary or that any delay involved in complying with such subsections would not be in the interests of the investing public or in the public interest. Compare section 72 of the Philippines Securities Regulation Code which authorises the SEC of the Philippines to issue, amend, and rescind rules and regulations and orders as necessary or appropriate.

34 See Alma Pekmezovic and Gordon Walker, 'Equity Crowdfunding in New Zealand' *C&SLJ* 63 (2015): 33.

Part III of the SCA deals with the powers of the SC. There is a general grant of power in section 38, which includes the power to issue rules, guidelines, notifications, directives, class orders, or orders under the SCA. Significantly, the SC has an unfettered discretionary exemption power in section 39 which states as follows:

> The Securities Commission may, in its discretion and upon such terms and conditions (if any) as it thinks appropriate, by notice in writing, exempt any person or class or persons from compliance with any of the provisions of this Act, the Capital Market Act 2015 and the Central Depositories Act 2015.

The Capital Markets Act 2015 (CMA) was certified on 6 December 2017. It consists of 16 Parts and 10 Schedules. Part I of the CMA contains the definition section. So, for example, the term, 'securities' is defined to include debentures, shares, and units in a unit trust. Part II of the CMA deals with the approval of a stock exchange and related requirements. Part II, Subdivision 3, makes provision for 'registered electronic facilities': sections 27–29. These latter sections could be used to enable ECF and P2PL platforms.

Part III of the CMA deals with licensing and regulation. A 'regulated activity' such as dealing in securities cannot be carried out without a capital market license: section 34. The term 'regulated activity' means any of the regulated activities specified in Part 1 of Schedule 2: dealing in securities; trading in derivatives; fund management; advising on corporate finance; investment advice and financial planning. This means that an ECF platform would constitute a regulated activity and require licensing absent an exemption.

In broad overview, Part IV (Issues of Securities) of the CMA requires an issuer to seek the approval of the SC before the issuance of securities. Section 116 states that the approval of the SC is required for, inter alia, a proposal to issue securities for listing, but this does not apply to proposals specified under Schedule 5, which excludes, inter alia, securities of a private company other than debentures and underwriting agreements. Part IV, Subdivision 3 of the CMA contains the prospectus requirements. The key provision is section 128 which contains the requirement to register a prospectus in relation to an issue of securities. Sections 129–152 contain the various requirements and prohibitions that attach where section 128 applies.

Offers Excluded from the Prospectus Requirements: CMA, Schedule 6

Part IV of the CMA also includes multiple provisions for the exclusion of securities transactions from the requirements of the CMA. Pursuant to section 125(1), an 'excluded offer or invitation' is one which is specified in Schedule 6 and where such offer or invitation 'may' be prescribed by the SC as such

'by order published in the National Gazette'. Section 125 catches an information memorandum.[35] On the face of it, however, specification in Schedule 6
alone is not sufficient for compliance. The subsection is expressed in the con-
junctive. Thus, there must be the requisite specification in Schedule 6 and a
prescription published in the National Gazette. The SC has discretion in this
regard and, presumably, a letter notifying the SC may be sufficient to exercise
that discretion in favour of the applicant. For example, an offer to persons outside PNG would appear to be self-evident.[36] A list of 21 excluded offers and
invitations appears in Schedule 6 of the CMA. They include underwriting
agreements, rights offers by unlisted companies, offers made exclusively to
persons outside PNG and an offer or invitation in respect of 'securities' of a
'private' company.

Issues Excluded from the Prospectus Requirements: CMA, Schedule 7

Pursuant to section 126, an 'excluded issue' is one specified in Schedule 7 where
such issue is made to a person or class of persons . . . as 'may' be prescribed by
the SC as such 'by order published in the National Gazette'. The list of excluded
issues largely follows the list appearing in Schedule 6 and includes the reference to a 'private' company. Schedule 7, Clause 12, states that an 'issue in
respect of the securities of a private company' is an excluded issue. On the face
of it then, ECF could be achieved by a combination of the Schedule 6 and 7
exclusions. In practice, this means that offers and issues by a private company
to no more than 50 persons are permissible.

Securities Commission Power to Amend Schedules: CMA, Section 470

In Part XVI (General) of the CMA, sections 466 and 467 are significant.
Section 466 gives the SC power to issue Guidelines and Practice Notes.
Section 467 contains the regulation-making power that resides with the Head
of State. Most important, section 470 gives the SC the power to amend
Schedules. This means that the SC has the power to amend Schedules 6 and 7
if deemed desirable.

Legal Reform Opportunities for ECF and P2PL in PNG

Existing PNG statutes point to multiple opportunities to create regulatory space
for AFPs, including ECF and P2PL. The statutory objectives in the SCA in

---

35 See CMA, sections 125(3)–(4).
36 CMA Sch. 6, Cl. 5.

section 7, for instance, provide a clear mandate to the SC for active consideration of alternative capital-raising mechanisms and the application of financial technologies to the capital market. Needless to add, economic sustainability and job creation are aims of the SDGs to which PNG is a signatory, and a similar emphasis appears in the PNG government meta-strategy, *Papua New Guinea Vision 2050*. Section 39, meanwhile, empowers the SC – in an appropriate case – to make an exemption for AFPs if it deemed it expedient to do so.

The definitions within the CMA exclude from the definition of debt securities 'any agreement for a loan where the lender and borrower are signatories to the agreement and where the lending of money is in the ordinary course of business of the lender . . .' This means that a moneylender or nonbank financial intermediary whose primary business is money-lending is not caught within the definition of a security under the CMA. In turn, this implies that P2PL (whether to business or consumer) is neither prohibited nor required to obtain a license by the CMA. To this extent, P2PL requires no regulatory change in PNG. By contrast, ECF remains subject to the CMA, because the issuance of equity securities is contemplated unless conducted via a private company to no more than 50 persons. To enable ECF to bring international investment, then, legislative amendments or regulatory exemptions are still needed.

The requirement, in Part IV of the CMA, that issuers obtain SC approval prior to issuing securities, is a particular obstacle to ECF. Fundraising via a prospectus carries significant compliance costs, which deter fundraising by MSMEs in particular. Legislative initiatives to lessen the compliance costs for such entities have been introduced in a number of jurisdictions. However, there are exceptions within Part IV, Subdivision 3, that point to a way ahead for PNG to continue to accommodate ECF. Notably, section 127 states that the 'provisions of this division as specified in Schedule 6 or Schedule 7' or as prescribed by the SC shall not apply to an 'excluded offer', an 'excluded invitation', and an 'excluded issue.'

However, Schedules 6 and 7 of the CMA do not follow the cognate exclusions in New Zealand or Australia. ECF and P2PL are not specifically excluded in sections 125–126 but there is no specific provision for these new fundraising mechanisms in the CMA. It would be possible, however, to enable them by providing exclusions in Schedules 6 and 7 and the promulgation of Guidelines under section 466 based on these exclusions. Ideally, the lists of exclusions should be amended to follow the New Zealand model appearing in Schedule 1 of the Financial Markets Conduct Act 2013 in order to give a regulatory imprimatur.

Conclusion

As far as PNG is concerned, there are no regulatory constraints within the relevant legislation to the introduction of ECF and P2PL. These innovations fall within the section 7 mandate of the SC and can be enabled by the provisions on registered electronic facilities in sections 27–29 of the CMA, the power to exempt AFPs in section 39 in the SCA, or via sections 125–126 of the CMA (since the SC could use Guidelines on the exclusions as noted above and has the power to modify Schedules 6 and 7 of the CMA via section 470). In the case of ECF, the proposed innovation would be best operated by a capital market licence holder under section 34 of the CMA enabled by the creation of a new class of 'prescribed intermediary' following the New Zealand model. As for P2PL, simple money lending activities are not caught by the provisions of the CMA as they are excluded from the definition of a debenture. They would, however, be subject to the applicable statutes and common law, including contract and consumer protection laws. Hence, there appears to be no immediate legal barrier to the creation of an online P2PL platform. If thought necessary to expedite reform, consideration could be given to amending Schedules 6 and 7 of the CMA to encompass ECF and P2PL by means of promulgated regulations. Of course, the relevant legislation is of very recent origin – the CMA only came into effect in December 2017 – so the regulator can hardly be accused of inertia.

Facilitating law reform for FinTech and MSME fundraising in Hong Kong would hardly be difficult. At most, a short amending Act is required; at the least, meaningful change can be achieved by administrative action by the Commission. The key requirements are policy leadership combined with political will or decisive administrative action. Policymaker or regulator inertia as regards ECF and P2PL also goes some way to explaining regulatory responses to initial coin offerings (ICOs) in Hong Kong. If policymakers are hesitant towards ECF and P2PL then it is unlikely that any form of crafted regulation to address ICOs will eventuate.[37]

In the case of Hong Kong, however, amending the provisions of the 17th Schedule of CWUMPO could constitute a small step towards addressing the challenges posed by ICOs. The reasoning runs as follows: on the one hand, the ICO phenomenon is partly driven by the high transaction costs involved in traditional initial public offerings and, on the other hand, by the fact that exemptions available under traditional securities regulation are limited. It is arguable that the space between these extremes is being filled by ICOs carried out in other, more permissive jurisdictions (regulatory arbitrage). However, if the exemptions in the 17th Schedule were relaxed, as has occurred elsewhere, then it could be expected that FinTech and other SMEs seeking first-round financing might make use of the alternative financing platforms and revised

---

37 The creation of an ECF regime in Hong Kong could be regarded as a first step towards the regulation of ICOs or, more accurately, security token offerings (STOs): see J. D. Alois, 'European Parliament Draft Legislation Shows Intent to Enable Crowdfunding Platforms to Host Initial Coin Offerings', *Crowdfund Insider,* 5 September 2018, accessible at www.crowdfundinsider.com.

exemptions in Hong Kong rather than going to other jurisdictions such as Singapore to raise funds.[38] The latter point has some added resonance in the context of perceived regional competition between Hong Kong and Singapore for recognition as a leading FinTech hub. In this regard, Hong Kong would need to lift the small offers exemption from the present HK$5 million to about HK$30 million simply to match the small offers exemption in Singapore.[39] A similar argument could be mounted as regards the introduction of ECF in Hong Kong; again the cap for such raising would need to be HK$30 million or higher to match Singapore.

In summary, facilitating law reform for FinTech and MSME fundraising in Hong Kong and PNG would not be difficult. At most, a short amending Act is required; at the least, meaningful change can be achieved by administrative action by the regulator. The key requirements are policy leadership combined with political will or decisive administrative action.

Acknowledgements

This publication was made possible by the NPRP award NPRP 11S-1119-170016 from the Qatar National Research Fund (a member of The Qatar Foundation). The statements made herein are solely the responsibility of the author.

---

38 For example, section 272A appearing in Part XIII, Subdivision 4, of the Securities and Futures Act (Singapore) makes provision for small offers of up to SG$5 million.
39 Ibid.

17

Facilitating SDGs by Tax System Reform

Benjamin Walker

Introduction

The Sustainable Developments Goals (SDGs) consist of 17 goals that countries can strive to achieve, many of which touch directly on tax matters. This chapter outlines the role tax plays in facilitating the SDGs. If countries are serious about achieving their SDGs, a comprehensive evidence-based approach to tax is needed to foster and complement other areas of development. The central aim of this chapter is the identification of major goals and key factors that impact these goals. This inquiry should aid all stakeholders in developing and implementing tax policy in developing countries. Tax system reform is needed in many developing countries to alleviate the negative effects of taxation and finance investment in education, health, and infrastructure.

The writer defines the term *tax system* broadly to include laws passed by the legislature and their enforcement by the tax administration. Tax often involves voluntary compliance and hence the enforcement of tax law plays a greater role than in other areas of law.

The chapter consists of four parts. First, the relevant SDGs and their interaction with tax are analysed. Here, the major areas of tax policy critical for developing countries are discussed. Second, an overview of tax and development is provided with specific case studies illustrating successful tax law reform. Third, technological advances are outlined that could offer countries opportunities to improve efficiency, transparency, and fairness. Fourth, some concluding remarks are offered connecting the key themes of the chapter.

Sustainable Development Goals: Harnessing Business to Achieve the SDGs through Finance, Technology, and Law Reform, First Edition. Edited by Julia Walker, Alma Pekmezovic, and Gordon Walker.

Sustainable Development Goals

Goal 3: Good Health and Well-Being

Goal 3 identifies 'weaknesses in tax systems' as a major obstacle for improving health outcomes. Governments cannot invest in health if they lack the resources. Hence, increases in tax collection could potentially improve outcomes. There is evidence to suggest that an increase in taxation leads to greater social spending in areas of health and education. For every $100 raised in taxation per capita, there is a $10 increase in health spending per capita.[1] Health and education are two areas for developing countries that require dramatic increases in spending. Developed countries consistently spend a greater proportion of their budget on these two areas than developing countries. A basic universal health system could, for example, promote better tax compliance as taxpayers can directly see the benefits.

Goal 8: Decent Work and Economic Growth

Goal 8 aims to 'promote sustained, inclusive and sustainable economic growth, full and productive employment and decent work for all'. The tax system deeply affects many factors that contribute to economic growth. However, numerous other non-tax-related factors impact economic growth such as innovative capacity, availability of capital, type of investment, skill level of workers and labour market flexibility.[2] Attempting to separate tax from other factors is difficult. Many Scandinavian countries have high Gross Domestic Product (GDP) growth rates while maintaining high tax/GDP ratios. Their non-tax-related factors are geared towards high GDP growth, conscientious culture, high social capital, and business friendly regulation.

The subgoals contained within Goal 8 are lofty, multi-faceted, and not entirely consistent. Subgoal 8.1 provides a more tangible target of 7% GDP growth rate per year for the least developed countries. The classical understanding is that tax creates a deadweight loss and, hence, reduces economic growth. The modern understanding is more nuanced as taxes can act as incentives and disincentives to certain behaviours. However, taxes are still generally viewed as harmful to economic growth. Countries need to consider the main tax categories of property, consumption, personal, and corporate taxes; the best mix of these categories depends on their particular situation. Corporate taxes are often seen as reducing investment into a country, thus, countries should focus on taxing labour. However, Goal 8 also focuses on full employment. Thus, taxing labour could potentially reduce full employment. Based on

---

1 Reeves et al., 'Financing Universal Healthcare Coverage: Effects of Alternative Tax Structures on Public Health Systems: Cross-National Modelling in 89 Low-Income and Middle-Income Countries', *The Lancet* 386 (2014): 274–280.

2 OECD, 'Tax Policy Reform and Economic Growth', *OECD Tax Policy Studies No. 20* (2010). Available at: https://doi.org/10.1787/9789264091085-en.

the efficiency characteristics of each tax category, taxes on property are generally considered the least harmful tax.

Fundamentally, it is important that a growth-oriented tax system is adopted to create few obstacles. Countries should carefully consider tax policies that attract both capital and skilled labour. The former would involve Intellectual Property (IP) regimes, Research & Development (R&D) credits, and special tax regimes for capital inflows. The later could include a special tax rate for expatriates, favourable deductions, and special residency rules (e.g. Netherlands and United Kingdom).

Developing countries have one advantage over developed countries – they have a far younger population. Most developed countries face long-term budget deficits due to an ageing population. Hence, they face the prospect of even higher tax rates or reduced social spending. Both are likely to cause social unrest. Developing countries could slowly develop their tax systems to foster economic growth by harnessing their young populations.

International tax policy should also be carefully considered. The Organisation for Economic Co-operation and Development (OECD) has actively promoted the use of Double Tax Conventions (DTCs) to improve economic outcomes. However, there is growing evidence[3] and debate[4] about whether DTCs are in the interests of developing countries. As capital-importing countries, they lose significant tax revenues as most distributive rules give the residence State greater taxing rights. Tax competition for investment could be a viable option for developing countries; however, a race to the bottom of tax rates can also erode tax bases.[5]

Goal 10: Reduce Inequality within and among Countries

Goal 10 is a response to the global perception of unfairness in the distribution of wealth. Two notable goals include:

> 10.1: By 2030, progressively achieve and sustain income growth of the bottom 40 percent of the population at a rate higher than the national average; and

> 10.4: Adopt policies, especially fiscal, wage, and social protection policies, and progressively achieve greater equality.

---

3 K. Brooks and R. Krever, 'The Troubling Role of Tax Treaties', in M. Geerten et al. (eds), 'Tax Design Issues Worldwide', *Series on International Taxation* 51 (Alphen aan den Rijn: Kluwer Law International, 2015): 159–178; T. Dagan, 'The Costs of International Tax Cooperation', *University of Michigan Law Public Law Research Paper 13* (2012).

4 T. Dagan, 'BRICS: Theoretical Framework and the Potential of Cooperation', in Y. Brauner and P. Pistone (eds), *BRICS and the Emergence of International Tax Coordination* (Amsterdam: IBFD, 2015): 15–32.

5 J. D. Wilson, 'Theories of Tax Competition', 52 *National Tax Journal* 2 (1999): 269. Evidence to the contrary: S. Cnossen, 'Tax Policy in the European Union', CED IFO Working Paper 758 (2002).

Inequality between countries has been declining since 1980. However, inequality within countries has slightly increased. Thus, subgoal 10.1 will be difficult to achieve. It suffers from the common 'planning fallacy', that is, that a government can simply turn levers to distribute wealth as it pleases. However, in free societies, attempting to control the distribution of wealth is extremely difficult, given the multitude of factors that cannot be controlled by a central authority. The inequality between countries is even more difficult to control as there is no central authority whatsoever.

One controllable factor is the tax system, and governments can introduce policies targeted at reducing inequality. However, they must accept that any tax measure could potentially have limited impact. Both listed subgoals require a progressive tax system. A progressive tax system is where higher income and wealth are taxed at a higher percentage. For example, Person A earns $100 and is taxed at 10%, leaving her with $90. Person B earns $500 and is taxed at 40%, leaving her with $300. Person B has a far greater tax burden (as a percentage of her income) as she earns more than Person A. A regressive system is where lower income and wealth is taxed at a higher percentage. Thus, Person A would face a higher tax burden (as a percentage of her income) than Person B. Such an outcome can arise where capital is taxed at lower levels than income. Hence, inequality increases. However, taxing capital generally harms economic growth; thus, Goals 8 and 10 could be considered mutually exclusive.

There is debate about whether inequality in general harms economic growth. The OECD and International Monetary Fund (IMF) both argue that inequality negatively affects economic growth.[6] However, the correlations are not causal. Others argue that such a sweeping assertion cannot be made due to the wide array of factors. Furthermore, there is evidence that economic growth and inequality are positively correlated; however, they are negatively correlated in extremely poor countries.[7] Therefore, Goals 8 and 10 are not mutually exclusive for these extremely poor countries.

The social protection policies stated at subgoal 10.4 would require contributions by wealthier elements in society to fund protection of poorer elements. Attempting to achieve high economic growth combined with a progressive tax system is a difficult task for developing countries. Developing countries should consider carefully whether such a progressive system could work in practice. Experience has taught many policymakers that a

---

6 F. Cingano, 'Trends in Income Inequality and its Impact on Economic Growth', OECD Social, Employment and Migration Working Papers No. 163 (2014), http://dx.doi. org/10.1787/5jxrncwxv6j-en; IMF, *Fiscal Policy and Income Inequality* (2014), http://www.imf. org/external/np/pp/eng/2014/012314.pdf.

7 Dorn et al. (eds), 'Globalization and Income Inequality Revisited', IFO Working Paper No. 247 (2018).

broad-based, low-tax rate model is the most effective method to promote economic growth and account for inequality, that is, tax every economic gain possible, but at a low rate.

Goal 12: Ensure Sustainable Consumption and Production Patterns

Goal 12 relates to the mass-consumption culture that has arisen in the past century, which produces a high percentage of waste. Goal 13 provides that countries take urgent action to combat climate change and its impacts. Subgoal 12c states:

> Rationalize inefficient fossil fuel subsidies that encourage wasteful consumption by removing market distortions, in accordance with national circumstances, including by restructuring *taxation* and phasing out those harmful subsidies, where they exist, to reflect their environmental impacts, taking fully into account the specific needs and conditions of developing countries and minimizing the possible adverse impacts on their development in a manner that protects the poor and the affected communities.

Thus, countries should consider restructuring tax systems. Both Goals 12 and 13 raise the issue of environmental taxes. Over the past 50 years there has been a growing consensus that human activity is having an adverse impact on the planet. Such predictions are alarming, especially when they are made from the natural sciences. There have been three significant international agreements relating to the environment. The UN Framework Convention on Climate Change (UNFCCC) was signed in 1992. Developed countries listed in Annex I committed to adopt policies to limit their emission of greenhouse gases. No mechanism was provided to achieve this goal, and it had limited impact on countries. In 1997, the Kyoto Protocol was adopted that introduced market-based trading systems as a mechanism to reduce greenhouse emissions. Again, only developed countries were obligated to limit greenhouse gases. In 2016, the landmark Paris Agreement was signed requiring both developed and developing countries to reduce greenhouse gases. There are no specified mechanisms, thus, there is potential for environmental taxes to become a policy tool to reduce greenhouse gases according to the Paris Agreement objectives and the SDGs. The environment is core to a number of the SDGs and countries must carefully consider whether environmental taxes are appropriate.

---

8 See C. Black, 'Considering the Taxation Implications of Australia's Carbon Pricing Mechanism', *Australian Tax Review 41* (2014): 136–153.

Only developed countries have introduced carbon taxes: Denmark, Finland, Japan, Norway, Sweden, Australia (later repealed)[8] and the United Kingdom. A sign of a successful system is reduced revenue as people shift to cleaner forms of energy. Only one developing country, South Africa, has seriously considered a carbon tax, but disagreements about implementation ultimately led to abandoning the idea. The biggest hurdle for developing countries is introducing a carbon tax that does not hurt economic growth.

Carbon taxes can apply at the upstream, midstream, or downstream of a resource production chain.[9] An upstream tax applies immediately when the resource is extracted based on volume or weight. This method is simple and covers all the pollution potential. A midstream tax applies usually at the point of refinement. This covers less pollution, however, it is quite effective in countries that are well developed. A downstream tax applies usually at the point of consumption or upon import. This is useful where a country has a large consumer base. Developing countries would benefit most likely from an upstream tax, as they have neither a large consumer base nor sufficient infrastructure.

A painful truth is that resource-rich countries tend to provide worse social services to their people than non-resource countries. Where a country relies too heavily on a carbon tax it could be counterproductive. Another issue is that once countries develop a certain level of economic development, priorities shift from basic human needs to more consideration for the environment. War, famine, and plague are three consistent attributes of human history that have only recent vanished for most of the global population.[10] It is perhaps difficult to imagine a carbon tax working for people who are afflicted by these three attributes in extremely poor countries. Therefore, the writer is sceptical of developing countries using environmental taxes as an effective tax to reduce dirty energy sources.

Goal 16: Peace, Justice and Strong Institutions

Goal 16 is a courageous goal for the UN. Goal 16.6 aims to 'develop effective, accountable and transparent institutions at all levels.' The institutions involved in taxation, namely the tax administration and the courts, should be a key focus on this goal. The issue of corruption is a major problem. Tax administrations are considered the third most corrupt institutions in Africa and account for more than 2% of GDP in lost revenue. Thus, any solutions must carefully consider corruption.

---

9 T. Falcao, 'Taking the Environmental Tax Agenda Forward: How the U.N. Committee of Experts Can Lead the Way', *Journals Tax Analysts* (2018).
10 Y. N. Harari, *Homo Deus: A Brief History of Tomorrow* (London: Harvill Secker, 2016).

Goal 17: Strengthen the Means of Implementation and Revitalize Global Partnership for Sustainable Development

Goal 17 is more concrete and obtainable than many of the other goals. Two subgoals are noteworthy:

> 17.1: Strengthen domestic resource mobilization, including through international support to developing countries, to improve domestic capacity for tax and other revenue collection; and
>
> 17.9: Enhance international support for implementing effective and targeted capacity building in developing countries to support national plans to implement all the Sustainable Development Goals, including through North-South, South-South and triangular cooperation.

Goal 17 is built upon international cooperation that could create tax systems that are more transparent, efficient, and fair to taxpayers. Domestic resource mobilisation is a key concept based on increasing the flow of taxes and other income to governments. At the same time, economic growth should gradually increase tax revenues. There are a number of global tax projects underlying Goal 17 that promote international cooperation.

The Addis Tax Initiative was launched at the Third International Financing for Development Conference in July 2015. Over 55 countries and organisations have signed up for the initiative. The central goals are to catalyse significant increases in domestic revenue and to improve the transparency, fairness, effectiveness, and efficiency of tax systems in partner countries.[11] The initiative is facilitated by the International Tax Compact, which was launched by the German Federal Ministry for Economic Cooperation and Development.

The most important international project is the Platform on Tax Collaboration.[12] The platform was created by the OECD, World Bank, IMF, and the UN. All four organisations provide assistance to developing countries, and this project provides a framework for sharing of information and consolidating research. In February 2018, a conference was held dedicated specifically to Taxation and SDGs. The goals of the platform are threefold:

1. Strengthening international tax cooperation;
2. Building Institutions through Medium Term Revenue Strategies (MTRS); and
3. Promoting partnerships and stakeholder engagement.

The focus on MTRS is an immediate focus for Angel Gurria (Secretary-General of the OECD). It is estimated that a tax/GDP ratio of 15% is required for the delivery of government services.[13] One third of developing countries

---

11 https://www.addistaxinitiative.net/.
12 http://www.oecd.org/ctp/platform-for-collaboration-on-tax.htm.
13 V. Gaspar et al., 'Tax Capacity and Growth: Is there a Tipping Point?', IMF Working Paper No. WP/16/234 (2015), https://www.imf.org/external/pubs/ft/wp/2016/wp16234.pdf.

fall below this threshold. Increasing tax revenue is tied directly to health and education expenditure, which is the most politically attractive method of selling more taxation. The returns on raising revenue for investment in health and education are large. The current international political dogma is focused on increased taxation. The international organisations all support this position. However, the blind focus on arbitrary targets may in fact harm countries that have different circumstances from one another. Countries should be wary of calls for 'cooperation', as it usually means 'do as we say or else'.

A Wider Picture of Development

Taxation is a large piece of the SDG puzzle. Implicit in the SDGs is the requirement for state financing via taxation to meet the gap in investment. A greater reliance on taxation as opposed to aid and natural resources broadly, creates a more accountable government.[14] Furthermore, as noted previously, countries with large mining sectors are often worse-off than other countries.[15] However, while we can remain optimistic, there is no causal relationship between greater taxation and a more accountable government.[16] Hence, a cautious approach is necessary. Private investment is also central to the SDG puzzle and factoring this variable complicates the picture. For the purposes of this chapter, it is necessary to focus purely on taxation and development more broadly. There is research that provides stimulating reading for stakeholders.

Taxes and Economic Development

The decreased ability to collect taxes goes hand in hand with low economic development, which is often referred to as Wagner's Law.[17] The tax/GDP ratios of developed countries and the tax/GDP ratios of developing countries are similar if one compares their equivalent GDP per capita levels.[18] For example, most western-European countries in the early twentieth century had the same GDP per capita of many developing countries in the early twenty-first century. Using the historical data, we can see equivalence in tax/GDP ratios. Thus, the lower tax/GDP ratios for developing countries are not unusual and are a natural consequence of lower economic development. Attempting to postulate

---

14 M. Moore, 'Tax and the Governance Dividend', ICTD Working Paper 37 (2015), https://assets .publishing.service.gov.uk/media/57a08988ed915d622c000275/ICTD-WP37.pdf.

15 R. Edwards, 'Mining Away the Preston Curve', *World Development* 78 (2016): 22–36, http:// www.sciencedirect.com/science/article/pii/S0305750X15002351.

16 P. Carter and A. Cobham, 'Are Taxes Good for Your Health?', Working Paper 2016/171 (2016), https://www.wider.unu.edu/publication/are-taxes-good-your-health.

17 A. T. Peacock and J. Wiseman, *The Growth of Public Expenditure in the United Kingdom* (New Jersey: Princeton University Press, 1961).

some grand political narrative to explain the current discrepancy is fruitless. Furthermore, developing countries actually spend more on health and education than developed countries at the same level of development. As a result, one cannot expect major increases in tax revenue without an equivalent increase in economic development.

Tax Effort

Tax effort measures how many resources are directed at collecting taxes, that is, how efficient a tax administration is at collecting taxes. It is defined as follows: tax-GDP ratio/tax capacity. Tax capacity is based on economic and institutional characteristics. Some developing countries exert more tax effort but collect less tax. However, the correlation between tax effort and tax collection is quite high (0.71).[19] Focusing purely on tax/GDP ratio is perhaps misguided and developing countries should consider better tax systems. Many companies in developing countries are already subject to high tax rates.[20] Many developing countries today rely heavily on taxing nonresident Multinational Enterprises (MNEs). Corporate taxes account for less than 10% of total taxes in most developed countries. Conversely, corporate taxes often account for up to 50% of total taxes in developing countries. Developing countries, therefore, have scope to develop other areas of taxes that require fewer resources and collect greater taxes, i.e. indirect taxes. Indirect taxes are collected when certain transactions on goods or services occur and an intermediary is responsible for collecting the tax.

Tax collection is also connected to wider institutional factors that affect government decisions. Effective tax law reform must consider the prevailing political scenario. Bird remarks that:

> The single most important ingredient for effective tax administration is clear recognition at the highest levels of politics of the importance and willingness to support good administrative practices, even if political friends are hurt.[21]

Thus, stakeholders need to consider means to incentivise politicians to support good practices. This dynamic will vary from country to country.

---

18 T. Piketty, *Capital in the Twenty-First Century* (Cambridge: Harvard University Press, 2014).

19 R. Fenochietto and C. Pessino, 'Understanding Countries' Tax Effort', IMF Working Paper No. WP/13/244 (2013), https://www.imf.org/external/pubs/cat/longres.aspx?sk=41132.0.

20 World Bank, *Paying Taxes* (2017), https://www.pwc.com/gx/en/services/tax/paying-taxes-2017.html.

21 R. M. Bird, 'Improving Tax Administration in Developing Countries', *Journal of Tax Administration* 1, no. 1 (2015): 23–45, http://jota.website/article/view/8.

Taxes and Spending

Any tax system must be analysed in conjunction with its spending policies. Spending by governments is tied to the willingness of taxpayers to comply with tax laws. If people perceive that governments are corrupt, they are less likely to pay taxes. A tax system may be progressive, but that does not guarantee reduced inequality if social spending is poorly directed. If spending is directed to wealthier individuals in society, inequality increases. One paper argues that 60–80% of the education budget in India is attributable to inefficiencies and rent-seeking by various stakeholders.[22] Zimbabwe has a relatively high tax/GDP ratio, but spends 85% of total revenue on government employee wages.[23] Where people feel they are receiving quality services from their governments, the social contract between people and State is enhanced. Latin America has seen declines in income equality and poverty that has formed a new middle class willing to pay taxes. However, there is always a fine line between responsible spending policies and reckless spending (e.g. the IMF has explicitly warned Brazil of excessive spending).[24]

Georgia

Georgia introduced a number of key reforms that substantially improved their tax system. In 2003, the tax/GDP ratio was 12%. After the 'Rose Revolution', the government embarked on major reforms to stamp out corruption and attract investment. One entity was established (State Revenue Service) that combined both tax and customs together. By 2009, the number of separate taxes was reduced from 21 to 6. Corporate income and personal income tax rates were reduced to a single rate. Most processes were automated and e-invoicing was introduced. Electronic information sharing was also established. Cameras were installed to monitor communications between taxpayers and tax officials. By 2012, tax revenue had increased four times in nominal terms and the tax/GDP rate was 25%. Georgia is a useful example for developing countries that have inherently large state institutions. It also illustrates the pitfall of viewing tax rates as the major determinant for tax collection. Georgia managed to double its tax/GDP ratio by reducing the number of taxes and their rates. Furthermore, a wider governmental commitment to stamping out corruption and improving government services led to an improvement in tax systems.

---

22 L. Pritchett and Y. Aiyar, 'Taxes: Price of Civilization or Tribute to Leviathan?' Centre for Global Development Working Paper 412 (2015), https://www.cgdev.org/publication/taxes-price-civilization-or-tribute-leviathan.

23 IMF, 'Staff Report for the 2016 Article IV Consultation and the Third Review of the Staff-Monitored Program – Press Release; Staff Report; and Statement by the Executive Director for Zimbabwe', IMF Country Report No. 16/109 (2016), https://www.imf.org/external/pubs/cat/longres.aspx?sk=43882.0.

24 IMF, 'Article IV Consultation—Press Release; Staff Report; and Statement by the Executive Director for Brazil', IMF Country Report No. 16/348 (2016), https://www.imf.org/external/pubs/ft/scr/2016/cr16348.pdf.

> **Rwanda**
>
> After the devastating conflict of the late twentieth century, Rwanda is a positive story for developing countries. In 2003, the Rwanda Revenue Authority introduced an e-Tax Information System. In 2005, a new income tax law was introduced with rates of 0%, 20%, and 30% with few exemptions. Furthermore, greater resources were provided for enforced collections and appeals processes. In 2006, a consumption tax was introduced on certain products. During this period, import duties were substantially decreased. The United Kingdom is a key player helping Rwanda improve its tax system. The results are impressive. The number of registered VAT taxpayers increased from 3,621 in 2007 to 11,702 in 2013. PAYE taxpayers increased from 7,323 in 2007 to 20,718 in 2013. The tax/GDP ratio has also moderately increased. Rwanda is different from Georgia because there were simply no tax laws. Georgia had large burdensome tax laws, and a corrupt tax administration that was hindering economic performance. Rwanda is an example for countries with few state institutions. Overall, a specialised approach to tax reform is required that considers the underlying economic, cultural, political, and societal factors. Recognising that a one-size-fits-all is not possible may cause disquietude, but international organisations must acknowledge this underlying fact before grand political dogmas are advanced.

Taxes and Technology

The digitalisation of business has caused widespread disruption to all areas of life. Disruption has forced governments to digitalise their services in order to maintain and improve their relevance. Taxing digitalised business has proved more difficult for governments as they are slow to respond to quick changes. Estonia is a remarkable developing country embracing technology and the recent avalanche of countries announcing plans to invest in cutting-edge technology is a welcome sign. Technology is potentially the greatest weapon for a developing country in the fight for better tax systems. Technology could solve a number of problems that tax administrations face such as international tax compliance, access to accurate and current data, corruption, tax fraud, and high operational costs. Furthermore, current technology exists that could also improve certain areas of tax law such as indirect taxes, payroll taxes, transfer pricing (TP), and exchange of information between tax administrations. Tax administrations must harness the power of technology to contribute towards achieving the SDGs.

Blockchain

Blockchain is an exciting technology that offers tax administrations enhanced coordination with taxpayers. The blockchain is simply a digital ledger of certain transactions that is generally seen as incorruptible. Blockchain offers greater transparency, automation, and clear rules. Confidentiality is a basic right of any taxpayer, and there are often issues where taxpayer information has been leaked to third parties. Blockchain could increase taxpayer confidentiality. The distributed ledgers could be made available only to concerned parties, ensuring a high degree of confidentiality for the taxpayer.

Smart contracts are a set of rules that govern transactions. These smart contracts can be encoded into the blockchain network to allow automated processes without the need of an intermediary. Most current tax reporting systems require periodic payments of tax whereby the tax administration will audit a low percentage of payments based on historic data. This process is costly and time consuming for all parties. There is often low trust between the taxpayer and the tax administration. This often leads to information asymmetries and often the assumption from tax officials that the taxpayer is hiding information. The corollary is a breakdown in tax morale and an unfair application of tax laws. Those who are not audited, win the tax audit lottery. Those who are audited, lose the tax audit lottery. The blockchain offers immediate payment of tax with real-time information immediately accessible. Thus, tax officials could cover more taxpayers with more information that ensures a fairer system for all stakeholders. Furthermore, the capital investment required to establish such a system is relatively low.

Artificial Intelligence

Artificial Intelligence (AI) has been highlighted as a potential solution for solving complex international direct tax problems.[25] AI could self-teach itself using predetermined search conditions based on a wide range of sources (i.e. tax databases) to solve the particular fact problem. This could potentially aid stakeholders to solve difficult questions. This writer is sceptical of such an approach. Such a system assumes tax laws are coherent and answers are determinate, which is simply not true.[26] Anti-avoidance rules often use the concept of 'spirit of the law', which is difficult to determine, and often changes over time. Tax planners are quick to reorganise facts to reduce tax liabilities. Furthermore, there are multiple ethical and procedural issues that arise if AI is relied upon more often than not. Therefore, AI is perhaps decades away from being a reality for tax systems.

Tax Law Reform

The combination of blockchain and smart contracts offer concrete improvements that are available today. As mentioned previously, developing

---

25 D. Deputy, G. Andersen, and B. Kuźniacki, 'Toward Frictionless Trade and Frictionless Compliance: The Challenges and Opportunities of Blockchain', *Journals Tax Analysts* (2018).
26 B. Bogenschneider, 'Manufactured Factual Indeterminacy and the Globalization of Tax Jurisprudence', *University College London J. Law & Jurisprudence* 4, no. 2 (2015): 250–270.

countries should assess whether indirect taxes could improve tax collection. Blockchain technology makes it an even more viable option. The blockchain provides two counterparties: the supplier of goods or services and the payer. Every transaction could carry two labels. The first label is the fee to be paid to the supplier. The second label is the tax applicable to the supply of the good or service. The second label could be paid immediately to the tax administration. The tax administration would also have access to the distributed ledger to assess the accuracy of the information. A smart contract could be encoded to simply perform this action for every transaction. This solution is viable, and many tax administrations are currently conducting feasibility studies. The technology does not solve issues of interpretation; however, it could reduce VAT fraud and offers far better information symmetries for tax administrations.

Payroll taxes are another area where blockchain can offer improved efficiencies. The employer can simply enter in the amount to be paid, which creates two labels, 'net amount' and 'tax applicable'. This can again be encoded using smart contracts without the need for an intermediary. The tax is collected immediately, and taxpayers do not use paper records. Some countries have multiple systems collecting payroll taxes; thus, it is imperative that only central authority can access the information.

Transfer pricing (TP) is currently a hot topic for tax administrations. Much of the BEPS activities conducted by MNEs occur in this area. MNEs price contracts in such a manner as to shift profit to the lowest tax jurisdiction. MNEs could use smart inter-company contracts using the blockchain to provide a transparent register of transactions. The tax administration could gain access and assess these contracts using real-time information. Tax administrations are often hampered by the lack of quality and relevant documentation for TP audits. Blockchain could offer tax administrations a reliable source of information. The problem of mispricing still remains, and stakeholders must acknowledge that technology does not solve all issues.

Exchange of information between tax administrations is a key tool in the fight against global tax avoidance and evasion. Without reliable information, governments are simply unable to effectively enforce their tax laws. Country-by-Country Reports were a key outcome of the ground-breaking Base Erosion and Profit Shifting (BEPS) project led by the OECD. Large MNEs are required to file certain information that is subsequently shared with the relevant countries. The underlying principle is to provide tax administrations with a complete picture of an MNE's business operations, rather than a fragmented picture. This theoretically should allow tax administrations to take more informed decisions about possible TP audits. Blockchain is again another potential tool. It allows MNEs to upload information that could be viewed by authorised viewers on the distributed ledgers; thereby avoiding any complicated and tedious information exchange mechanism.

Recent Developments

There are encouraging examples of developing countries adopting digital tax measures. In 2015, Russia required VAT transactional data with any electronic Value Added Tax ('VAT') return. Domestic VAT revenues subsequently rose 12%. In 2017, India established a VAT system that requires detailed transactional data. Hungary is currently introducing live invoice reporting and Costa Rica has recently made e-invoicing mandatory for B2B transactions. All these developments are encouraging for developing countries embracing technology. Developing countries have a host of examples to learn and understand their own problems.

Conclusion

The SDGs are ambitious targets for countries to achieve. While the UN can easily set the targets, it is ultimately individual countries that must take the required steps to achieve these goals. A multitude of controllable and uncontrollable factors will dictate whether a country achieves the SDGs. Tax is one central factor that countries cannot exclude. Despite sparse reference to tax in the SDGs, tax heavily impacts nearly each SDG.

The chapter has analysed the link between taxes and SDGs 3, 8, 10, 12, 13, 16, and 17. A number of insights can be drawn from the analysis. The impact of tax systems is likely to vary widely. A business-friendly tax approach may increase economic growth (SDG 8), while simultaneously increasing inequality, contrary to SDG. It may also increase environmental degradation (SDGs 12 and 13). Environmental taxes may correspondingly decrease economic growth while improving the environment. Governments may have no choice but to prioritise certain SDGs over others. International cooperation and networks formed by the OECD, UN, IMF, and World Bank are perfect points of information for developing countries to potentially tackle some of these issues. Tax and development is a complex field of research with a multitude of factors one must consider. However, two key observations can be made. First, sound tax policy must be considered in conjunction with an analysis of wider political and societal factors. The blind pursuit of more taxes is spurious and is often not suitable for each country. Furthermore, governments must consider the connection between their spending and taxpayer behaviour, that is, prudent spending is correlated with higher tax collection. Second, governments should focus more on better tax systems. This includes goals to reduce corruption, inefficient reporting systems, prudent tax measures, a mixture of tax categories, and transparency. Technology currently exists that can revolutionise tax systems to achieve these goals (e.g. blockchain). Transparency over time can become a wont in many countries. Small steps over time with great assiduity will vastly improve tax systems and contribute to the SDGs.

18

Facilitating the SDGs by Competition and Consumer Law and Policy Reform: Aspirations and Challenges in Papua New Guinea

Brent Fisse

Introduction

Competition and consumer law and policy reforms in Papua New Guinea (PNG) are significant in improving economic and social welfare and thereby in helping to achieve the Sustainable Development Goals (SDGs).[1]

The PNG Department of Treasury initiated the Consumer and Competition Framework Review ('Review') in 2014 to examine the laws and institutions that protect consumers and promote competition in PNG and to make recommendations for their improvement. The review was undertaken with the assistance of the Asian Development Bank.[2] A comprehensive Final Report was published in 2017,[3] and the National Executive Committee approved the Final Report and its recommendations in March 2018. One recommendation was that a National Competition Policy for PNG be formulated and introduced after consultation on a draft, which was published for consultation in March 2018.[4]

The first section of this chapter outlines the main features of the competition and consumer reforms proposed in PNG ('Proposed PNG Reforms') and relates these initiatives to SDG 8 and SDG 9. Further sections address

---

1 United Nations, 'Transforming Our World: The 2030 Agenda for Sustainable Development', A/RES/70/1 (September 2015). See further Michael J. Trebilcock and Mariana Mota Prado, *Advanced Introduction to Law and Development* (Cheltenham, UK: Edward Elgar, 2014); Daniel Sokol, Thomas K. Cheng, and Ioannis Lianos (eds), *Competition Law and Development* (Stanford: Stanford Law Books, 2013).
2 The author was a member of the ADB review team led by Dr A. Simpson. The views expressed here are those of the author only.
3 PNG, Department of Treasury, *Consumer and Competition Framework Review: Final Report and Recommendations* (2017) at: https://docs.wixstatic.com/ugd/43809e_43ccc327d7224b1b9a4 07de0d95f6e74.pdf.
4 https://docs.wixstatic.com/ugd/43809e_2e65d4fa95444c24a2511b02dfc0f940.pdf.

Sustainable Development Goals: Harnessing Business to Achieve the SDGs through Finance, Technology, and Law Reform, First Edition. Edited by Julia Walker, Alma Pekmezovic, and Gordon Walker.
© 2019 John Wiley & Sons Ltd. Published 2019 by John Wiley & Sons Ltd.

five of the challenges that arise in developing competition and consumer law and policy fit for purpose in PNG and capable of facilitating SDG 8 and SDG 9:

1. Tailoring law and policy to the particular needs and circumstances of PNG;
2. Removing statutory and regulatory barriers to entry;
3. Designing competition rules that are practical and avoid excessive technicality;
4. Harnessing consumer protection laws to protect and promote small business in ways that competition rules cannot; and
5. Using enforcement mechanisms that have some chance of working in PNG.

Proposed PNG Competition and Consumer Reforms and SDGs

The Final Report of the Consumer and Competition Framework Review (2017) sets out many proposed changes for improving competition and consumer protection in PNG:

- Part II explores the protection of consumers in PNG and makes recommendations for the improvement of the existing consumer protection regime.
- Part III proposes a National Competition Policy for PNG and modernisation of existing competition laws under the ICCC Act.
- Part IV examines the contribution that consumer protection and competition law can make to the economic empowerment of women as consumers, employees, and entrepreneurs.
- Part V examines the regulatory contracts framework that applies to the providers of ports, electricity, third-party motor vehicle insurance, and postal services, and makes recommendations for better regulation of those sectors.
- Part VI explores the price control and price monitoring measures that operate under the Price Regulation Act and makes recommendations for the more targeted application of these measures.
- Part VII considers selected features of the business environment that affect the ability of PNG businesses to compete regionally and internationally, and makes or endorses recommendations for improvement of those features.

The draft National Competition Policy for PNG (2018) has the following core elements:

- Competition Policy Objectives
- Competition Principles
- Coordination of Initiatives

- Reviewing and Rectifying Statutory Impediments to Competition
- Public Procurement
- Institutional Arrangements
- Consumer Protection
- Competition Legislation
- Price Monitoring and Control
- International Trade
- Timeframe and Resources
- Progress Review.

The draft National Competition Policy complements other policies, including the National Strategy for Responsible Sustainable Development for Papua New Guinea,[5] which states that: 'Competition needs to be promoted across the economy, including in key service sectors such as telecommunications, electricity, and transport. This will require strengthening the role of the [ICCC] in investigating the competitiveness of markets and prosecuting anti-competitive behaviour'. The National Strategy for Responsible Sustainable Development also recognised consumer protection as being an important part of competition policy.

Another part of the reform initiative is capacity building for the Independent Consumer and Competition Commission (ICCC). That work includes the *ICCC Capability Assessment Report* and a programme of internal ICCC training.

The proposed PNG competition and consumer reforms are particular means, among many others, of facilitating the pursuit of SDG 8 and SDG 9. Studies have shown that effective competition regimes are likely to have positive impacts on the level of per capita GDP and economic growth. Conceptually, competition and consumer laws and policies are linked with 'consumer welfare' and/or 'total welfare'. Those concepts are economic categories within the broad precept of social development.

The Final Report and the Draft National Competition Policy relate to SDG 8.2 ('Achieve higher levels of economic productivity through diversification, technological upgrading and innovation, including through a focus on high-value added and labour-intensive sectors'). They also relate to SDG 8.3 ('Promote development-oriented policies that support productive activities, decent job creation, entrepreneurship, creativity and innovation, and encourage the formalization and growth of micro-, small-, and medium-sized enterprises, including through access to financial services').

---

5 http://www.planning.gov.pg/images/dnpm/pdf/StaRS.pdf.

The Final Report and the Draft National Competition Policy also reflect SDG 9. They relate most closely to:

- SDG 9.1 ('Develop quality, reliable, sustainable and resilient infrastructure, including regional and transborder infrastructure, to support economic development and human well-being, with a focus on affordable and equitable access for all');
- SDG 9.2 ('Promote inclusive and sustainable industrialization and, by 2030, significantly raise industry's share of employment and gross domestic product, in line with national circumstances, and double its share in least developed countries'); and
- SDG 9.3 ('Increase the access of small-scale industrial and other enterprises, in particular in developing countries, to financial services, including affordable credit, and their integration into value chains and markets').

Tailoring Law and Policy to the Particular Needs and Circumstances of PNG

The SDGs seek to impel solutions tailored to the needs and circumstances of each particular country. That underlying philosophy is mirrored by the Proposed PNG Reforms.

The approach taken heeds Kathryn McMahon's warning about the mantra of 'convergence'.[6] That mantra is often recited at the shallow end of the literature on competition law and policy in developing economies but is unconvincing and misleading:

> While important efforts have been made by international agencies to provide technical advice to developing countries, much of the work programme of these organisations is directed towards the facilitation of global mergers and unilateral enforcement, which are largely in the interests of the developed countries. The recognition of the multiple and contextual goals required by developing economies is not easily accommodated within calls for greater international convergence and standardisation of competition norms in accordance with one model of neoclassical economics, despite reference to 'informed divergence'. The challenge is to develop an approach to international and domestic competition law which is responsive to the diverse needs and context of developing economies.[7]

---

6 Kathryn McMahon, 'Competition Law and Developing Economies: Between "Informed Divergence" and International Convergence', in Ariel Ezrachi (ed.), *Research Handbook on International Competition Law* (Cheltenham, UK: Edward Elgar, 2012), 209.
7 Ibid., 236–237.

The Proposed PNG Reforms are built from the ground up and are the result of extensive consultation. They take as their starting point existing PNG laws and practices and seek to heed local views as to what might usefully be done to improve them. This approach is the antithesis of off-the-shelf templates or Western models.

One highlight of the Proposed PNG Reforms is the use of focus groups to ascertain how well consumer protection laws were working. Focus group discussion sessions were run with women consumers and mixed groups of consumers in six rural and urban areas.[8] The findings were disturbing and a spur for corrective action:

> [M]any (possibly most) consumers are unaware of the existence of the ICCC and of the role that it performs. Many of those consumers who had heard of the ICCC did not understand its functions or felt that it was difficult or impossible for them to contact the ICCC from their villages. Many also believed that making a complaint would not result in any useful outcome. . . .
>
> Many PNG consumers also feel that suppliers of goods and services, when approached directly, are unresponsive to their complaints. . . .
>
> The reports indicate that consumers would like to be able to make a personal approach to an enforcement agency to make a complaint. Consumers would also like a point of contact in their own locality to obtain advice. As the majority of PNG's citizens live in rural villages, it is unrealistic to expect that the ICCC can spread its resources widely enough to enable face-to-face meetings to occur throughout the whole country. Opportunities to make complaints can be improved, however, by the ICCC being active in spreading information about consumer rights and the role of the ICCC, using telephone hotlines, community radio and TV, sms broadcasts, websites, social media, community meetings or such other methods as will be effective.[9]

Another localising feature of the Proposed PNG Reforms is the thrust towards the use of Village Courts to help provide fast, simple, and inexpensive resolution of consumers' disputes. In PNG, the majority of people live in widely dispersed small and often isolated villages and cannot be expected to travel to

---

8 Institute of National Affairs, PNG, *Report on Focus Group Study: Consumer Protection in Papua New Guinea* (November 2016).
9 Final Report, 41–42.

the main cities to make complaints or to attend hearings. As one response, the Final Report recommended that:

> . . . Village Court Magistrates be empowered (legally and by training) to administer consumer protection laws, in less serious matters, in order that consumers outside the main centres can have recourse to local dispute resolution. Village Court Magistrates should be paid by the Government (to help ensure their independence); trained in the laws they administer (including consumer protection); trained to perform properly their functions of adjudicating and mediating disputes; and should be overseen by the District Court.[10]

That recommendation reflects the assessment of the Ministry of Justice in *A Just, Safe and Secure Society: A White Paper on Law and Justice in Papua New Guinea* (2007).

A further example of focusing on local needs and circumstances is the Final Report's exploration of the potential for the PNG consumer and competition framework to provide better protection for women and members of disadvantaged groups as consumers, employees, and business owners and to help expand women's economic opportunities in the private sector.[11] Significant difficulties are outlined and recommendations are made for ameliorating them. The recommendations include proposals for addressing gender imbalances in the public procurement process by making the process gender-equitable and thereby promoting women's economic empowerment. These recommendations are well-directed, given the importance of public procurement in the PNG economy, the extensive role of small business in the economy, and the preponderance of women in small business in PNG.

Removing Statutory and Regulatory Barriers to Entry

No matter how good frontline competition and consumer laws may be, their contribution to SDGs may be undermined by barriers to entry erected by industry-specific legislation and delegated legislation or by regulatory practices.[12]

One of many examples in PNG is Section 72 of the Motor Vehicles (Third Party Insurance) Act 1974, which requires the Minister to publish in the *National Gazette* a nomination for an insurer to offer insurance products of the defined type. This has resulted in the creation and protection of a monopoly provider of motor vehicle insurance, for no good reason.

---

10 Final Report, 62–63.
11 Final Report, Part IV.
12 See e.g., OECD, *Economic Policy Reforms 2014, Going for Growth Interim Report*, chapter 2, at http://www.oecd.org/economy/going-for-growth-2014.htm.

Another example is Section 10 of the Postal Services Act 1996, which provides that 'Post PNG has the exclusive right to carry letters' in PNG and has a range of other exclusive rights, such as the right to insure postal articles and to sell postage stamps.

This dimension of competition policy is large and important but hard to grapple with. Statutory and regulatory barriers to entry tend to be widely scattered in legal crannies and defy easy discovery with even the most advanced research tools. They are often created inconspicuously by lawmakers looking after vested interests or lacking due appreciation of what is required to foster a competitive market economy. There is rarely a champion to unearth impediments to competition and agitate for their removal. This side of the competition and consumer moons is dark and intractable.

The Final Report could not be expected to undertake all the research needed to uncover the many possible statutory and regulatory barriers to entry in PNG[13] but made several constructive recommendations.

Recommendation 190 is that the advisory role of the ICCC be specified under the ICCC Act as including:

a) Advising any Minister (not solely the Minister for Treasury);
b) Advising other agencies (not just the Minister);
c) Advising on the ICCC's own initiative (not just on request); and
d) Proposing new legislation to the Treasurer on its own initiative (not just responding to proposals).

Recommendation 191 is that the National Working Group on Improving Business and Investment Climate (or an equivalent body) be resourced and supported by the government, with revised specific Terms of Reference, including an unequivocal mandate to identify impediments to competition and propose legal, administrative, or other appropriate solutions to remove such impediments.

The Final Report discusses the significant barriers to entry created by State Owned Enterprises (SOEs).[14] A range of important and essential services in PNG is provided by SOEs – namely power, water, telecommunications, and port services, among others. Most SOEs face little or no competition in the markets they supply. They have these competitive advantages:

• The ADB 'Finding Balance' study showed that during 2002–2009 the average cost of debt of SOEs in PNG was 4.5% compared with an average commercial debt rate of 11.4%;[15]

---

13 See Institute of National Affairs, PNG, *The Business and Investment Environment in Papua New Guinea in 2012: Private Sector Perspective* (2013).
14 Final Report, Part V, Part VIID.
15 Asian Development Bank, *Finding a Balance: Benchmarking the Performance of State-Owned Enterprises in Papua New Guinea* (2012), 4.

- SOEs receive ongoing equity contributions from the government that are provided to finance assets, retire debt, or simply absorb accumulated losses;
- SOEs often enjoy greater access to, or bidding advantages in, tenders for government contracts; and
- Some SOEs enjoy statutory monopolies that are intended partly to give them revenue to fund loss-making community service obligations CSOs.

Several recommendations in the Final Report seek to remove or at least reduce these competitive advantages.

Recommendation 187 is that the ICCC and Kumul Consolidated Holdings (a government-owned entity that controls the SOEs) be required to negotiate and agree to Competitive Neutrality Principles binding on all SOEs and that the ICCC should have the function of investigating and reporting publicly on possible infringements. Competitive neutrality obliges SOEs to compete on a level playing field with privately owned enterprises. Competitive neutrality requires that SOEs not enjoy advantages or privileges that are unavailable to privately owned enterprises.

Recommendation 188 urges the government to implement other recommendations for withdrawing state ownership from commercial enterprises where possible, restructuring SOEs to allow greater private sector participation, implementing the Public Private Partnership Act, giving SOEs a full commercial orientation, and ensuring that community service obligations are contracted out to the private sector and delivered on a cost-recovery basis.

Recommendations 187 and 188 are especially aspirational and require a degree of economic rationality that may exceed political will. SOEs are an expedient avenue for achieving political popularity, by keeping electricity prices below their real cost. They also generate much-needed government revenue.

Designing Competition Rules That Are Practical and Avoid Excessive Technicality

Effective competition rules are needed to promote the economic growth that is essential to achieving the SDGs. Unfortunately, the 'substantial lessening of competition' test ('SLC' test) that is a cornerstone of competition regulation around the world is ill-defined and uncertain. Despite occasional erudite pretence to the contrary, no one really knows what is meant by 'substantial'. This uncertainty plagues attempts in developing economies to use competition law as a means of improving economic and social welfare. If businesses and regulators do not know what is meant by an SLC, their efforts to enforce the SLC test or to comply with it will lack direction or get bogged down. The Proposed PNG Reforms recognise this problem and attempt to address it. However, much work has yet to be done to inject practical meaning into the SLC test.

The case law offers limited guidance beyond telling us that 'substantial' does not mean 'large' or 'big'. The opportunity to clarify the law was not taken by the High Court of Australia in *Rural Press Ltd v ACCC* (2003), where it was stated that 'substantial' means 'meaningful or relevant to the competitive process'.[16]

Vacuity of that kind is useless when trying to apply the substantial lessening of competition in the real world. Practical elucidation is needed. As Tom Leuner has argued:

> . . . it is better to understand and debate the fundamentals of the effects which will meet that standard, than to rely upon the vagaries of instinctual responses to competition law. Although many commentators debate the possible causes of competition effects and the factors that play a role in assessing the likelihood of competition effects, there is a need to focus on what will ultimately be indicative of a breach.[17]

Leuner has advocated the use of guideline thresholds on: (a) the degree of harm to competition, (b) the critical duration of harm to competition, and (c) the probability of harm to competition. The thresholds suggested as a starting point are (a) a price increase threshold of 5%, (b) a critical duration threshold of 18 months, and (c) a probability threshold of 30%. Leuner concedes the difficulty of trying to measure any of the dimensions of substantiality precisely but contends that an approximate framework of the kind suggested is 'a roadmap of what a substantial lessening of competition looks like' and 'will assist the development of more consistent decision-making and hopefully lead to more debate in relation to the underlying policy issues'.

Market share thresholds can be useful. They are used to provide safe harbours under several EU block exemptions, including those relating to technology transfer agreements, vertical restraints, and horizontal cooperation agreements.[18] For example, under the technology transfer block exemption, a

---

16 216 CLR 53 at 71 (2003) per Gummow, Hayne, and Heydon JJ.

17 Tom Leuner, 'Time and the Dimensions of Substantiality', *Australian Business Law Review* 36 (2008): 327, 365–366.

18 European Commission, Commission Regulation (EC) No 772/2004 on the application of Article 101(3) of the Treaty to categories of technology transfer agreements, OJ 2004 L123/11 (TTBER); see further Jonathan Faull and Ali Nikpay, *The EU Law of Competition* (Oxford: Oxford University Press, 3rd ed., 2014), chapter 10C. Market share thresholds are also used in European Commission, Commission Regulation 230/2010 on the Application of Article 101(3) of the Treaty on the Functioning of the European Union to Categories of Vertical Agreements and Concerted Practices [2010] OJ L102/1 (VBER); see further Jonathan Faull and Ali Nikpay, *The EU Law of Competition* (Oxford: Oxford University Press, 3rd ed., 2014), chapter 9B.

market share threshold of 20% applies in the case of agreements between competitors and a market share threshold of 30% in the case of agreements between
non-competitors. Case-by-case rule of reason assessment is required outside
the safe harbours. The fact that market shares exceed a threshold does not give
rise to any presumption of liability.

Other rules of thumb are possible, including those geared to the volume of
commerce likely to be foreclosed by the conduct in question, or the likelihood
of any significant price increase (e.g., 5% or more over a period of three months
or more). For instance, the following rule of thumb has been used in the United
States in the context of exclusive dealing:

> In general, exclusive dealing will not be found illegal under U.S. anti-
> trust law if it does not foreclose more than 30% of all effective distri-
> bution channels. However, exclusive dealing affecting more than 30%
> of all effective distribution channels is neither automatically nor even
> presumptively illegal. Indeed, in most instances, foreclosure must be
> above 50% in order to raise any competitive concern.[19]

Such an approach offends purists,[20] but developing economies do not have
the resources necessary to engage in protracted disputes over competition
effects in a market, let alone to pay high economists' and lawyers' fees for the
privilege of doing so.

The Final Report recommends that the meaning of 'substantial' in the SLC
test be explained in ICCC guidelines and that the guidelines include worked
examples to illustrate in a practical way the kinds of circumstances in which
there is likely to be a 'substantial lessening of competition'.[21] The ICCC has
done useful work on guidelines in other areas including merger review, but has
yet to tackle the SLC test. The challenge is considerable – competition regulators around the world have yet to produce any useful guidelines on the SLC
test. Fog prevails, without any lights.

---

19 US Department of Justice and US Federal Trade Commission, *Exclusive Dealing/Single
Branding* (response to ICN questionnaire), at: http://www.internationalcompetitionnetwork.org/
uploads/questionnaires/uc%20pp/us%20response%20exclusive%20dealing.pdf. See further
American Bar Association, *Antitrust Law Developments (Seventh)*, Vol. 1 (Chicago: American Bar
Association, 2012), 211–220. In practice, such rules of thumb are often used notwithstanding the
much purer 'qualitative substantiality' test laid down in *Tampa Electric Co v Nashville Coal Co*,
365 US 320 at 329 (1961).
20 See, e.g., Rachel Trindade, Alexandra Merrett, and Rhonda Smith, '2014 – The Year of SLC',
The State of Competition 21 (2014).
21 Final Report, 76.

Harnessing Consumer Protection Laws to Protect and Promote Small Business

Small businesses often look to competition law for assistance with how they are treated by large suppliers, usually by relying on prohibitions of misuse of market power or abuse of dominance.[22] Small business is a main artery of the economy and an important target under SDG 8.3.[23]

The appeal to competition law by small business is difficult to understand except as desperation. The prohibitions of the misuse of market power and the abuse of dominance seek to promote competition, not to protect particular market participants. The elements of those prohibitions are also often difficult to establish. The element of market power or dominance can be difficult to prove and may require expert economic evidence. The element of misuse or abuse can raise questions of interpretation and difficulties in application. Consumer protection laws, including prohibitions of misleading or deceptive conduct or unconscionable conduct, may be more helpful to small business. They are concerned with promoting fair trading, including fair trading by large suppliers with small businesses. They do not require market power or dominant market power. Nor are they defined in the troublesome terms of misuse or abuse of market power.

Small business should look more to consumer law for protection against oppressive conduct by big business. As Stephen King has explained:

> . . . small businesses often lack the resources and sophistication of big companies. This makes small business vulnerable to unconscionable and unfair conduct in the market place. We already have a set of rules to protect consumers from such behaviour. So the real starting point for helping small business is in the consumer laws, not the competition laws.[24]

In Australia, the difficulty of establishing liability for misuse of market power under Section 46 of the Competition and Consumer Act has led to increased reliance on the prohibition of unconscionable conduct (Section 21 of the

---

22 A frequent but misguided claim by small business representatives in Australia is that the effects test in Section 46 of the *Competition and Consumer Act 2010* (Cth) as amended in 2017 will assist them substantially.

23 See generally Andrew Simpson and Brent Fisse, 'Competition for Private Sector Development: Small Enterprises and Competition Policy in Pacific Islands Countries', in Michael T. Schaper and Cassey Lee (eds), *Competition Law, Regulation and SMEs in APEC: Understanding the Small Business Perspective* (Singapore: ISEAS Publishing, 2016), chapter 22.

24 Stephen King, 'Why the Australian Consumer Law Can Help Small Business', *The Conversation,* 14 November 2013.

Australian Consumer Law), as in the context of dealings between supermarkets and suppliers. In proceedings successfully brought by the ACCC against Coles Supermarkets Australia Pty Ltd in 2014,[25] the Federal Court, by consent, made declarations that Coles engaged in unconscionable conduct in 2011 in its dealings with suppliers. The Court also ordered Coles to pay pecuniary penalties of $10 million. Coles also entered into a court-enforceable undertaking with the ACCC to provide redress to more than 200 suppliers (payments totalling $12.3 million resulted).[26]

However, claims based on the prohibition of unconscionable conduct have failed in some other cases. Soon after the Coles case, the ACCC did not succeed in similar proceedings against Woolworths.[27] In both cases, the supermarkets were charged with demanding uncontracted payments from suppliers, with threats of escalation and adverse repercussions. It is difficult to understand why Woolworths escaped liability when Coles did not.[28]

The meaning of 'unconscionable' in the context of dealings with consumers has been clarified a little by the Full Court of the Federal Court of Australia. In *ACCC v Lux Distributors Pty Ltd*,[29] a case relating to the sale of vacuum cleaners to elderly people in their homes, it was held that a 'normative standard of conscience' is to be applied. This standard does not require a high level of obloquy[30] but is 'permeated with accepted and acceptable community values'.[31] In some contexts, such values are contestable. In this case, however, they were 'honesty and fairness in the dealing with consumers'.[32]

In PNG, the Fairness of Transactions Act provides for mediation and, if that fails, review by a court of a 'transaction' that 'was not genuinely mutual or was manifestly unfair to a party'. This Act has been relied upon in some private claims. However, the ICCC does not formally have standing under the Act. The Final Report recommends that the Fairness of Transactions Act be amended by adding the power for the ICCC to initiate mediation under the Act and to bring proceedings on a representative basis on behalf of parties that may have been treated unfairly.[33]

---

25 *ACCC v Coles Supermarkets Australia Pty Ltd* [2014] FCA 1405.

26 'Coles to Pay Suppliers $12m', *Australian Financial Review*, 1 July 2015, 1.

27 *ACCC v Woolworths Limited* [2016] FCA 1472.

28 See further Caron Beaton-Wells, 'Supermarket Unconscionability – The Difference Two Years Can Make" (15 December 2016) at: https://law.unimelb.edu.au/news/clen/supermarket-unconscionability-the-difference-two-years-can-make.

29 FCAFC 90 [2013].

30 Contrast *Attorney-General (NSW) v World Best Holdings Ltd* [2005] NSWCA 261 at [124].

31 FCAFC 90 at 23 [2013].

32 Ibid.

33 Final Report, 83.

It may be asked whether the Proposed PNG Reforms go far enough to protect the interests of small business against unfair or oppressive conduct. One possible approach would be to deal with the problem squarely by a general prohibition of conduct in trade that is 'unfair'.[34] The terms 'unfair' and 'unconscionable' are not synonymous: conduct that is unfair or unreasonable is not for those reasons alone unconscionable. An unfairness test is used in some jurisdictions, including the European Union. The concept of unfairness is better understood by business and the community than the mystic jargon 'unconscionable'.

Using Enforcement Mechanisms That Have Some Chance of Working in PNG

Competition and consumer laws have been enforced in PNG by the ICCC, but not nearly with the intensity and consistency of enforcement in more established and better resourced regimes, including those in Australia and New Zealand. An effective enforcement regime is essential if competition and consumer laws are relied on to support SDG 8 and SDG 9.

The Final Report recommends that competition and consumer law enforcement be strengthened in various ways, most notably by:

- Giving the ICCC power to prosecute consumer protection offences independently of the Public Prosecutor;
- Enabling the ICCC to seek civil remedies in consumer protection matters as well as in competition matters;
- Giving the ICCC power to issue 'infringement notices' against traders (the effect of an infringement notice would be to alert the recipient that it will be liable to be prosecuted unless it takes immediate steps to put an end to conduct that the ICCC has identified as the law);
- Creating the power for the ICCC to bring a 'representative action' on its own initiative on behalf of a group of persons who have been affected by conduct that violates consumer protection laws;
- Equipping the courts with the power in consumer protection cases to make a broad variety of orders similar to those available in competition cases, including:

  - Orders to award compensation to a consumer who has suffered loss;
  - Injunctions;

---

34 See further Eileen Webb, 'Why an Unfairness Test Might Be a Better Way to Tackle Big Business Bullies', *The Conversation*, 16 December 2015; European Union, Directive 2005/29/EC of the European Parliament and of the Council of 11 May 2005 concerning unfair business-to-consumer commercial practices in the internal market ('Unfair Commercial Practices Directive').

- Corrective advertising orders;
- Orders requiring traders who make assertions to prove the truth of them; and
- Orders banning repeat offenders from management of businesses;

- Giving the ICCC and the courts power to accept court-enforceable undertakings;
- Reviewing and increasing maximum penalties (the standard maximum penalty for a breach of a competition rule should be increased to K20 million and a provision should be made for an alternative maximum penalty of double the gain or double the loss likely to be caused by a breach);
- Enabling a court to order a defendant to take specified precautions against repetition of a breach of the ICCC Act; and
- Making admissions of fact in litigation by the ICCC, or agreed by a party in a settlement with the ICCC, should be admissible as evidence in private actions for damages or other remedies.

These recommendations seek to rectify weaknesses or gaps in existing enforcement mechanisms and are to be welcomed. Along with other changes, including those proposed in relation to investigative powers, and other initiatives, including the ICCC internal training programme, they are calculated to make a difference.

The Final Report covers much ground but stops short of tackling some difficult problems. One of these problems is that fines or monetary penalties against corporations have serious limitations, including that of being vulnerable to being passed on to consumers rather than having a deterrent impact on the managers responsible for the breach subject to penalty.[35] Effective competition is a constraint against such pass-on but much of the PNG economy is not subject to effective competition. What can and should be done to address the limitations of fines and monetary penalties against corporations is a large topic in itself.[36] However, PNG and other developing economies should look sceptically at US and EU approaches to monetary penalties, given that those penalties are often huge yet still tend to be treated as mere licence fees for conducting business as usual. Imposing high fines or monetary penalties on PNG corporations would generate revenue for the government but is likely to be a misallocation of resources. The SDGs require economic growth, not the transfer of wealth to the government at the expense of consumers.

---

35 Brent Fisse, 'Australian Cartel Law: Biopsies', Sydney Law School Research Paper No. 18/27 (17 May 2018), at: https://papers.ssrn.com/sol3/papers.cfm?abstract_id=3180392.
36 Ibid.

Conclusion

Competition and consumer laws are among many particular means of achieving the SDGs. However, making such laws work in developing economies is much easier said than done. The PNG experience with competition and consumer reform illustrates the challenges that need to be met before competition and consumer laws can be expected to support the SDGs effectively.

First, off-the-shelf or Western models are most unlikely to work. Solutions must be tailored to the local needs and circumstances of each particular country, which requires a ground-up approach with extensive consultation, public education, and capacity-building.

Second, frontline competition and consumer laws may be undermined by barriers to entry erected by industry-specific legislation and delegated legislation or by regulatory practices. This is a widespread problem and very difficult to resolve.

Third, competition laws typically rely heavily on the 'substantial lessening of competition' test ('SLC' test). Businesses and regulators need to know what is meant by the SLC test; otherwise their efforts to enforce the test or to comply with it will lack direction or get bogged down. Yet no one really knows what is meant by the key element 'substantial', so much work is needed to inject practical meaning into the SLC test.

Fourth, the appeal to competition law by small businesses faced with exploitation by big business is often misguided. The prohibitions of misuse of market power and the abuse of dominance seek to promote competition, not to protect particular market participants, and are defined accordingly. Consumer protection laws, including prohibitions of misleading or deceptive conduct or unconscionable conduct, are likely to be more helpful to small business because they are concerned with promoting fair trading.

Finally, an effective enforcement regime is essential if competition and consumer laws are expected to support SDG 8 and SDG 9. Many useful improvements may be feasible, as the Proposed PNG Reforms show. Ultimately, however, fundamental problems remain to be overcome. One is the need to avoid the limitations of fines and monetary penalties against corporations, including the danger of pass-on to consumers and, as result, wealth transfer by them to government. That is an example (one of many) where adoption of Western models would be inimical to economic growth, and difficult to reconcile with the SDGs.

Resolution Adopted by the General Assembly
on 25 September 2015

From Resolution adopted by the General Assembly on 25 September 2015 (without reference to a Main Committee (A/70/L.1): 70/1. Transforming Our World: The 2030 Agenda for Sustainable Development, by The General Assembly (Seventieth Session, Agenda items 15 and 116, A/RES/70/1, 21 October 2015), © 2015 United Nations. Reprinted with the permission of the United Nations.

[without reference to a Main Committee (A/70/L.1)]

70/1. Transforming our world: the 2030 Agenda for Sustainable Development

The General Assembly

Adopts the following outcome document of the United Nations summit for the adoption of the post-2015 development agenda:

Transforming Our World: The 2030 Agenda for Sustainable Development

Preamble

This Agenda is a plan of action for people, planet and prosperity. It also seeks to strengthen universal peace in larger freedom. We recognize that eradicating poverty in all its forms and dimensions, including extreme poverty, is the greatest global challenge and an indispensable requirement for sustainable development.

All countries and all stakeholders, acting in collaborative partnership, will implement this plan. We are resolved to free the human race from the tyranny of poverty and want and to heal and secure our planet. We are determined to take the bold and transformative steps which are urgently needed to shift the

From Resolution adopted by the General Assembly on 25 September 2015 (without reference to a Main Committee (A/70/L.1): 70/1. Transforming Our World: The 2030 Agenda for Sustainable Development, by The General Assembly (Seventieth Session, Agenda items 15 and 116, A/RES/70/1, 21 October 2015), © 2015 United Nations. Reprinted with the permission of the United Nations.

world on to a sustainable and resilient path. As we embark on this collective journey, we pledge that no one will be left behind.

The 17 Sustainable Development Goals and 169 targets which we are announcing today demonstrate the scale and ambition of this new universal Agenda. They seek to build on the Millennium Development Goals and complete what they did not achieve. They seek to realize the human rights of all and to achieve gender equality and the empowerment of all women and girls. They are integrated and indivisible and balance the three dimensions of sustainable development: the economic, social and environmental.

The Goals and targets will stimulate action over the next 15 years in areas of critical importance for humanity and the planet.

People
We are determined to end poverty and hunger, in all their forms and dimensions, and to ensure that all human beings can fulfil their potential in dignity and equality and in a healthy environment.

Planet
We are determined to protect the planet from degradation, including through sustainable consumption and production, sustainably managing its natural resources and taking urgent action on climate change, so that it can support the needs of the present and future generations.

Prosperity
We are determined to ensure that all human beings can enjoy prosperous and fulfilling lives and that economic, social and technological progress occurs in harmony with nature.

Peace
We are determined to foster peaceful, just and inclusive societies which are free from fear and violence. There can be no sustainable development without peace and no peace without sustainable development.

Partnership
We are determined to mobilize the means required to implement this Agenda through a revitalized Global Partnership for Sustainable Development, based on a spirit of strengthened global solidarity, focused in particular on the needs of the poorest and most vulnerable and with the participation of all countries, all stakeholders and all people.

The interlinkages and integrated nature of the Sustainable Development Goals are of crucial importance in ensuring that the purpose of the new Agenda is realized. If we realize our ambitions across the full extent of the Agenda, the lives of all will be profoundly improved and our world will be transformed for the better.

Declaration

Introduction

1. We, the Heads of State and Government and High Representatives, meeting at United Nations Headquarters in New York from 25 to 27 September 2015 as the Organization celebrates its seventieth anniversary, have decided today on new global Sustainable Development Goals.

2. On behalf of the peoples we serve, we have adopted a historic decision on a comprehensive, far-reaching and people-centred set of universal and transformative Goals and targets. We commit ourselves to working tirelessly for the full implementation of this Agenda by 2030. We recognize that eradicating poverty in all its forms and dimensions, including extreme poverty, is the greatest global challenge and an indispensable requirement for sustainable development. We are committed to achieving sustainable development in its three dimensions – economic, social and environmental – in a balanced and integrated manner. We will also build upon the achievements of the Millennium Development Goals and seek to address their unfinished business.

3. We resolve, between now and 2030, to end poverty and hunger everywhere; to combat inequalities within and among countries; to build peaceful, just and inclusive societies; to protect human rights and promote gender equality and the empowerment of women and girls; and to ensure the lasting protection of the planet and its natural resources. We resolve also to create conditions for sustainable, inclusive and sustained economic growth, shared prosperity and decent work for all, taking into account different levels of national development and capacities.

4. As we embark on this great collective journey, we pledge that no one will be left behind. Recognizing that the dignity of the human person is fundamental, we wish to see the Goals and targets met for all nations and peoples and for all segments of society. And we will endeavour to reach the furthest behind first.

5. This is an Agenda of unprecedented scope and significance. It is accepted by all countries and is applicable to all, taking into account different national realities, capacities and levels of development and respecting national policies and priorities. These are universal goals and targets which involve the entire world, developed and developing countries alike. They are integrated and indivisible and balance the three dimensions of sustainable development.

6. The Goals and targets are the result of over two years of intensive public consultation and engagement with civil society and other stakeholders around the world, which paid particular attention to the voices of the poorest and most vulnerable. This consultation included valuable work done by the Open Working Group of the General Assembly on Sustainable Development Goals and by the United Nations, whose Secretary-General provided a synthesis report in December 2014.

Our vision

7. In these Goals and targets, we are setting out a supremely ambitious and transformational vision. We envisage a world free of poverty, hunger, disease and want, where all life can thrive. We envisage a world free of fear and violence. A world with universal literacy. A world with equitable and universal access to quality education at all levels, to health care and social protection, where physical, mental and social well-being are assured. A world where we reaffirm our commitments regarding the human right to safe drinking water and sanitation and where there is improved hygiene; and where food is sufficient, safe, affordable and nutritious. A world where human habitats are safe, resilient and sustainable and where there is universal access to affordable, reliable and sustainable energy.

8. We envisage a world of universal respect for human rights and human dignity, the rule of law, justice, equality and non-discrimination; of respect for race, ethnicity and cultural diversity; and of equal opportunity permitting the full realization of human potential and contributing to shared prosperity. A world which invests in its children and in which every child grows up free from violence and exploitation. A world in which every woman and girl enjoys full gender equality and all legal, social and economic barriers to their empowerment have been removed. A just, equitable, tolerant, open and socially inclusive world in which the needs of the most vulnerable are met.

9. We envisage a world in which every country enjoys sustained, inclusive and sustainable economic growth and decent work for all. A world in which consumption and production patterns and use of all natural resources – from air to land, from rivers, lakes and aquifers to oceans and seas – are sustainable. One in which democracy, good governance and the rule of law, as well as an enabling environment at the national and international levels, are essential for sustainable development, including sustained and inclusive economic growth, social development, environmental protection and the eradication of poverty and hunger. One in which development and the application of technology are climate-sensitive, respect biodiversity and are resilient. One in which humanity lives in harmony with nature and in which wildlife and other living species are protected.

Our shared principles and commitments

10. The new Agenda is guided by the purposes and principles of the Charter of the United Nations, including full respect for international law. It is grounded in the Universal Declaration of Human Rights,[1] international human rights treaties, the Millennium Declaration[2] and the 2005 World

---

1 Resolution 217 A (III).
2 Resolution 55/2.

Summit Outcome.[3] It is informed by other instruments such as the Declaration on the Right to Development.[4]

11. We reaffirm the outcomes of all major United Nations conferences and summits which have laid a solid foundation for sustainable development and have helped to shape the new Agenda. These include the Rio Declaration on Environment and Development,[5] the World Summit on Sustainable Development, the World Summit for Social Development, the Programme of Action of the International Conference on Population and Development,[6] the Beijing Platform for Action[7] and the United Nations Conference on Sustainable Development. We also reaffirm the follow-up to these conferences, including the outcomes of the Fourth United Nations Conference on the Least Developed Countries, the third International Conference on Small Island Developing States, the second United Nations Conference on Landlocked Developing Countries and the Third United Nations World Conference on Disaster Risk Reduction.

12. We reaffirm all the principles of the Rio Declaration on Environment and Development, including, inter alia, the principle of common but differentiated responsibilities, as set out in principle 7 thereof.

13. The challenges and commitments identified at these major conferences and summits are interrelated and call for integrated solutions. To address them effectively, a new approach is needed. Sustainable development recognizes that eradicating poverty in all its forms and dimensions, combating inequality within and among countries, preserving the planet, creating sustained, inclusive and sustainable economic growth and fostering social inclusion are linked to each other and are interdependent.

Our world today

14. We are meeting at a time of immense challenges to sustainable development. Billions of our citizens continue to live in poverty and are denied a life of dignity. There are rising inequalities within and among countries. There are enormous disparities of opportunity, wealth and power. Gender inequality remains a key challenge. Unemployment, particularly youth unemployment, is a major concern. Global health threats, more frequent

---

3 Resolution 60/1.

4 Resolution 41/128, annex.

5 *Report of the United Nations Conference on Environment and Development, Rio de Janeiro, 3–14 June 1992*, vol. I, *Resolutions Adopted by the Conference* (United Nations publication, Sales No. E.93.I.8 and corrigendum), resolution 1, annex I.

6 *Report of the International Conference on Population and Development, Cairo, 5–13 September 1994* (United Nations publication, Sales No. E.95.XIII.18), chap. I, resolution 1, annex.

7 *Report of the Fourth World Conference on Women, Beijing, 4–15 September 1995* (United Nations publication, Sales No. E.96.IV.13), chap. I, resolution 1, annex II.

and intense natural disasters, spiralling conflict, violent extremism, terrorism and related humanitarian crises and forced displacement of people threaten to reverse much of the development progress made in recent decades. Natural resource depletion and adverse impacts of environmental degradation, including desertification, drought, land degradation, freshwater scarcity and loss of biodiversity, add to and exacerbate the list of challenges which humanity faces. Climate change is one of the greatest challenges of our time and its adverse impacts undermine the ability of all countries to achieve sustainable development. Increases in global temperature, sea level rise, ocean acidification and other climate change impacts are seriously affecting coastal areas and low-lying coastal countries, including many least developed countries and small island developing States. The survival of many societies, and of the biological support systems of the planet, is at risk.

15. It is also, however, a time of immense opportunity. Significant progress has been made in meeting many development challenges. Within the past generation, hundreds of millions of people have emerged from extreme poverty. Access to education has greatly increased for both boys and girls. The spread of information and communications technology and global interconnectedness has great potential to accelerate human progress, to bridge the digital divide and to develop knowledge societies, as does scientific and technological innovation across areas as diverse as medicine and energy.

16. Almost 15 years ago, the Millennium Development Goals were agreed. These provided an important framework for development and significant progress has been made in a number of areas. But the progress has been uneven, particularly in Africa, least developed countries, landlocked developing countries and small island developing States, and some of the Millennium Development Goals remain off-track, in particular those related to maternal, newborn and child health and to reproductive health. We recommit ourselves to the full realization of all the Millennium Development Goals, including the off-track Millennium Development Goals, in particular by providing focused and scaled-up assistance to least developed countries and other countries in special situations, in line with relevant support programmes. The new Agenda builds on the Millennium Development Goals and seeks to complete what they did not achieve, particularly in reaching the most vulnerable.

17. In its scope, however, the framework we are announcing today goes far beyond the Millennium Development Goals. Alongside continuing development priorities such as poverty eradication, health, education and food security and nutrition, it sets out a wide range of economic, social and environmental objectives. It also promises more peaceful and inclusive

societies. It also, crucially, defines means of implementation. Reflecting the integrated approach that we have decided on, there are deep interconnections and many cross-cutting elements across the new Goals and targets.

The new Agenda

18. We are announcing today 17 Sustainable Development Goals with 169 associated targets which are integrated and indivisible. Never before have world leaders pledged common action and endeavour across such a broad and universal policy agenda. We are setting out together on the path towards sustainable development, devoting ourselves collectively to the pursuit of global development and of "win-win" cooperation which can bring huge gains to all countries and all parts of the world. We reaffirm that every State has, and shall freely exercise, full permanent sovereignty over all its wealth, natural resources and economic activity. We will implement the Agenda for the full benefit of all, for today's generation and for future generations. In doing so, we reaffirm our commitment to international law and emphasize that the Agenda is to be implemented in a manner that is consistent with the rights and obligations of States under international law.

19. We reaffirm the importance of the Universal Declaration of Human Rights, as well as other international instruments relating to human rights and international law. We emphasize the responsibilities of all States, in conformity with the Charter of the United Nations, to respect, protect and promote human rights and fundamental freedoms for all, without distinction of any kind as to race, colour, sex, language, religion, political or other opinion, national or social origin, property, birth, disability or other status.

20. Realizing gender equality and the empowerment of women and girls will make a crucial contribution to progress across all the Goals and targets. The achievement of full human potential and of sustainable development is not possible if one half of humanity continues to be denied its full human rights and opportunities. Women and girls must enjoy equal access to quality education, economic resources and political participation as well as equal opportunities with men and boys for employment, leadership and decision-making at all levels. We will work for a significant increase in investments to close the gender gap and strengthen support for institutions in relation to gender equality and the empowerment of women at the global, regional and national levels. All forms of discrimination and violence against women and girls will be eliminated, including through the engagement of men and boys. The systematic mainstreaming of a gender perspective in the implementation of the Agenda is crucial.

21. The new Goals and targets will come into effect on 1 January 2016 and will guide the decisions we take over the next 15 years. All of us will work to implement the Agenda within our own countries and at the regional and global levels, taking into account different national realities, capacities and levels of development and respecting national policies and priorities. We will respect national policy space for sustained, inclusive and sustainable economic growth, in particular for developing States, while remaining consistent with relevant international rules and commitments. We acknowledge also the importance of the regional and subregional dimensions, regional economic integration and interconnectivity in sustainable development. Regional and subregional frameworks can facilitate the effective translation of sustainable development policies into concrete action at the national level.

22. Each country faces specific challenges in its pursuit of sustainable development. The most vulnerable countries and, in particular, African countries, least developed countries, landlocked developing countries and small island developing States, deserve special attention, as do countries in situations of conflict and post-conflict countries. There are also serious challenges within many middle-income countries.

23. People who are vulnerable must be empowered. Those whose needs are reflected in the Agenda include all children, youth, persons with disabilities (of whom more than 80 per cent live in poverty), people living with HIV/AIDS, older persons, indigenous peoples, refugees and internally displaced persons and migrants. We resolve to take further effective measures and actions, in conformity with international law, to remove obstacles and constraints, strengthen support and meet the special needs of people living in areas affected by complex humanitarian emergencies and in areas affected by terrorism.

24. We are committed to ending poverty in all its forms and dimensions, including by eradicating extreme poverty by 2030. All people must enjoy a basic standard of living, including through social protection systems. We are also determined to end hunger and to achieve food security as a matter of priority and to end all forms of malnutrition. In this regard, we reaffirm the important role and inclusive nature of the Committee on World Food Security and welcome the Rome Declaration on Nutrition and the Framework for Action.[8] We will devote resources to developing rural areas and sustainable agriculture and fisheries, supporting smallholder farmers, especially women farmers, herders and fishers in developing countries, particularly least developed countries.

---

8 World Health Organization, document EB 136/8, annexes I and II.

25. We commit to providing inclusive and equitable quality education at all levels – early childhood, primary, secondary, tertiary, technical and vocational training. All people, irrespective of sex, age, race or ethnicity, and persons with disabilities, migrants, indigenous peoples, children and youth, especially those in vulnerable situations, should have access to lifelong learning opportunities that help them to acquire the knowledge and skills needed to exploit opportunities and to participate fully in society. We will strive to provide children and youth with a nurturing environment for the full realization of their rights and capabilities, helping our countries to reap the demographic dividend, including through safe schools and cohesive communities and families.

26. To promote physical and mental health and well-being, and to extend life expectancy for all, we must achieve universal health coverage and access to quality health care. No one must be left behind. We commit to accelerating the progress made to date in reducing newborn, child and maternal mortality by ending all such preventable deaths before 2030. We are committed to ensuring universal access to sexual and reproductive health-care services, including for family planning, information and education. We will equally accelerate the pace of progress made in fighting malaria, HIV/AIDS, tuberculosis, hepatitis, Ebola and other communicable diseases and epidemics, including by addressing growing anti-microbial resistance and the problem of unattended diseases affecting developing countries. We are committed to the prevention and treatment of non-communicable diseases, including behavioural, developmental and neurological disorders, which constitute a major challenge for sustainable development.

27. We will seek to build strong economic foundations for all our countries. Sustained, inclusive and sustainable economic growth is essential for prosperity. This will only be possible if wealth is shared and income inequality is addressed. We will work to build dynamic, sustainable, innovative and people-centred economies, promoting youth employment and women's economic empowerment, in particular, and decent work for all. We will eradicate forced labour and human trafficking and end child labour in all its forms. All countries stand to benefit from having a healthy and well-educated workforce with the knowledge and skills needed for productive and fulfilling work and full participation in society. We will strengthen the productive capacities of least developed countries in all sectors, including through structural transformation. We will adopt policies which increase productive capacities, productivity and productive employment; financial inclusion; sustainable agriculture, pastoralist and fisheries development; sustainable industrial development; universal access to affordable, reliable, sustainable and modern energy services; sustainable transport systems; and quality and resilient infrastructure.

28. We commit to making fundamental changes in the way that our societies produce and consume goods and services. Governments, international organizations, the business sector and other non-State actors and individuals must contribute to changing unsustainable consumption and production patterns, including through the mobilization, from all sources, of financial and technical assistance to strengthen developing countries' scientific, technological and innovative capacities to move towards more sustainable patterns of consumption and production. We encourage the implementation of the 10-Year Framework of Programmes on Sustainable Consumption and Production Patterns. All countries take action, with developed countries taking the lead, taking into account the development and capabilities of developing countries.

29. We recognize the positive contribution of migrants for inclusive growth and sustainable development. We also recognize that international migration is a multidimensional reality of major relevance for the development of countries of origin, transit and destination, which requires coherent and comprehensive responses. We will cooperate internationally to ensure safe, orderly and regular migration involving full respect for human rights and the humane treatment of migrants regardless of migration status, of refugees and of displaced persons. Such cooperation should also strengthen the resilience of communities hosting refugees, particularly in developing countries. We underline the right of migrants to return to their country of citizenship, and recall that States must ensure that their returning nationals are duly received.

30. States are strongly urged to refrain from promulgating and applying any unilateral economic, financial or trade measures not in accordance with international law and the Charter of the United Nations that impede the full achievement of economic and social development, particularly in developing countries.

31. We acknowledge that the United Nations Framework Convention on Climate Change[9] is the primary international, intergovernmental forum for negotiating the global response to climate change. We are determined to address decisively the threat posed by climate change and environmental degradation. The global nature of climate change calls for the widest possible international cooperation aimed at accelerating the reduction of global greenhouse gas emissions and addressing adaptation to the adverse impacts of climate change. We note with grave concern the significant gap between the aggregate effect of parties' mitigation pledges in terms of global annual emissions of greenhouse gases by 2020 and aggregate emission pathways consistent with having a likely chance of holding the increase in global average temperature below 2 degrees Celsius, or 1.5 degrees Celsius above pre-industrial levels.

---

9 United Nations, *Treaty Series*, vol. 1771, No. 30822.

32. Looking ahead to the twenty-first session of the Conference of the Parties in Paris, we underscore the commitment of all States to work for an ambitious and universal climate agreement. We reaffirm that the protocol, another legal instrument or agreed outcome with legal force under the Convention applicable to all parties shall address in a balanced manner, inter alia, mitigation, adaptation, finance, technology development and transfer and capacity-building; and transparency of action and support.

33. We recognize that social and economic development depends on the sustainable management of our planet's natural resources. We are therefore determined to conserve and sustainably use oceans and seas, freshwater resources, as well as forests, mountains and drylands and to protect biodiversity, ecosystems and wildlife. We are also determined to promote sustainable tourism, to tackle water scarcity and water pollution, to strengthen cooperation on desertification, dust storms, land degradation and drought and to promote resilience and disaster risk reduction. In this regard, we look forward to the thirteenth meeting of the Conference of the Parties to the Convention on Biological Diversity to be held in Mexico.

34. We recognize that sustainable urban development and management are crucial to the quality of life of our people. We will work with local authorities and communities to renew and plan our cities and human settlements so as to foster community cohesion and personal security and to stimulate innovation and employment. We will reduce the negative impacts of urban activities and of chemicals which are hazardous for human health and the environment, including through the environmentally sound management and safe use of chemicals, the reduction and recycling of waste and the more efficient use of water and energy. And we will work to minimize the impact of cities on the global climate system. We will also take account of population trends and projections in our national rural and urban development strategies and policies. We look forward to the upcoming United Nations Conference on Housing and Sustainable Urban Development to be held in Quito.

35. Sustainable development cannot be realized without peace and security; and peace and security will be at risk without sustainable development. The new Agenda recognizes the need to build peaceful, just and inclusive societies that provide equal access to justice and that are based on respect for human rights (including the right to development), on effective rule of law and good governance at all levels and on transparent, effective and accountable institutions. Factors which give rise to violence, insecurity and injustice, such as inequality, corruption, poor governance and illicit financial and arms flows, are addressed in the Agenda. We must redouble our efforts to resolve or prevent conflict and to support post-conflict countries, including through ensuring that women have a role in peacebuilding and State-building. We call for further effective measures and actions to be taken, in

conformity with international law, to remove the obstacles to the full realization of the right of self-determination of peoples living under colonial and foreign occupation, which continue to adversely affect their economic and social development as well as their environment.

36. We pledge to foster intercultural understanding, tolerance, mutual respect and an ethic of global citizenship and shared responsibility. We acknowledge the natural and cultural diversity of the world and recognize that all cultures and civilizations can contribute to, and are crucial enablers of, sustainable development.

37. Sport is also an important enabler of sustainable development. We recognize the growing contribution of sport to the realization of development and peace in its promotion of tolerance and respect and the contributions it makes to the empowerment of women and of young people, individuals and communities as well as to health, education and social inclusion objectives.

38. We reaffirm, in accordance with the Charter of the United Nations, the need to respect the territorial integrity and political independence of States.

Means of implementation

39. The scale and ambition of the new Agenda requires a revitalized Global Partnership to ensure its implementation. We fully commit to this. This Partnership will work in a spirit of global solidarity, in particular solidarity with the poorest and with people in vulnerable situations. It will facilitate an intensive global engagement in support of implementation of all the Goals and targets, bringing together Governments, the private sector, civil society, the United Nations system and other actors and mobilizing all available resources.

40. The means of implementation targets under Goal 17 and under each Sustainable Development Goal are key to realizing our Agenda and are of equal importance with the other Goals and targets. The Agenda, including the Sustainable Development Goals, can be met within the framework of a revitalized Global Partnership for Sustainable Development, supported by the concrete policies and actions as outlined in the outcome document of the third International Conference on Financing for Development, held in Addis Ababa from 13 to 16 July 2015. We welcome the endorsement by the General Assembly of the Addis Ababa Action Agenda,[10] which is an

---

10 The Addis Ababa Action Agenda of the Third International Conference on Financing for Development (Addis Ababa Action Agenda), adopted by the General Assembly on 27 July 2015 (resolution 69/313, annex).

integral part of the 2030 Agenda for Sustainable Development. We recognize that the full implementation of the Addis Ababa Action Agenda is critical for the realization of the Sustainable Development Goals and targets.

41. We recognize that each country has primary responsibility for its own economic and social development. The new Agenda deals with the means required for implementation of the Goals and targets. We recognize that these will include the mobilization of financial resources as well as capacity-building and the transfer of environmentally sound technologies to developing countries on favourable terms, including on concessional and preferential terms, as mutually agreed. Public finance, both domestic and international, will play a vital role in providing essential services and public goods and in catalysing other sources of finance. We acknowledge the role of the diverse private sector, ranging from micro-enterprises to cooperatives to multinationals, and that of civil society organizations and philanthropic organizations in the implementation of the new Agenda.

42. We support the implementation of relevant strategies and programmes of action, including the Istanbul Declaration and Programme of Action,[11] the SIDS Accelerated Modalities of Action (SAMOA) Pathway[12] and the Vienna Programme of Action for Landlocked Developing Countries for the Decade 2014–2024,[13] and reaffirm the importance of supporting the African Union's Agenda 2063 and the programme of the New Partnership for Africa's Development,[14] all of which are integral to the new Agenda. We recognize the major challenge to the achievement of durable peace and sustainable development in countries in conflict and post-conflict situations.

43. We emphasize that international public finance plays an important role in complementing the efforts of countries to mobilize public resources domestically, especially in the poorest and most vulnerable countries with limited domestic resources. An important use of international public finance, including official development assistance (ODA), is to catalyse additional resource mobilization from other sources, public and private. ODA providers reaffirm their respective commitments, including the commitment by many developed countries to achieve the target of 0.7 per cent of gross national income for official development assistance (ODA/GNI) to developing countries and 0.15 per cent to 0.2 per cent of ODA/GNI to least developed countries.

---

11 *Report of the Fourth United Nations Conference on the Least Developed Countries, Istanbul, Turkey, 9–13 May 2011* (A/CONF.219/7), chaps. I and II.

12 Resolution 69/15, annex.

13 Resolution 69/137, annex II.

14 A/57/304, annex.

44. We acknowledge the importance for international financial institutions to support, in line with their mandates, the policy space of each country, in particular developing countries. We recommit to broadening and strengthening the voice and participation of developing countries – including African countries, least developed countries, landlocked developing countries, small island developing States and middle-income countries – in international economic decision-making, norm-setting and global economic governance.

45. We acknowledge also the essential role of national parliaments through their enactment of legislation and adoption of budgets and their role in ensuring accountability for the effective implementation of our commitments. Governments and public institutions will also work closely on implementation with regional and local authorities, subregional institutions, international institutions, academia, philanthropic organizations, volunteer groups and others.

46. We underline the important role and comparative advantage of an adequately resourced, relevant, coherent, efficient and effective United Nations system in supporting the achievement of the Sustainable Development Goals and sustainable development. While stressing the importance of strengthened national ownership and leadership at the country level, we express our support for the ongoing dialogue in the Economic and Social Council on the longer-term positioning of the United Nations development system in the context of this Agenda.

Follow-up and review

47. Our Governments have the primary responsibility for follow-up and review, at the national, regional and global levels, in relation to the progress made in implementing the Goals and targets over the coming 15 years. To support accountability to our citizens, we will provide for systematic follow-up and review at the various levels, as set out in this Agenda and the Addis Ababa Action Agenda. The high-level political forum under the auspices of the General Assembly and the Economic and Social Council will have the central role in overseeing follow-up and review at the global level.

48. Indicators are being developed to assist this work. Quality, accessible, timely and reliable disaggregated data will be needed to help with the measurement of progress and to ensure that no one is left behind. Such data is key to decision-making. Data and information from existing reporting mechanisms should be used where possible. We agree to intensify our efforts to strengthen statistical capacities in developing countries, particularly African countries, least developed countries, landlocked developing countries, small island developing States and middle-income countries. We are committed to developing broader measures of progress to complement gross domestic product.

A call for action to change our world

49. Seventy years ago, an earlier generation of world leaders came together to create the United Nations. From the ashes of war and division they fashioned this Organization and the values of peace, dialogue and international cooperation which underpin it. The supreme embodiment of those values is the Charter of the United Nations.

50. Today we are also taking a decision of great historic significance. We resolve to build a better future for all people, including the millions who have been denied the chance to lead decent, dignified and rewarding lives and to achieve their full human potential. We can be the first generation to succeed in ending poverty; just as we may be the last to have a chance of saving the planet. The world will be a better place in 2030 if we succeed in our objectives.

51. What we are announcing today – an Agenda for global action for the next 15 years – is a charter for people and planet in the twenty-first century. Children and young women and men are critical agents of change and will find in the new Goals a platform to channel their infinite capacities for activism into the creation of a better world.

52. "We the peoples" are the celebrated opening words of the Charter of the United Nations. It is "we the peoples" who are embarking today on the road to 2030. Our journey will involve Governments as well as parliaments, the United Nations system and other international institutions, local authorities, indigenous peoples, civil society, business and the private sector, the scientific and academic community – and all people. Millions have already engaged with, and will own, this Agenda. It is an Agenda of the people, by the people and for the people – and this, we believe, will ensure its success.

53. The future of humanity and of our planet lies in our hands. It lies also in the hands of today's younger generation who will pass the torch to future generations. We have mapped the road to sustainable development; it will be for all of us to ensure that the journey is successful and its gains irreversible.

Sustainable Development Goals and targets

54. Following an inclusive process of intergovernmental negotiations, and based on the proposal of the Open Working Group on Sustainable Development Goals,[15] which includes a chapeau contextualizing the latter, set out below are the Goals and targets which we have agreed.

---

15 Contained in the report of the Open Working Group of the General Assembly on Sustainable Development Goals (A/68/970 and Corr.1; see also A/68/970/Add.1–3).

55. The Sustainable Development Goals and targets are integrated and indivisible, global in nature and universally applicable, taking into account different national realities, capacities and levels of development and respecting national policies and priorities. Targets are defined as aspirational and global, with each Government setting its own national targets guided by the global level of ambition but taking into account national circumstances. Each Government will also decide how these aspirational and global targets should be incorporated into national planning processes, policies and strategies. It is important to recognize the link between sustainable development and other relevant ongoing processes in the economic, social and environmental fields.

56. In deciding upon these Goals and targets, we recognize that each country faces specific challenges to achieve sustainable development, and we underscore the special challenges facing the most vulnerable countries and, in particular, African countries, least developed countries, landlocked developing countries and small island developing States, as well as the specific challenges facing the middle-income countries. Countries in situations of conflict also need special attention.

57. We recognize that baseline data for several of the targets remains unavailable, and we call for increased support for strengthening data collection and capacity-building in Member States, to develop national and global baselines where they do not yet exist. We commit to addressing this gap in data collection so as to better inform the measurement of progress, in particular for those targets below which do not have clear numerical targets.

58. We encourage ongoing efforts by States in other forums to address key issues which pose potential challenges to the implementation of our Agenda, and we respect the independent mandates of those processes. We intend that the Agenda and its implementation would support, and be without prejudice to, those other processes and the decisions taken therein.

59. We recognize that there are different approaches, visions, models and tools available to each country, in accordance with its national circumstances and priorities, to achieve sustainable development; and we reaffirm that planet Earth and its ecosystems are our common home and that "Mother Earth" is a common expression in a number of countries and regions.

Sustainable Development Goals

Goal 1.	End poverty in all its forms everywhere
Goal 2.	End hunger, achieve food security and improved nutrition and promote sustainable agriculture
Goal 3.	Ensure healthy lives and promote well-being for all at all ages

Goal 4.   Ensure inclusive and equitable quality education and promote lifelong learning opportunities for all

Goal 5.   Achieve gender equality and empower all women and girls

Goal 6.   Ensure availability and sustainable management of water and sanitation for all

Goal 7.   Ensure access to affordable, reliable, sustainable and modern energy for all

Goal 8.   Promote sustained, inclusive and sustainable economic growth, full and productive employment and decent work for all

Goal 9.   Build resilient infrastructure, promote inclusive and sustainable industrialization and foster innovation

Goal 10. Reduce inequality within and among countries

Goal 11. Make cities and human settlements inclusive, safe, resilient and sustainable

Goal 12. Ensure sustainable consumption and production patterns

Goal 13. Take urgent action to combat climate change and its impacts[*]

Goal 14. Conserve and sustainably use the oceans, seas and marine resources for sustainable development

Goal 15. Protect, restore and promote sustainable use of terrestrial ecosystems, sustainably manage forests, combat desertification, and halt and reverse land degradation and halt biodiversity loss

Goal 16. Promote peaceful and inclusive societies for sustainable development, provide access to justice for all and build effective, accountable and inclusive institutions at all levels

Goal 17. Strengthen the means of implementation and revitalize the Global Partnership for Sustainable Development

---

[*]Acknowledging that the United Nations Framework Convention on Climate Change is the primary international, intergovernmental forum for negotiating the global response to climate change.

Goal 1. End poverty in all its forms everywhere

1.1   By 2030, eradicate extreme poverty for all people everywhere, currently measured as people living on less than $1.25 a day

1.2   By 2030, reduce at least by half the proportion of men, women and children of all ages living in poverty in all its dimensions according to national definitions

1.3   Implement nationally appropriate social protection systems and measures for all, including floors, and by 2030 achieve substantial coverage of the poor and the vulnerable

1.4   By 2030, ensure that all men and women, in particular the poor and the vulnerable, have equal rights to economic resources, as well as access to basic services, ownership and control over land and other forms of property, inheritance, natural resources, appropriate new technology and financial services, including microfinance

1.5 By 2030, build the resilience of the poor and those in vulnerable situations and reduce their exposure and vulnerability to climate-related extreme events and other economic, social and environmental shocks and disasters

　1.a Ensure significant mobilization of resources from a variety of sources, including through enhanced development cooperation, in order to provide adequate and predictable means for developing countries, in particular least developed countries, to implement programmes and policies to end poverty in all its dimensions

　1.b Create sound policy frameworks at the national, regional and international levels, based on pro-poor and gender-sensitive development strategies, to support accelerated investment in poverty eradication actions

Goal 2. End hunger, achieve food security and improved nutrition and promote sustainable agriculture

2.1 By 2030, end hunger and ensure access by all people, in particular the poor and people in vulnerable situations, including infants, to safe, nutritious and sufficient food all year round

2.2 By 2030, end all forms of malnutrition, including achieving, by 2025, the internationally agreed targets on stunting and wasting in children under 5 years of age, and address the nutritional needs of adolescent girls, pregnant and lactating women and older persons

2.3 By 2030, double the agricultural productivity and incomes of small-scale food producers, in particular women, indigenous peoples, family farmers, pastoralists and fishers, including through secure and equal access to land, other productive resources and inputs, knowledge, financial services, markets and opportunities for value addition and non-farm employment

2.4 By 2030, ensure sustainable food production systems and implement resilient agricultural practices that increase productivity and production, that help maintain ecosystems, that strengthen capacity for adaptation to climate change, extreme weather, drought, flooding and other disasters and that progressively improve land and soil quality

2.5 By 2020, maintain the genetic diversity of seeds, cultivated plants and farmed and domesticated animals and their related wild species, including through soundly managed and diversified seed and plant banks at the national, regional and international levels, and promote access to and fair and equitable sharing of benefits arising from the utilization of genetic resources and associated traditional knowledge, as internationally agreed

2.a Increase investment, including through enhanced international cooperation, in rural infrastructure, agricultural research and extension services, technology development and plant and livestock gene banks in order to enhance agricultural productive capacity in developing countries, in particular least developed countries

2.b Correct and prevent trade restrictions and distortions in world agricultural markets, including through the parallel elimination of all forms of agricultural export subsidies and all export measures with equivalent effect, in accordance with the mandate of the Doha Development Round

2.c Adopt measures to ensure the proper functioning of food commodity markets and their derivatives and facilitate timely access to market information, including on food reserves, in order to help limit extreme food price volatility

Goal 3. Ensure healthy lives and promote well-being for all at all ages

3.1 By 2030, reduce the global maternal mortality ratio to less than 70 per 100,000 live births

3.2 By 2030, end preventable deaths of newborns and children under 5 years of age, with all countries aiming to reduce neonatal mortality to at least as low as 12 per 1,000 live births and under-5 mortality to at least as low as 25 per 1,000 live births

3.3 By 2030, end the epidemics of AIDS, tuberculosis, malaria and neglected tropical diseases and combat hepatitis, water-borne diseases and other communicable diseases

3.4 By 2030, reduce by one third premature mortality from non-communicable diseases through prevention and treatment and promote mental health and well-being

3.5 Strengthen the prevention and treatment of substance abuse, including narcotic drug abuse and harmful use of alcohol

3.6 By 2020, halve the number of global deaths and injuries from road traffic accidents

3.7 By 2030, ensure universal access to sexual and reproductive health-care services, including for family planning, information and education, and the integration of reproductive health into national strategies and programmes

3.8 Achieve universal health coverage, including financial risk protection, access to quality essential health-care services and access to safe, effective, quality and affordable essential medicines and vaccines for all

3.9 By 2030, substantially reduce the number of deaths and illnesses from hazardous chemicals and air, water and soil pollution and contamination

3.a Strengthen the implementation of the World Health Organization Framework Convention on Tobacco Control in all countries, as appropriate

3.b Support the research and development of vaccines and medicines for the communicable and non-communicable diseases that primarily affect developing countries, provide access to affordable essential medicines and vaccines, in accordance with the Doha Declaration on the TRIPS Agreement and Public Health, which affirms the right of developing countries to use to the full the provisions in the Agreement on Trade-Related Aspects of Intellectual Property Rights regarding flexibilities to protect public health, and, in particular, provide access to medicines for all

3.c Substantially increase health financing and the recruitment, development, training and retention of the health workforce in developing countries, especially in least developed countries and small island developing States

3.d Strengthen the capacity of all countries, in particular developing countries, for early warning, risk reduction and management of national and global health risks

Goal 4. Ensure inclusive and equitable quality education and promote lifelong learning opportunities for all

4.1 By 2030, ensure that all girls and boys complete free, equitable and quality primary and secondary education leading to relevant and effective learning outcomes

4.2 By 2030, ensure that all girls and boys have access to quality early childhood development, care and pre-primary education so that they are ready for primary education

4.3 By 2030, ensure equal access for all women and men to affordable and quality technical, vocational and tertiary education, including university

4.4 By 2030, substantially increase the number of youth and adults who have relevant skills, including technical and vocational skills, for employment, decent jobs and entrepreneurship

4.5 By 2030, eliminate gender disparities in education and ensure equal access to all levels of education and vocational training for the vulnerable, including persons with disabilities, indigenous peoples and children in vulnerable situations

4.6 By 2030, ensure that all youth and a substantial proportion of adults, both men and women, achieve literacy and numeracy

4.7 By 2030, ensure that all learners acquire the knowledge and skills needed to promote sustainable development, including, among others, through education for sustainable development and sustainable lifestyles, human rights, gender equality, promotion of a culture of peace and non-violence, global citizenship and appreciation of cultural diversity and of culture's contribution to sustainable development

    4.a Build and upgrade education facilities that are child, disability and gender sensitive and provide safe, non-violent, inclusive and effective learning environments for all

    4.b By 2020, substantially expand globally the number of scholarships available to developing countries, in particular least developed countries, small island developing States and African countries, for enrolment in higher education, including vocational training and information and communications technology, technical, engineering and scientific programmes, in developed countries and other developing countries

    4.c By 2030, substantially increase the supply of qualified teachers, including through international cooperation for teacher training in developing countries, especially least developed countries and small island developing States

Goal 5. Achieve gender equality and empower all women and girls

5.1 End all forms of discrimination against all women and girls everywhere

5.2 Eliminate all forms of violence against all women and girls in the public and private spheres, including trafficking and sexual and other types of exploitation

5.3 Eliminate all harmful practices, such as child, early and forced marriage and female genital mutilation

5.4 Recognize and value unpaid care and domestic work through the provision of public services, infrastructure and social protection policies and the promotion of shared responsibility within the household and the family as nationally appropriate

5.5 Ensure women's full and effective participation and equal opportunities for leadership at all levels of decision-making in political, economic and public life

5.6 Ensure universal access to sexual and reproductive health and reproductive rights as agreed in accordance with the Programme of Action of the International Conference on Population and Development and the Beijing Platform for Action and the outcome documents of their review conferences

5.a   Undertake reforms to give women equal rights to economic resources, as well as access to ownership and control over land and other forms of property, financial services, inheritance and natural resources, in accordance with national laws

5.b   Enhance the use of enabling technology, in particular information and communications technology, to promote the empowerment of women

5.c   Adopt and strengthen sound policies and enforceable legislation for the promotion of gender equality and the empowerment of all women and girls at all levels

Goal 6. Ensure availability and sustainable management of water and sanitation for all

6.1   By 2030, achieve universal and equitable access to safe and affordable drinking water for all

6.2   By 2030, achieve access to adequate and equitable sanitation and hygiene for all and end open defecation, paying special attention to the needs of women and girls and those in vulnerable situations

6.3   By 2030, improve water quality by reducing pollution, eliminating dumping and minimizing release of hazardous chemicals and materials, halving the proportion of untreated wastewater and substantially increasing recycling and safe reuse globally

6.4   By 2030, substantially increase water-use efficiency across all sectors and ensure sustainable withdrawals and supply of freshwater to address water scarcity and substantially reduce the number of people suffering from water scarcity

6.5   By 2030, implement integrated water resources management at all levels, including through transboundary cooperation as appropriate

6.6   By 2020, protect and restore water-related ecosystems, including mountains, forests, wetlands, rivers, aquifers and lakes

6.a   By 2030, expand international cooperation and capacity-building support to developing countries in water- and sanitation-related activities and programmes, including water harvesting, desalination, water efficiency, wastewater treatment, recycling and reuse technologies

6.b   Support and strengthen the participation of local communities in improving water and sanitation management

Goal 7. Ensure access to affordable, reliable, sustainable and modern energy for all

7.1   By 2030, ensure universal access to affordable, reliable and modern energy services

7.2 By 2030, increase substantially the share of renewable energy in the global energy mix

7.3 By 2030, double the global rate of improvement in energy efficiency

7.a By 2030, enhance international cooperation to facilitate access to clean energy research and technology, including renewable energy, energy efficiency and advanced and cleaner fossil-fuel technology, and promote investment in energy infrastructure and clean energy technology

7.b By 2030, expand infrastructure and upgrade technology for supplying modern and sustainable energy services for all in developing countries, in particular least developed countries, small island developing States and landlocked developing countries, in accordance with their respective programmes of support

Goal 8. Promote sustained, inclusive and sustainable economic growth, full and productive employment and decent work for all

8.1 Sustain per capita economic growth in accordance with national circumstances and, in particular, at least 7 per cent gross domestic product growth per annum in the least developed countries

8.2 Achieve higher levels of economic productivity through diversification, technological upgrading and innovation, including through a focus on high-value added and labour-intensive sectors

8.3 Promote development-oriented policies that support productive activities, decent job creation, entrepreneurship, creativity and innovation, and encourage the formalization and growth of micro-, small- and medium-sized enterprises, including through access to financial services

8.4 Improve progressively, through 2030, global resource efficiency in consumption and production and endeavour to decouple economic growth from environmental degradation, in accordance with the 10-Year Framework of Programmes on Sustainable Consumption and Production, with developed countries taking the lead

8.5 By 2030, achieve full and productive employment and decent work for all women and men, including for young people and persons with disabilities, and equal pay for work of equal value

8.6 By 2020, substantially reduce the proportion of youth not in employment, education or training

8.7 Take immediate and effective measures to eradicate forced labour, end modern slavery and human trafficking and secure the prohibition and elimination of the worst forms of child labour, including recruitment and use of child soldiers, and by 2025 end child labour in all its forms

8.8 Protect labour rights and promote safe and secure working environments for all workers, including migrant workers, in particular women migrants, and those in precarious employment

8.9   By 2030, devise and implement policies to promote sustainable tourism that creates jobs and promotes local culture and products

8.10 Strengthen the capacity of domestic financial institutions to encourage and expand access to banking, insurance and financial services for all

8.a   Increase Aid for Trade support for developing countries, in particular least developed countries, including through the Enhanced Integrated Framework for Trade-related Technical Assistance to Least Developed Countries

8.b   By 2020, develop and operationalize a global strategy for youth employment and implement the Global Jobs Pact of the International Labour Organization

Goal 9.   Build resilient infrastructure, promote inclusive and sustainable industrialization and foster innovation

9.1   Develop quality, reliable, sustainable and resilient infrastructure, including regional and transborder infrastructure, to support economic development and human well-being, with a focus on affordable and equitable access for all

9.2   Promote inclusive and sustainable industrialization and, by 2030, significantly raise industry's share of employment and gross domestic product, in line with national circumstances, and double its share in least developed countries

9.3   Increase the access of small-scale industrial and other enterprises, in particular in developing countries, to financial services, including affordable credit, and their integration into value chains and markets

9.4   By 2030, upgrade infrastructure and retrofit industries to make them sustainable, with increased resource-use efficiency and greater adoption of clean and environmentally sound technologies and industrial processes, with all countries taking action in accordance with their respective capabilities

9.5   Enhance scientific research, upgrade the technological capabilities of industrial sectors in all countries, in particular developing countries, including, by 2030, encouraging innovation and substantially increasing the number of research and development workers per 1 million people and public and private research and development spending

9.a   Facilitate sustainable and resilient infrastructure development in developing countries through enhanced financial, technological and technical support to African countries, least developed countries, landlocked developing countries and small island developing States

9.b   Support domestic technology development, research and innovation in developing countries, including by ensuring a conducive policy environment for, inter alia, industrial diversification and value addition to commodities

9.c Significantly increase access to information and communications technology and strive to provide universal and affordable access to the Internet in least developed countries by 2020

Goal 10. Reduce inequality within and among countries

10.1 By 2030, progressively achieve and sustain income growth of the bottom 40 per cent of the population at a rate higher than the national average

10.2 By 2030, empower and promote the social, economic and political inclusion of all, irrespective of age, sex, disability, race, ethnicity, origin, religion or economic or other status

10.3 Ensure equal opportunity and reduce inequalities of outcome, including by eliminating discriminatory laws, policies and practices and promoting appropriate legislation, policies and action in this regard

10.4 Adopt policies, especially fiscal, wage and social protection policies, and progressively achieve greater equality

10.5 Improve the regulation and monitoring of global financial markets and institutions and strengthen the implementation of such regulations

10.6 Ensure enhanced representation and voice for developing countries in decision-making in global international economic and financial institutions in order to deliver more effective, credible, accountable and legitimate institutions

10.7 Facilitate orderly, safe, regular and responsible migration and mobility of people, including through the implementation of planned and well-managed migration policies

10.a Implement the principle of special and differential treatment for developing countries, in particular least developed countries, in accordance with World Trade Organization agreements

10.b Encourage official development assistance and financial flows, including foreign direct investment, to States where the need is greatest, in particular least developed countries, African countries, small island developing States and landlocked developing countries, in accordance with their national plans and programmes

10.c By 2030, reduce to less than 3 per cent the transaction costs of migrant remittances and eliminate remittance corridors with costs higher than 5 per cent

Goal 11. Make cities and human settlements inclusive, safe, resilient and sustainable

11.1 By 2030, ensure access for all to adequate, safe and affordable housing and basic services and upgrade slums

11.2 By 2030, provide access to safe, affordable, accessible and sustainable transport systems for all, improving road safety, notably by expanding public transport, with special attention to the needs of those in vulnerable situations, women, children, persons with disabilities and older persons

11.3 By 2030, enhance inclusive and sustainable urbanization and capacity for participatory, integrated and sustainable human settlement planning and management in all countries

11.4 Strengthen efforts to protect and safeguard the world's cultural and natural heritage

11.5 By 2030, significantly reduce the number of deaths and the number of people affected and substantially decrease the direct economic losses relative to global gross domestic product caused by disasters, including water-related disasters, with a focus on protecting the poor and people in vulnerable situations

11.6 By 2030, reduce the adverse per capita environmental impact of cities, including by paying special attention to air quality and municipal and other waste management

11.7 By 2030, provide universal access to safe, inclusive and accessible, green and public spaces, in particular for women and children, older persons and persons with disabilities

    11.a Support positive economic, social and environmental links between urban, peri-urban and rural areas by strengthening national and regional development planning

    11.b By 2020, substantially increase the number of cities and human settlements adopting and implementing integrated policies and plans towards inclusion, resource efficiency, mitigation and adaptation to climate change, resilience to disasters, and develop and implement, in line with the Sendai Framework for Disaster Risk Reduction 2015–2030, holistic disaster risk management at all levels

    11.c Support least developed countries, including through financial and technical assistance, in building sustainable and resilient buildings utilizing local materials

Goal 12. Ensure sustainable consumption and production patterns

12.1 Implement the 10-Year Framework of Programmes on Sustainable Consumption and Production Patterns, all countries taking action, with developed countries taking the lead, taking into account the development and capabilities of developing countries

12.2 By 2030, achieve the sustainable management and efficient use of natural resources

12.3 By 2030, halve per capita global food waste at the retail and consumer levels and reduce food losses along production and supply chains, including post-harvest losses

12.4 By 2020, achieve the environmentally sound management of chemicals and all wastes throughout their life cycle, in accordance with agreed international frameworks, and significantly reduce their release to air, water and soil in order to minimize their adverse impacts on human health and the environment

12.5 By 2030, substantially reduce waste generation through prevention, reduction, recycling and reuse

12.6 Encourage companies, especially large and transnational companies, to adopt sustainable practices and to integrate sustainability information into their reporting cycle

12.7 Promote public procurement practices that are sustainable, in accordance with national policies and priorities

12.8 By 2030, ensure that people everywhere have the relevant information and awareness for sustainable development and lifestyles in harmony with nature

12.a Support developing countries to strengthen their scientific and technological capacity to move towards more sustainable patterns of consumption and production

12.b Develop and implement tools to monitor sustainable development impacts for sustainable tourism that creates jobs and promotes local culture and products

12.c Rationalize inefficient fossil-fuel subsidies that encourage wasteful consumption by removing market distortions, in accordance with national circumstances, including by restructuring taxation and phasing out those harmful subsidies, where they exist, to reflect their environmental impacts, taking fully into account the specific needs and conditions of developing countries and minimizing the possible adverse impacts on their development in a manner that protects the poor and the affected communities

Goal 13. Take urgent action to combat climate change and its impacts*

13.1 Strengthen resilience and adaptive capacity to climate-related hazards and natural disasters in all countries

13.2 Integrate climate change measures into national policies, strategies and planning

13.3 Improve education, awareness-raising and human and institutional capacity on climate change mitigation, adaptation, impact reduction and early warning

---

*Acknowledging that the United Nations Framework Convention on Climate Change is the primary international, intergovernmental forum for negotiating the global response to climate change.

13.a Implement the commitment undertaken by developed-country parties to the United Nations Framework Convention on Climate Change to a goal of mobilizing jointly $100 billion annually by 2020 from all sources to address the needs of developing countries in the context of meaningful mitigation actions and transparency on implementation and fully operationalize the Green Climate Fund through its capitalization as soon as possible

13.b Promote mechanisms for raising capacity for effective climate change-related planning and management in least developed countries and small island developing States, including focusing on women, youth and local and marginalized communities

Goal 14. Conserve and sustainably use the oceans, seas and marine resources for sustainable development

14.1 By 2025, prevent and significantly reduce marine pollution of all kinds, in particular from land-based activities, including marine debris and nutrient pollution

14.2 By 2020, sustainably manage and protect marine and coastal ecosystems to avoid significant adverse impacts, including by strengthening their resilience, and take action for their restoration in order to achieve healthy and productive oceans

14.3 Minimize and address the impacts of ocean acidification, including through enhanced scientific cooperation at all levels

14.4 By 2020, effectively regulate harvesting and end overfishing, illegal, unreported and unregulated fishing and destructive fishing practices and implement science-based management plans, in order to restore fish stocks in the shortest time feasible, at least to levels that can produce maximum sustainable yield as determined by their biological characteristics

14.5 By 2020, conserve at least 10 per cent of coastal and marine areas, consistent with national and international law and based on the best available scientific information

14.6 By 2020, prohibit certain forms of fisheries subsidies which contribute to overcapacity and overfishing, eliminate subsidies that contribute to illegal, unreported and unregulated fishing and refrain from introducing new such subsidies, recognizing that appropriate and effective special and differential treatment for developing and least developed countries should be an integral part of the World Trade Organization fisheries subsidies negotiation[16]

---

16 Taking into account ongoing World Trade Organization negotiations, the Doha Development Agenda and the Hong Kong ministerial mandate.

14.7 By 2030, increase the economic benefits to small island developing States and least developed countries from the sustainable use of marine resources, including through sustainable management of fisheries, aquaculture and tourism

14.a Increase scientific knowledge, develop research capacity and transfer marine technology, taking into account the Intergovernmental Oceanographic Commission Criteria and Guidelines on the Transfer of Marine Technology, in order to improve ocean health and to enhance the contribution of marine biodiversity to the development of developing countries, in particular small island developing States and least developed countries

14.b Provide access for small-scale artisanal fishers to marine resources and markets

14.c Enhance the conservation and sustainable use of oceans and their resources by implementing international law as reflected in the United Nations Convention on the Law of the Sea, which provides the legal framework for the conservation and sustainable use of oceans and their resources, as recalled in paragraph 158 of "The future we want"

Goal 15. Protect, restore and promote sustainable use of terrestrial ecosystems, sustainably manage forests, combat desertification, and halt and reverse land degradation and halt biodiversity loss

15.1 By 2020, ensure the conservation, restoration and sustainable use of terrestrial and inland freshwater ecosystems and their services, in particular forests, wetlands, mountains and drylands, in line with obligations under international agreements

15.2 By 2020, promote the implementation of sustainable management of all types of forests, halt deforestation, restore degraded forests and substantially increase afforestation and reforestation globally

15.3 By 2030, combat desertification, restore degraded land and soil, including land affected by desertification, drought and floods, and strive to achieve a land degradation-neutral world

15.4 By 2030, ensure the conservation of mountain ecosystems, including their biodiversity, in order to enhance their capacity to provide benefits that are essential for sustainable development

15.5 Take urgent and significant action to reduce the degradation of natural habitats, halt the loss of biodiversity and, by 2020, protect and prevent the extinction of threatened species

15.6 Promote fair and equitable sharing of the benefits arising from the utilization of genetic resources and promote appropriate access to such resources, as internationally agreed

15.7 Take urgent action to end poaching and trafficking of protected species of flora and fauna and address both demand and supply of illegal wildlife products

15.8 By 2020, introduce measures to prevent the introduction and significantly reduce the impact of invasive alien species on land and water ecosystems and control or eradicate the priority species

15.9 By 2020, integrate ecosystem and biodiversity values into national and local planning, development processes, poverty reduction strategies and accounts

15.a Mobilize and significantly increase financial resources from all sources to conserve and sustainably use biodiversity and ecosystems

15.b Mobilize significant resources from all sources and at all levels to finance sustainable forest management and provide adequate incentives to developing countries to advance such management, including for conservation and reforestation

15.c Enhance global support for efforts to combat poaching and trafficking of protected species, including by increasing the capacity of local communities to pursue sustainable livelihood opportunities

Goal 16. Promote peaceful and inclusive societies for sustainable development, provide access to justice for all and build effective, accountable and inclusive institutions at all levels

16.1 Significantly reduce all forms of violence and related death rates everywhere

16.2 End abuse, exploitation, trafficking and all forms of violence against and torture of children

16.3 Promote the rule of law at the national and international levels and ensure equal access to justice for all

16.4 By 2030, significantly reduce illicit financial and arms flows, strengthen the recovery and return of stolen assets and combat all forms of organized crime

16.5 Substantially reduce corruption and bribery in all their forms

16.6 Develop effective, accountable and transparent institutions at all levels

16.7 Ensure responsive, inclusive, participatory and representative decision-making at all levels

16.8 Broaden and strengthen the participation of developing countries in the institutions of global governance

16.9 By 2030, provide legal identity for all, including birth registration

16.10 Ensure public access to information and protect fundamental freedoms, in accordance with national legislation and international agreements

16.a Strengthen relevant national institutions, including through international cooperation, for building capacity at all levels, in particular in developing countries, to prevent violence and combat terrorism and crime

16.b Promote and enforce non-discriminatory laws and policies for sustainable development

Goal 17. Strengthen the means of implementation and revitalize the Global Partnership for Sustainable Development

Finance

17.1 Strengthen domestic resource mobilization, including through international support to developing countries, to improve domestic capacity for tax and other revenue collection

17.2 Developed countries to implement fully their official development assistance commitments, including the commitment by many developed countries to achieve the target of 0.7 per cent of gross national income for official development assistance (ODA/GNI) to developing countries and 0.15 to 0.20 per cent of ODA/GNI to least developed countries; ODA providers are encouraged to consider setting a target to provide at least 0.20 per cent of ODA/GNI to least developed countries

17.3 Mobilize additional financial resources for developing countries from multiple sources

17.4 Assist developing countries in attaining long-term debt sustainability through coordinated policies aimed at fostering debt financing, debt relief and debt restructuring, as appropriate, and address the external debt of highly indebted poor countries to reduce debt distress

17.5 Adopt and implement investment promotion regimes for least developed countries

Technology

17.6 Enhance North-South, South-South and triangular regional and international cooperation on and access to science, technology and innovation and enhance knowledge sharing on mutually agreed terms, including through improved coordination among existing mechanisms, in particular at the United Nations level, and through a global technology facilitation mechanism

17.7 Promote the development, transfer, dissemination and diffusion of environmentally sound technologies to developing countries on favourable terms, including on concessional and preferential terms, as mutually agreed

17.8 Fully operationalize the technology bank and science, technology and innovation capacity-building mechanism for least developed countries by 2017 and enhance the use of enabling technology, in particular information and communications technology

Capacity-building

17.9 Enhance international support for implementing effective and targeted capacity-building in developing countries to support national plans to implement all the Sustainable Development Goals, including through North-South, South-South and triangular cooperation

Trade

17.10 Promote a universal, rules-based, open, non-discriminatory and equitable multilateral trading system under the World Trade Organization, including through the conclusion of negotiations under its Doha Development Agenda

17.11 Significantly increase the exports of developing countries, in particular with a view to doubling the least developed countries' share of global exports by 2020

17.12 Realize timely implementation of duty-free and quota-free market access on a lasting basis for all least developed countries, consistent with World Trade Organization decisions, including by ensuring that preferential rules of origin applicable to imports from least developed countries are transparent and simple, and contribute to facilitating market access

Systemic issues

Policy and institutional coherence

17.13 Enhance global macroeconomic stability, including through policy coordination and policy coherence

17.14 Enhance policy coherence for sustainable development

17.15 Respect each country's policy space and leadership to establish and implement policies for poverty eradication and sustainable development

Multi-stakeholder partnerships

17.16 Enhance the Global Partnership for Sustainable Development, complemented by multi-stakeholder partnerships that mobilize and share knowledge, expertise, technology and financial resources, to support the achievement of the Sustainable Development Goals in all countries, in particular developing countries

17.17 Encourage and promote effective public, public-private and civil society partnerships, building on the experience and resourcing strategies of partnerships

Data, monitoring and accountability

17.18 By 2020, enhance capacity-building support to developing countries, including for least developed countries and small island developing States, to increase significantly the availability of high-quality, timely and reliable data disaggregated by income, gender, age, race, ethnicity, migratory status, disability, geographic location and other characteristics relevant in national contexts

17.19 By 2030, build on existing initiatives to develop measurements of progress on sustainable development that complement gross domestic product, and support statistical capacity-building in developing countries

Means of implementation and the Global Partnership

60. We reaffirm our strong commitment to the full implementation of this new Agenda. We recognize that we will not be able to achieve our ambitious Goals and targets without a revitalized and enhanced Global Partnership and comparably ambitious means of implementation. The revitalized Global Partnership will facilitate an intensive global engagement in support of implementation of all the Goals and targets, bringing together Governments, civil society, the private sector, the United Nations system and other actors and mobilizing all available resources.

61. The Agenda's Goals and targets deal with the means required to realize our collective ambitions. The means of implementation targets under each Sustainable Development Goal and Goal 17, which are referred to above, are key to realizing our Agenda and are of equal importance with the other Goals and targets. We shall accord them equal priority in our implementation efforts and in the global indicator framework for monitoring our progress.

62. This Agenda, including the Sustainable Development Goals, can be met within the framework of a revitalized Global Partnership for Sustainable Development, supported by the concrete policies and actions outlined in the Addis Ababa Action Agenda, which is an integral part of the 2030 Agenda for Sustainable Development. The Addis Ababa Action Agenda supports, complements and helps to contextualize the 2030 Agenda's means of implementation targets. It relates to domestic public resources, domestic and international private business and finance, international development cooperation, international trade as an engine for development, debt and debt sustainability, addressing systemic issues and science, technology, innovation and capacity-building, and data, monitoring and follow-up.

63. Cohesive nationally owned sustainable development strategies, supported by integrated national financing frameworks, will be at the heart of our efforts. We reiterate that each country has primary responsibility for its own economic and social development and that the role of national

policies and development strategies cannot be overemphasized. We will respect each country's policy space and leadership to implement policies for poverty eradication and sustainable development, while remaining consistent with relevant international rules and commitments. At the same time, national development efforts need to be supported by an enabling international economic environment, including coherent and mutually supporting world trade, monetary and financial systems, and strengthened and enhanced global economic governance. Processes to develop and facilitate the availability of appropriate knowledge and technologies globally, as well as capacity-building, are also critical. We commit to pursuing policy coherence and an enabling environment for sustainable development at all levels and by all actors, and to reinvigorating the Global Partnership for Sustainable Development.

64. We support the implementation of relevant strategies and programmes of action, including the Istanbul Declaration and Programme of Action, the SIDS Accelerated Modalities of Action (SAMOA) Pathway and the Vienna Programme of Action for Landlocked Developing Countries for the Decade 2014–2024, and reaffirm the importance of supporting the African Union's Agenda 2063 and the programme of the New Partnership for Africa's Development, all of which are integral to the new Agenda. We recognize the major challenge to the achievement of durable peace and sustainable development in countries in conflict and post-conflict situations.

65. We recognize that middle-income countries still face significant challenges to achieve sustainable development. In order to ensure that achievements made to date are sustained, efforts to address ongoing challenges should be strengthened through the exchange of experiences, improved coordination, and better and focused support of the United Nations development system, the international financial institutions, regional organizations and other stakeholders.

66. We underscore that, for all countries, public policies and the mobilization and effective use of domestic resources, underscored by the principle of national ownership, are central to our common pursuit of sustainable development, including achieving the Sustainable Development Goals. We recognize that domestic resources are first and foremost generated by economic growth, supported by an enabling environment at all levels.

67. Private business activity, investment and innovation are major drivers of productivity, inclusive economic growth and job creation. We acknowledge the diversity of the private sector, ranging from micro-enterprises to cooperatives to multinationals. We call upon all businesses to apply their creativity and innovation to solving sustainable development challenges. We will foster a dynamic and well-functioning business sector, while protecting labour rights and environmental and health standards in accordance with

relevant international standards and agreements and other ongoing initiatives in this regard, such as the Guiding Principles on Business and Human Rights[17] and the labour standards of the International Labour Organization, the Convention on the Rights of the Child[18] and key multilateral environmental agreements, for parties to those agreements.

68. International trade is an engine for inclusive economic growth and poverty reduction, and contributes to the promotion of sustainable development. We will continue to promote a universal, rules-based, open, transparent, predictable, inclusive, non-discriminatory and equitable multilateral trading system under the World Trade Organization, as well as meaningful trade liberalization. We call upon all members of the World Trade Organization to redouble their efforts to promptly conclude the negotiations on the Doha Development Agenda.[19] We attach great importance to providing trade-related capacity-building for developing countries, including African countries, least developed countries, landlocked developing countries, small island developing States and middle-income countries, including for the promotion of regional economic integration and interconnectivity.

69. We recognize the need to assist developing countries in attaining long-term debt sustainability through coordinated policies aimed at fostering debt financing, debt relief, debt restructuring and sound debt management, as appropriate. Many countries remain vulnerable to debt crises and some are in the midst of crises, including a number of least developed countries, small island developing States and some developed countries. We reiterate that debtors and creditors must work together to prevent and resolve unsustainable debt situations. Maintaining sustainable debt levels is the responsibility of the borrowing countries; however we acknowledge that lenders also have a responsibility to lend in a way that does not undermine a country's debt sustainability. We will support the maintenance of debt sustainability of those countries that have received debt relief and achieved sustainable debt levels.

70. We hereby launch a Technology Facilitation Mechanism which was established by the Addis Ababa Action Agenda in order to support the Sustainable Development Goals. The Technology Facilitation Mechanism will be based on a multi-stakeholder collaboration between Member States, civil society, the private sector, the scientific community, United Nations entities and other stakeholders and will be composed of a United Nations inter-agency task team on science, technology and innovation for the Sustainable Development Goals, a collaborative multi-stakeholder

---

17 A/HRC/17/31, annex.
18 United Nations, *Treaty Series*, vol. 1577, No. 27531.
19 A/C.2/56/7, annex.

forum on science, technology and innovation for the Sustainable Development Goals and an online platform.

- The United Nations inter-agency task team on science, technology and innovation for the Sustainable Development Goals will promote coordination, coherence and cooperation within the United Nations system on science, technology and innovation-related matters, enhancing synergy and efficiency, in particular to enhance capacity-building initiatives. The task team will draw on existing resources and will work with 10 representatives from civil society, the private sector and the scientific community to prepare the meetings of the multi-stakeholder forum on science, technology and innovation for the Sustainable Development Goals, as well as in the development and operationalization of the online platform, including preparing proposals for the modalities for the forum and the online platform. The 10 representatives will be appointed by the Secretary-General, for periods of two years. The task team will be open to the participation of all United Nations agencies, funds and programmes and the functional commissions of the Economic and Social Council and it will initially be composed of the entities that currently integrate the informal working group on technology facilitation, namely, the Department of Economic and Social Affairs of the Secretariat, the United Nations Environment Programme, the United Nations Industrial Development Organization, the United Nations Educational, Scientific and Cultural Organization, the United Nations Conference on Trade and Development, the International Telecommunication Union, the World Intellectual Property Organization and the World Bank.
- The online platform will be used to establish a comprehensive mapping of, and serve as a gateway for, information on existing science, technology and innovation initiatives, mechanisms and programmes, within and beyond the United Nations. The online platform will facilitate access to information, knowledge and experience, as well as best practices and lessons learned, on science, technology and innovation facilitation initiatives and policies. The online platform will also facilitate the dissemination of relevant open access scientific publications generated worldwide. The online platform will be developed on the basis of an independent technical assessment which will take into account best practices and lessons learned from other initiatives, within and beyond the United Nations, in order to ensure that it will complement, facilitate access to and provide adequate information on existing science, technology and innovation platforms, avoiding duplications and enhancing synergies.

- The multi-stakeholder forum on science, technology and innovation for the Sustainable Development Goals will be convened once a year, for a period of two days, to discuss science, technology and innovation cooperation around thematic areas for the implementation of the Sustainable Development Goals, congregating all relevant stakeholders to actively contribute in their area of expertise. The forum will provide a venue for facilitating interaction, matchmaking and the establishment of networks between relevant stakeholders and multi-stakeholder partnerships in order to identify and examine technology needs and gaps, including on scientific cooperation, innovation and capacity-building, and also in order to help to facilitate development, transfer and dissemination of relevant technologies for the Sustainable Development Goals. The meetings of the forum will be convened by the President of the Economic and Social Council before the meeting of the high-level political forum under the auspices of the Council or, alternatively, in conjunction with other forums or conferences, as appropriate, taking into account the theme to be considered and on the basis of a collaboration with the organizers of the other forums or conferences. The meetings of the forum will be co-chaired by two Member States and will result in a summary of discussions elaborated by the two co-Chairs, as an input to the meetings of the high-level political forum, in the context of the follow-up and review of the implementation of the post-2015 development agenda.
- The meetings of the high-level political forum will be informed by the summary of the multi-stakeholder forum. The themes for the subsequent multi-stakeholder forum on science, technology and innovation for the Sustainable Development Goals will be considered by the high-level political forum on sustainable development, taking into account expert inputs from the task team.

71. We reiterate that this Agenda and the Sustainable Development Goals and targets, including the means of implementation, are universal, indivisible and interlinked.

Follow-up and review

72. We commit to engaging in systematic follow-up and review of the implementation of this Agenda over the next 15 years. A robust, voluntary, effective, participatory, transparent and integrated follow-up and review framework will make a vital contribution to implementation and will help countries to maximize and track progress in implementing this Agenda in order to ensure that no one is left behind.

73. Operating at the national, regional and global levels, it will promote accountability to our citizens, support effective international cooperation in achieving this Agenda and foster exchanges of best practices and mutual learning. It will mobilize support to overcome shared challenges and identify new and emerging issues. As this is a universal Agenda, mutual trust and understanding among all nations will be important.

74. Follow-up and review processes at all levels will be guided by the following principles:

a) They will be voluntary and country-led, will take into account different national realities, capacities and levels of development and will respect policy space and priorities. As national ownership is key to achieving sustainable development, the outcome from national-level processes will be the foundation for reviews at the regional and global levels, given that the global review will be primarily based on national official data sources.

b) They will track progress in implementing the universal Goals and targets, including the means of implementation, in all countries in a manner which respects their universal, integrated and interrelated nature and the three dimensions of sustainable development.

c) They will maintain a longer-term orientation, identify achievements, challenges, gaps and critical success factors and support countries in making informed policy choices. They will help to mobilize the necessary means of implementation and partnerships, support the identification of solutions and best practices and promote the coordination and effectiveness of the international development system.

d) They will be open, inclusive, participatory and transparent for all people and will support reporting by all relevant stakeholders.

e) They will be people-centred, gender-sensitive, respect human rights and have a particular focus on the poorest, most vulnerable and those furthest behind.

f) They will build on existing platforms and processes, where these exist, avoid duplication and respond to national circumstances, capacities, needs and priorities. They will evolve over time, taking into account emerging issues and the development of new methodologies, and will minimize the reporting burden on national administrations.

g) They will be rigorous and based on evidence, informed by country-led evaluations and data which is high-quality, accessible, timely, reliable and disaggregated by income, sex, age, race, ethnicity, migration status, disability and geographic location and other characteristics relevant in national contexts.

h) They will require enhanced capacity-building support for developing countries, including the strengthening of national data systems and evaluation programmes, particularly in African countries, least developed countries, small island developing States, landlocked developing countries and middle-income countries.

i) They will benefit from the active support of the United Nations system and other multilateral institutions.

75. The Goals and targets will be followed up and reviewed using a set of global indicators. These will be complemented by indicators at the regional and national levels which will be developed by Member States, in addition to the outcomes of work undertaken for the development of the baselines for those targets where national and global baseline data does not yet exist. The global indicator framework, to be developed by the Inter-Agency and Expert Group on Sustainable Development Goal Indicators, will be agreed by the Statistical Commission by March 2016 and adopted thereafter by the Economic and Social Council and the General Assembly, in line with existing mandates. This framework will be simple yet robust, address all Sustainable Development Goals and targets, including for means of implementation, and preserve the political balance, integration and ambition contained therein.

76. We will support developing countries, particularly African countries, least developed countries, small island developing States and landlocked developing countries, in strengthening the capacity of national statistical offices and data systems to ensure access to high-quality, timely, reliable and disaggregated data. We will promote transparent and accountable scaling-up of appropriate public-private cooperation to exploit the contribution to be made by a wide range of data, including earth observation and geospatial information, while ensuring national ownership in supporting and tracking progress.

77. We commit to fully engage in conducting regular and inclusive reviews of progress at the subnational, national, regional and global levels. We will draw as far as possible on the existing network of follow-up and review institutions and mechanisms. National reports will allow assessments of progress and identify challenges at the regional and global level. Along with regional dialogues and global reviews, they will inform recommendations for follow-up at various levels.

National level

78. We encourage all Member States to develop as soon as practicable ambitious national responses to the overall implementation of this Agenda. These can support the transition to the Sustainable Development Goals and build on existing planning instruments, such as national development and sustainable development strategies, as appropriate.

79. We also encourage Member States to conduct regular and inclusive reviews of progress at the national and subnational levels which are country-led and country-driven. Such reviews should draw on contributions from indigenous peoples, civil society, the private sector and other stakeholders, in line with national circumstances, policies and priorities. National parliaments as well as other institutions can also support these processes.

Regional level

80. Follow-up and review at the regional and subregional levels can, as appropriate, provide useful opportunities for peer learning, including through voluntary reviews, sharing of best practices and discussion on shared targets. We welcome in this respect the cooperation of regional and subregional commissions and organizations. Inclusive regional processes will draw on national-level reviews and contribute to follow-up and review at the global level, including at the high-level political forum on sustainable development.

81. Recognizing the importance of building on existing follow-up and review mechanisms at the regional level and allowing adequate policy space, we encourage all Member States to identify the most suitable regional forum in which to engage. United Nations regional commissions are encouraged to continue supporting Member States in this regard.

Global level

82. The high-level political forum will have a central role in overseeing a network of follow-up and review processes at the global level, working coherently with the General Assembly, the Economic and Social Council and other relevant organs and forums, in accordance with existing mandates. It will facilitate sharing of experiences, including successes, challenges and lessons learned, and provide political leadership, guidance and recommendations for follow-up. It will promote system-wide coherence and coordination of sustainable development policies. It should ensure that the Agenda remains relevant and ambitious and should focus on the assessment of progress, achievements and challenges faced by developed and developing countries as well as new and emerging issues. Effective linkages will be made with the follow-up and review arrangements of all relevant United Nations conferences and processes, including on least developed countries, small island developing States and landlocked developing countries.

83. Follow-up and review at the high-level political forum will be informed by an annual progress report on the Sustainable Development Goals to

be prepared by the Secretary-General in cooperation with the United Nations system, based on the global indicator framework and data produced by national statistical systems and information collected at the regional level. The high-level political forum will also be informed by the *Global Sustainable Development Report*, which shall strengthen the science-policy interface and could provide a strong evidence-based instrument to support policymakers in promoting poverty eradication and sustainable development. We invite the President of the Economic and Social Council to conduct a process of consultations on the scope, methodology and frequency of the global report as well as its relation to the progress report, the outcome of which should be reflected in the ministerial declaration of the session of the high-level political forum in 2016.

84. The high-level political forum, under the auspices of the Economic and Social Council, shall carry out regular reviews, in line with General Assembly resolution 67/290 of 9 July 2013. Reviews will be voluntary, while encouraging reporting, and include developed and developing countries as well as relevant United Nations entities and other stakeholders, including civil society and the private sector. They shall be State-led, involving ministerial and other relevant high-level participants. They shall provide a platform for partnerships, including through the participation of major groups and other relevant stakeholders.

85. Thematic reviews of progress on the Sustainable Development Goals, including cross-cutting issues, will also take place at the high-level political forum. These will be supported by reviews by the functional commissions of the Economic and Social Council and other intergovernmental bodies and forums which should reflect the integrated nature of the Goals as well as the interlinkages between them. They will engage all relevant stakeholders and, where possible, feed into, and be aligned with, the cycle of the high-level political forum.

86. We welcome, as outlined in the Addis Ababa Action Agenda, the dedicated follow-up and review for the financing for development outcomes as well as all the means of implementation of the Sustainable Development Goals which is integrated with the follow-up and review framework of this Agenda. The intergovernmentally agreed conclusions and recommendations of the annual Economic and Social Council forum on financing for development will be fed into the overall follow-up and review of the implementation of this Agenda in the high-level political forum.

87. Meeting every four years under the auspices of the General Assembly, the high-level political forum will provide high-level political guidance on the Agenda and its implementation, identify progress and emerging challenges and mobilize further actions to accelerate implementation. The next high-level political forum under the auspices of the General Assembly will be

held in 2019, with the cycle of meetings thus reset, in order to maximize coherence with the quadrennial comprehensive policy review process.

88. We also stress the importance of system-wide strategic planning, implementation and reporting in order to ensure coherent and integrated support to the implementation of the new Agenda by the United Nations development system. The relevant governing bodies should take action to review such support to implementation and to report on progress and obstacles. We welcome the ongoing dialogue in the Economic and Social Council on the longer-term positioning of the United Nations development system and look forward to taking action on these issues, as appropriate.

89. The high-level political forum will support participation in follow-up and review processes by the major groups and other relevant stakeholders in line with resolution 67/290. We call upon those actors to report on their contribution to the implementation of the Agenda.

90. We request the Secretary-General, in consultation with Member States, to prepare a report, for consideration at the seventieth session of the General Assembly in preparation for the 2016 meeting of the high-level political forum, which outlines critical milestones towards coherent, efficient and inclusive follow-up and review at the global level. The report should include a proposal on the organizational arrangements for State-led reviews at the high-level political forum under the auspices of the Economic and Social Council, including recommendations on voluntary common reporting guidelines. It should clarify institutional responsibilities and provide guidance on annual themes, on a sequence of thematic reviews, and on options for periodic reviews for the high-level political forum.

91. We reaffirm our unwavering commitment to achieving this Agenda and utilizing it to the full to transform our world for the better by 2030.

4th plenary meeting
25 September 2015

Instruments mentioned in the section entitled "Sustainable Development Goals and targets"

World Health Organization Framework Convention on Tobacco Control (United Nations, *Treaty Series*, vol. 2302, No. 41032)

Sendai Framework for Disaster Risk Reduction 2015–2030 (resolution 69/283, annex II)

United Nations Convention on the Law of the Sea (United Nations, *Treaty Series*, vol. 1833, No. 31363)

"The future we want" (resolution 66/288, annex)

Index

Sustainable Development Goals: Harnessing Business to Achieve the SDGs through Finance, Technology, and Law Reform, First Edition. Edited by Julia Walker, Alma Pekmezovic, and Gordon Walker.
© 2019 John Wiley & Sons Ltd. Published 2019 by John Wiley & Sons Ltd.